Additions and Corrections to the W.P.A. Inventory of Washington County, Ohio: MARIETTA

Jana Sloan Broglin

HERITAGE BOOKS
2025

HERITAGE BOOKS
AN IMPRINT OF HERITAGE BOOKS, INC.

Books, CDs, and more—Worldwide

For our listing of thousands of titles see our website
at
www.HeritageBooks.com

Published 2025 by
HERITAGE BOOKS, INC.
Publishing Division
5810 Ruatan Street
Berwyn Heights, MD 20740

(Originally Titled)
INVENTORY OF THE COUNTY ARCHIVES OF OHIO
Prepared by
The Historical Records Survey
Division of Women's and Professional Projects
Works Progress Administration

No. 84. WASHINGTON COUNTY (MARIETTA)

Columbus, Ohio
The Historical Records Survey
April 1938

International Standard Book Number
Paperbound: 978-0-7884-4953-6

The Historical Records Survey

Luther H. Evans, National Director
John O. Marsh, State Director

Division of Women's and Professional Projects

Ellen S. Woodward, Assistant Administrator
Mildred M. Thrasher, State Director

WORKS PROGRESS ADMINISTRATION

Harry L. Hopkins, Administrator
Carl Watson, State Administrator

The *Inventory of the County Archives of Ohio* is one of a number of bibliographies of historical materials prepared throughout the United States by workers on the Historical Records Survey of the Work Projects Administration. The publication herewith presented, an inventory of the archives of Washington County, is number 84 of the Ohio series.

The Historical Records Survey Program was undertaken in the winter of 1935-1936 for the purpose of providing useful employment to needy unemployed historians, lawyers, teachers, and research and clerical workers. In carrying out this objective, the project was organized to compile inventories of historical materials, particularly the unpublished government documents and records which are basic in the administration of local government, and which provide invaluable data for students of political, economic, and social history. The archival guide herewith presented is intended to meet the requirements of the day-to-day administration by the officials of the county, and also the needs of lawyers, businessmen, and other citizens who require facts from the public records for the proper conduct of their affairs. The volume is so designed that it can be used by the historian in his research in unprinted sources in the same way he uses the library card catalog for printed sources.

The inventories produced by the Historical Records Survey attempt to do more than give merely a list of records– they attempt further to sketch in the historical background of the county or other unit of government, and to describe precisely and in full detail the organization and functions of the government agencies whose records they list. The county, town, and other local inventories for the entire county will, when completed, constitute an encyclopedia of local government as well as a bibliography of local archives.

The successful conclusion of the work of the Historical Records Survey, even in a single county, would not be possible without the support of public officials, historical and legal specialists, and many other groups in the community. Their cooperation is greatly acknowledged.

The survey program was organized by Luther H. Evans, and operates as a nation-wide project in the Division of Women's and Professional Projects, of which Mrs. Ellen S. Woodward, Assistant Administrator, is in charge.

HARRY L. HOPKINS
Administrator

PREFACE
2nd Edition

In 1929 after the stock market crash along with the Great Depression which followed, President Herbert Hoover and his successor Franklin D. Roosevelt formulated relief projects, the most successful was the establishment of the Works Progress Administration (WPA).

Established as the Works Projects Administration in 1935, the WPA was the largest of the many programs developed during Roosevelt's "New Deal." In 1939, the agency's name was changed to Works Progress Administration, and continued as such until its demise in 1943.

The Federal Writers' Project, a division of the WPA (known as Federal Project Number One) created jobs for many unemployed librarians, clerks, researchers, editors, and historians. The workers went to courthouses, town halls, offices in large cities, vital statistics offices and inventoried records. Besides indexing works, many records were transcribed. One of these many projects was the *Inventory of the County Archives* which has benefitted genealogists and historians. The inventories listed the records, either by volumes or file boxes and years per record type, within the office. Although the WPA oversaw this project, the information for each volume of records may differ significantly by the information submitted.

The information herein is verbatim except for obvious spelling errors. Records listed may have met the requirement for retention and have been destroyed as per the records retention act, while other records are considered permanent records. (*See:* **https://codes.ohio.gov/ohio-revised-code** Ohio Revised Code, sections 149.31 and 149.34). Records once considered "open" to the public, such as lunacy, idiotic, and juvenile cases, may be "closed" due to a revision of state laws. However, the records may be opened to family members with adequate proof of lineage.

The addresses and website section of this edition list an up-to-date location guide to each office mentioned, if located.

This project was to encompass all of Ohio's 88 counties although approximately 30 of these inventories have been located while others may be missing or never done.

Jana Sloan Broglin
Fellow, Ohio Genealogical Society
Swanton, Ohio
2025

PREFACE
1st Edition

The Historical Records Survey began operation in Ohio in February 1936, and has been under the technical supervision of the State Archivist and Curator of History, Ohio State Archaeological and Historical Society. General regulations and procedures applicable to all the project units in the forty-eight states have been followed in Ohio. In the sixteen districts of the Works Progress Administration in Ohio, the project was organized and operated by the district supervisors of the Writers' Project. In November 1936, the Survey became an independent part of Federal Project No. 1.

The objective of the Survey in Ohio has been the preparation of complete inventories of the records of the state and of each county, city, other local governmental unit. Although a condensed form of entry is used, information is given as to the limiting dates of all extant records, the contents of individual series, and location of records in statehouse, county courthouse, or other depository.

The *Inventory of the County Archives of Ohio* will, when completed, consist of a set of 88 volumes with a separate number for each county in the state. The units of the series are numbered according to the position of the county in an alphabetical list of the counties. Thus, the inventory herewith presented for Washington County is number 84. The inventory of the State archives and of municipal and other local records constitute separate publications.

The principle followed in the inventory of the county records has been to place a record in the office of origin rather than in the office of deposit. The records are arranged with those of the executive branch of the county government first, followed by judicial, law enforcing, fiscal, and miscellaneous agencies. Minor agencies are placed in the general arrangement according to function rather than according to constitutional or statutory responsibility to a major subdivision. The legal development of each office or agency has been treated in a prefatory section preceding the inventory of the records of the office.

The Historical Records Survey was inaugurated in Washington County in May 1936, under the direction of Emerson Hansel, District Supervisor of the project, and the final careful rechecking of the county records was completed in February 1938 by George Reichert. The wholehearted cooperation of the county officials with the project workers has meant much in the thoroughness and completeness of the result. For the accuracy of the inventory, the project personnel in Washington County is entirely responsible. The research for the historical data was conducted by Dr. James H. Rodabaugh of the project. Members of the state editorial staff of the Historical Records Survey, under the supervision of Russell S. Drum, Assistant State Director in charge of the administrative details of the project, and Miss Winifred Smith, State Editor, compiled, arranged, indexed, edited, and reproduced the volume for distribution among public and semipublic institutions and organizations.

The various units of the *Inventory of the County Archives of Ohio* will be issued in mimeographed or printed form for free distribution to state and local public officials and public libraries in Ohio, and to a limited number of libraries and government agencies outside the state. Requests for information concerning particular units of the *Inventory* should be addressed to the Historical Records Survey, Old Post Office Building, State and Third Streets, Columbus, Ohio.

John O. Marsh
State Director
The Historical Records Survey

Columbus, Ohio
April 30, 1938

ABBREVIATIONS, SYMBOLS, AND EXPLANATORY NOTES

adm. . . . . administration
am.. . . . . amended
Arch. . . . . Archaeological
Art. . . . . Article
c. . . . . copyright
capias . . . . a warrant or order for arrest of a person, typically issued by the judge or magistrate in a case.
CCC. . . . . Civilian Conservation Corps
certiorari. . . . . to be more fully informed
cf . . . . compare
chap(s) . . . . chapter(s)
comp. . . . . compiler
Const. . . . . Constitution
ed(s) . . . . editor(s)
edn. . . . . edition
et al. . . . . (et alii), and others
(et) passim . . . . and here and there
ex officio . . . . as a result of one's status or position
et seq. . . . . and following
fee simple . . . . full and irrevocable ownership
G. C. . . . . General Code
habeas corpus . . . . protection against illegal imprisonment
ibid. . . . . the same reference
loc. cit. . . . . (*loco citato)* in the place cited
N.P. . . . . The Ohio NISI PRIUS REPORTS
n.p. . . . . no place of publication shown
n. s. . . . . new series
nolle prosequi . . . . notice of abandonment by a plaintiff or prosecutor of all or part of a suit or action
O.L. . . . . *Laws of Ohio*
op. cit. . . . . (*opere citato*) In the work cited
posse comitatus. . . . . a group of citizens called upon to assist the sheriff
praecipes. . . . . a written request for action
prima facie . . . . on the first impression

pro rata . . . . in proportion
procedendo . . . . sends case from appellate court to a lower court
pt. . . . . part
quo warranto. . . . . by what authority or warrant
replevins . . . . return of personal property wrongfully taken or held by a defendant
R.S. . . . . Revised Statutes
sec(s) . . . . section(s)
sic . . . . thus, following copy
supersedeas . . . . a stay of enforcement of a judgment pending appeal
v. . . . . versus
venires . . . . a group of people summoned for jury duty
vol(s) . . . . volume(s)
WPA . . . . Works Progress/Projects Administration
writ . . . . a formal, legal document, a decree
x . . . . by
— . . . . current, to date
4-H . . . . (Four - H)

ABBREVIATIONS, SYMBOLS, AND EXPLANATORY NOTES

Each chapter or section of "County Offices and their Records" consists of an essay describing the legal status and functions of one department of county government and an inventory of the records of that department.

Each record constitutes a separate entry. Entries are arranged under topical headings and subheadings.

Each entry sets forth, insofar as applicable, the following:

1. Entry number. Entries are numbered consecutively throughout the inventory.
2. The exact title as it appears on the record, or if the record has no title a supplied title in brackets. If the title of the record is non-descriptive, misleading, or incorrect an additional title (in capitals and lowercase letters), also enclosed in brackets, has been supplied.
3. Dates show inclusive years or parts of years covered by the record. Breaks in dates indicate that the record is missing or was not kept between dates shown. A dash in place of the final date indicates an open record. If no current entries have been made the date of the last entry is noted. Where no statement is made that the record was discontinued at the last date shown, it could not be definitely established that such was the case. Where no comment is made on the absence of prior and subsequent records, no definite information could be obtained.
4. Quantity, given in chronological order wherever possible.
5. Labeling. Numbers and letters within parentheses indicate labeling on volumes, file boxes, or other containers.
6. Variations in title. The current or most recent title is used but significant variations are shown with dates for which each was used.
7. Change of agency. Occasionally a record is discontinued as a county record and kept by some other agency.
8. Description. A statement of the nature and purpose of the record and of what the record shows. As the contents of a record may vary, over time the description may differ somewhat from the record at any one period. Wherever feasible, changes in content are shown with dates. In map and plat entries the names of author and publisher and the scale are omitted only when not available.

9. Arrangement. Records said to be alphabetically arranged are frequently alphabetized only as to initial letter of the surname. This is true especially where there is a secondary arrangement.
10. Indexing. Self-contained indexes are described in the entry. Separate indexes constitute separate entries with cross references to and from the record entry.
11. Nature of recording. Changes are indicated with dates.
12. Condition. No statement is made if good or excellent.
13. Number of pages. Averaged for the series.
14. Dimensions show size of volumes, maps, file boxes, or other containers and are expressed in inches in every instance. The dimensions of volumes are given in order of height, width, and thickness; of file boxes in order of height, width, and depth.
15. Location. Rooms referred to are in the county courthouse unless some other building is specified.

Title line cross references are used to complete series where a record is kept separately for a period of time or in other records for different periods of time. They are also used in all artificial entries which are made to show, under their proper office, records kept in the same volume or file with records of another office. In both instances, the description of the master entry shows the title and entry number of the record from which the cross reference is made. Dates shown in the description of the master entry are for the part or parts of the record contained therein, and are shown only when they vary from those of the master entry. Artificial entries show only title, dates, and description.

Separate third paragraph cross references from entry to entry, are used to show prior, subsequent, or related records which are not a part of the same series. If, however, both entries are under the same subject headings, no third paragraph references are made. "See also" references from subject headings refer to entries in the same department which contain records logically belonging under that heading but which have been classified under an equally appropriate heading.

Washington County, the first to be erected in the Northwest Territory, was established by proclamation of Governor Arthur St. Clair on July 26 or 27 1788 (Salmon P. Chase, comp., *Statutes of Ohio and the Northwestern Territory, 1788-1833*, Cincinnati, 1833-1835, III, 2096); The discrepancy in dates is either to the fact that one day elapsed after the proclamation was prepared before its public announcement, or to a clerical error of the secretary in entering the proclamation in his records; (*cf.* C. E. Carter, ed., *The Territorial Papers of the United States: Northwest Territory*, Washington, 1934-1936, III, 279, note on page 16). At first its boundaries, extending from the Ohio River to Lake Erie and from the Pennsylvania line to the Cuyahoga and Scioto Rivers, enclosed territory covering more than half of the state of Ohio. In 1792 that area was first diminished when a parcel of it was transferred to Hamilton County. The formation of new counties year after year steadily decreased Washington County's size, until in 1851 the present boundaries were defined. (Randolph Chandler Downes, "Evolution of Ohio County Boundaries," *Ohio Arch. and Hist. Quarterly,* XXXVI, 1927, 340-477). It is located in the southeastern portion of the state and bounded on the North by Monroe, Noble, and Morgan Counties, on the west by Morgan and Athens, and on the southeast by the Ohio River which, at this point, separates West Virginia and Ohio. Washington county's area of 630 square miles contained a population in 1930 of 42,437, of which 14,285 lived in the county seat, Marietta (Secretary of State *Ohio Fifteenth Federal Census*, 1930, 9, 11).

The Muskingum Valley was apparently a favorite habitat of the Indians, both of prehistoric and historic kinds. There are in Washington County 115 archaeological sites, including 102 mounds, seven village sites, and six enclosures, practically all of which are located along the Muskingum River. The Marietta Works, covering nearly 80 acres, is said to be one of the best examples of the complex type of enclosure. (Wm. C. Mills, *Archaeological Atlas of Ohio,* Columbus, 1914, 84). In the historic period the Muskingum Valley was the land of the Delawares, though they were there by the consent of the Wyandots (H. C. Shetrone, "The Indian in Ohio," *Ohio Arch. and Hist. Quarterly,* XXVII, 1919. 274-510).

The desire for the possession of the Ohio Valley was a cause of an imperialistic race between France and Great Britain. France, whose claims dated back to the exploration of LaSalle, sent Celeron de Bienville in 1749 through the Ohio region to plant leaden plates as physical evidence of French jurisdiction. One of these was planted at the site of Marietta, where it was found in 1798 (S. P.

Hildreth, *Pioneer History: being an account of the first examinations of the Ohio Valley, and the early settlements of the Northwest Territory* Cincinnati, 1848, 21; George M. Wrong, *The Conquest of New France,* Allen Johnson, ed., *The Chronicles of America Series,* New Haven, 1918-1921, X, 146-147). In the middle of the eighteenth century the colonial rivalry between the French and English flared into open warfare, as a result of which the French were driven from American soil by the Treaty of Paris in 1763.

Add the close of the American Revolution the Ohio Valley passed into the hands of the states of the United States. The colony and later state of Virginia claimed possession of the Northwest Territory on the basis of charters issued to the London Company by King James I in 1606 and 1609 (W. E. Peters, *Ohio Lands and Their Subdivisions.* 2d edn., Athens, 1918, 105-106). During the Revolution the Continental Congress asked the states to cede their lands to the federal government for the common benefit of the nation. In October 1783 Virginia complied, giving up her claims to the territory northwest of the Ohio River with the exception of certain reserved lands. (*Ibid.,* 106-108). Immediately plans were made for the disposal of this vast domain, and on May 20, 1785, the famous Land Ordinance was passed establishing the rectangular system of surveys and reserving certain lands for the support of education and others for the future disposal of Congress (*Journals of the Continental Congress*, Library of Congress edn., XXVIII, 375). This act also authorized the survey and sale of the first "Seven Ranges" of eastern Ohio. The three eastern ranges of townships in Washington County lay in Range V, VI, and VIII of the Seven Ranges (C. E. Sherman, *Ohio Land Subdivisions, Ohio Cooperative Topographic Survey,* III, 1925, 39). These lands, although the first to be opened to the public, were, nevertheless, not the location of the first permanent settlement in Ohio.

The early settlement of Washington County is the story of a speculative Enterprise, and is intricately bound up with the passage of the Ordinance of 1787. The end of the Revolution found many of the soldiers impoverished and the federal and state governments unable to pay them. In 1783 the Newburgh Petition of 285 Continental Army officers was forwarded to Congress, asking for western lands upon which they might settle and also a government for those lands (Archer Butler Hulbert, ed., *The Records of the Original Proceedings of the Ohio Company*, Marietta, 1917, I, xciii). Benjamin Tupper, an army officer, returned to Massachusetts, after participating in the survey of the Seven Ranges, with glowing accounts of fine lands in the Ohio Valley. He and General Rufus Putnam, who also had a first-hand knowledge of the West, succeeded in calling together delegates representing those interested in obtaining western lands. At the Tavern of the Bunch of Grapes in Boston, 11 delegates met on March 1, 1786, and formed the Ohio Company of Associates. Putnam, Samuel Parsons, of Connecticut, and the Reverend Manasseh Cutler, a disgruntled Massachusetts preacher (*ibid.*, lvi), were authorized to seek to buy land from the Confederation Congress. Parsons approached Congress first, but, due to an apparent lack of interest in the project and the fact that the Constitutional Convention was then in session, a quorum could not be reached.

On July 5, 1787, Cutler, of the Ohio Company, arrived in New York, not only seeking a new home for Revolutionary soldiers but also seeking for himself a new means of making a living (*ibid.,* lvii). The agent of the Ohio Company was an able diplomat. Through his position he was destined to aid in passing an ordinance providing government for the Northwest, namely, the Ordinance of 1787. The prospect of settlement made an act of government of prime importance, and that is, perhaps, the extent of Cutler's or the Ohio Company's real influence in the passage of the Ordinance.

This act, the legality of which may be doubted (Frederic L. Paxson, *History of the American Frontier, 1763-1893*, Boston and N. Y., 1924, 69); Payson Jackson Treat, "Origin of the National Land System under the Confederation" *Amer. Hist. Assn. Annual Report,* 1905, I, 233-239), was, like the Federal Constitution being prepared at the time, in reality a conservative instrument reacting against the lack of control permitted by the Jeffersonian Resolutions of 1784 as the constitution was to react against the anarchy existing under the Articles of Confederation. Where as the Resolutions of 1784 would have permitted local self-government in the territories from the beginning, the Ordinance of 1787 gave no share to the people in the first governmental stage and nullified the influence of popular representation in the second stage by granting the governor an absolute veto. In addition, in the latter stage a property qualification of 50 acres of land was required of voters, 200 acres of representatives and 500 acres of members of the council. This second stage bears a strong resemblance to the administration of government of a British royal province, similar to that of Massachusetts under its charter of 1691. (*Cf.* Eugene Halloway Roseboom and Francis Phelps Weisenburger, *A History of Ohio*, N. Y., 1934, 75; Carter, *op. cit.,* II, 41, and note on page 6).

Article II of the compact of the Ordinance of 1787 contains a provision guaranteeing property and stating that "in the just preservation of rights and property it is understood and declared, that no law ought ever to be made, or have force in the said territory, that shall in any manner whatever interfere with, or effect private contracts or engagements" (Carter, *op. cit.,* II, 46). The Ohio Company, whose grant was now pending, desired protection for the pyramid of contracts which it was about to erect and disposing of its lands. Furthermore, the members of the company and prospective buyers and, in fact, all property holders, were disturbed by the turn of affairs since the war. The masses, oppressed by debts, bad money, and heavy taxes, began to register their dissatisfaction openly and with force. In September 1786 an armed mob numbering several hundred stormed the legislature at Exeter, New Hampshire, demanding, among other things, paper money and distribution of property (Andrew Cunningham McLaughlin, *The Confederation and the Constitution,* A. B. Hart, ed., *The American Nation: A History*, N. Y., 1904-1918, X, 147). The Rhode Island government, in the hands of the radical element virtually wiped out private debts by making them payable in worthless currency (*ibid.*, 149-150). The rebellion which really startled the conservatives was that led by Daniel Shays in Massachusetts late in the year 1786, threatening the foundations of that state's government (*ibid.,* chapter x). Several of the Ohio company associates lived in the areas where this rebellion took place. Cutler opposed it, and Tupper took active part in defending Springfield against Shay's mob (*Dictionary of American Biography*, N. Y. 1928-1937, XIX, 52). The prospective owners of a large estate in the West naturally sought protection of their right to hold it (W. P. Cutler, "Private Contract Provision in the Northwest Ordinance of 1787," *Mag. of Amer. Hist.,* XXII, 1889, 483-486). The security of property stood foremost in the mind of Richard Henry Lee, delegate to congress from Virginia and member of the committee which drew up the Ordinance of 1787. Writing to Washington two days after the passage of the ordinance, he observed, "It seemed necessary, for the security of property among uninformed, and perhaps licentious people. . . that a strong toned government should exist, and the rights of property be clearly defined" (quoted in Carter, II, 46).

The East feared the expansion of the West would destroy eastern dominance in national politics, and conservatives like Governeur Morris, Rufus King, and Elbridge Gerry tried various means in the Constitutional Convention to prevent the equality of new states (H. C. Hockett, *Western Influence on Political Parties to 1825, Ohio State Univ. Bull.,* XXII, no. 3, chapter ii). Nathan Dane, a member of Congress from Massachusetts, wrote Rufus King after the passage of the Ordinance of 1787, declaring it contained a better system of government than the old one of 1784. A population of 60,000, he felt, was too small to demand statehood; yet "each State in the common course of things must become important soon after it shall have that number of inhabitants. The Eastern State of the three will probably be the first, and more important than the rest, and will no doubt be settled chiefly by Eastern people; and there is, I think, full and equal chance of the adopting Eastern politics." (Quoted in C. B. Galbreath, "The Ordinance of 1787, Its Origin and Authorship," *Ohio Arch. and Hist. Quarterly,* XXXIII, 1924, 163).

On the other hand, the South chose to take advantage of this opportunity to play for western political support. To this end the southern delegates in Congress even agreed to support the anti-slavery provision in the Ordinance of 1787. In the first place the financial condition of the country made it imperative that no opportunity to dispose of the public lands be lost. Immediately after the Revolution the South was wrought up by Spain's refusal to permit free navigation of the Mississippi River. Many Southerners feared the North and East would be willing to sacrifice that right for commercial privileges of benefit to their own sections. Therefore the South, in order to weaken the North politically "neglected no opportunity of increasing the population and importance of the Western territory," hoping to draw to it inhabitants of the poor soils of New England. (Frederick D. Stone, "The Ordinance of 1787," *Penn. Mag. of Hist. and Biog.,* XIII, 1889, 309-340). William Grayson, one of the delegates from Virginia and temporary president of congress when the Ordinance passed, declared: "If the Mississippi was yielded to Spain. . .the migration to the western country would be stopped and the Northern States would not only retain their inhabitants, but preserve their superiority and influence over those of the South." (*ibid.,* 331). Besides these political considerations, the South supported the Ordinance with its anti-slavery clause thinking it would be advantageous to that section to have a monopoly on cheap labor. Grayson explained to James Monroe that "The clause respecting slavery was agreed to by the southern members for the purpose of preventing tobacco and indigo being made on the northwest side of the Ohio, as well as for other political reasons" (Galbreath, *loc. cit.,* 167). If any selection was responsible for the passage of the ordinance of 1787 it was the South. Grayson was one of the moving spirits in Congress at the time. The committee reporting the Ordinance was composed of three Southerners, and one each from New York and Massachusetts. Five of the eight states which passed the ordinance were of the South (*Journals of the Continental Congress,* Library of Congress edn., XXII, 343).

The Ordinance of 1787, it has been pointed out, was connected with the promotion of a land speculation. This may account for certain ambiguous phrases in the document which have received great fame and perhaps undeserved praise. The general impression, and a faulty one, has been that the Ordinance effectively fostered religion and education in the Northwest. In Article III of its bill of rights is found this declaration: "Religion, Morality and knowledge being necessary to good government and the happiness of mankind, schools and means of education shall forever be encouraged." (Carter, *op. cit.* II, 457). Could a phrase be more equivocal and yet more pregnant with the promise of a Canaan? Congress in general was not interested in education in the territory. The immediate concern was to provide governmental administration. By the above abstract phrase Congress probably intentionally escaped any obligation to promote education and religion. The foundations of the public system of education had been laid in the West by the Land Ordinance of 1785. But Congress at that time specifically refused to provide for religion. (Stone, *loc. cit*). The statements, however, were good advertising material for the land speculators some of whom were members of Congress. With the administrative ordinance out of the way, Congress turned to the request of the Ohio Company.

July 20, only seven days after the passage of the Ordinance, Cutler recorded in his journal: "Colonel Duer came to me with proposals from a number of the principal characters in the city [New York] to extend the contract and take in another company, but that it should be kept a profound secret [and], offered me generous conditions if I would accomplish this business for them." (William Parker Cutler and Julia Perkins Cutler, *Life, Journals and Correspondence of Rev. Manassah Cutler*, Cincinnati, 1888, I, 494). Duer, through his position as Secretary of the Board of Treasury, was in an advantageous position to engineer this land-grab. On July 27, Cutler's petition was granted with all his terms, some of which had formerly been opposed, but included, in addition to 1,781,760 acres for the Ohio Company, an option on nearly 5,000,000 acres which Cutler declared was "for a private speculation in which many of the principal characters in America are concerned. Without connecting this speculation," he continued, "similar terms and advantages could not have been obtained for the Ohio Company." (*Ibid.*, I, 305; Hulbert, I, lxxvi). Participants in the additional speculative Enterprise, the Scioto Company, included a number of the leading financiers of the United States, Great Britain, and Europe, and some in important positions in the American Government. Besides Duer, Samuel Osgood also on the Board of Treasury, was one of the Scioto group. (Archer Butler Hulbert, "The Methods and Operations of the Scioto Group of Speculators," *Miss. Valley Hist. Review*, I, 1914-1915, 502-515). Winthrop

Sargent was secretary of the Ohio Company enacted with Cutler in completing the purchase. Two of the new judges chosen to go to the Northwest Territory, Parsons and Varnum, and Governor St. Clair where stockholders of the Ohio Company. (Paxson, *op. cit.,* 69); E. C. Dawes, "The Beginning of the Ohio Company and the Scioto Purchase," *Ohio Arch. and Hist. Quarterly*, IV, 1895, 1-29). Delegates to Congress, Arthur Lee and Edward Carrington were shareholders, and Alexander Hamilton, friend of Duer, owned five shares and part of another (Albion Morris Dyer, *First Ownership of Ohio Lands*, Boston, 1911, 60ff).

On October 27, 1787 the title to the Ohio Company's lands passed from the United States to the company. Immediately plans were laid for the establishment of a settlement within the purchase. The original proprietors and settlers during the years 1788-1790, came from the states of New Hampshire, Massachusetts, Rhode Island, and Connecticut *(ibid.).* During the winter of 1787-1788 the surveyors and workmen were employed by the company and instructed to proceed to western Pennsylvania. They gathered together at Sumrill's Ferry, where a large boat was built. On April 7, the party of 42 arrived at the mouth of the Muskingum. (Hildreth, *Pioneer History,* 188-191). During the following summer and coming years this boat, first known as the *Adventure Galley* and later as the *Mayflower*, was sailed up the Ohio to bring loads of immigrants to the Muskingum settlement. (*ibid.*, 192).

The new settlement, at first called Adelphi, was changed on July 2 to Marietta, an abbreviation of the name of the French queen, Marie Antoinette (*ibid.,* 208, 213). A veneration for the classics was shown in the planning of the town; the new garrison with block houses at the corners was called Campus Martius; the smaller square in the town was named *Capitolium,* and the larger, *Quadranaou;* And the road leading from the Muskingum to Quadranao was given the name *Sara Via* (*ibid.,* 214). During the year 1788 a total of 133 males arrived at Marietta. Among them were the officials appointed to administer the government of the territory. During the next year 152 men and 51 families arrived, and in 1790 there were around 200 arrivals (H. Z. Williams and Bro., pub., *History of Washington County, Ohio,* Cleveland, 1881, 51, 57-59). Immigrants were meanwhile passing down the Ohio to Kentucky. Many of them were desirous of settling in the Ohio Company purchase. In a direct violation of the company's policy, the agents in 1789 agreed to donate 100 acres to each person settling in regions selected by the agents. In the next two years explorations were made and four settlements were commenced. (Randolph Chandler Downes, *Frontier Ohio 1788-1803, Ohio Historical Collections* III, Columbus, 1935, 60-61). Belpre was founded in 1789 and settled by 40 associates. Newbury was settled at the same time (C. E. Dickinson, *A History of Belpre: Washington County, Ohio,* Parkersburg, W. Va., 1920, 8-9, 37). Waterford and Wolf Creek settlements were also made in these years (S. P. Hildreth, *Memoirs of the Early Pioneer Settlers of Ohio,* Cincinnati, 1854, 104).

Migration into Ohio was virtually stopped in 1790 by the outbreak of the Indian Wars which continued until 1795. Marietta had been more or less protected by the presence of Fort Harmar, located on the west side of the Muskingum at its mouth. However, in 1790 the troops were ordered to Fort Washington, and only a small company under Captain Haskell was left to protect the Ohio Company settlements during the wars. (A. A. Graham, "The Military Posts, Forts and Battlefields Within the State of Ohio," *Ohio Arch. and Hist. Quarterly*, III, 1890-1891. 300-311). In 1791 President Washington reported to Congress there were not more than 307 men in the Muskingum settlements capable of bearing arms ([Jacob] Burnet, *Notes on the Early Settlement of the North-Western Territory*, Cincinnati, 1847, 114-115). Early in January 1791 Indians made a surprise attack on the Big Bottom settlement, located on the Muskingum in present Morgan County, and massacred 13 people. The fear of the Indians led the company to petition Congress to create a buffer community. In answer, the act of April 21, 1792 set aside the so-called Donation Tract north of the Ohio Company purchase. In this tract parcels of 100 acres were given to each male who would actually settle there within five years after the passage of the act. Part of present Washington County was included in the Donation Tract. (Sherman, *op. cit.*, 59).

The Indian Wars came to an end in 1795 with Wayne's Treaty of Greenville which removed the Indian menace from southern Ohio. Immediately thereafter, on February 1, 1796, the Ohio Company partitioned its land among the shareholders (Peters, *op. cit.,* 254-255). Immigrants began to swarm into the region north of the Ohio River, and many came into the Ohio Company's lands. Squatters seeking lands crowded Marietta in the spring of 1797. (Downes, *Frontier Ohio,* 76). The immigrants, wherever they came from, were men who had not made a success of their lives in their former habitats and were seeking to better their conditions. Cutler, for example, wrote: "I have suffered exceedingly in ye war, and after it was over, by paper money and ye high price of articles of living. My salary small and family large, for several years I thought ye people had not done me justice, and I meditated leaving them" (Hulbert, *Records of the Ohio Company,* I, lvii). To easterners without property the West offered an opportunity to enjoy that privilege. Most of the first settlers were New Englanders who had lost what fortunes they had in the Revolution (Burnet, *op. cit.,* 42-44).

Many of the squatters, however, and those who settled on the free lands, were Pennsylvanians and Kentuckians and of Scotch-Irish extractions. In the early years of Washington County's history the New England element was very strong in the population. At the time of the War of 1812, this group sided with the citizens of the New England states in opposing the war. They believed the government could have secured a satisfactory treaty from Britain and opposed the administration's favoritism toward France. (Williams, *op. cit.,* 134). By 1800 the population of Washington County had grown to 5,427. In the next 30 years that total increased to 11,731, While the physical size of the county was being reduced by the erection of new counties. (*Compendium of the Eleventh Census of the United States*, 1890, pt. i, 36). Marietta, however, numbered only 1,207 in 1830 (Secretary of State, *Ohio Fifteenth Federal Census*, 1930, 9). A new element in the population, the Germans, began to arrive in considerable numbers from Germany in the summer of 1833 after the German Revolution had been crushed (Bernard Peters, "The German Pioneers," *Ohio Arch. and Hist. Quarterly*, II, 1888-1889, 52-59). However, some Germans (Pennsylvania-Dutch) had already migrated into the county from Pennsylvania (*ibid).*, and there were also some Germans among the first garrison at Fort Harmar (Albert Bushnell Hart, "The Westernization of New England," *Ohio Arch. and Hist. Quarterly*, II, 1888-1889, 52-59). Scotchmen were included in this second period of immigration. In 1828, Naham Ward, of Marietta, went to Scotland where he published *A Brief Sketch of the State of Ohio*, as a result of which the Scottish population in Washington County increased, particularly around Barlow. Ward was also influential in inducing Germans to settle in Washington County. Later migrations brought Catholic German and Irish immigrants who settled in Muskingum, Watertown, Adams, and Warren Townships particularly. (Williams, *op. cit.*, 100). By 1850 the population of the county had increased to 23,540 (*Compendium of the Eleventh Census of the United States,* 1890, pt. i, 36). In 1900 Washington County attained its population peak with 48,245, from which figure there has been a steady decrease (Secretary of State, *Ohio Fifteenth Federal Census*, 1930, 11).

In the absence of a legally established government (Governor St. Clair did not arrive until July 1788) the original pioneers of Marietta organized their own squatter government. A board of police was set up which drew up regulations for the community. (Downes, *Frontier Ohio*, 128). Soon after his arrival St. Clair provided government by proclaiming the erection of Washington County. Officials named to the principal county offices were Ebenezer Sprout, sheriff; Return Jonathan Meigs, prothonotary to the court of common pleas; Enoch Parsons, register of deeds; Rufus Putnam, judge of probate; and Rufus Putnam, Benjamen [sic] Tupper, and Archibald Crary, judges of the court of common pleas (Carter, *op. cit.,* III, 278-292). After Ohio attained statehood the first county officers were as follows: Edward W. Tupper, clerk of court of common pleas; DudleyWoodbridge, recorder; Jabez True, treasurer; Joel Bowen, coroner; Matthew Backus, prosecutor; John Clark, sheriff; Isaac Pierce, W. R. Putnam, and Simeon Deming, county commissioners; and Calvin Pease, president, and Griffin Greene, Joseph Buell, and Joseph Wood, associate judges of the court of common pleas (Williams, *op. cit.,* 112-113). The first court of Washington County was held at the residence of Eben Battelle and then in the northwest blockhouse of Campus Martius (Thomas J. Summers, *History of Marietta*, Marietta, 1903, 149). A courthouse measuring 45 by 39 feet and two stories high was constructed in 1798. Its walls, three feet thick, were made of double tiers of logs 18 inches square. A new building, started in the early twenties, was enlarged and improved in 1854 and again in 1876. (Williams, *op. cit.,*109). In 1900 the old courthouse was torn down and a new one was completed by the fall of 1902 (Summers, *op. cit.,* 153, 156). The village of Marietta was incorporated in 1800 by an act providing for an annual town meeting to elect a council, clerk, treasurer, assessors, overseers, highway supervisors, since viewers, and collectors (Downes, *Frontier Ohio*, 154-155).

Washington County settlers at first tended to resist the strong arm of Governor St. Clair; unsuccessfully they sought to convince him the Ordinance of 1787 did not give him veto power. They opposed the strict interpretation of the requirement that the territorial code of laws was to be adopted from codes of the eastern states. There was a more or less general disregard shown for law and the constituted authorities. (Randolph Chandler Downes, "The Statehood Contest in Ohio," *Miss. Valley Hist. Review,* XVIII, 1931-1932, 155-171). When, however, the increase of population in the valleys of the Scioto and Miami Rivers began to threaten the political supremacy of Marietta in the government of the territory, the Mariettans turned to the strong support of St. Clair. New Englanders and others at Cincinnati, joined the Marietta forces in a Federalist party coalition against the Republican Virginians who had settled Chillicothe and the Scioto Valley. Each town was anxious that the new state boundaries be such that it would become a capital. St. Clair suggested lines such that Marietta and Cincinnati might both have become capitals while the Republican-inclined populace of the Virginia Military

District and the back-country of Ohio would have been so divided as to secure the supremacy of the Federalist Part. (Downes, *Frontier Ohio,* 188-200). The success of the statehood movement meant defeat for the Federalist Party, and in 1803 the Republican organization of Washington County was successful in defeating the Marietta Federalists (*ibid.,* 218-219).

As in all other early Ohio counties agriculture was the principal industry in Washington County. An unglaciated plateau, generally a rough surface, covers Southeastern Ohio. The unglaciated soils are the poorest in the state. (Roderick Peattie, *Geography of Ohio, Geological Survey of Ohio*, Bull. XXVII, 4th series, Columbus, 1923, 3, 13, 50). The immediate valleys of the Muskingum and Ohio Rivers are fertile and productive. In the county are a total of 32,640 acres of rich alluvial soil which raises the average quality of his lands above the average of those in other southern Ohio counties. (*Report of the Geological Survey of Ohio*, Columbus, 1874, II, 156-157). It is estimated that 30 percent of the total area of the county is very steep and broken and 60 percent is hilly to very hilly. This fact has led the federal government to include the eastern townships and a couple of western townships in the Muskingum Purchase Unit for reforestation. Four western townships have been included in the Hocking Valley Purchase Unit. This, of course, necessitates moving a number of the people from those sub-marginal lands. (*A Study of the Public Schools of Washington County*, Ohio Study of Local School Units, mimeographed, Columbus, 1937, 4).

Grains, particularly like corn, made up the first crops harvested. In the second year of the settlement wheat was raised. Harvesting was accomplished with the sickle and later the cradle, and the grain was thrashed with a flail or under the Hooves of horses or oxen. (Peattie, *op. cit.,* 56). Among the early products raised in the Muskingum and Ohio bottoms were cotton and rice (Williams, *op. cit.,* 96). Flax was first grown at Belpre in 1790 (Dickinson, *A History of Belpre,* 43-44). Fine cattle were brought over the mountains by Colonel Israel Putnam in 1788 and again in 1795. Largely through his influence Belpre became an important farming center in early Ohio, especially noted for its dairy products. Sheep-raising was introduced before the opening of the nineteenth century. Paul Fearing was one of the first to develop the sheep-raising industry. Israel Putnam, the younger, imported Merino sheep sometime before 1810. (*Ibid.,* 44; Williams, 98). Washington County, however, was not able to keep up with the agricultural developments in the other portions of the state. Southeastern Ohio is decidedly below the normal for the state in agricultural worth. In 1930, about 82 percent of the county's area was included in farmlands. Only 29.6 percent of the farmlands, however, were tilled. In 1935, according to statistics prepared by the department of rural economics of Ohio State University, the average income for the 4,032 farms in Washington County was $484 in contrast to the state average of $1,122. The income per acre was $5.53 in contrast to $12.53 for the state. (*A Study of the Public Schools of Washington County op. cit.,* 5-7). The presence of some rich alluvial soils and a large amount of poor and hilly soils has led to economic and social distinctions between the inhabitants of those respective areas (Peattie, *op. cit.,* 58).

The first manufacturing Industries in the county arose out of the necessities of the West isolated as it was from the East. The Ohio Company donated lands to builders of mills in the purchase (Downes, *Frontier Ohio,* 120). The Wolf Creek settlement was made in 1789 for the purpose of erecting mills. In March 1790 a grist mill and a sawmill were in operation. (Hildreth, *Pioneer History*, 419-424).The first tannery was established at Marietta in 1791 (Dickinson, *op. cit.,* 252). The important industry of early Marietta was shipbuilding which began about 1800. In that year a company was formed and a break of 104 tons, named the *St. Clair*, was constructed. Loaded with a cargo of pork and flour she sailed from Marietta in May 1801. At Havana the flour was sold at $40 a barrel subject to a $20 duty, and a load of sugar was taken on. The *St. Clair* then proceeded to Philadelphia where it was sold. This was the first rigged vessel on the Ohio, and it was commanded by Abraham Whipple, a naval commander during the Revolution. (Hildreth, *Memoirs of the Early Pioneer Settlers*, 159-160; Charles Henry Ambler, *A History of Transportation in the Ohio Valley*, Glendale, Cal., 1932, 85-87). Between 1800 and 1808 24 ships were built at Marietta, ranging from 70 to 350 tons. Jefferson's Embargo, passed late in 1807, crippled American commerce and killed the ship building industry at Marietta, which explains in part the opposition of the pioneers to the War of 1812. The Embargo also dealt a severe blow to the complimentary industry of rope making. There were three rope works in operation at Marietta supplying the rigging and cordage for the ships. Ship building was resumed in 1844 and continued for 22 years. (Williams, *History of Washington County,* 376-377).

In the decade 1820-1830 boat building became an important industry in Washington County. Harmar and Marietta were the chief locations of this industry. Steamboats were constructed not only for river traffic but also for sea commerce. This industry continued a profitable one throughout most of the nineteenth century. (*Ibid.,* 378-379). After the turn of the mid-century among the industrial establishments in the county were chair, lock, and bucket factories; iron, gas, and boiler works; foundries and breweries (*ibid*, 370-372). An industry of importance in the present century, the oil business, got a start early in the nineteenth century. Oil was discovered in Washington County shortly after settlement began. It was sold at first as "Seneca Oil," used for medicinal purposes, illumination, and lubrication. (Peattie, *op. cit.,* 70). Marietta became one of the earliest distributors of oil. The principal supply, however, came from West Virginia. The firm of Bosworth, Wells and Company began this business in 1847 and carried it on till 1860, shipping oil to Pittsburgh, New York, Philadelphia, St. Louis, Peoria, Chicago, and Cincinnati. In the fall of 1860 promoters, particularly from Pennsylvania, began to develop the Duck Creek Valley oil fields at Macksburg. During the next four or five years a great speculation in land was experienced and some lands sold for as high as $1,500 an acre. (J. A. Bownocker, *The Occurrence and Exploitation of Petroleum and Natural Gas in Ohio, Geological Survey of Ohio,* Bull. 1, 1st ser., Columbus, 1903, 148-150), In the 1920s Marietta revived somewhat because of the petroleum resources nearby (Peattie, 91). There is, however, relatively little industrial activity in Washington County today. In 1930 only 2,400 were employed in manufacturing and 1,091 in mining, whereas 4,828 were employed in agriculture (*A Study of the Public Schools of Washington County*). In 1935 the total tax duplicate of the county was 35,188,075, ranking 44th in the state (Auditor of State of Ohio, *Annual Report*, 1935, 552).

The New England settlers of the Ohio Company lands brought with them the Congregational church. The first sermon at Marietta is said to have been preached by the Reverend Daniel Breck on Sunday July 20, 1788. About 300 were present, the services having attracted a considerable number from across the Ohio River (Rev. C. E. Dickinson, "The First Church Organization in the Oldest Settlement in the Northwest Territory," *Ohio Arch. and Hist. Quarterly,* II, 1888-1889, 280-298). Breck stayed about a month, when Manassas Cutler arrived and preached for three Sundays. After that various laymen preached until the regular pastor, the Reverend Daniel Story, arrived from Boston in the spring of 1789. Story's salary was paid by the Ohio Company. The congregation was organized in December 1796 with principles such that both Congregationalists and Presbyterians might subscribe to it. (C. F. Martzolff, "Early Religious Movements in the Muskingum Valley," *Ohio Arch. and Hist. Quarterly,* XXV, 1916, 183-190). Presbyterianism was at first submerged through its connection with the Congregational church which continued under the Plan of Union of 1801. In 1804, however, 35 persons withdrew from the Congregational Church probably to join the

Presbyterians. On February 20, 1804 the Reverend Stephen Lindley was employed as minister of the Presbyterian church in Marietta. (Williams, *History of Washington County,* 384). A New England religious influence of unorthodox nature was seen in Marietta in 1806 with the arrival of some Unitarians (*ibid.,* 391).

Methodism met with strong opposition at Marietta. The Reverend Robert Manley preached the first sermon there in 1799, but he received no warm welcome. A few small classes were formed in the region and a circuit was organized, the second in the Northwest Territory. (*Ibid.,* 382; Francis I. Moats, "The Rise of Methodism in the Middle West," *Miss. Valley Hist. Review*, XV, 1928-1929. 69-88). Camp meetings were held in 1804 and 1805 under the leadership of George Atkins. Some Mariettans joined their meeting: houses were stoned, windows broken, and chimneys stopped up, smoking out the worshipers. In 1806 a third camp meeting was held at Harmar, conducted by John Sale and Peter Cartwright. A great Revival was held in 1809-1810. (Williams, *History of Washington County*, 383). A Baptist church was organized in 1797 at the Rainbow settlement on the Muskingum about 12 miles above Marietta. The Baptists organized in Marietta in 1818, the Universalists in 1817, and the Episcopalians in 1826. (*Ibid.,* 385-.87). The German and Irish migrations to Washington County led to the establishment of the Evangelical, United Brethren, Lutheran, and the Roman Catholic churches. At the last religious census there were 15,8004 church members in the county, including 5,222 Methodists (Episcopal), 2,122 Roman Catholics, 1,305 Presbyterians, 1,239 Congregationalists, and 500 or more members in each of the following churches: Baptist, Church of Christ, Disciples of Christ, Evangelical, and the United Brethren (Bureau of Census, *Religious Bodies*: 1926, I, 657).

Elementary schools were opened in the Ohio company settlements a year after the arrival of the settlers, when the directors of the company appropriated money for the instruction of children at Marietta, Belpre, and Waterford (Robert E. Chaddock, *Ohio Before 1850: A Study of the Early Influence of Pennsylvania and Southern Populations in Ohio*, Columbia University, *Studies*, XXXI, no. 2, 141). Major Anselm Tupper taught the first school at Marietta in the winter of 1789-1790. It was held in a block house in Campus Martius. In the summer of 1789 Bathsheba Rouse, of Massachusetts, opened the first school for younger children at Belpre. Daniel Mayo, a Harvard graduate, taught the older children at Belpre in one of the block houses in 1789 and for several years thereafter. (W. Ross Dunn, "Education in Territorial Ohio," *Ohio Arch. and Hist. Quarterly*, XXXV, 1926, 322-379), Higher education early received support in Washington County. A stock company was organized in 1797 to erect and promote the Muskingum Academy. That institution was opened in 1800, with David Putnam, a graduate of Yale, as teacher. After passing through several transformations that school ultimately became Marietta College in 1835. By 1935 that historic institution had physical assets of nearly $1,000,000 and an endowment of over $1.25 million. (Arthur G. Beach, *A Pioneer College: The Story of Marietta*, n. p., 1935, *passim*).

Ohio counties were laid out to fit the needs of an Agricultural Society of the nineteenth century. The last Ohio County was created in 1851 and there have been no changes in boundaries for over half a century. The counties now range in population from 10,000 to 1,200,000. Approximately 70 of Ohio's 88 counties may be considered rural. (R. E. Heiges, *The Office of Sheriff in the Rural Counties of Ohio,* Findlay, Ohio, 1933, 52). The median population is approximately 30,000 but over half of the people live in eight large urban counties.

The county is a creation of the state for the execution of state policy and have such powers as the state confers upon it. It has, however, had to provide an ever-increasing number of local services similar to those rendered by municipalities and its legal status is therefor changing. The county eventually may become relatively less the agent of the state and tend to approximate the municipal corporation in the character of its activities and in its legal status. (Report of Governor's Commission, *The Reorganization of County Government in Ohio,* 1934, 3, 28-29).

The board of county Commissioners is the central feature of the structure of the county government. The functions of this board touch either directly or indirectly every other branch and department. The board is the agency in whose name actions for and against the county are brought. This board empowered to determine certain policies for the conduct of county affairs such as adoption of the budget, establishment of services left optional by law, and the authorization of improvements. Thus in a limited sense it constitutes the legislative branch. The board also functions as the central administrative body although much of the administration, centered in other elective offices, is beyond its control. The county auditor was originally made secretary of the board and still functions as such in a majority of the counties. Later provisions of the law permitted the board to appoint its own clerk, thus removing this duty from the auditor. (*Ibid.,* 58-59).

There are three types of financial functions performed by county officers and employees: tax administration, handling of the fiscal affairs of the county, and the trusteeship of funds held for individuals in court procedure. The principal financial authorities are the board of commissioners, the auditor, and the treasurer. The commissioners levy taxes, appropriate funds, and authorized payments. The auditor's primary duties are the keeping of accounts, the issuance of warrants, the valuation of real estate, and the preparation of the tax list. The treasurer collects taxes, receives and has custody of county moneys, and disburses upon warrant from the auditor. (*Ibid.,* 71).

There are three strictly clerical officers whose work consists mainly of the preparation and custody of records: the recorder, the clerk of courts, and the judge of the probate court. All three have some part in the recording of documents and instruments affecting the title of property and of other documents presented for record. The last two have as their principal duty the keeping of court records; the clerk of courts serving both as clerk of the court of appeals and the common pleas court, and the probate court looking after its own records. (Report of Governor's Commission, *op. cit.,* 179).

It is the duty of the recorder to copy, index, and file documents authorized to be recorded in his office. These consist almost entirely of chattel mortgages and instruments affecting the title to real estate (*ibid.,* 180). The system of recording is prescribed by Statute. With the exception of a few urban counties recording is done by typewriter with considerable use of printed forms. The photographic method of copying is now in use in Clark, Cuyahoga, Hamilton, Lucas, Montgomery, and Summit Counties.

The principal records of the clerk of courts are prescribed by Statute. They include an appearance docket, an execution docket, a journal of the orders of the court, a complete record of proceedings, a system of indexes, and a file of original papers (51 O. L. 107 The clerk is responsible for a variety of non-judicial record work of which the filing and indexing of automobile bills of sale was a major item. The bill of sale law was repealed by an act effective January 1, 1938, requiring the clerk to issue a certificate of title and to file a duplicate of the certificates (G. C. sec. 6290-6). At present the clerk acts as the agent of the state for the sale of hunting and fishing licenses and also issues auctioneers and ferry licenses.

The probate judge is by statute a clerk of his own court. The constitution permits the combination of a probate and common pleas courts in counties of less than 60,000 population. In this case the judge of common pleas becomes *ex-officio* the clerk of the probate division and two separate offices are retained for keeping records. Such mergers now exist in three counties: Adams, Henry, and Wyandot. (Report of Governor's Commission, *op. cit.,* 182-183).

Listed below, with amendments, are some notable provisions adopted at the conventions of 1851 and 1912 which affected the organization of county government:

"Laws may be passed to secure to mechanics, artisans, laborers, subcontractors and material men, they're just dues by direct lien up on the property, upon which they have bestowed labor or for which they have furnished material" (Art. II, sec. 33, 1851). "All nominations for elective state, district, county and municipal offices shall be made at direct primary election or by petition as provided by law. . ." (Art. V, sec. 7, 1912 "The General Assembly shall provide by general law for the organization and government of counties, and may provide by general law alternative forms of county government. No alternative form shall become operative in any county until submitted to the electors thereof and approved by a majority of those voting. . .Municipalities and townships shall have authority, with the consent of the county, to transfer to the county any of their powers or to revoke the transfer of any such power, under regulations provided by general law, but the rights of initiative and referendum shall be secured to. . .every measure, , , giving or withdrawing such consent." (Art. X, sec. 1, amendment adopted 1933). "Appointments and promotions in the civil service of the state, the several counties, and cities, shall be made according to merit and fitness, to be ascertained, as far as practical, by competitive examinations" (Art. XV, sec. 10, 1912). "Elections for state and county officers shall be held on the first Tuesday after the first Monday in November in the even numbered years." (Art. XVII, sec. 1, amendment adopted 1905).

The aim of the survey has been to make information available regarding the records which have accumulated over a period of more than 130 years. Survey workers have not made a study of the functions of the county offices with a view toward recommending any reorganization of county government but in the report of the Governor's Commission (*op. cit.,* 186-187) recommendations were made bearing upon the record system as follows:

1. County charters and optional forms of government should provide for a department of records and court service to take over the functions of the recorder and clerk of courts, the non-judicial record work of the probate court, and the functions of the sheriff as a court officer (see also Heiges, *op. cit.,* 55-56).
2. The issuance of licenses should be transferred from the clerk of courts to the department of finance.
3. Wider use should be made of the photographic process of recording in large counties.
4. Legislation should be adopted permitting the destruction of chattel mortgages and automobile bills of sale after they have ceased to have effect.
5. The requirements of three systems of indexes of cases in the clerk's office should be eliminated from the code and only the index of pending suits and living judgments should be required.
6. Provisions should be made in the rules of the common pleas court for service of process by mail and that method should be brought into general use (see also Heiges, *op. cit.,* 60-61).

Following the report of the governor's commission, a new law (116 O. L. 132-133) was passed in 1933 permitting any county to adopt a charter or an alternative form of government, as provided in section 3 of Article X of the Constitution of Ohio, if it does not interfere with or restrict in any manner a charter which has been adopted by any municipal government. The electors may establish by charter provision a civil service commission or personnel department. In April 1935 (116 O. L. 134) the legislature also provided that the electors of any county may establish by charter provision accounting department of health.

HOUSING, CARE, AND ACCESSIBILITY OF THE RECORDS

The first courthouse in Washington County was built in 1798, under the superintendence of Dudley Woodbridge, Esquire, and Architect Griffin Greene. It was built on a lot given to the county by Dudley Woodbridge. Contracts were made with Joshua Wells to frame and raise the building, with Joshua Shipman to weatherboard and shingle it, with James Lawton to do the mason work, and with Gilbert Duvol, Jr., to furnish the iron-grating, spikes, bolts, and other hardware, totaling 3,000 pounds, for which he was to have 16 cents per pound. The main building was 45 feet in length and 39 in breadth, two stories high. Walls were three feet thick and made of double tiers of yellow poplar logs, 18 inches square, neatly hewn and dovetailed at the corners of the building. The logs were so laid as to break joints, like masonry, and were held together by heavy iron bolts. The front room in the upper story was the courtroom. It was 40 by 30 feet in dimension, lighted by seven windows and heated by two large fireplaces.

The two lower rooms were occupied by the jailer and his family. A passage between them led to the jail in the rear part of the structure which, like the courthouse proper, was very strongly built. The jury rooms were in the rear of the courtroom over the jail. The roof over the old courthouse corresponded with the rest of the building, being constructed of very heavy timbers, and covered with thick shingles about three feet in length. A cupola, surrounding the roof, houses a bell which was later placed in the courthouse constructed in 1822. For many years this bell was rung regularly at nine o'clock in the morning, at noon, and at nine o'clock in the evening, and was tolled upon the occasion of the death of any inhabitant. It bore the inscription, "-1802- Barazilia Davidson, Norwich, Connecticut."

As early as 1819 the necessity of a new building became apparent, and after the subject had been agitated for some time a committee was appointed by a citizens meeting to report upon the matter. They committee consisted of two years little or no action was taken, but in 1821 the commissioners advertised for a plan, and employed Joseph Holden to collect the materials for building. It was decided that the building should contain four principal offices, each to be 16 feet square, and that the dimensions of the whole structure should be 48 feet each way. Much opposition to the location arose, and there was considerable discussion as to the relative merits of various sites. The commissioners were annoyed with scores of petitions and personal appeals for location in a dozen different places. Some wished the building to be erected upon the elevated square on Washington Street, some upon the lot where Judge Ewart had lived, then known as the Thierry property, and others on

Fifth Street, but a few weeks later a majority of the citizens assembled at a meeting and voted in favor of the Thierry property as the location. The Commissioners changed their plan in conformance with the general desire, but a few weeks later decided on the corner of Putnam and Second Streets on a lot donated by Colonel Ebenezer Sproat. The work was begun so soon that opponents to that location had no time to affect another change. The lot was previously used as a place for the punishment of criminals; the pillory, stocks, and whipping post stood there. (H. Z. Williams and Bro., pub., *History of Washington County*, Cleveland, 1881, 108-109).

The courthouse was ready for occupancy in 1823. No changes were made in this building until 1854 when an addition on the north was constructed and again in 1879 the main building was improved by adding a front 24 by 48 feet in dimension. This courthouse was used by the county until August 1900 when it was torn down to make way for the present one. (Thomas J. Summers, *History of Marietta*, Marietta, 1903).

In 1848 a jail was built on the site of the first courthouse. It was the one jail in the history of the county which was separate from the courthouse.

It has been historically stated that the building was located a little distance back from Putnam Street through the influence of Governor Meigs, in order that the view from the home of a friend be not obscured. However a petition in the county auditor's office signed by Dudley Woodbridge and 18 others not including Governor Meigs requesting that the building be set back "where it will be most ornamental to the town and equally convenient for the inhabitants of the county" seems to disprove this contention.

In 1900 the contract was let for the construction of a new courthouse. Immediately the old building was torn down and the site prepared for construction. On April 9, 1901 the cornerstone was laid and work continued until the building was ready for occupancy in the summer of 1902. The building still houses most of the offices of the various departments of county government and provides such facilities as are described in the following paragraphs.

Commissioners. The county commissioner's office is located on the south side of the first floor of the courthouse with entrance from the lobby and a door connecting it with the county auditor's office. The greater part of the commissioners' bound records are filed in this room, with the unbound records filed in the auditor's inner office. This room houses not only the commissioner's office but also the offices of the administrator of aid for the blind and the dog warden, and their records. Space and equipment provided these departments are ample for the needs of the officials and the convenience of the public. The room is well lighted and ventilated and is free from both dust and dampness. Unbound commissioners' records prior to 1930 and some old bound records are located in store room No. 3 on the third floor of the county courthouse.

Recorder. The recorder's office, located in the northeast corner of the first floor, consists of three rooms: the main office and record file room, the typing room, and the supply store room. All records, except a few of the older ones which are in store rooms Nos. 1 and 3 on the third floor, are filed in the main office. Steel roller-type equipment is provided for bound records and steel file boxes for unbound records. Space and equipment provided this office are adequate for the needs of the office and for the use of the records by the public. The rooms are well lighted and ventilated and are free from dust and dampness.

Clerk of Courts. The clerk's records, which include the records of the court of common pleas and all appellate courts, and those of the coroner, are housed in three rooms in the northwest corner of the second floor; the main office, the typists' workroom, and the record file room. A large percent of both bound and unbound records are located in the record storerooms on the third floor of the county courthouse. The space and equipment provided this department are ample for the use of officials or other persons wishing to use the records. Adequate steel-roller type equipment with sliding doors is provided for bound records and steel file boxes for unbound records. Lighting and ventilating facilities at the atmospheric conditions are satisfactory.

Probate Court. This department consists of three rooms in the northeast corner of the first floor; the probate court main office, the probate judge's private office, and the record file room. Records are filed in the main office as well as in the record file room. Space provided this department is ample both for the needs of the office and the convenience of the public. However, the filing equipment which consists of steel roller-type shelving for bound records and steel file boxes for unbound records is satisfactory as to type but is quite inadequate. Because of this fact most of the unbound records are filed in chronological order without regard to type of case. This method requires less space and eliminates the transferring of records. The rooms are well lighted and well ventilated and are free from dust and dampness. All records of aid to dependent children are located in the record file room which also houses the office of the administrator. A large percent of bound and unbound records of the probate court are located in the storerooms on the third floor of the courthouse.

Sheriff. The sheriff's office is located in the southeast corner on the second floor of the courthouse. The one room provides adequate space and equipment for the needs of this office. Built-in shelving is provided for filing bound records, and steel file boxes for unbound records. The room is well lighted and well ventilated and free from dust and dampness.

Prosecuting Attorney. The office of prosecuting attorney is the private office of the attorney elected to the position of county prosecutor. At the time the survey was in progress the county prosecutors records were located in the office of the prosecutor, sixth floor, First National Bank Building, Putnam and Second Streets, Marietta.

Treasurer. The treasurer's office, consisting of one room, is located in the northwest corner of the first floor of the courthouse. Space and equipment provided this office are adequate for the needs of the office and the convenience of the public. Steel filing equipment is provided by two built-in record vaults and one steel safe. A number of records are reported as missing which may be located in the record vault on which the combination was accidentally set a short time previous to the survey. No one in the office or in Marietta could be located who knows the combination. Some of the older treasurer's records are located in the store room No. 3 on the third floor of the courthouse; there are also some records housed in the auditor's office. The rooms are well lighted and ventilated and are free from dust and dampness.

Auditor. The auditor's department consists of two rooms located on the west side and southwest corner on the first floor of the courthouse. The rooms, a large main office room and a small private office (auditor's inner office), are well lighted and ventilated and are free from dampness and dust. The space and equipment provided are ample for the needs of the office and the convenience of the public. Steel roller-type shelving is provided for bound records and steel file boxes for unbound records. Records of the budget commission, board of revision, sinking fund trustees, soldiers' relief commission, and unbound records of the county commissioners are housed in the auditor's offices. Unbound records prior to 1930 are located in the record storerooms Nos. 1 and 3 on the third floor of the courthouse. A large number of old bound records are also located in the storerooms. Some of the county treasurer's records are housed in the auditor's office.

County Board of Education. The office of the county board of education is located on the west side of the second floor of the courthouse. It consists of two rooms: the main office and the county superintendent of schools' private office. The rooms are well lighted and ventilated and are free from dust and dampness. The space and equipment provided this office are ample for the needs of the office and the convenience of the public. Some of the records of this office are located in storeroom number one No. 1 on the third floor of the courthouse.

Board of Health. The office of the county board of health is located on the east side of the second floor of the courthouse and consists of two rooms: the main office and reception room, and the conference and laboratory room. The rooms are well lighted and ventilated and are free from dust and dampness. The space and steel filing equipment provided this department are ample for the needs of the office and the convenience of the public.

Children's Home. Records of the children's home are housed in the office of the superintendent of the institution. The superintendent's office is provided with two steel safes in which the institution's records are kept. The office is located on the first floor of the main building and is well lighted and ventilated. The Washington County children's home is located one mile north of Marietta on east side of State Route 77.

County Home. Records of the Washington County home are housed in the office of the superintendent of the institution. The office is located on the west side of the first floor of the institution building. No adequate means of filing or caring for records is provided this office, the records being kept in desk drawers and on desks and tables. The office is well lighted and ventilated and is free from dust and dampness. The Washington County infirmary is located about two and one half miles southeast of Marietta just north of US 50.

Relief Administration. The office of the Washington County relief administration is located on the east side of the county courthouse. This office is well lighted and ventilated and is free from dust and dampness. The space provided this office is very crowded. The equipment provided is adequate for the needs of the office and the convenience of the public. The records of this office are all unbound records and metal filing cabinets are provided for filing records.

Aid for the Aged. The office of aid for the aged is located on the east side of the first floor of the courthouse. This office consists of one room and is very crowded, with no privacy for interviews. The equipment provided this office is ample for the needs of the office and the convenience of the public. The room is well lighted and ventilated and is free from dust and dampness.

Board of Elections. The office of the county board of elections is located in Room 526, First National Bank Building, Putnam and Second Streets. The office consists of one room, well lighted and ventilated and free from dust and dampness. For the needs of this office and the convenience of the public steel filing equipment is provided for filing the records.

Engineer. The office of the county engineer consisting of two rooms is located in the northeast corner of a basement of the courthouse. The rooms are well lighted and ventilated and are free from dampness. Space and equipment provided this office are ample for the needs of the office and the convenience of the public. Steel roller-type shelving is provided for bound records and metal file boxes for unbound records. Records are located in both the main office and the work room.

Agricultural Extension Agent. The office of the county agricultural extension agent is located in the southeast corner of the basement of the courthouse. The office consists of two rooms, well lighted and ventilated in are free from dust and dampness. The space and equipment provided this office are ample for the needs of the office and the convenience of the public. The records of this office are of the unbound type and metal file cases are provided for filing records.

There are three stories for old or inactive records located in the northwest corner of the third floor. These rooms are numbered 1, 2, and 3, and reference is made to them by number and giving the location of the records house in them. These records, dating as early as 1788 or as late as 1932, includes records of the County Commissioners, auditor, treasurer, recorder, clerk of courts, court of quarter sessions, supreme, district, circuit, common please, and probate courts, and the board of education. These records, not grouped as to office or as to type of record, were arranged in part by workers of the Historical Records Survey.

HOUSING, CARE, AND ACCESSIBILITY OF THE RECORDS

Wooden shelving is provided for bound records. The unbound records of earlier dates are arranged in bundles, later dates in cardboard file boxes and heavy paper jackets. The space provided is ample for the proper filing of the records, but more shelving is needed. All three rooms are well lighted by both natural and artificial light. A large amount of dust has collected and many of the records have been slightly damaged by moisture caused by leaks which have developed in the roof at some point in the past.

No accommodations are provided for the convenience of the public in making a search or check of the records.

COURTHOUSE FLOOR PLANS

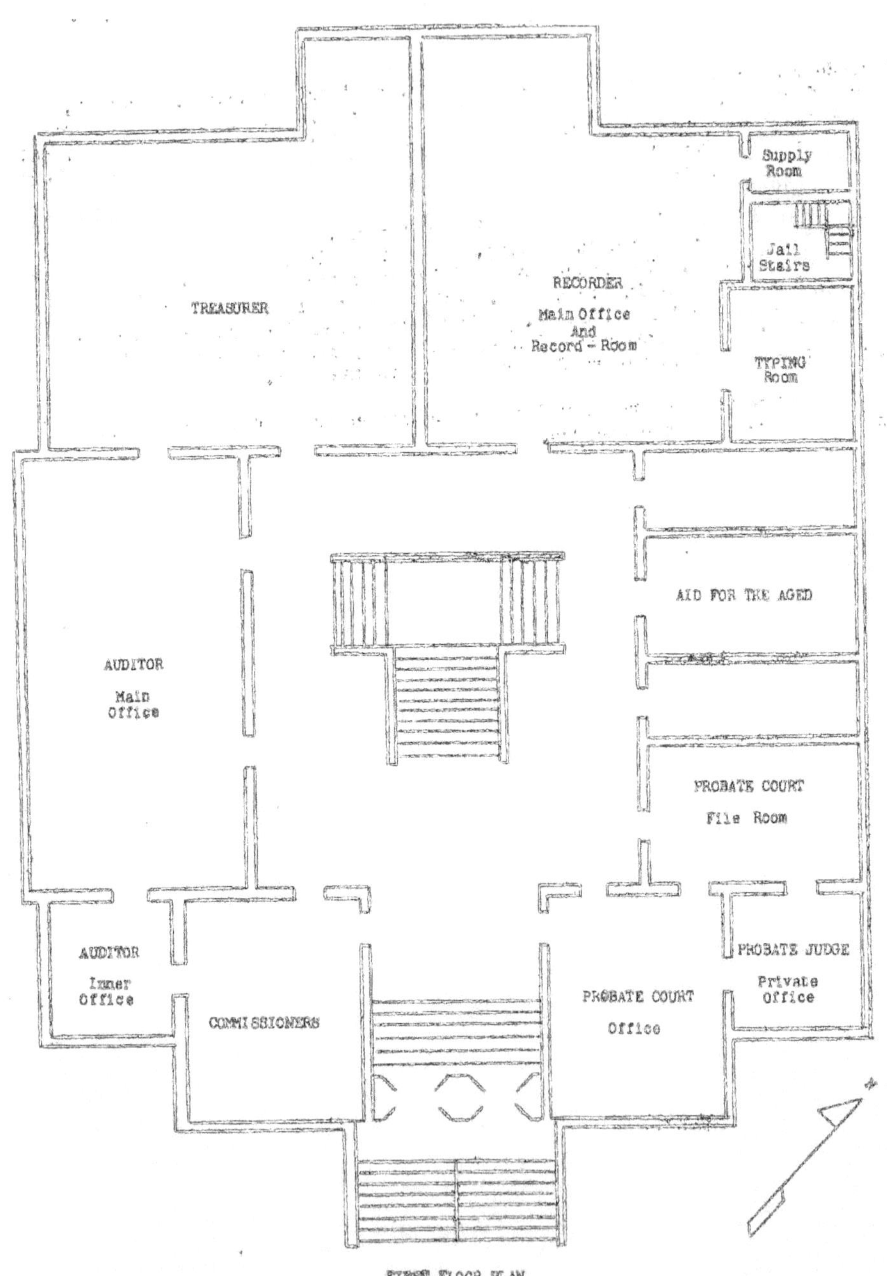

FIRST FLOOR PLAN
WASHINGTON COUNTY COURTHOUSE

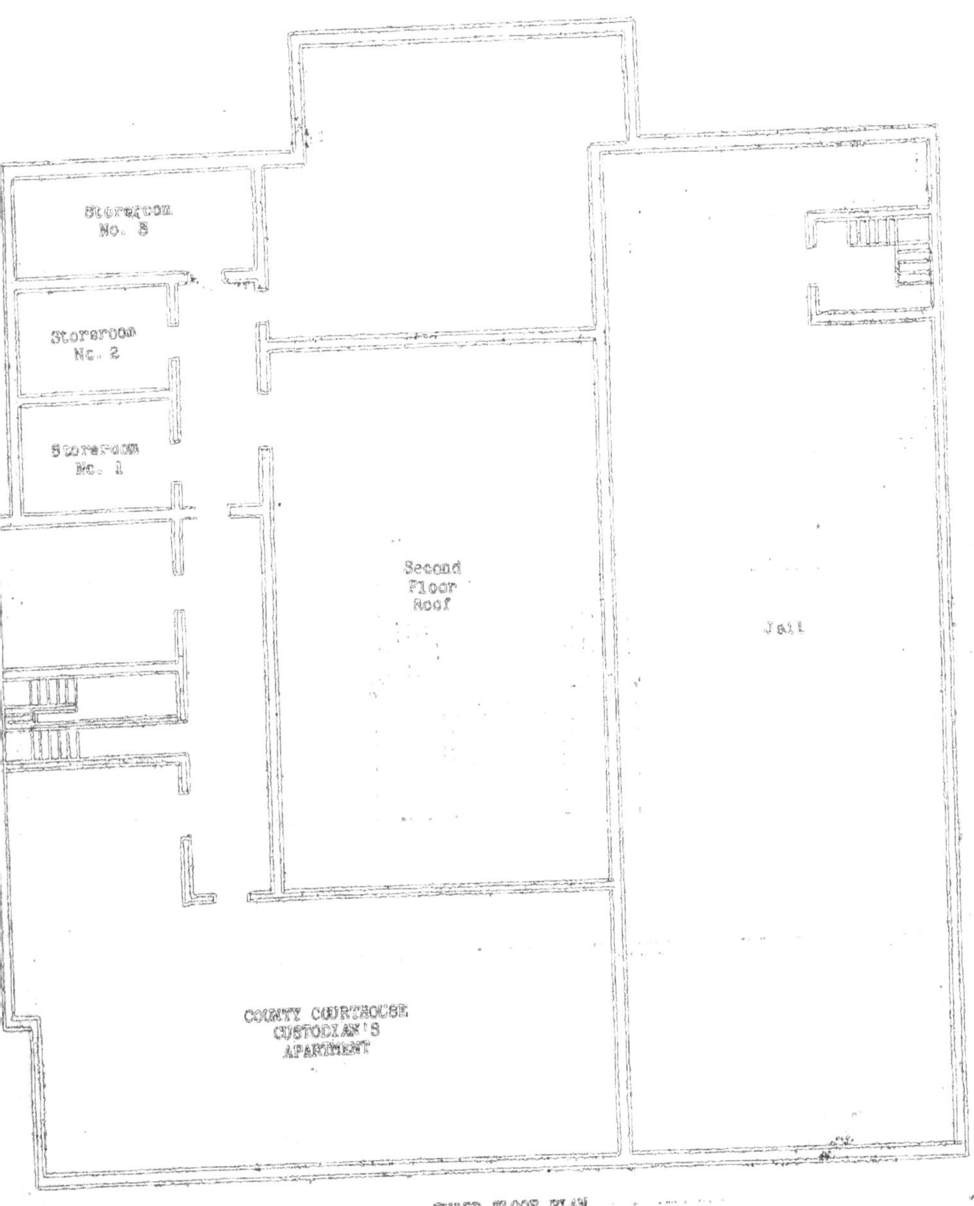

THIRD FLOOR PLAN
WASHINGTON COUNTY COURTHOUSE
MARIETTA, OHIO

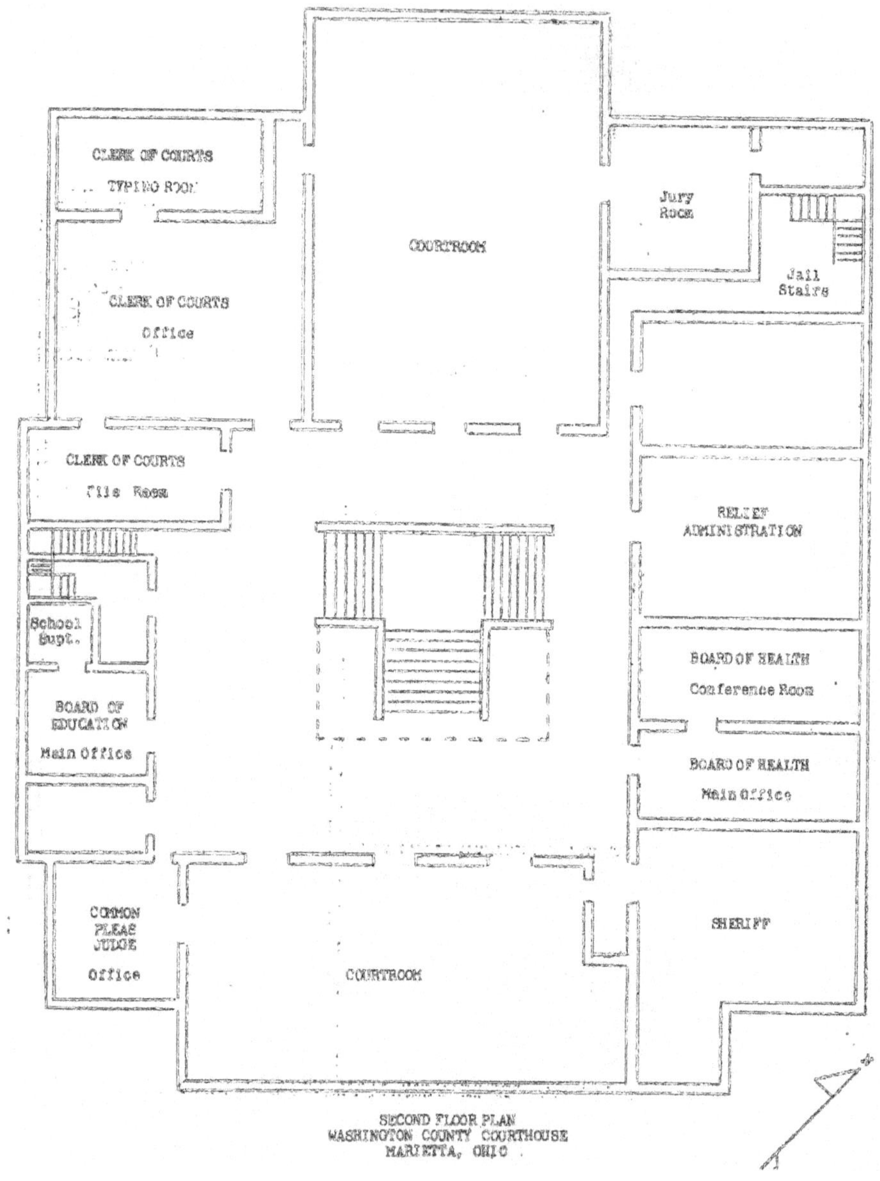

SECOND FLOOR PLAN
WASHINGTON COUNTY COURTHOUSE
MARIETTA, OHIO

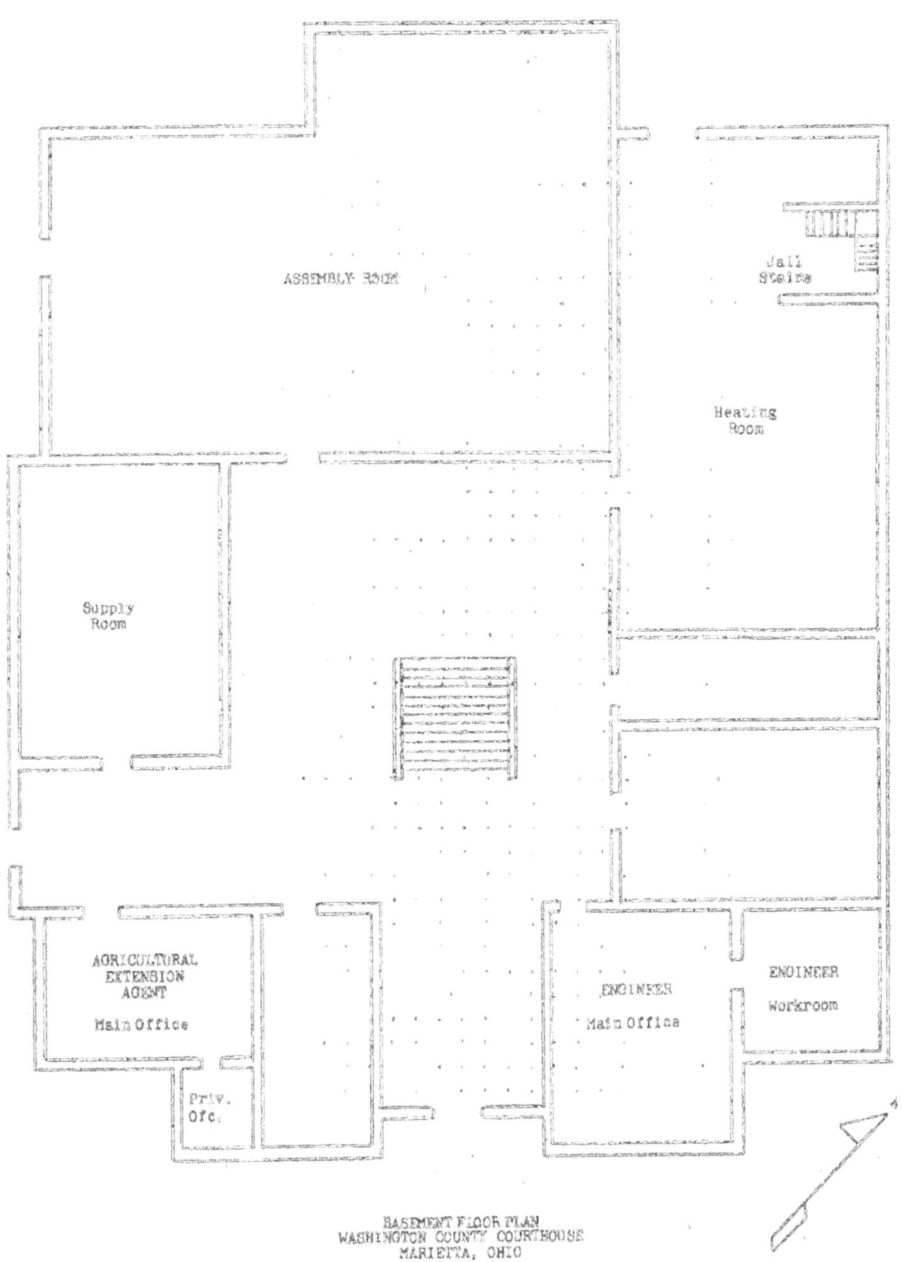

BASEMENT FLOOR PLAN
WASHINGTON COUNTY COURTHOUSE
MARIETTA, OHIO

The local government system for the Northwest Territory comprising the present state of Ohio established the office of county commissioners. This office, created by the territorial act of 1792, consisted of two appointive commissioners who are directed to compile a tax list, levy taxes for the county, and draft plans for and supervise the construction of a "court-house, jail, pillory, whipping-post, and several stocks." (Theodore Calvin Pease, *Laws of the Northwest Territory 1788-1800, Ill. State Bar Assn., Law Ser.*, I, Springfield, 1925, 78).

The governmental system established in 1802, under the first constitution of Ohio, made no provision for the office of county commissioners and its existence is due entirely to statutory enactment. By an act of the legislature passed in 1804, the territorial office was recreated and was to be composed of three members elected for three-year terms (2 O. L. 150). Four years later the commissioners were made a corporate body invested with the power to sue and be sued (5 O. L. 97). They were required to keep a record of their proceedings; to assess taxes for the support of the county; appoint a county treasurer; and to supervise the construction of bridges (8 O. L. 48). They were paid on a per diem basis. Moreover, during the same period they were given the task of constructing courthouses, jails, and offices for the clerk of courts, court of common pleas, sheriff, auditor, and the treasurer (2 O. L. 154-157; 29 O. L. 316). Of these earlier duties the commissioners retain all but one; that of appointing a county treasurer. However, since 1831 they have been authorized to examine and compare the accounts of the county treasurer and county auditor and to examine the condition of county finances.

Besides the duties regarding construction and finance, the commissioners were given the task of constructing local highways when so authorized by the legislature. During the first 30 years of Ohio history the duties of the commissioners in this respect were local in nature. But as the system of road construction expanded they were given the additional duty of converting free turnpikes into state roads (44 (O. L. 74). During the forties and fifties private companies were authorized by the legislature to construct plank roads (44 O. L. 126-127). When those companies were caught in the stringency of a financial depression in1857, the commissioners were authorized to purchase their holdings. If such a transaction were made, the transfer signed by the president of the company was to be deposited with the county auditor. (54 O. L. 198). In the seventies the commissioners, although earlier subjected to regulatory measures by the legislature, were prohibited from levying taxes for roads to exceed three mills on the dollar on the taxable property in the county (69 O. L. 11). Later, in 1885, they were authorized to levy taxes not to exceed five mills on the dollar on all taxable property in the county for the maintenance of roads which had been damaged by excessive wear or were damaged from other causes (G. C. sec. 7419).

With the development of modern means of transportation, scientific principles were applied to road construction and maintenance. Although the county surveyor, now the county engineered had in earlier years furnished the commissioners with estimates for bridge construction, it was not until the latter part of the nineteenth century that they were authorized to utilize his scientific knowledge in road construction. (78 O. L. 285; 98 O. L. 245-247). After the opening of the present century the surveyor was directed to appoint a maintenance engineer, with the consent of the commissioners, to supervise the repairing of improved roads in the county (108 O. L. pt. i, 497).

Although the county commissioners have never been closely associated with the administration of criminal justice, their earlier duties regarding the construction of county jails qualified them, in the earlier period, for additional duties in this respect. During the middle of the nineteenth century the commissioners of Cuyahoga County were authorized to employ persons on construction work who were confined in the county jails. (37 O. L. 54). While this provision was repealed by the criminal code adopted in 1853, other earlier functions applicable to all counties were continued. Since 1843 the commissioners have provided equipment and fixtures for places of incarceration, food and clothing for prisoners, and have appointed a jail physician. (41 O. L. 74; 87 O. L. 186). Since 1869 they have been authorized to offer a reward for the detection or apprehension of any person charged with a felony in the county. (66 O. L. 321). Since 1892 the commissioners in any county where there is no workhouse may, under certain conditions, release or parole an indigent person confined in the jail (89 O. L. 408; 113 O. L. 203). With the extension of modern crime into the rural areas in the form of small-town bank robbing, the commissioners were given the duty of furnishing motorcycles to the sheriff and his deputies in an attempt to compete with the high-powered equipment used by modern gangs. One of the latest functions in this respect is the contracting with radio stations for the broadcasting of descriptions of fleeing criminals (G. C. sec. 13431-1).

Besides providing for those who have violated the laws, the commissioners were given the duty of caring for persons who, because of poverty or physical or mental defects, became public charges Since 1816 they have established and maintained "poor houses." (14 O. L. 477). Since 1908 the commissioners have been authorized to issue warrants for the relief of the blind from $100 to $400 per year (G. C. sec. 2969). Since 1913 they have been authorized, in any county containing a city which has an infirmary, to contract with the director of public safety for the care of the county's indigent (G. C. sec. 2419-1). In 1933 the commissioners were designated as a board to administer the state law providing aid for the aged (115 O. L. pt. ii, 431-439). Two years later, in 1935, the commissioners were authorized to provide non-institutional support, care, assistance, or relief for the indigent in the county and were authorized to establish a suitable agency or office for such purposes (116 O. L. 134).

In addition to furnishing financial aid to the civilian population the commissioners were authorized, in 1886, to levy a tax for the relief of indigent Union soldiers, sailors, or marines of the Civil War, or if such veterans were deceased, for their dependents (83 O. L, 232). In 1919 the provisions of the original act were amended to include all indigent veterans of the World War (108 O. L. pt. i, 633). The commissioners were authorized also, in 1884, to defray the funeral expenses of any honorably discharged soldier, sailor, or marine who died indigent. Ten years later the provisions of the act were extended to include the mother, wife, or widow of any soldier, sailor, or marine; and the war nurses. (90 O. L. 177).

The humanitarian duty of caring for the county's dependent and neglected children was delegated to the county commissioners. Since 1866 they have been authorized to establish and maintain a children's home. At the beginning of the present century, when the treatment of children was undergoing a remarkable change, they were authorized to place dependent and neglected children in private homes or institutions where they would receive food, clothing, and medical and dental treatment (109 O. L. 533). The development of the juvenile court system added new responsibilities. In order to completely segregate juvenile offenders from adults being tried in the regular criminal courts, the commissioners were authorized to provide a separate building, to be known as the "juvenile court."

The commissioners, by the authority conferred upon them to construct public buildings, were given duties regarding educational advancement. Since 1871 they have been authorized to accept the quests for the construction of county libraries, and since 1913 to issue bonds, after submitting such questions to the voters, for the construction of libraries, or to contract with existing libraries for the use of people in the county (G. C. secs. 2454, 2434-1; 110 O. L. 242). Moreover, during the same period, they were authorized to provide and maintain civic centers in the county and to employ an expert director to supervise and administer them (G.

C. sec. 2457-4).

Other duties not closely related to the original ones have been added from decade to decade. For example, in 1850 the commissioners were authorized to subscribe to one leading newspaper of each political party in the county and cause them to be bound and deposited with the county auditor as public archives. (48 O. L. 65). The newspapers on file in the auditor's office have not been listed in this inventory as they are to be subject of a separate publication. Amendment to the original act, passed in 1923, provided for the preservation of such newspapers for a period of ten years, after which they may be removed to the Ohio State Archaeological and Historical Society library. (110 O. L. 4). They have been authorized also to promote historical research by appropriating annually a sum not to exceed $100 to defray the expenses of compiling and publishing historical data for historical societies not incorporated for profit. (G. C. sec. 2457-1).

During the early years of the twentieth century the commissioners were given the duty of providing facilities for county sanitation, which, in previous years had been sadly neglected. In 1917 they were authorized to lay out, establish, and maintain one or more sewer districts within the county. Since 1917 no sewer or sewage treatment works may be constructed outside of any incorporated municipality by any person, persons, firms, or corporations until the plans have been approved by the commissioners. (G. C. sec. 6602-1; 107 O. L. 440).

Then, too, during the same period the commissioners were authorized to provide facilities for the treatment of tuberculosis. In 1913 they were empowered to appoint, with the approval of the state department of health, one or more instructing and visiting nurses to visit homes or places housing tubercular patients, and since 1917 have been authorized to establish tuberculosis dispensaries and provide by tax levies the necessary funds for their establishment and maintenance. (G. C. sec. 3153, 3153-5). Meantime they were authorized to cooperate with the commissioners of other counties for the establishment of a district tubercular hospital (100 O. L. 87).

Finally, the county commissioners have acted in a supervisory capacity over other county officials. Since the middle of the nineteenth century they have been authorized to compare the annual reports and statements made to them by the prosecuting attorney, clerk of courts, sheriff, and treasurer; take measures to rectify errors, correct discrepancies, and record in their journal the results of such examinations. (G. C. sec. 2504; R. S. 886; 48 O. L. 66). Such reports were filed with the county auditor who has custody of their official acts and proceedings.

Moreover in the latter part of the same century the commissioners were given their present duty of visiting hospitals, detention hones, private asylums, and any other institution exercising a reformatory or correctional influence over individuals, and reporting on the sanitary conditions and the treatment of inmates. These reports, filed with the county prosecutor, are open to the inspection and examination of the public (G. C. sec. 2499; 92 O. L. 212).

The county commissioners offer a typical example of an office, which, designed primarily for an agricultural society, has expanded to meet the needs and requirements of modern society. At present the commissioners are elected for a four-year term (108 O. L. pt. ii, 1300).

Journals

1. COMMISSIONERS' JOURNAL
1797—. 20 volumes.

Minutes of meetings and proceedings of the board of county commissioners under territorial government, 1797-1803, and under county government, 1813—. Volume for 1797-1810 contains a record copy of all petitions including petitions to establish roads; copy of all resolutions passed by the board record of commissioners' appointment of county officials; itemized account of bills for payment from public funds, with record of date order was issued on the county treasury for payment; reports of assessors and tax collectors; and record of tax levies. [Record of Common Pleas Court], 1805, entry 207. Volumes for 1810— contain a record of proceedings in laying out and establishing roads; fixing damages to land by construction of roads; appraising property and fixing the tax thereon; allowing appropriation for the building and improving of bridges, ditches, and culverts; appointing of land viewers; establishing the location of ferries and the rate of transportation across the various rivers; and proceedings in relation to the children's home and the agricultural society. Contains: Infirmary Journal 1935—, entry 5; Contract Record, 1797-1912, entry 32; Journal, 1935—, entry 505 (Blind Relief) Record, December 19112-May 1936, entry 638. Chronologically arranged by dates of entries. For index to bills, 1877-1904, see entry 3; otherwise no index 17 99-1908; for index 1909—, see entry 2; for index to infirmary and children's home bills, see entry 463. 1797-1913, handwritten; 1913— typed. Average 500 pages. 18 x 13 x 3. Commissioners' office, south wall.

2. GENERAL INDEX TO COMMISSIONERS' JOURNAL
1909—. 10 volumes.

Index to Commissioners' Journal showing surnames and names of principals, volume and page numbers of record, amount in dollars and cents, and for what purpose. Arranged under tabs by names of departments, alphabetically thereunder by subjects or names of principals, and chronologically thereunder by dates of entries. 1909-1928, handwritten; 1928—, handwritten and typed. Average 300 pages. 18.5 x 12.5 x 3. Commissioners's office, south wall.

3. GENERAL INDEX TO COMMISSIONERS' JOURNAL, BILLS
1877-1904. 1 volume. No prior records.

Index to bills as recorded in Commissioners' Journal, entry 1, showing name of creditor, volume and page numbers of record, date bill filed, amount of bill, and nature of bill. Alphabetically arranged by names of creditors and chronologically thereunder by dates of filing. Handwritten on printed forms. 480 pages. 18 x 12 x 2.5. Storeroom 3.

For subsequent records, see entry 462.

4. MINUTES
1931. 1 file box (E6).

Notes of special meetings of the Washington County commissioners showing dates of meetings, names of commissioners, and record of business transacted. Chronologically arranged by dates of meetings. For index, see entry 397. Handwritten. 13 x 5 x 10. Auditor's inner office.

5. INFIRMARY JOURNAL
1913-1934. 2 volumes. 1865-1912 in Journal, entry 605; 1935— in Commissioners' Journal, entry 1.

Record copy of minutes of meetings of county commissioners sitting as the board of infirmary directors showing date of meeting; record of business; itemized account of bills and claims considered and allowed showing bill number, date of bill, name of creditor, for what, amount of bill, and amount allowed; and copies of annual inventories of infirmary equipment and furnishings showing appraised valuation. Chronologically arranged by dates of meetings. No index. Typed. Average 570 pages. 16 x11 x 2.75. Auditor's office.

Reports

6. REPORTS

1852—. 34 bundles and 4 file boxes.

Original annual reports to county commissioners by county officials showing date of report and date filed, what office, record of office expense and detailed itemized account of fees, fines, costs, and sundries collected. Chronologically arranged by dates of filing. 1852-1930, no index; for index, 1930—, see entry 197. 1852-1914, typed on printed forms. Bundles, 4 x 3.5 x 9.5; file boxes, 10 x 4.5 x 14. 23 bundles, 1852-1929, storeroom 3; 4 file boxes, 1930—, Auditor's inner office.

For duplicate copies of prosecuting attorneys reports, see entry 325; of sheriff's reports, see entry 336; of treasurer's reports, see entry 384; of auditor's reports, see entry 521.

7. SOLDIERS' RELIEF

1915—. 1 file box (A9).

Original copy of the soldiers' relief commission report to county commissioners recommending assistance to those entitled thereto under the provisions of state act and showing name of person, amount to be paid each month, relationship of soldier, sailor, or marine, and address of recipient. Chronologically arranged by dates of reports. No index. Handwritten on printed forms. 13 x 5 x 10. Auditor's inner office.

For other records, see entries 37, 636, 637.

8. [CLERK OF COURTS' REPORTS]

1793-1825. In Road Record, entry 679.

Record copy of annual reports by the clerk of courts to the county commissioners on the amount of fines and costs assessed and common pleas court, number of days court was held, judges' per diem, and total amount due judges.

For subsequent records, see entry 9.

9. RECORD

1856-1882. 1 volume. Subsequent records missing.

Record copy of annual reports by clerk of courts, prosecuting attorney, probate judge, and sheriff to county commissioners showing number of cases filed in county courts, number of cases disposed of, number of cases still pending, number of arrests made, number of prisoners conveyed to penal institutions, number of incompetents conveyed to state institutions, number of prisoners registered in county jail, number of meals served to prisoners in county jail, cost of feeding prisoners in county jail, total amount of fines and costs assessed, amount of fines and costs collected, and total witness and juror fees per diem, and mileage. Chronologically arranged by years. No index. Handwritten. 290 pages. 15 x 10 x 1.5. Storeroom 3.

For prior records of clerk of courts reports, see entry 8.

10. ANNUAL REPORTS

1904—. 4 bundles and 1 file box.

Record copy of county commissioners detailed annual reports of receipts and expenditures accounting funds showing date of report, abstract of tax duplicate of county giving property value, tax rate and total property tax assessed, amount of special assessments, amount of liquor (1904-1919) and cigarette tax assessments, amount of receipts for all other sources, and total cash receipts; also amount distributed to state, county, townships, municipalities, and schools, amount appropriated to each fund or department, detailed account of expenditures by such county office or department, balance or deficit of each fund or department appropriation, total balance of all funds, and total indebtedness of county. Chronologically arranged by years. 1904-1933, no index; for index, 1933—, see entry 397. Handwritten on printed forms. Bundles, 3 x 4 x 10; file box, 10 x 4.5 x 14. 4 bundles, 1904-1932, storeroom 3; 1 file box, 1933—, Auditor's inner office.

11. REPORTS OF COUNTY DOG WARDEN

1928—. 1 file box (U5)

Original reports of county dog warden to the board of county commissioners of claims for damages to livestock inflicted by dogs showing name and address of claimants; township; number of animals and their kind grade, quality, and value of same; nature of injury, amount of damages claimed less deduction for carcasses or pelts sold or used, and net damages claims; and dog warden's estimate of net amount of injury. Chronologically arranged by dates of reports. For index, see entry 397. Handwritten on printed forms. 13 x 5 x 10. Auditor's inner office.

For dog warden's duplicates, see entry 706.

12. SHERIFF'S STATEMENTS

1859—. 34 bundles and 3 file boxes.

Original monthly reports to the county commissioners from the sheriff on number of meals served to county jail inmates giving date, name of prisoner or other person, cost of meal, and number of meals. Chronologically arranged by dates of reports. 1859-1928, no index; for index,1929—, see entry 397. 1859-1928, handwritten on printed forms; 1929—, typed on printed forms. Bundles, 3 x 3.5 x9; file boxes, 13 x 5 x 10. 34 bundles, 1859-1928, storeroom 3; 3 file boxes, 1929—, Auditor's inner office.

13. [CHILDREN'S HOME TRUSTEES' REPORTS]

1877-1912. In Children's Home Reports and Vouchers, entry 467.

Annual reports from the trustees of the children's home to the county commissioners showing number of children in the home according to last report, number admitted during the year, number discharged from the home during the year, and number in the home at time of report; also itemized account of receipts and expenditures, balance at time of report; and date filed.

For subsequent records, see entry 14.

14. CHILDREN'S HOME REPORTS

1913—. 2 file boxes.

Reports of the superintendent of the children's home to the board of county commissioners showing number of inmates, statistics for the year, number of inmates from other counties, list of expenditures, to whom paid and for what purpose, voucher number and amount, total cash received during the year, total amount on hand at close a fiscal year, and signatures of trustees. Chronologically arranged by dates of reports. For index, see entry 397. Handwritten on printed forms. 13 x 5 x 10. 5. Auditor's inner office.

For prior records, see entry 13.

15. REPORTS, INFIRMARY DIRECTORS

1871-1912. 4 bundles.

Original semi-annual reports from infirmary directors to the county commissioners showing date of report, number of inmates registered in institution according to last report, number registered since last report, number of births and deaths since last report, number discharged since last report, and number of inmates at time of report; also itemized account of receipts and expenditures for period of report, detailed inventory of infirmary property, and date of filing. Chronologically arranged by dates of filing. No index. Handwritten on printed forms.4 x 3.5 x 8. Storeroom 3.

For subsequent records, see entry 16.

16. REPORTS, INFIRMARY SUPERINTENDENTS

1913—. 2 file boxes (I2, I3).

Original semi-annual reports from infirmary superintendent to the county commissioners showing date of report, number of inmates registered in institution according to last report, number registered since last report, number of births and deaths since last report, number discharged since last report, and number of inmates at time of report; also itemized account of receipts and expenditures for period of report, detailed inventory of infirmary property, and date of filing. Chronologically arranged by dates of filing. For index, see entry 397. Handwritten on printed forms. 13 x 5 x 10. Auditor's inner office.

For prior records, see entry 15.

17. FINANCIAL STATEMENTS

1904—. 29 jackets and 3 file boxes (F10-F12).

Original monthly financial statements by the county auditor to county commissioners showing receipts from all sources to each fund, expenditures authorized by voucher or warrant against each fund, credit balance to each fund at beginning of report period, credit balance to each fund on date of statement, record of transfer of funds, and dates of filing. Chronologically arranged by dates of filing.1904-1929, no index; for index, 1929—, see entry 397. Handwritten on printed forms. Jackets 3.5 x 4.5 x 9; file boxes, 10 x 4.5 x 14. 29 jackets, 1904-1928, storeroom 3; 3 file boxes, 1929—, Auditor's inner office.

18. DOCTORS' CERTIFICATES

1916—.1 file box (D5).

Original reports to county commissioners by physicians on tubercular patients showing date of examination, name of patient, kind of tuberculosis suffered by patient, and recommendation for proper treatment and nursing for patient at a sanitarium. Chronologically arranged by dates of examinations. For index, see entry 397. Handwritten on printed forms. 13 x 5 x 10. Auditor's inner office.

Road Records
(See also entries 677-683)

19. ROAD RECORDS

1794—. 1,221 bundles and 24 file boxes.

Original petitions filed with county commissioners by freeholders of county for establishing roads including original reports of viewers appointed to view route petitioned for, original reports by county engineer of surveys made of route petitioned showing sketch of proposed route and survey data, estimate of cost of establishing road, and date filed. Chronologically arranged by dates of filing. 1794-1885, no index; for index, 1886—, see entry 397. Handwritten. Bundles, 5 x 4 x 8; file boxes, 10 x 4.5 x 14. 1,221 bundles, 1794-1930, storeroom 3; 24 file boxes, 1886—, Auditor's inner office.

20. RESOLUTIONS

1916—. 1 file box (D4).

Records of resolutions adopted by board of county commissioners for the purchase of road building materials, support of county agricultural agents' work in Washington County, purchase of road graders for certain townships, and for building of roads which have been petitioned for. Chronologically arranged by dates of filing. For index, see entry 397. Typed on printed forms.13 x 5 x 10. Auditor's inner office.

For prior records, see entry 677.

21. ROAD PETITIONS TO CONSTRUCT OR IMPROVE ROADS

1916—. 6 volumes.

Record copy of petitions to the board of commissioners for the building of new roads and the improvement of old ones showing date, name of road, route of proposed road, names of owners of land through which road extends, and signatures of the petitioners. Chronologically arranged by dates of entries. No index. Handwritten on printed forms. Average 25 pages. 16 x 10 x .5. Commissioners' office, south wall.

For prior records, see entry 677.

22. PETITIONS REFUSED

1831—. 17 bundles and 1 file box.

Original petitions filed by freeholders with commissioners asking for the establishing, extending, changing, or vacating of public roads and designating proposed road, with signatures of petitioners and data filing. Chronologically arranged by dates of filing. 1831-1914, no index; for index, 1915—, see entry 397. Handwritten. Bundles, 4 x 3.5 x 8; file box, 10 x 4.5 x 14. 1 bundles, 1831-1914, storeroom 3; 1 file box, 1915—, Auditor's inner office.

23. BONDS

1826-1909. 21 bundles.

Surety bonds which have been filed with county commissioners by petitioners for establishing, vacating, or changing roads and showing date of bond, name of road, amount of bond, and signatures of petitioners filing bond. Chronologically arranged by dates of bonds. No index. Handwritten.4 x 3.5 x 8. Storeroom 3.

For other records, see entries 24, 382, 528-537.

24. BONDS IN PETITION FOR COUNTY ROADS

1904—. 1 file box. Last bond filed 1933.

Record showing names of petitioners, names of bondsmen, amount of bond furnished, date bond signed by bondsmen, outline of street or road, and presentation of petition to county commissioners. Chronologically arranged by dates of petitions. For index, see entry 397. Handwritten on printed forms. 10 x 4.5 x 14. Auditor's inner office.

For other records, see entries, 23, 382, 528-537.

25. SPECIAL ASSESSMENTS FOR STATE HIGHWAYS

1931-1932. 9 volumes. Prior records missing; discontinued.

Commissioners record of special assessments against landholders for the building of state highways showing name of owner, class, rate, range, township, and road numbers, acreage, number of lot, description of lands, name of town or township, classification, number of acres taxed, value, assessment, and date paid. Chronologically arranged by dates of entries. No index. Handwritten on printed forms. Average 100 pages. 25 x 20 x 1. Commissioners' office, east wall.

Agreements and Contracts

26. CONTRACTS

1915—. 1 file box (F4).

Original contracts entered into by the board of county commissioners and the township trustees with physicians for the care of ill, indigent persons showing date of contact, name of physician, and annual compensation. Chronologically arranged by dates of filing for index, see entry 397. Typed on printed forms. 13 x 5 x 10. Auditor's inner office.

27. BRIDGE CONTRACTS

1912-1915. 2 file boxes (E1, F1).

Agreements entered into by contractors and board of county commissioners for construction of bridges according to plans and specifications showing date of contract, name of contractor, and conditions of contract. Chronologically arranged by dates of contracts. For index, see entry 397. Handwritten on printed forms. 13 x 5 x 10. Auditor's inner office.

28. AGREEMENTS

1920-1930. 1 file box. (A5).

Original agreements entered into between landowners and county commissioners. Easement agreements for establishing highways by which all claims to further compensation and damage in connection with the opening, construction, and improvement of the road are waived. Chronologically arranged by dates of filing. For index, see entry 397. Typed on printed forms. 13 x 5 x 10. Auditor's inner office.

29. CONTRACTS, ROAD AND BRIDGE

1887-1932. 49 jackets.

Original contracts entered into by county commissioners with contractors for furnishing material and labor in construction and repair of county roads and bridges showing date of contract, what road or bridge, specifications of material and work to be performed, amount of contract, name of contractor, amount of bond filed by contractor, and date contract to be fulfilled. Chronologically arranged by dates of filing. No index. Handwritten on printed forms. 4.5 x 4.5 x 10. Storeroom 3.

30. CONTRACTS

1796-1921. 132 bundles and 21 jackets.

Original contracts and agreements entered into by county commissioners with firms and individuals to furnish material or labor, or both, in construction or repair of county roads, bridges, and buildings showing date of contract, name of contractor, conditions of contract, date contract to be completed, and amount of contract. Chronologically arranged by dates of contracts. No index. Handwritten on printed forms. Bundles, 3.5 x 3.5 x 8; jackets, 3.5 x 4.5 x 9. Storeroom 3.

31. ROAD AND HIGHWAY CONTRACTS

1917—. 1 file box (R6).

Original contracts between county commissioners and firms and individuals for road construction and repair showing date of contract, conditions of contract, name of road, and length of improvements. Chronologically arranged by dates of filing. For index, see entry 397. Handwritten on printed forms. 13 x 10 x 5. Auditor's inner office.

32. CONTRACT RECORD

1913—. 2 volumes. 1797-1912 in Commissioners' Journal, entry 1.

Record showing contract number, estimate of quantity of material, and cost of improvement as furnished by county engineer; date advertised, record of bids submitted, date and contract awarded, name of contractor, date work to start, date to be completed, amount of contract, and record of payments to contractor on account. Numerically arranged by contract numbers. Alphabetical index by names of contractors. Handwritten on printed forms. Average 330 pages. 16 x 11 x 1.75. Auditor's office.

Estimates and Specifications

33. ESTIMATES AND SPECIFICATIONS

1811-1917. 379 bundles.

Original estimates and specifications by county surveyor on construction and repair of county roads, bridges, and buildings as filed with county commissioners showing date filed, what improvement, estimate of amount of material required, hours of labor, estimated total cost, specifications as to type of construction, and grade of material to be used. Chronologically arranged by dates of filing. No index. 1811-1862, handwritten; 1863-1917, handwritten on printed forms. 4 x 3.5 x 9. Storeroom 3.

34. ESTIMATES
1912—. 22 file boxes (G3).
Records of estimates for repairs to county buildings showing date, amount of estimate, what building, and estimate by county surveyor. Chronologically arranged by dates of submission. For index, see entry 397. Typed on printed forms. 13 x 5 x 10. Auditor's inner office.

35. CONSTRUCTION BIDS ON COUNTY BRIDGES
1913—. 1 file box (B4).
Last entry 1933.
Original bids submitted by contractors for the building and erection of bridges showing date, name and address of contractor, amount of bid, and itemized total of all items. Chronologically arranged by dates of bids. For index, see entry 397. Handwritten and typed on printed forms. 13 x 5 x 10. Auditor's inner office.

Relief Records

36. MOTHERS' PENSIONS
1915-1936. 11 file boxes.
Probate court findings and orders on making allowances for mothers' pensions showing date filed, name of applicant, number of dependent children, and amount of grant per month. Chronologically arranged by dates of filing. For index, see entry 397. Handwritten on printed forms. 13 x 5 x 10. Auditor's inner office.

For subsequent records of aid to dependent children, see entries 655-659; for other records, see entries 318-320.

37. APPLICATIONS FOR SOLDIERS' RELIEF
1886—. 58 jackets and 1 file box (D6).
Original applications for relief filed with the county commissioners by indigent ex-soldiers, sailors, and marine; and by war nurses, (1894—) showing name of applicant, date of applications, birthplace, present address, member of what company and regiment or vessel, service record, statement of applicant sustaining

claim for need of relief, date of filing, and (1913—) amount allowed. Contains [Applications for Soldiers' Relief by Surviving Relatives], 1894—, entry 38. Chronologically arranged by dates of filing. 1886-1912, no index; for index, 1913—, see entry 397. 1886-1912, handwritten on printed forms; 1913-1915, handwritten and typed on printed forms; 1916—, typed on printed forms. Jackets, 3.5 x 4.5 x 9; file box, 13 x 5 x 10. 68 jackets, 1886-1915, Storeroom 3; 1 file box, 1913—, Auditor's inner office..

38. [APPLICATIONS FOR SOLDIER'S RELIEF BY SURVIVING RELATIVES]

1894—. In Applications for Soldiers' Relief, entry 37.

Applications for soldiers' relief by an indigent ex-soldier's parent, wife, widow, or minor child for relief from soldiers' relief fund giving date, name of applicant, age and in what year born, relationship of applicant to deceased soldier, name of company and regiment in which he served, date of soldier's death, present address of applicant, amount of income or earnings (if any), and signature of applicant.

39. BLIND RELIEF APPLICATIONS

1892-June 1936. 4 jackets and 1 file box (B7

Original applications to county commissioners for relief of needy blind showing date, name and sex of applicant, affidavit showing applicant is, by reason of loss of eyesight, unable to provide self with the necessities of life and has not sufficient means for maintenance, and length of residence in state of Ohio; also record of written evidence of blindness showing date, name and sex of applicant, local address, supporting testimony of competent witnesses, and copy of medical certificate. Chronologically arranged by dates of filing. 1892-1924, no index; for index, 1925-1936, see entry 397. Handwritten on printed forms. Jackets, 3.5 x 4.5 x 9; file box, 13 x 5 x 10. 4 jackets, 1892-1925, Storeroom 3; 1 file box, 1925-June 1936, Auditor's inner office.

For subsequent records, see entries 638-341.

Business Administration of Office

Appropriations

40. ANNUAL APPROPRIATION RESOLUTIONS

1929—. 3 volumes. Prior records missing.

Departmental budget showing expenditure classification, expenditures last year, appropriation for current year, request for next year, amount approved by county commissioners for budget, actual expenditures, and appropriation for following year; also shows title of position, name of person now holding position, present rate of pay, rate of pay for next year, and amount requested for next year by county commissioners. Chronologically arranged by dates of entries. No index. Handwritten on printed forms. Average 25 pages. 14 x 8.5 x .25. Auditor's inner office.

41. APPROPRIATIONS

1930—. 4 file boxes (B4, C6, G2, G4). Prior records missing.

Original appropriation orders by the county commissioners showing date and appropriation order number for trustees of the different townships, to be used for repair and maintenance of county roads, showing amount of appropriation by the order of board of county commissioners. Chronologically arranged by dates of appropriations. For index, see entry 397. Handwritten on printed forms. 13 x 5 x 10. Auditor's inner office.

42. APPROPRIATION CERTIFICATES

1925—. 1 file box (A4). Prior records missing.

Certificates to county auditor by board of county commissioners of appropriations for: treatment of tuberculosis, soldiers' relief, mothers' pensions, maintenance of county and children's homes, experiment farm, salaries for clerks of county officials, and general operating expense. Chronologically arranged by dates of appropriations. For index, see entry 397. Handwritten on printed forms. 13 x 5 x 10. Auditor's inner office.

Bills and Accounts

43. [TREASURY RECEIPTS]

1793-1825. In Road Record (First Series), Entry 679.

Copy of commissioners' account of annual receipts and expenditures from the county treasury.

44. CLASSIFICATION BLOTTER

1901-1912. 2 volumes. Prior records missing; discontinued.

Auditor's classification of expenditures of county funds from which county commissioners make up their annual report showing for each fund, names of payees, order numbers, purpose, amounts, and classified as to material, labor, fees, debt payments, interest, salaries, and sundries. Alphabetically arranged by names of funds. No index. Handwritten or printed forms. Average 110 pages. 16 x 14 x .75. Auditor's inner office.

45. SHEEP CLAIMS

1890-1932. 14 file boxes.

Original claims filed for compensation for sheep killed or injured by dogs showing date claim filed, name of claimant, number of sheep killed, number of sheep injured, value, testimony of witnesses, amount allowed, and order number. Chronologically arranged by dates of filing. No index. Handwritten on printed forms. 4.5 x 4.5 x 10. Storeroom 3.

For subsequent records, see entry 46; for records of claims, see entry 47.

46. ANIMAL CLAIMS

1931—. 3 file boxes (C5, D3, D5).

Original animal claims presented to the trustees of the various townships for damages done by the killing or injury of horses sheep, cattle, swine, mules, and goats by dogs, showing number of animals, kind, grade, quality, value, nature of injury, township, amount, and names and addresses of owners and of witnesses. Chronologically arranged by dates of filing. For index, see entry 397. Handwritten on printed forms. 13 x 5 x 10. Auditor's inner office.

For prior records of sheep claims, see entry 45; for other records see entry 461.

47. SHEEP CLAIM RECORD

1892—. 3 volumes. Prior record is missing.

Record of claims for sheep killed or injured by dogs showing claim number, name of claimant, number killed, number injured, amount claimed for killed, amount claimed for injured, total claim, amount allowed, order number, names of witnesses, and amount of fees and mileage to witnesses. Numerically arranged by claim numbers. No index. Handwritten on printed forms. Average 390 pages. 16 x 11 x 2.5. 1 volume, 1892-1917, Storeroom 3; 2 volumes, 1917—, Commissioners' office.

For original claims, see entries 45, 46.

48. COUNTY ORDERS, STUBS

1807-1816. 6 volumes.

Record stubs of orders issued by county commissioners for payment of bills and claims from county funds showing order number, date, name of payee, amount of order, and for what. Numerically arranged by consecutive order numbers. No index. Handwritten on printed forms. Average 139 pages. 6.5 x 2.5 x 1. Storeroom 3.

49. BILLS

1803—. 1,417 bundles, 97 jackets, and 62 file boxes.

Original bills and claims filed with commissioners by creditors of county for payment showing date of bill, for what, amount, name of creditor, and date filed. Chronologically arranged by dates of filing. 1802-1928, no index; for index, 1929—, see entry 397. Handwritten. Bundles, 4.5 x 3.5 x 7; jackets, 3.5 x 4.5 x 9; file boxes, 1929—, Auditor's inner office.

Soldiers' Burial Record

50. SOLDIERS' BURIAL RECORD

1891—. 4 volumes. Prior records missing.

Report of burial commission to the county commissioners on the burial of indigent soldiers and sailors, their wives, widows, mothers, and children, showing name of decedent, if soldier or sailor, what rank, company and regiment or vessel, relationship of decedent to soldier or sailor, township or town, date of death, itemized statement of burial expenses, copy of report by township or ward committee on claim, and date approved by county commissioners. Chronologically arranged by dates approved. Alphabetically indexed by names of decedents.

Handwritten on printed forms. Average 230 pages. 14 x 10 x 1.25. 1 volume, 1901-1910, Storeroom 3; 3 volumes, 1891-1900, 1911—, Auditor's inner office.

Miscellaneous

51. TAX LIST

1795-1819. 16 bundles. Prior records missing; discontinued as commissioners' record.

Annual returns of property subject to tax made by listers and filed with county commissioners showing town or township, name of owner, number of tracts of land, value of each, value of chattels, and total value for taxation. Chronologically arranged by years. No index. Handwritten. 4 x 3.5 x 8. Storeroom 3.

For other records, see entry 408.

52. LAND TAX LIST

1817. 1 volume.

List of lands subject to taxation showing township or town, name of owner, number of acres, lot number, range, section, watercourse, original proprietor, valuation, and amount of tax. Contains delinquent land tax list for 1816. Arranged by townships or towns and alphabetically thereunder by names of owners. No index. 200 pages. 15 x 9 x 1. Storeroom 3.

For other records, see entry 408.

53. [RETURNS OF LANDS OR TAXATION]

1803-1812. In Journal, entry 203.

Record of returns of lands for taxation showing name of owners, number of acres in each tract, lot, range, township, and section numbers, tax rate, kind of title to land, and watercourse.

54. WARRANTY DEEDS

1869—. 1 file box. (D2).

Warranty deeds to real property to county commissioners for building roads and other purposes showing date, names of grantor and grantee, name of state, county, and township, location and description of land and road, and lot, section, range, and township numbers. Chronologically arranged by dates deeds were drawn. 1869-

1881, no index; for index, 1822—, see entry 397. Handwritten on printed forms. 13 x 5 x 10. Auditor's inner office.

55. TAVERN AND FERRY FEES

1804-1821. 1 bundle. Discontinued.

Original resolutions passed by board of county commissioners fixing the fees taxed on licenses to operate taverns and ferries in Washington County. Chronologically arranged by years. No index. Handwritten. 4 x 3.5 x 8. Storeroom 3.

56. EXPERIMENT FARM PETITIONS

1912. 1 file box (D1).

Original petitions to county commissioners, signed by more than five percent of the electors, praying for the establishment of an experimental farm, and to issue bonds for the purchase and equipment of such farm. This farm has been established south of Marietta on State Route 97. No systematic arrangement. For index, see entry 497. Handwritten on printed forms. 13 x 5 x 10. Auditor's inner office.

57. OIL AND GAS LEASE

1934. 1 file box (D8).

Original agreement made between the county commissioners of Washington County as lessor, and lessees, for the drilling of oil and gas on the land owned by the county and known as County Home Land and showing date and signatures of the county commissioners as lessors, and signatures of lessees. Chronologically arranged by dates of agreements. For index, see entry 397. Typed on printed forms. 13 x 5 x 10. Auditor's inner office.

58. REGISTER

1929—. 1 volume.

Register of persons paying visits to the county commissioners showing date, name, and township address. Chronologically arranged by dates registered. No index. Handwritten on printed forms. 500 pages. 16 x 12 x 2.5. Commissioners' office.

The office of county recorder, although not unknown as an early English institution for the registration of land titles, developed in colonial America, where, because of the mobility of the restless pioneers, changes in land titles were frequent and some system was needed to protect purchasers against previous encumbrances. Public land registers, established in most of the colonies during the colonial period and continued by the states following independence, provided as a model of land registration for the territory of which the present state of Ohio was then a part. Thus the office of county recorder was established by an act of the Northwest Territory, August 1, 1795. This act, adopted from the Pennsylvania code, provided for the appointment by the governor of a recorder in each county whose principal duty was the recording of deeds. (Pease, *op. cit.,* I, 197-199).

When Ohio entered the union in 1802 no constitutional provision was made for the continuance of the office, but the legislature during its first session passed an act providing for a recorder in each county to be appointed by the judges of the court of common pleas for a seven-year term (1 O. L. 136). The recorder continued to be an appointive officer until 1829, when, by an act of the legislature, he became elected for a three-year term (27 O. L. 65). The tenure of office remained at three years until the constitutional amendment on November 7, 1905, which provided for the election of all county officers in the even-numbered years (*Ohio Const.,* XVIII, sec. 2). The term of office was fixed at two years, and so continued until the amendment of 1933, which extended the tenure of the incumbent until January 1937, at which time the recorder, elected at the regular election in November 1936, began to serve a four-year term (115 O. L. 191).

The first county recorder was directed by statute to record "all deeds, mortgages and conveyances of lands and tenements," lying within his county, and also all instruments and writings required by law to be recorded (1 O. L. 137). In 1805 he was directed to record all plats and maps of newly laid-out villages and new subdivisions of towns and villages (3 O. L. 213-215). In 1835 he was permitted, when authorized by the county commissioners, to transcribe from the records of other counties all deeds, mortgages, and other instruments or writing for the sale or conveyance of lands, tenements, or hereditaments affecting land titles in his county (33 O. L. 8; 35 O. L. 10-11).

Since the establishment of the office many duties besides those of recording land titles have been added. The present practice of recording powers of attorney began in 1818 (16 O. L. 155-156). Although the mechanics of Cincinnati were authorized to file mechanics' liens with the recorder as early as 1823 it was not until

1840 that the privilege was extended to the laborers of Washington County ((21 O. L. 8-10; 41 O. L. 66). Successive acts in 1865, 1872, 1881, 1884, 1904, and 1923 added new duties to the office in the recording of soldiers' discharges (62 O. L. 59), copies of certificates of compliance authorizing insurance companies not incorporated under the laws of Ohio to transact business in the state, and certified copies of renewal as granted by such companies to their agents (69 O. L. 32, 150; 97 O. L. 405), limited partnership agreements (78 O. L. 248), stallion keepers' liens (81 O. L. 43), oil and gas leases (85 O. L. 179), partition fence records (97 O. L. 140), and federal tax liens (110 O. L. 252). The recording of chattel mortgages and conditional sales began in 1846. Such instruments were to be deposited with the township clerk where the mortgagor was a resident. In all townships, however, in which the recorder maintained his office such instruments were to be deposited with him. (44 O. L. 61). Since 1906 chattel mortgages have been filed with the county recorder exclusively. It is provided that in order to be valid against subsequent mortgages, the chattel mortgage must be deposited with the county recorder of the county where the mortgagor resides at the time of its execution, and to retain its validity the mortgage must be renewed every three years. (G. C. sec. 8565). In 1936 the legislature passed an act authorizing the recorder to destroy such instruments six years after the time of refiling has expired (116 O. L. 324).

In the latter part of the nineteenth century an important extension of the method of recording land titles was provided by an act of the general assembly. The "Torrens System," as provided by the act of 1896 (92 O. L. 220), was declared unconstitutional by the supreme court of Ohio as being contrary to section 16 of the bill of rights of the state constitution (56 O. S. 575). The act of 1913, amended in 1913 and 1915, provides for the examination of land titles by the recorder and the issuance, if the title proved to be held in fee simple, of a certificate of title by the courts. The official certificate became the title of ownership and is indefeasible. However, in the event an interest is found in the land, after the issuance of the certificate, a claim is allowed to the legal claimant from a fund created for that purpose at the time of registration. (G. C. secs. 8572-34 - 8572-56: 106 O. L. 225: 115 O. L. 445-447). This system, although adopted by a few counties, not including Washington, is not used as widely as it might be because of the difficulty of replacing the traditional complicated system.

The recorder, like other county officials, had been required in earlier years to keep records of the business of his office, but it was not until the middle of the nineteenth century that the legislature, looking forward to some uniformity in land registration, enacted measures prescribing the form and contents of such records. Since 1850 the recorder has been required to keep a record of deeds in which is recorded all deeds, powers of attorney, and other instruments of writing for the unconditional sale of land, tenements, or hereditaments (48 O. L. 64). The same year saw the beginning of a record of mortgages in which was recorded all mortgages, powers of attorney, and other instruments of writing by which land, tenements, or hereditaments "shall or maybe mortgaged" or otherwise conditionally sold; and a record of plats in which was to be recorded all plats and maps of the town lots and of the subdivisions thereof, and of other divisions or surveyed lands, in like regular succession according to the priority of their presentation (48 O. L. 64). Since 1851 the recorder has been required to keep a separate record of deeds and mortgages denominated respectfully as "Record of Deeds" and "Record of Mortgages" (49 O. L. 103). Fourteen years later, in 1865, began the separate recording of leases in which the recorder was and is required to record all leases and powers of attorney for the execution of leases (62 O. L. 170). The present practice of keeping a daily register of deeds and a daily register of mortgages had its beginning in 1896. In this record are entered in alphabetical order the names of the grantors of all deeds and mortgages affecting real estate (92 O. L. 268).

Although indexes had been prepared in earlier years, the present system of indexing had its beginning in 1851 and took practically its present form in 1896 (49 O. L. 103; 92 O. L. 268; 102 O. L. 277). At present the recorder, at the beginning of each day's business, is required to make and maintain a general alphabetical index, direct and reverse, of all names of both parties of all instruments recorded by him. The indexes show the kind of instruments, date, range, township and section, the survey number and number of acres, or lot and sublot numbers and the part thereof, of each tract of lot of land described in any such instrument of writing; the name of the grantor is entered in the direct index under the appropriate letter and followed on the same line by the name of the grantee; the name of the grantee is entered in the reverse index under the appropriate letter and followed on the same line the name of the grantor. (G. C. sec, 2764).

Since 1859 the county commissioners have been authorized to provide sectional indexes to the records of all real estate in the county, beginning with some designated year and continuing through a period of years as may be specified (G. C. Sec. 2766; 64 O. L. 256; 76 O. L. 49; 102 O. L. 289).

The present duties of the recorder do not differ, in the main, from those prescribed in the middle of the nineteenth century. His records, bound in large bulky volumes, are open to the inspection of the public and are transferred to his successor.

Real Property Transfers

Deeds and Land Grants

59. OHIO COMPANY'S RECORD
1792-1796. 1 volume.

Copy of deeds to tracts (called shares at five shillings per share) of land granted to Rufus Putnam, Manasseh Cutler, Robert Oliver, and Griffin Greene in trust for the Ohio Company of Associates; this land being granted by letters patent from the president of the United States (George Washington) to the Ohio Company in the territory Northwest of the Ohio River in the County of Washington, and being two tracts containing a total of 964,285 acres. Deeds show name of grantee, description of lot or lots drawn, number of shares, names of witnesses, copy of notarization, date file, and date recorded. Chronologically arranged by dates of recordings. Alphabetically indexed by names of grantees. Handwritten on printed forms. 510 pages. 12.5 x 7.5 x 3.25. Recorder's office.

60. [Ohio Company's Land Contract]
June 18, 1805. 4 leaves.

Duplicate copy of contract between the board of treasury of the United States and Manasseh Cutler and Winthrop Sargent, agents for the Ohio Company of Associates, for the grant of territory Northwest of the Ohio River showing names of parties to the contract, description of tracts with boundary lines designated, number of acres, amount of consideration, reservations for support of schools and religion, signatures of agents, of registrar of the treasury, and the secretary of the treasury, and departmental seal. Handwritten. Writing legible; paper faded and slightly torn. 8 pages. 14.75 x 9.5. Auditor's office, safe.

61. REGISTER OF CONVEYANCES
December 1859—. 26 volumes. (1-26 Title varies; Volumes 1-3, Book of Entry.

Daily register of instruments filed for record showing date, kind of instrument names of grantee and grantor, to whom delivered, of whom received, fee, and consecutive instrument number; volumes 4-26, January 1880—, shows deeds to agricultural lands, town lots, and consideration; mortgages on agricultural lands, town lots, and amount received; cancellation of mortgages on agricultural lands and town lots; also leases on minerals, leaseholders, assignment consideration, miscellaneous instruments, date, and to whom delivered. Chronologically arranged by dates of filing. No index. Handwritten on printed forms. Average 250 pages. 17.75 x 14 x 2. 3 volumes, 1859-1879, Storeroom 3; 23 volumes, 1880—, Recorder's office.

62. DAILY REGISTER OF DEEDS

July 1896—. 7 volumes. (1-7).

Daily record of deeds conveying real estate filed for recording showing instrument number, name of grantor and grantee, date and hour filed, and remarks. Alphabetically arranged by names of grantees and chronologically thereunder by dates of filing. No index. Handwritten on printed forms. Average 320 pages. 16 x 11 x 1.75. Recorder's office.

63. DEED RECORD

1788— . 215 volumes. (1-215).

Record copy of deeds, liens, and other instruments conveying title to real estate located in Washington County including easements for highways and roads showing name of grantor and grantee, kind and date of instrument, amount of consideration, description of real estate transferred. Contains: Lease Records, in volumes 1-57, 1788-1864, entry 69; Record of Mortgages, 1788-April 1850, entry 74; Lien Record [Mechanics'], 1840-1883, entry 78; Plat Books, 1788-1849, entry 88; Record Power of Attorney, 1788-1897, entry 101. Volume 1, March 10, 1788-September 1794 is a transcribed volume; all other volumes are original. Chronologically arranged by dates of filing. September 1794-June 1807, alphabetically indexed by names of grantors in each volume; for separate indexes, see entry 64-66. 1788-November 1810, Handwritten; November 1910—, typed. 1788-April 1834, average 470 pages. 15.5 x 10 x 3; April 1834—, average 630 pages. 18 x 11.5 x 3.5. Recorder's office.

64. INDEX OF RECORDS

March 1788-January 1840. 3 volumes. Discontinued.

Abstract of transfers and index to Deed Record volumes 1 to 30, 1788-January 1840, entry 63, showing names of grantor and grantee, date of instrument, kind of instrument, volume and page numbers of record, range, township, section, and lot numbers, acreage, number of acres sold, and description of tract sold. Alphabetically arranged by names of grantors and chronologically thereunder by dates of instruments. Handwritten on printed forms. Average 300 pages. 18 x 11.5 x 1.5. Recorder's office.

65. INDEX TO DEEDS, DIRECT

1788—. 15 volumes. (1-15).

Direct index to Deed Record, entry 63, showing consecutive instrument numbers, date recorded, name of grantor and grantee, volume and page numbers of record, section, township, range, and lot numbers, acreage, and town or township. Alphabetically arranged by names the grantors and chronologically thereunder by dates of recording. Handwritten on printed forms. Average 570 pages. 18 x 12 x 3. Recorder's office.

66. INDEX TO DEED RECORD, REVERSE

1788—, 15 volumes. (1-15).

Reverse index to Deeds Record, entry 63, showing consecutive instrument numbers, date recorded, name of grantee and grantor, volume and page numbers of records, section, township, range, and lot numbers, acreage, and town or township. Alphabetically arranged by names of grantees and chronologically thereunder by dates of recording. Handwritten on printed forms. Average 570 pages. 18 x 12 x 3. Recorder's office.

67. DEEDS

1790-1930. 15 file boxes. No subsequent records.

Original deeds to real estate filed for recording which have not been called for showing instrument number, name of grantor and grantee, date of deed, amount of consideration, description of real estate transferred, signature of grantor and witnesses, notarization, date filed for record, and date recorded. Chronologically arranged by years and alphabetically thereunder by names of grantees. No index. 1790-1910, handwritten and handwritten on printed forms; 1911—, typed on printed forms. 10 x 4.5 x 14. Recorder's office.

68. ABSTRACT OF TITLE [Transfers]

1815-1893. 3 volumes. (A-C) No prior records; discontinued.

Record of transfers of real estate showing date of transfer, town or township, names the grantor and grantee, acreage, lot number, and consideration; and record of leases, mortgages, or liens against the property. Chronologically arranged by dates of transfers. Alphabetically indexed by names of grantors. Handwritten. Average 330 pages. 12 x 7.5 x 1.5. Recorder's office.

Leases

69. LEASE RECORD

January 1865. 88 volumes. (58-145) 1788-1864 in Deed Record, entry 63.

Record copy of leases of lands for agricultural purposes and for prospecting for minerals, gas, and oil; buildings for dwelling, business, or manufacturing purposes; also of machinery and equipment; all leases show date of lease, name of grantor and grantee, conditions of lease, copy and notarization, date filed, and date recorded. Chronologically arranged by dates of recordings. For indexes, see entries 70 and 71. January 1865-February 1911, handwritten; February 1911—, typed. Average 630 pages. 17 x 11.5 x 3.25. Recorder's office.

70. INDEX TO LEASES, DIRECT

April 1864—. 6 volumes. (1-6).

Direct index to Lease Record and volume 57 of Deed Record, entry 63, showing names of grantor and grantee, volume and page numbers of lease or deed record, section, township, range, lot numbers, acreage, and kind of lease. Alphabetically arranged by names the grantors and chronologically thereunder by dates of filing. Handwritten on printed forms. Average 600 pages. 18 x 12 x 3.5. Recorder's office.

71. INDEX TO LEASES, REVERSE

April 1864—. 6 volumes. (1-6).

Reverse index to Lease Record and to volume 57 of Deed Records, entry 63, showing names of grantee and grantor, volume and page numbers of lease or deed records, date filed, section, township, range, and lots numbers, acreage, and kind of lease. Alphabetically arranged by names that grantees and chronologically thereunder by dates of filing. Handwritten on printed forms. Average 600 pages. 18 x 12 x 3.5. Recorder's office.

72. LEASES

1872-1926. 3 file boxes.

Original leases filed for recording that have not been called for, showing instrument number, date of lease, name of grantor and grantee, conditions of lease, signatures of grantor and witnesses, notarization, date filed for record, and date recorded. Alphabetically arranged by names of grantees. No index. 1872-1907, handwritten on printed forms; 1907-1926, handwritten and typed on printed forms. 10 x 4.5 x 14. Recorder's office.

Mortgages

73. DAILY REGISTER OF MORTGAGES

July 1896—. 5 volumes. (1-5).

Daily record of mortgage deeds filed for record showing consecutive instrument number, name of grantor and grantee, and date and hour of filing. Alphabetically arranged by names of grantors. No index. Handwritten on printed forms. Average 400 pages. 16 x 11 x 2. Recorder's office.

74. RECORDS OF MORTGAGES

May 1850—. 118 volumes. (1-118). 1788-April 1850 in Deed Record, entry 53.

Record copy of mortgage deeds conveying conditional title to real estate as security for value received, showing instrument number, name of grantor and grantee, date of mortgage, amount secured, conditions of mortgage, description of real estate covered by mortgage deed, names of witnesses, copy of notarization, date filed for record, and date recorded. Record of cancellation of mortgage noted on side margin of page; also contains a record of releases noted on margin. Chronologically arranged by dates of recording. For indexes, see entry 75 and 76. May 1850-November 1910, handwritten; November 1910—, typed. Average 630 pages. 18 x 11.5 x 3.25. Recorder's office.

75. INDEX TO MORTGAGES, DIRECT
1850—. 10 volumes. (1-10).

Direct index to Record of Mortgages showing consecutive instrument number, date recorded, names of grantor and grantee, volume and page numbers of record, section, township, range, and lot numbers, acreage, and town or township. Alphabetically arranged by names of grantors and chronologically thereunder by dates of recording. Handwritten on printed forms. Average 620 pages. 18 x 12 x 3.25. Recorder's office.

76. INDEX TO MORTGAGES, REVERSE
1850—. 10 volumes. (1-10).

Reverse index to Record of Mortgages showing consecutive instrument number, names of grantee and grantor, dates recorded, volume and page numbers of record, section, township, range, lot numbers, acreage, and town or township. Alphabetically arranged by names of grantees and chronologically thereunder by dates of recording. Handwritten on printed forms. Average 620 pages. 18 x 12 x 3.25. Recorder's office.

77. MORTGAGES
1864-1929. 2 file boxes. No subsequent records.

Original mortgage deeds filed for recording and which have not been called for, showing instrument number, names of mortgagor and mortgagee, date of mortgage, conditions of mortgage, amount of mortgage, signature of mortgagee and witnesses, notarization, and date of recording. Alphabetically arranged by names of mortgagee and the chronologically thereunder by years. No index. 1864-1914, handwritten; 1915-1929, typed on printed forms. 10 x 4.5 x 14. Recorder's office.

Liens

78. LIEN RECORD [Mechanics']
January 1884—. 6 volumes. (1-6). 1840-1883 in Deed Record, entry 63.

Record copy of mechanics' liens filed and recorded showing name of creditor and debtor, itemized account of labor and material furnished, and for what construction or improvements, copy of notarization of claim, date of filing, and date of recording. Chronologically arranged by dates of recording. Alphabetically indexed by name of creditors and debtors. 1884-February 1927, handwritten; April 1927—, typed. Average 420 pages. 16 x 11 x 2.25. Recorder's office.

79. INDEX TO LIENS, DIRECT
April 1861—. 6 volumes. (1-6).
Direct index to Lien Record [Mechanics'] and to liens recorded in Deed Record, 1864-1883, entry 63, showing names of creditor and debtor, date filed, volume and page numbers of record, amount and kind of lien, and date paid. Alphabetically arranged by creditors and chronologically thereunder by dates of filing. Handwritten on printed forms. Average 600 pages. 18 x 12 x 3.5. Recorder's office.

80. INDEX TO LIENS, REVERSE
April 1864—. 6 volumes. (1-6).
Reverse index to Lien Record [Mechanics'] and to liens recorded in Deed Record, 1864-1883, entry 63, showing names of debtor and creditor, date filed, volume and page numbers of record, amount and kind of lien, and date paid. Alphabetically arranged by names of debtors and chronologically thereunder by dates of filing. Handwritten on printed forms. Average 600 pages. 18 x 12 x 3.5. Recorder's office.

81. FEDERAL TAX LIEN INDEX
April 1925—. 1 volume.
Index record showing recorder's number, name of taxpayer, residence, collector's notice number, date and hour of filing, amount of tax assessed, penalty, collector's serial number, certificate of discharge, amount of tax assessed and paid, and date and hour of filing certificate of discharge. Alphabetically arranged by names of taxpayers and chronologically thereunder by dates of filing. No index. Handwritten on printed forms. 250 pages. 16 x 17 x 1.25. Recorder's office.

82. CORPORATION RECORDS
January 1931—. 1 volume. No prior records.
Record copy of notice issued by state tax commission of payment of franchise and excise tax and discharge of lien showing date, name of taxpayer, amount of tax assessed, penalty, total amount assessed and paid, date paid, date of filing, and date of recording. Chronologically arranged by dates of filing. Typed on printed forms. 430 pages. 16 x 10.5 x 2.25. Recorder's office.

83. EXERCISE AND FRANCHISE TAX LIEN INDEX AND INDEX TO CORPORATION RECORD
January 1930—. 1 volume.
Index record showing recorder's file number of notice of lien, name of public utility or corporation, date and hour filed, amount of tax, penalty, total, recorder's file number, notice of payment of tax and date of discharge of lien, date tax paid, date and hour of filing notice of payment of tax and discharge of lien, and volume and page numbers of Corporation Records, entry 82. Alphabetically arranged by names of public utilities or corporations and chronologically thereunder by dates of filing. Handwritten on printed forms. 250 pages. 16 x 16 x 1.5. Recorder's office.

84. PERSONAL TAX LIEN RECORD
1933—. 1 volume.
Record of treasurer's cumulative delinquent duplicate of taxes other than real estate taxes showing tax district, name of taxpayer, years delinquent, volume and page numbers of Treasurer's General Personal Tax Duplicate, entry 348, year filed, amount of tax, penalty, total amount due, and date paid. Alphabetically arranged by names of taxpayers and chronologically thereunder by years of filing. Handwritten on printed forms. 160 pages. (Loose-leaf) 10 x 12 x 1. Recorder's office.

85. INDEX TO PERSONAL TAX LIEN RECORD AND CERTIFICATES OF RELEASE OR PARTIAL DISCHARGES
1933—. 1 volume.
Index record showing certificate number, name of taxpayer, volume and page numbers of Personal Tax Lien Record, entry 84, record of releases, and record of partial discharges. Alphabetically arranged by names of taxpayers. Typed on printed forms. 150 pages. (Loose-leaf) 11.5 x 14 x 1. Recorder's office.

86. INDEX TO NOTICES OF LIENS SURVEY TO RECOGNIZANCES
August 1929—. 1 volume.
Index record showing recorder's file number, date and hour of filing of lien, names of sureties and defendant, amount of recognizance, description of real estate, notice of discharge of recognizance, and date and hour of filing notice of discharge of recognizance. Alphabetically arranged by names of sureties and chronologically thereunder by dates of filing. Handwritten on printed forms. 250 pages. 16 x 17 x 1.25. Recorder's office.

Plats and Surveys

87. OHIO COMPANY'S LANDS

1786-1819. 1 volume.

Record copy of minutes of meeting held March 1, 1786, at Boston, Massachusetts, for the purpose of forming a company of associates to purchase lands and make a settlement in the western country showing names of officers elected, names of members of the association (The Ohio Company), copies of minutes of subsequent meetings held at Boston, Massachusetts, and minutes of meeting held at Marietta, first meeting December 1788; also plats and maps of the several agencies created in Washington County which later became townships; plats and maps showing boundary and division lines with area on each tract and list of original proprietors; also name a proprietor, lot of number and area of lot owned; also subsequent surveys of towns and townships with plat maps showing boundary lines of townships and lots (tracts of land),streams, roads, lot number, area of each tract, section lines, section numbers, with description of plat survey showing kind of landmark at starting point, each boundary or lot line, course of line, number chains and links, remarks, together with a list of original proprietors of each plat survey, showing lot number, name of proprietor and section, range, and township numbers. Surveys under direction of Rufus Putnam. This record was transcribed in 1906 by John W. Lansley, county recorder, from the original which is now located in Campus Martius Museum. Chronologically arranged by dates of meetings or surveys. No index. Handwritten; plats and maps, hand sketched. Scales vary, 1 inch equals 40 feet to 1 inch equals 40 chains. 298 pages. 20 x 14 x 1.75. Recorder's office.

88. PLAT BOOKS

1850—. 5 volumes. (1-5). 1788-1849 in Deed Record, entry 63.

Plat maps, surveyor's description, and survey data of all additions, subdivisions, and allotments platted in Washington County subsequent to 1850, showing name of Plat, boundary lines of plat, lot lines, streets and alleys, streams and railroads, lot dimensions, lot number, names of lot owners at time of platted, date recorded, date surveyed and platted, and name of surveyor. Chronologically arranged by dates recorded. Handwritten and hand sketched. Scales vary, 1 inch equals 100 feet to 1 inch equals 20 rods; scale is given on only a few plats. 1 volume, 1850-1904, 220 pages 17.5 x 12 x 1.5; 4 volumes, 1871—, Average 60 pages 24 x 30 x 1.25. Recorder's office.

89. INDEX TO PLAT BOOKS
1850—. 1 volume.
Index to Plat Books showing name of plat, of what township or town, and volume and page numbers of record. Alphabetically arranged by names of plats. Handwritten on printed forms. 300 pages. 16 x 11 x 1.5. Recorder's office.

90. LINE FENCE RECORD
November 1905—. 1 volume.
Record copy of petitions to township trustees by landowners asking for a division or partition of line fences, separating adjoining lands, and assignment to each landowner his share of the fence to maintain, showing names of litigants, what township, description of adjoining lands and dividing lines, date filed or record, and date recorded. Chronologically arranged by dates of recordings. Alphabetically indexed by names of petitioners. Handwritten. 420 pages. 18 x 12 x 2.25. Recorder's office.

Personal Property Transfers

91. CHATTEL MORTGAGE RECORD
January 1881—. 2 volumes. (1, 2 Prior records missing.
Record copy of chattel mortgages and conditional bills of sale recorded, showing names of grantor and grantee, amount of mortgage, itemized list of property mortgaged, conditions of mortgage, copy of notarization, date filed for record, dates recorded, and copy of cancellation of mortgage. Chronologically arranged by dates of recording. Alphabetically indexed by names of mortgagors in each volume; also separate indexes, entries 92-95. Handwritten. Average 310 pages. 14 x 8.5 x 1.5. Recorder's office.

92. CHATTEL MORTGAGE INDEX, DIRECT AND REVERSE
March 1878-June 1930. 12 volumes. (1-12).
Direct and reverse index record to chattel mortgages showing name of mortgagor and mortgagee, town or township, date of instrument, date filed, date refiled,

amount, volume and page numbers of Chattel Mortgages Record, entry 91, and dates cancelled; also includes conditional sales index, 1878, and May 1885-June 1923. Alphabetically arranged by names of mortgagors and mortgagees and chronically thereunder by dates of filing (direct index front half of volumes; reverse index back have of volumes). Handwritten on printed forms. Average 400 pages. 17 x 12 x 2.25. Recorder's office.

For subsequent records, see entries 93 and 94.

93. CHATTEL MORTGAGE INDEX, DIRECT

July 1930—. 3 volumes. (13-15).

Direct index showing names of mortgagor and mortgagee, instrument number, date of instrument, date filed, amount of mortgage, date refiled, and date cancelled. Alphabetically arranged by names of mortgagors and chronologically thereunder by dates of filing. Handwritten on printed forms. 280 pages. 14.5 x 16.5 x 2. Recorder's office.

For prior records, see entry 92.

94. CHATTEL MORTGAGE INDEX, REVERSE

July 1930—. 3 volumes. (13-15).

Reverse index showing names of mortgagee and mortgagor, instrument number, date of instrument, date filed, amount of mortgage, date refiled, and date cancelled. Alphabetically arranged by mortgagees and chronologically thereunder by dates of filing. Handwritten on printed forms. Average 280 pages. 14.5 x 16.5 x 2. Recorder's office.

For prior records, see entry 92.

95. INDEX OF CONDITIONAL SALES

August 1885-June 1923. 1 volume. Discontinued.

Direct and reverse index to conditional sales recorded in Chattel Mortgage Record, entry 91, showing instrument number, amount, date of instrument, date filed, and date cancelled. Alphabetically arranged by names of grantors and grantees and chronologically thereunder by dates of filing. Handwritten on printed forms. 300 pages. 13 x 5 x 1.5. Recorder's office.

For other indexes, see entries 92-94.

96. CHATTEL MORTGAGES

1911—. 38 file boxes.

Original chattel mortgages given as security for value received showing instrument number, date of mortgage, names of mortgagor and mortgagee, amount secured, itemized list of chattels, terms of mortgage, signature of mortgagee, and dates of filing and recording. Alphabetically arranged by names of mortgagors and chronologically thereunder by dates of filing. Typed on printed forms. 10 x 4.5 x 14. Recorder's office.

Corporations and Partnerships

97. TRADERS' RECORD

May 1884- March 1886. 1 volume. Discontinued.

Registration record of individual and partnership traders' names as required by act passed by general assembly showing date filed, kind of business, business address, name of business, name of each member of firm, address of each member of firm, and date of recording. Chronologically arranged by dates of recording. Alphabetically indexed by names of firms. Handwritten on printed forms. 280 pages. 18 x 11.5 x 2.5. Recorder's office.

98. RECORD OF INCORPORATIONS AND LIMITED PARTNERSHIPS

1864-September 1906. 1 volume.

Record copy of incorporation and limited partnership agreements showing name of incorporation or limited partnership, date incorporated or partnership formed, nature of business, amount of capital stock, names of stockholders or partners, number of shares held by each stockholder or partner, place of business, date filed, and date of recording. Chronologically arranged by dates of recording. Alphabetically indexed by names of corporations or partnerships. Handwritten. 230 pages. 13 x 8 x 1.25. Recorder's office.

99. [Religious Societies]

1820-1830. In Marriage Record, entry 293.

Record of organizations of religious societies showing name of secretary, date of organization, and names of official members.

100. RECORD OF INCORPORATED SOCIETIES

1846- May 1893. 1 volume. Discontinued.

Record copy of articles of incorporation of societies including churches, civic organizations, and academies showing name of organization, purpose of organization, address, date of organization, names of organizers, names of officers, date filed for record, and dates of recordings. Chronologically arranged by dates of recording. No index. Handwritten. 200 pages. 13 x 8.5 x 1.25. Recorder's office.

Grants of Authority

101. RECORD POWER OF ATTORNEY

1898—. 2 volumes. (1-2). 1788-1897 in Deed Record, entry 63.

Record copy of grant of authority to act for the grantor in matters set forth in instrument showing names of grantor and grantee, enumeration of duties to perform, date of instrument, signatures at grantor and witnesses, copy of notarization, date filed for record, and date recorded. Chronologically arranged by dates of recording. Alphabetically indexed by names of grantors showing names of grantees. 1898-March 1927, handwritten; April 1927—, typed. Average 600 pages. 18 x 12 x 3. Recorder's office.

102. CERTIFICATES OF COMPLIANCE

1823—. 29 bundles and 9 file boxes.

Certificates issued by state department of insurance and filed with county recorder certifying the named company has complied with insurance regulations, showing name of company, home office, kind of insurance, with itemized financial statement of company, date of certificate, and date filed. Chronologically arranged by dates of filing. No index. 1892-1900, handwritten on printed forms; 1900—, typed on printed forms. Bundles, 3.5 x 3 x 7.5; file boxes, 10 x 4.5 x 14. 29 bundles, 1892-1920, Storeroom 1. 9 file boxes, 1921—, Recorder's office.

103. INSURANCE AGENTS' LICENSES

1903—. 17 bundles and 11 file boxes.

Record copies of licenses issued by state department of insurance to insurance agents and filed with county recorder showing name of company, home office, name of agent, address, date of license, and date filed. Chronologically arranged by dates of filing. No index. Typed on printed forms. Bundles, 4.5 x 3 x 7.5; file boxes, 10 x 4.5 x 14. 17 bundles, 1903-1920, Storeroom 1; 11 file boxes, 1921—, Recorder's office.

Business Administration of Office

104. RECORD OF FEES
January 1907—. 13 volumes. (1-13).
Recorder's daily record of fees for services rendered showing date, by whom paid, volume and page numbers of book where recorded, kind of instrument, total fee, recording fee, filing fee, cancellation, searches, and sundries. Chronologically arranged by dates of entries. No index. Handwritten on printed forms. Average 320 pages. 16 x 11 x 1.5. Recorder's office.

105. RECORDER'S CASH BOOK AND RECORD OF FEES
January 1907—. 13 volumes. (1-13).
Daily record of cash receipts for recording, filing, and searching, showing consecutive number except chattel mortgages, consecutive chattel mortgage number, by whom paid, kind of instrument or service, total fee, fee for recording, filing, cancellation, searches, and sundries. Chronologically arranged by dates of entries. No index. Handwritten on printed forms. Average 320 pages. 18 x 11.5 x 2.5. Recorder's office.

106. EX OFFICIO SERVICE
1921-1930. 1 volume. Discontinued.
Record of request for services to be performed by recorder showing date of request, kind of record to copy or search, fee, signature of person securing service, and volume and page numbers of Record of Fees, entry 104, and Recorder's Cash Book and Record of Fees, entry 105. Chronologically arranged by dates of requests. Handwritten on printed forms. 300 pages. 18 x 12 x 1.5. Recorder's office.

Reports

107. CONVEYANCE STATISTICS
1906—. 32 reports and 1 file box. No prior records.
Recorder's record copy of annual reports to secretary of state on conveyances in

Washington County showing number of deeds recorded, number acres, consideration, and average price per acre; number leases recorded, number acres, and consideration; mortgages other than railroad mortgages, number recorded, number acres, and amount secured; cancellation of mortgages, number cancelled, number of acres, and amount secured. Each item is classified as agricultural land, city or town property, or mineral and oil land. Chronologically arranged. No index. Handwritten on printed forms. 10 x 4.5 x 14. Recorder's office.

108. TRANSFERS OF TAXABLE PROPERTY

1820—. 36 reports in 1 file box. No prior records.

Recorder's copy of semiannual reports to state tax commission of transfers of taxable property showing date of report, date of conveyance, names the grantor and grantee, description of property, and volume and page numbers of records. Chronologically arranged by dates of reports. No index. Handwritten on printed forms. 10 x 4.5 x 14. Recorder's office.

Miscellaneous

109. PROTEST RECORD

1870-1873. 1 volume, Discontinued.

Record copy of protest entered by notaries public with nonpayment of promissory notes, bills of exchange, drafts, and bank checks on their maturity, or, on presentation for payment, showing date of protests, name of notary public, name of bank or holder of instrument, reason for nonpayment, copy of instrument protested, and date of recording. Chronologically arranged by dates of recording. No index. Handwritten on printed forms. 180 pages. 10 x 8 x 1. Recorder's office.

110. SOLDIERS' DISCHARGE RECORD

September 1861—. 4 volumes. (1-4).

Record copy of official discharges from the United States army or navy of soldiers and sailors enlisted for the War of Rebellion, Spanish-American War, Philippine Insurrection, and World War, with discharges of regular army enlistments, show ing name of soldier or sailor, rank, company, regiment or vessel, physical description of soldier, date of discharge, where discharged, reason for discharge, service record, name of commanding officer, and date of recording. Volumes 1 and 2, discharges of Civil War soldiers. Volume 3, discharges of Spanish-American War, Philippine

Insurrection, and regular army or navy enlistments. Volume 4, discharges of World War soldiers and sailors. Chronologically arranged by dates of recording. Alphabetically indexed by names of soldiers or sailors. 2 volumes, September 1861-June 1898, handwritten; 1 volume, April 1900-April 1932, handwritten on printed forms; 1 volume, March 1919—, typed on printed forms. 2 volumes, 1861-1892, 440 pages 16 x 11 x 2.25; 1 volume, 1900-1932, 400 pages 18 x 12 x 2.25; 1 volume, 1919—, 860 pages 17 x 10.5 x 5. Recorder's office.

111. RECORD OF DEATHS, SOLDIERS AND SAILORS, WASHINGTON COUNTY RESIDENTS

May 1861-October 1879. 1 volume. Discontinued.

Record of deaths of soldiers and sailors who were residents of Washington County enlisted in Union Army, showing name of decedent, company, regiment or vessel, date of death, place of death, cause of death, date of enlistment, age, marital status, color, place of residence, and place of burial. Alphabetically arranged by names of decedents. No index. Handwritten on printed forms. 330 pages. 18 x 12 x 2. Recorder's office.

112. RECORD OF BURIAL OF CIVIL WAR VETERANS

1926. 1 volume.

Record of burial of Civil War veterans in the following cemeteries in Washington County: Oak Grove, Mound, Harmar, Valley, Catholic, Rainbow, Rockland, Green Lawn, Beverly, Round Bottom, Putnam, Bethel, Watertown, Waterford, Universalist, New Matamoras, Bartlett, Barlow, Warren Chapel, Churchtown, Lower Newport, Gravel Bank, Smith at Aurelius, Grerman at Aurelius, Macksburg, Coal Run, Stanley, Layman, Mt. Liberty, Antioch, Decatur, Chapel, Presbyterian at Decatur Rake, Bloomfield, Point Pleasant, Newport, Newberry, and Bells Ridge showing name of veteran, company, regiment, branch of service, rank, date of death, cemetery lots number. Arranged by names of cemeteries and alphabetically thereunder by names of veterans. No index. Handwritten. 460 pages. 18 x 12 x 2.5. Recorder's office.

113. MISCELLANEOUS RECORD

November 1910—. 1 volume.

Record copies of instruments and documents including miscellaneous wills, affidavits as to dates of birth, history of the acquisition of the Daughters of American Revolution lot in Mound Cemetery on which to locate the monument to Revolutionary War soldiers, leases of buildings for dwelling and business purposes, right away agreements for joint use of private roadway, copies of land contracts, bills of sale of merchandise by assignee, waiver of prior rights to mechanics' lien proceedings, copies of nurses' certificate granted by state board of medical examiners, separate agreement between husband and wife, and copies of assignments for benefit of creditors, showing date of instrument, names of principles, title of instrument, date filed for record, and date recorded. Chronologically arranged by dates of recording. Alphabetically indexed by names of grantors or principles. Typed. 630 pages. 18 x 15 x 3.25. Recorder's office.

The office of clerk of courts, an ancient English institutions originating before the time of Edward I (Sir Frederick Pollock and Frederic William Maitland, *The History of English Law Before the Time of Edward I,* Cambridge, 18 95, I, 184) was transplanted to America during the colonial period. The American Revolution made no radical change in the political heritage derived from England, and the office was continued by the states. The duties of the office were modified, however, because of a separation, in the newer states, of administrative and judicial functions, which under the English system had been combined.

The sections of the Ohio constitution of 1802 creating the judicial system for the state provided for the appointment of a clerk of courts by the judges of the court of common pleas. He was to serve a seven-year term, but was subject to removal by the appointing power for a breach of good behavior. (*Ohio Const. 1802*, Art. III, sec. 9). The constitution of 1851 made the office of clerk elective for a three-year term (*Ohio Const,* Art. IV, sec. 6). A constitutional amendment in 1905 provided that the term of all elective offices shall be for an even number of years not exceeding four. In compliance with this amendment, the general assembly passed an act fixing the term of office of the clerk at two years. (98 O. L. 273). The term remained at two years until 1935 when it was extended to four years (116 O. L. pt. ii, 184). The remuneration of the office was by fees until 1906 when the legislature prescribed a definite salary (98 O. L. 94, 117).

The duties of the clerk of courts, like those of other county officers, are prescribed by statute. In 1853 a code of civil procedure was adopted summarizing the duties and forming the basis for the present ones in most respects similar to those prescribed during the earlier years of the office. The clerk of courts was directed to issue all writs and orders for provisional remedies; endorse the date upon all papers filed in his office; keep the journal, record books, and papers appertaining to the court and record its proceedings, and keep at least five books to be called the appearance docket, the trial docket and a printed duplicate of the trial docket, the journal, the record, and execution docket. (51 O. L. 107; 51 O. L. 158-159; 78 O. L. 105; 79 O. L. 115; 86 O. L. 174). The present practice of keeping an index, direct and reverse, to judgments began in Washington County in 1852 although not prescribed until 1866. (63 O. L. 10; 75 O. L. 103; 78 O. L. 88; 82 O. L. 39; 86 O. L. 26). In 1871, the clerk was made official custodian of the law reports and books furnished by the state for the use of the court and bar, and was made liable for their destruction (68 O. L. 109).

Some of the duties of the clerk as defined by the civil code of 1853 are still effective, others have been added by subsequent legislation. Thus, for example, in 1858 the clerk was directed to receive a notary commissions for record (55 O. L. 13; 93 O. L. 406; 115 O. L. 117). He was required, also, to receive for record special police commissions (1867), timber trade-marks (1883), partnership agreements (1894), index to judgments of federal courts (1898), marks of ownership [trade-marks] (1911), motor vehicle bills of sale (1921), and certificates of judgments to operate as a lien (1933) (64 O. L. 60; 80 O. L. 195; 91 O. L. 357; 92 O. L. 25; 93 O. L. 285; 102 O. L. 513-514; 109 O. L. 333; 116 O. L. 274). On the other hand, many of the earlier duties of the clerk have been transferred to other departments of local government or have been abolished. The clerk issued marriage licenses and ministers' licenses until 1851, after that date they have been issued by the probate court. Moreover the clerk issued peddlers' license until the decade of the sixties, since that time they have been issued by the auditor (59 O. L. 67). The practice of recording in the office of the clerk, the name of black or mulatto persons to be used as certificates of freedom was, of course, discontinued after the close of the War between the States in 1865.

In 1856 the clerk was directed by the legislature to preserve a list of births, marriages, and deaths as returned to his office by the assessor, and to transmit on or before the first day of June annually a copy of such statistics to the secretary of state. From these county lists, the secretary of state prepared tabular statements showing the vital statistics in each county. The clerk received 10 copies of the report, one of which he was required to preserve in his office. (53 O. L. 73-75). The clerk was relieved of the task of collecting and preserving vital statistics, when, in 1867 such powers and duties were vested in the probate judge (64 O. L. 63-64).

The clerk of courts was given other duties and addition to those of serving the court of common pleas and receiving documents for record. Since 1850 he has been required to report each year to the county commissioners all fines assessed by the court in criminal cases, together with the names of the parties to each case, and the amount of money he has paid to the treasurer (48 O. L. 66; 58 O. L. 69; 86 O. L. 239). Moreover, since 1867 he has been required to report annually to the secretary of state the number of crimes committed in his county, the number of pending cases, and the amount of fines collected (64 O. L. 17). An act of 1927, amended the act of 1867, directed the clerk to report on any matters which the secretary of state might require, and to forward a duplicate copy of his report on crime in his county to the state board of clemency (112 O. L. 203). (The state board of clemency was abolished in 1831).

The clerk of courts, like the county prosecuting attorney, is one of the most important persons in the judicial system. His significance and influence, however, were not recognized until recent years.

General Indexes

114. JUDGMENT INDEX, DIRECT
1852—. 7 volumes. (1 unnumbered, 1-6).

Direct index of judgment creditors showing name of judgment debtor, date, judgment decree, nature of suit, case number, volume and page numbers of Execution Docket, entry 196, Journal, entry 203, and Final Record, enter 204, nature of suit, date of execution, and date judgment satisfied. Alphabetically arranged by names of judgment creditors. Handwritten on printed forms. Average 600 pages. 16 x 11 x 3. Clerk of courts' office.

115. JUDGMENT INDEX, REVERSE
1852—. 7 volumes. (1unnumbered, 1-6).

Reverse index of judgment debtors showing name of judgment creditor, date judgment decree, nature of suit, case number, volume and page numbers of Execution Docket, entry 196, Journal, entry 203, and Final Record, entry 204, nature of suit, date of execution, and date judgment satisfied. Alphabetically arranged by names of judgment debtors and chronologically thereunder by dates of decrees. Handwritten on printed forms. Average 600 pages. 16 x 11 x 3. Clerk of courts' office.

116. INDEX TO LIVING JUDGMENTS
1873-1878. 1 volume.

Index to living judgments showing names of judgment creditor and debtor, volume and page numbers of Appearance Docket, entry 194, and Execution Docket, entry 196, and date execution issued. Alphabetically arranged by names of judgment creditors and chronologically thereunder by dates executions issued. Handwritten on printed forms. 400 pages. 18 x 12 x 2. Storeroom 2.

For subsequent records, see entry 117.

117. INDEX TO PENDING SUITS AND LIVING JUDGMENTS
1884—. 22 volumes. (1 A-L - 11 A-L; 1 M-Z - 11 M-Z).

Index showing names of plaintiffs and defendants, also volume and page numbers of Execution Docket, entry 196, and Criminal Docket, entry 198, or of Civil Docket, entry 199. Alphabetically arranged by names of plaintiffs. Handwritten on printed forms. Average 540 pages. 16 11 2.75. Clerk of courts 'office.

For prior index of living judgments, see entry 116.

Docket and Clerk's Entries

118. EXECUTION DOCKET
1861—. 6 volumes. (3-8). Prior records missing.

Docket of executions to satisfy judgments rendered by justice of the peace courts of Washington County showing name of justice, township, date judgment returned, names the litigants, date transcript filed, amount of judgment, date paid, and itemized cost bill. Chronologically arranged by dates of filing. Alphabetically indexed by names of judgment creditors. Handwritten. Average 480 pages. 16 x 11 x 2.5. Clerk of courts' office.

119. SUMMONS AND PRAECIPE DOCKET
1803-1848. 11 volumes.

Record of summonses issued by clerk of courts showing date issued, names of litigants, name of attorney, on whom issued, and date of sheriff's return. Contains Praecipe Docket, entry 120. Chronologically arranged by dates issued. No index. Handwritten. Average 90 pages. 9 x 7 x .5. Storeroom 2.

For original writs, see entries 125 and 126.

120. PRAECIPE DOCKET
1848—. 9 volumes. (1-9). 1803-1848 in Summons and Praecipe Docket, entry 119.

Clerk of courts' record of praecipes issued showing names of litigants, kind of action, kind of writ, date issued, and name of attorney. Chronologically arranged by dates issued. No index. Handwritten on printed forms. Average 280 pages. 14 x 9 x 1.5. 6 volumes, 1848-1922, Storeroom 2; 3 volumes, 1922—, Clerk of courts' office.

For original praecipes, see entry 125.

121. WITNESS DOCKET
1856-1885. 9 volumes.

Record of witnesses subpoenaed in criminal and civil causes showing term of court, names of litigants, case number, volume and page numbers of Criminal Docket, entry 198 or Civil Docket, entry 199, date of trial, names of plaintiff and defense witnesses, date subpoena issued, number of days, mileage, and total fee; also contains list of witnesses subpoenaed to appear before grand jury showing court term, names of witnesses, dates subpoena issued, number of days, mileage, and total fee. Chronologically arranged by dates of courts terms. No index. Handwritten on printed forms. Average 280 pages. 18 x 8 x 1.5. Storeroom 2.

For subsequent records, criminal cases, see entry 128; civil cases, see entry 129.

122. WITNESS DOCKET, GRAND JURY
1925—. 1 volume. -1924 in Witness Book, Criminal, entry 128.

Record of witnesses subpoenaed to appear before the grand jury showing term of court, names of witnesses, dates subpoenaed, date reported, number of days and attendance, mileage, total amount of fees, date certificate for fees issued, and certificate number. Chronologically arranged by dates of court terms. No index. Handwritten on printed forms. 180 pages. 16 x 11 x 1.5. Clerk of courts' office.

123. JUDGMENT DOCKET
May 1935—. 1 volume.

Clerk of courts' record of judgment lien certificates showing what court, case number, names a judgment creditor and judgment debtor, amount of judgment, date judgment rendered, date of filing, and date judgment satisfied. Chronologically arranged by dates of filing. Alphabetical index, direct, by names of judgment creditors, and reverse, by names of judgment debtors. Typed on printed forms. 440 pages. 18 x 11 x 2.5. Clerk of courts' office.

124. CASE RECEIPT RECORD
1919—. 1 volume.

Record of filing cases in common pleas court showing case number, names of litigants, what paper filed, date filed, date of sheriff's return, and name of attorney filing cause. Chronologically arranged by dates of filing. No index. Handwritten on printed forms. 480 pages. 13.5 x 8 x 2. Clerk of courts' office.

Court Writs and Jury and Witness Books

125. PRAECIPES

1803-1861. 78 bundles. 1862— in Original Records, Civil, entry 211 and Criminal Records, entry 212.

Copies of praecipes issued by clerk of courts in cases filed in county courts showing date of issue, case number, names of the litigants, on whom issued, name of attorney, and date of sheriff's return. Chronologically arranged by dates issued. No index. 1803-1844, handwritten; 1844-1861, handwritten on printed forms. 4 x 2.5 x 7. Storeroom 3.

For records of praecipes, see entries 119 and 120.

126. SUMMONSES

1804-1937. 9 bundles. 1838— in Original Records, Civil, entry 211, and Criminal Records, entry 212.

Original summonses issued in cases filed in county courts by clerk of courts showing date issued, names of litigants, kind of action, on whom issued, date to appear, name of attorney, and date of sheriff's return. Chronologically arranged by dates issued. No index. Handwritten. 4 x 2 x 8. Storeroom 3.

For record of summonses, see entry 119.

127. JURY BOOK

1886—. 7 volumes. (1 unnumbered, 1-6).

Record of grand and petit jury venires: showing court term, date subpoenaed, name, township or city ward, address, date reported, number of days, mileage, total fee, and date certificate for fees issued; petit jury showing court term, what case, nature of case, trial date, dates subpoenaed, name, township or city ward, address, date reported, number of days, mileage, total fee, and date certificate for fees issued. Chronologically arranged by dates of court terms. No index. Handwritten on printed forms. Average 430 pages. 16 x 11 x 2.25. 6 volumes, 1886-1931, Store room 2; 1 volume, 1931—, Clerk of courts' office.

128. WITNESS BOOK, CRIMINAL

1886—. 7 volumes. (1-7).

Record of witnesses subpoenaed in criminal cases showing name of defendant, case number, volume and page numbers of Criminal Docket, entry 198, date of trial, names of witnesses for state and for defendant, number of certificate for fees, dates subpoenaed, date witness reported, date discharged, number of days, mileage, total fees, and date certified to auditor. Contains witness docket, Grand Jury, -1924, entry 122, showing term of court, names of witness subpoenaed, number of certificate for fees, date subpoenaed, date witness reported, date discharge, number of days, mileage, total fee, and date certified to auditor. Chronologically arranged by dates of court terms or trials. Alphabetically indexed by names of defendants. Handwritten on printed forms. Average 140 pages. 16 x 11 x 1. 6 volumes, 1886-1925, Storeroom 2; 1 volume, 1925—, Clerk of courts' office.

For prior records, see entry 121.

129. WITNESS BOOK, CIVIL

1886—. 12 volumes. (1-12).

Record of witnesses subpoenaed in civil cases showing name of litigants, volume and page numbers of Civil Docket, entry 199, case number, trial date, names of witnesses for plaintiff and defendant, date subpoenaed, date witness reported, date discharge, number of days, mileage, and total fees. Chronologically arranged by trial dates. Alphabetically indexed by names of plaintiffs and defendants. Handwritten on printed forms. Average 140 pages. 16 x 11 x 1. 9 volumes, 1886-1928, Storeroom 2; 3 volumes, 1928—, Clerk of courts' office.

For prior records, see entry 121.

130. BILLS OF EXCEPTIONS

1874—. 613 bills.

Bills of exceptions filed on appeal from decision or verdict asking for review of case, on error or other grounds, showing names of litigants, date filed, from what court, to what court appealed, name of party filing exceptions, with transcript of testimony and the depositions, volume and page numbers of Appearance Docket, entry 194, and date motion overruled. No systematic arrangement; each bill bound separately. No index. 1874-1893, handwritten; 1894—, typed. Average 30 pages. 14 x 8.5 x .25 to 750 pages 14 x 8.5 x 3. 517 bills, 1874-1932, Storeroom 1; 96 bills, 1932—, Clerk of courts' office.

131. EXECUTIONS

1803—. 217 bundles and 62 file boxes.

Original execution orders to satisfy judgments rendered showing date issued, case number, names of litigants, kind of action, amount of judgment, date of sheriff's return, cost bill on execution, and date of filing. Chronologically arranged by dates issued. No index. 1803-1844, handwritten; 1844—, handwritten on printed forms. Bundles, 4 x 3.5 x 8; 21 file boxes, 4.5 x 4.5 x 9.5; 41 file boxes, 10 x 4.5 x 14. 217 bundles, 1803-1906, Storeroom 3; 21 file boxes, 1893-1909, Storeroom 1; 41 file boxes, 1910—, Clerk of courts' office.

Motor Vehicles

132. MOTOR VEHICLE BILLS OF SALE AND SWORN STATEMENTS OF OWNERSHIP

August 1921-December 31, 1937. 371 file boxes. Discontinued; motor registration law amended, effective January 1, 1938.

Duplicate copies of motor vehicle bills of sale or sworn statements of ownership showing consecutive instrument number, date of transfer, names of grantor and grantee, name of manufacturer, factory and motor numbers, year, horsepower, make, type, and model, oath of grantor, and date of filing; also if used vehicle, name of original purchaser, and names of subsequent owners. Numerically arranged by consecutive instruments numbers. Typed on printed forms. 4.5 x 4.5 x 9.5. 91 file boxes, August 1921-April 1929, Storeroom 2; 80 file boxes, April 1929-December 31, 1937, Clerk of courts' office.

For subsequent records, see entries 135 and 136.

133. INDEX, MOTOR VEHICLE BILLS OF SALE AND SWORN STATEMENT OF OWNERSHIP, DIRECT

1921-December 31, 1937. 8 volumes. Discontinued.

Direct index showing names of grantor and grantee, date filed, instrument number, make of vehicle, horsepower, type, model, motor and manufacturer's numbers, and if new or used vehicle. Alphabetically arranged by names of grantors and chronologically thereunder by dates of filing. Handwritten on printed forms. Average 540 pages. 14 x 16 x 3. Clerk of courts' office.

134. INDEX, MOTOR VEHICLE BILLS OF SALE AND SWORN STATEMENT OF OWNERSHIP, REVERSE
1921-December 31, 1937. 8 volumes. Discontinued.
Reverse index showing names of grantee and grantor, date filed, instrument number, make of vehicle, horsepower, type, model, motor and manufacturer's numbers, and if new or used vehicle. Alphabetically arranged by names of grantees and chronologically thereunder by dates of filing. Handwritten on printed forms. Average 540 pages. 14 x 16 x 3. Clerk of courts' office.

135. CERTIFICATE OF TITLE, CASH BOOK
January 1, 1938—. 1 volume.
Record of registration of certificates of title to motor vehicles showing date filed, certificate number, names of purchaser and vendor, total fee, issuing fee, notation of lien fee, memorandum of certificate fee, cancellation of lien fee, certified copy fee, acknowledgment fee, amount of fee to state, and amount of fee to county. Alphabetically arranged by names of purchasers and chronologically thereunder by dates of filing. No index. Handwritten on printed forms. 500 pages. 18 x 16 x 2.5. Clerk of courts' office.

For prior records, see entry 132.

136. CERTIFICATE OF TITLE, MOTOR VEHICLE
January 1, 1938—. 22 file boxes (A-Z).
Duplicate certificates of title to motor vehicles showing consecutive certificate number, date of certificate, names of purchaser and vendor, if new or used vehicle, make, type, model, motor number, date purchased, amount of lien, and fee. Alphabetically arranged by names of purchasers and chronologically thereunder by dates of certificates. No index. Typed on printed forms. 10 x 7 x 22. Clerk of courts' office.

For prior records, see entry 132.

Licenses and Permits

137. LICENSES AND PERMITS
1792-1861. 67 bundles.
Record of licenses and permits issued by order of common pleas quarter sessions court, 1792-1802, common pleas court, 1803-1899, and by clerk of courts, 1839-

1861, showing date, name of licensee, business or residence, kind and term of license, and amount of fee. Tavern, ferry, and all merchandising licenses are included, 1792-1830, and 1839-1861; tavern and ferry licenses only were recorded, 1831-1838. Chronologically arranged by dates of entries. No index. 1792-1844, handwritten; 1845-1861, handwritten on printed forms. 4.5 x 3 x 7.5. Storeroom 3.

138. [TAVERN AND FERRY LICENSES]

1803-1812. In Journal, entry 203.

Record of permits to keep taverns and operate ferries showing date, name of licensee, term of license, and amount of fee.

139. [MISCELLANEOUS PERMITS]

1802-1812. In Marriage Record, entry 293.

Record of licenses issued to operate taverns and ferries and to sell merchandise, showing kind of license and name of licensee.

140. AUCTIONEERS' LICENSE RECORD

1861-1929. 1 volume. Last entry 1929. Prior records missing.

Record of licenses issued to sell chattels and merchandise at public auctions showing name and licensee, license number, date issued, names of sureties on bond, amount of bond, term of license, and fee. Chronologically arranged by dates issued. Alphabetically indexed by names of licensees. Handwritten on printed forms. 380 pages. 16 x 10 x 2. Clerk of courts' office.

141. RECORD OF NOTARIES' COMMISSIONS

1855—. 13 volumes. (3 volumes, unnumbered, 4-13).

Record copy of commissions granted by governor of Ohio to perform the duties of notary public showing name of appointee, date of appointment, term of appointment, names of governor and secretary of state, copy of office of notary, and date recorded. Chronologically arranged by dates appointed. Alphabetically indexed by names of appointees. 1855-1870, handwritten; 1871–, handwritten on printed forms. 2 volumes average 110 pages 9 x 7 x .5; 11 volumes average 380 pages 14 x 9 x 2. 6 volumes, 1855-1905, Storeroom 2; 3 volumes, 1905-1920, Storeroom 1; 4 volumes, 1920—, Clerk of courts' office.

142. RECORD OF JUSTICES' OATHS AND MAYORS' CERTIFICATIONS

1866—. 4 volumes. (1-4).

Record of oaths of office by justices of the peace showing name of justice, township, date of commission, copy of oath of office, name of attesting official, date of oath, and date recorded; also record of mayors' certificates of election and qualifications showing name of official elected, what corporation, date term of office begins, copy of corporation clerk's certificate of election and qualifications for the office, and date recorded. Chronologically arranged by dates of recording. Alphabetically indexed by names of officials. Handwritten on printed forms. Average 300 pages. 14 x 9 x 1.75. 3 volumes, 1866-1919, Storeroom 2; 1 volume 1919—, Clerk of courts' office.

143. RECORD OF RAILROAD POLICEMEN'S COMMISSIONS

June 1885—. 1 volume. Last entry February 1934.

Record copy of commissions issued by governor of Ohio to individuals appointed to act as police on railroad property showing name of appointee, name of railroad company, date issued, signature of governor and secretary of state, copy of oath by appointee, and date recorded. Chronologically arranged by dates issued. Alphabetically indexed by names of appointees. Handwritten on printed forms. 140 pages. 16 x 11 x .75. Clerk of courts' office.

144. HUNTERS' LICENSE RECORD

1913-1925. 4 volumes. (1-4).

Record of hunters' licenses issued showing license number, date of issue, name of applicant, age, occupation, address, nativity, physical description of licensee, and fee. Alphabetically arranged by names of applicants and chronologically thereunder by dates issued. No index. Handwritten on printed forms. Average 240 pages. 16 x 11 x 1.25. Storeroom 2.

For subsequent records, see entry 146.

145. FISHING LICENSES

1919-1925. 1 volume.

Record of licenses issued to fish with rod and reel showing name of licensee, license number, date of issue, age, occupation, address, nativity, and physical description of licensee, and fee. Alphabetically arranged by names of licensees and chronologically thereunder by dates issued. No index. Handwritten on printed forms. 300 pages. 16 x 11 x 1.25. Storeroom 2.

For subsequent records, see entry 146.

146. INDEX TO HUNTERS' AND FISHING LICENSES
1926—. 2 volumes.

Index record showing name and address of licensee, date license issued, license number, and fee. Chronologically arranged by years and alphabetically thereunder by names of licensees. Handwritten on printed forms. Average 780 pages. 10 x 12 x 4. Clerk of courts' office.

For prior records of hunters' licenses, see entry 144; of fishing licenses, see entry 145.

147. RECORD OF REAL ESTATE BROKERS AND SALESMEN
1927—. 2 volumes. (1, 2).

Register of licenses issued to brokers and salesmen to sell, trade, and buy real estate for clients, showing date of issue, name of broker or salesman, address, by whom employed, license number, and fee. Alphabetically arranged by names of licensees. No index. Handwritten on printed forms. Average 160 pages. 13 x 7.5 x 1. Clerk of courts' office.

148. EMBALMERS' LICENSE RECORD
1903-1925. 1 volume. Discontinued.

Record copy of certificates issued to applicants by state board of embalming examiners granting license to embalm and prepare for burial, transportation or cremation of dead human bodies, showing license number, name of licensee date, issued, and date recorded. Chronologically arranged by dates of recording. Alphabetically indexed by names of licensees. Handwritten on printed forms. 290 pages. 13.5 x 8 x 1.25. Clerk of courts' office.

149. OPTOMETRIST RECORD
July 1920—. 1 volume.

Copies of certificates issued by Ohio state board of optometry to applicants passing the examination for optometrists showing license number, name of licensee, date of issue, names of president and secretary of board of optometry and photograph of licensee. Chronologically arranged by dates issued. Alphabetically indexed by names of licensees. Handwritten on printed forms. 140 pages. 10.5 x 8.5 x .75. Clerk of courts' office.

Partnerships

150. RECORD OF PARTNERSHIPS
1895—. 1 volume.
Register of partnerships showing name of partnership, certificate number, names of partners, and date of filing. Alphabetically arranged by names of partnerships. No index. Handwritten on printed forms. 180 pages. 14 x 10 x 1. Clerk of courts' office.

Elections

151. POLL LISTS AND TALLY SHEETS
1812-1897. 82 bundles. No prior or subsequent records found.
Precinct poll list and tally sheets of annual elections. Poll list shows name of electors casting ballots. Tally sheets show number of votes received by each candidate for election and date filed with clerk of courts. Chronologically arranged by years. No index. 1812-1863, handwritten; 1864-1897, handwritten on printed forms. 5 x 3.5 x 8. 54 bundles, 1806-1879, Storeroom 3; 28 bundles, 1880-1897, Storeroom 2.

152. POLL LIST AND TALLY SHEETS (Justices of the Peace)
1806-1900. 51 bundles. No prior or subsequent records found.
Precinct poll list and tally sheets of elections of justices of the peace. Poll list shows name of electors casting ballots at elections. Tally sheets show number of votes received by each candidate for election and date filed with clerk of courts. Chronologically arranged. No index. Handwritten. 4.5 x 3.5 x 8. Storeroom 3.

153. POLL LIST AND TALLY SHEETS
October 12, 1851. 1 bundle.
Precinct poll list and tally sheets of election on adoption of new state constitution and amendments. Poll list show names of electors casting ballots. Tally sheets show number of votes cast for and number against adoption and filed with clerk of courts. No systematic arrangement. No index. Handwritten on printed forms. 6.5 x 3.5 x 8. Storeroom 3.

154. ABSTRACTS OF VOTES

1870-1891. 1 volume. Subsequent records confidential.

Abstracts of votes cast at annual elections, for each candidate for election, showing date of election, township and city wards, number of votes cast in each township and city ward for candidates for each office, and total county votes. Chronologically arranged by election dates. No index. Handwritten on printed forms. 225 pages. 22 x 15.5 x 1.25. Storeroom 2.

155. POLL BOOKS AND TALLY SHEETS, GENERAL ELECTIONS

1930—. 600 volumes.

Precinct poll lists of electors casting ballots at general elections showing precinct and name and address of elector. Tally sheets show number of votes received by each candidate for election to office and each proposal voted on including bond issues and constitutional amendments. Alphabetically arranged by names of electors. No index. Handwritten on printed forms. Average 28 pages. 26 x 14 x .25. 375 volumes, 1930-1934, Storeroom 2; 225 volumes, 1935—, Clerk of courts' office.

156. POLL BOOKS AND TALLY SHEETS, PRIMARY ELECTIONS

1830—. 300 volumes.

Precinct poll books and tally sheets primary elections: poll books showing names and addresses of republican and democratic electors casting ballots; tally sheets showing number of votes received by each candidate for nomination on each party ticket. Alphabetically arranged by names of electors. No index. Handwritten on printed forms. Average 30 pages. 26 x 14 x .25. 225 volumes, 1930-1934, Storeroom 2; 75 volumes, 1936—, Clerk of courts' office.

Naturalization

157. NATURALIZATION, PETITIONS AND RECORD

1906—. 1 volume.

Petitions of aliens to become naturalized citizens of the United States on regular forms prescribed by United States department of commerce and labor, bureau of immigration and naturalization, with affidavits of citizens of United States affirming the petitions of the aliens; also oaths of allegiance by aliens on receipt of final papers. Chronologically arranged by dates of filing petitions. Alphabetically indexed by names of aliens. Handwritten on printed forms. 100 pages. 18 x 12 x .5. Storeroom 2.

For prior records, see entries 286 and 287.

Business Administration of Office

158. RECORD OF TREASURER'S RECEIPTS

1845-1854. 1 volume. No prior or subsequent records found.

Clerk of courts' receipts from county treasurer for fees and cost paid into treasury showing date of receipt, for what, what cause, and amount paid in. Chronologically arranged by dates of receipts. No index. Handwritten. 200 pages. 9 x 7 x 1. Storeroom 2.

159. LEDGER (Record of Court Costs and Payments)

1884-1885. 1 volume. Only record of this type found.

Clerk of courts' record of court costs showing volume and page numbers of Appearance Docket, entry 194 and of Journal, entry 203, names of litigants, date posted, and amount of cost and fees; also distribution of costs and fees showing to whom paid, for what, and amount. Chronologically arranged by dates posted. Alphabetically indexed by names of plaintiffs. Handwritten on printed forms. 330 pages. 14 x 9 x 1.5. Storeroom 3.

160. CASH BOOK

August 1842-February 1851. 1 volume. No other records found.

Clerk of courts' record of cash receipts showing date, from whom, for what service, and amount. Chronologically arranged by dates received. No index. Handwritten on printed forms. 400 pages. 14 x 8.5 x 2. Storeroom 2.

161. CASH JOURNAL
1877—. 18 volumes. (1-18).

Clerk of courts' journal of cost and fees in court cases showing names of litigants, case number, volume and page numbers of Witness Book, Criminal, entry 128, Witness Book, Civil, entry 129, Appearance Docket, entry 194, Execution Docket, entry 196, or Criminal Docket, entry 198, names of attorneys, court term, amount of judgment or fine, itemized bill of cost and fees, and date paid. Chronologically arranged by dates of court terms. Alphabetically indexed by names of plaintiffs and defendants. Handwritten on printed forms. Average 500 pages. 16 x 11 x 3. 10 volumes, 1877-1912, Storeroom 2; 8 volumes, 1912—, Clerk of courts' office.

162. ALIMONY RECORD
1909—. 3 volumes. (1-3).

Record of alimony payments to clerk of courts and by clerk of courts to payees showing case number, names of litigants, amount of alimony allowed, terms of payments, to whom payable, with record of payments made on order, and signature of payee or agent. Chronologically arranged by dates of entries. Alphabetically indexed by names of plaintiffs. Handwritten on printed forms. Average 240 pages. 16 x 11 x 1.25. 1 volume, 1909-1921, Storeroom 2; 2 volumes, 1921—, Clerk of courts' office.

163. FEE BOOK
1907-1912. 1 volume.

Clerk of courts' record of fees showing case number, by whom paid, to whom due, and total fee; amount due county, clerk, sheriff, witnesses, judgments, and sundries; also date paid and to whom paid. Chronologically arranged by dates paid. No index. Handwritten on printed forms. 220 pages. 18 x 14 x 1.25. Storeroom 2.

For subsequent records, see entry 164.

164. CASH BOOK
1913—. 12 volumes.

Clerk of courts' record of cash receipts and fees showing date, by whom paid, to whom due, and total; amount due county, clerk, sheriff, witnesses, jury, and sundry fund; also date paid out, to whom paid, for what, case number, and amount.

Chronologically arranged by dates received. Handwritten on printed forms. Average 310 pages. 16 x 11 x 1.75. 3 volumes, 1913-1919, Storeroom 2; 9 volumes, 1919—, Clerk of courts' office.

For prior records, see entry 163.

165. RECORD OF ACCRUED FEES

1907—. 7 volumes. (1-7).

Clerk of courts' record of fees accrued showing date accrued, case number, in what matter, to whom charged, total fees, civil causes, criminal causes, due from county, transcripts and copies, certificates, sundries, date paid, and classified as to source. Chronologically arranged by dates accrued. 1907-September 1917, alphabetically indexed by names of debtors; 1917—, no index. Handwritten on printed forms. Average 220 pages. 17 x 11 x 1.25. 1 volume, 1907-1917, Storeroom 2; 6 volumes, October 1917—, Clerk of courts' office.

166. RECORD OF MONEY PAID INTO COUNTY TREASURY

1889—. 3 volumes.

Clerk of courts' record of money paid into county treasury showing to whom money belongs, amount, what court record, volume and page numbers of record, and case number; also date money paid into treasury, case number, and volume and page numbers of Appearance Docket, entry 194. Alphabetically arranged by names of payees and chronologically thereunder by dates of entries. No index. Handwritten on printed forms. Average 320 pages. 14 x 8 x 1.75. 1 volume, 1889-1906, Storeroom 2; 2 volumes, 1906—, Clerk of courts' office.

Miscellaneous

167. STRAY BOOK

1801-1924. 3 volumes. Discontinued.

Record of strayed animals which have been penned and of report filed with clerk of courts showing date penned, description of animal, name and address of person holding stray, and date filed. Chronologically arranged by dates of filing. Handwritten. Average 220 pages. 11.5 x 8.5 x 1.5. 2 volumes, 1801-1878, Storeroom 3; 1 volume, 1874-1924, Clerk of courts' office.

For original reports, see entry 168.

168. ESTRAYS

1791-1834. 6 bundles.

Original reports of stray domestic animals penned by residents of Washington County showing date of report, name of person reporting penned stray, description of stray, and date stray penned. Chronologically arranged by dates reported. No index. Handwritten. 3.5 x 3 x 7. Storeroom 3.

For record of reports, see entry 167.

169. SALE OF STRAYS

1794-1846. 3 bundles.

Copies of advertisements posted for sale at public auctions of penned stray domestic animals for feed bill showing description of animal, name of person holding animal, date of sale, place of holding sale, amount of bill for feed and care, and date filed with clerk of courts. Chronologically arranged by dates of filing. No index. Handwritten. 3 x 3.5 x 8. Storeroom 3.

170. DECLARATION AND SCHEDULE

1820-1831. 1 bundle.

Original declaration and schedule of property and income by ex-Revolutionary War soldiers and sailors as provided by an act congress, May 1820, which provided a pension for such soldiers and sailors who were indigent or enfeebled by age, showing date of declaration, companies served in, length of service, inventory or schedule of chattels and income, number of dependents, and date filed. Chronologically arranged by dates of filing. No index. Handwritten. 5 x 3.5 x 8. Storeroom 3.

171. RECORD OF BONDS

1828-1861. 1 volume.

Clerk of courts' record copy of bonds filed by the following county officials: sheriff, coroner, surveyor, and prosecuting attorney, showing date of bond, name of principal, what office, names of sureties, amount of bond, and date filed. Chronologically arranged by dates of filing. Handwritten. 280 pages. 13.5 x 8 x 1.5. Storeroom 2.

For other official bond records, see entries 379-381 and 524-527.

172. RECORD OF PAPERS REMOVED
1905—. 2 volumes.

Clerk of courts' record of court papers which have been removed from files showing names of litigants, date removed, what papers, by whom removed, volume and page numbers of Appearance Docket, entry 194, case number, and date returned. Chronologically arranged by dates removed. No index. Handwritten on printed forms. Average 300 pages. 14 x 8 x 1.5. 1 volume, 1905-1924, Storeroom 1; 1 volume, 1924—, Clerk of courts' office.

173. [REGISTRATION OF NEGROES]
1805-1809. In Marriage Record, entry 293.

Registration of negro and mulatto persons brought into Washington County showing name, age, and sex.

174. EX OFFICIO SERVICE RECORD
1921—. 3 volumes.

Record of service requested showing dates, name of record or paper to copy, kind of certificate, kind of instrument acknowledged, affidavit to what or disposition in what case, amount of fee, signature of person requesting service, and volume and page numbers of Cash Book, entry 164. Chronologically arranged by dates of request. No index. Handwritten on printed forms. Average 150 pages. 16 x 11 x 1. 1 volume, 1921-1927, Storeroom 2; 2 volumes, 1927—, Clerk of courts' office.

175. [TAX COLLECTORS ACCOUNTS]
1793-1825. In Road Record (First Series), entry 679.

Copy of itemized annual account of the tax collector for Washington County showing amount of tax collections on real and personal property, amount of tax defaulted, amount on tax duplicate, and amount of commission for collections.

176. QUADRENNIAL ENUMERATION
1879-1909. 252 volumes. No other records found.

List of male inhabitants over twenty-one years of age as returned to clerk of courts by township and district assessors showing name, color, occupation, and address. Alphabetically arranged by names of inhabitants. No index. written on printed forms. Average 40 pages. 10 x 8 x .25. Storeroom 2.

177. ENUMERATION, SOLDIERS AND SAILORS

1908. 31 volumes.

List of soldiers and sailors (living) who enlisted in Mexican War, War of Rebellion, Spanish-American War, and Philippine Insurrection, showing township, ward, name of soldier or sailor, what war, branch of service, rank, company or battery, regiment or vessel, and post-office address. No systematic arrangement. No index. Handwritten on printed forms. Average 36 pages. 7.5 x 4 x .25. Storeroom 2.

178. [DISTRIBUTION OF STATUTE BOOKS]

1788-1841. In Marriage Record, entry 293.

Record of distribution of statute books showing name of recipient, title of book, and number of copies.

For subsequent records, see entry 179.

179. APPOINTMENT OF LAWS

1823-1850. 1 bundle. Discontinued.

Clerk of courts' record of distribution of laws of Ohio to county and township officials and attorneys showing date, name of recipient, official title, and what book. Chronologically arranged by years. No index. Handwritten. 4.5 x 3.5 x 8. Storeroom 3.

For prior records, see entry 178.

180. STATISTICAL REPORTS

1870—. 6 bundles and 31 pamphlets.

Record copies of statistical (judicial) reports by clerk of courts to secretary of state showing number of divorce suits filed, number pending at beginning of year, number decided during year, and number still pending; number of cases under each ground or action, amount of fines, cost assessed, amount forfeited, and recognizance; number cases of civil judgments; total amount of judgments found; total amount jury fees, civil and criminal; total number of prosecutions for crimes against the person showing number under each offense; total number of prosecutions for crimes against property showing number under each offense; total number of prosecutions for offenses against public peace and health with number under each offense; total number of prosecutions for offenses against public justice and policy with number under each offense; total number of prosecutions for offenses against public chastity and morality with number under each offense;

number convictions for crime or offenses of lower grade then charged in indictment; number inquests held by coroner or justice of the peace; number cases pending in common pleas and circuit or appeals court at beginning of year (July 1); number of cases filed during year, and number of cases pending; also nativity of persons naturalized. Chronologically arranged to by years. No index. Handwritten on printed forms. Bundles, 3.5 x 4 x 10; pamphlets, average 16 pages 17 x 13 x .25. Six bundles and 21 pamphlets, 1870-1927, Storeroom 3; 10 pamphlets, 1927—, Clerk of courts' office.

181. REPORTS, CORONER'S INQUESTS

1824—. 20 bundles, 22 jackets, and 15 file boxes. No prior records.

Transcripts of proceedings by coroner's inquests in cases of homicidal, accidental, or sudden deaths filed with clerk of courts, showing name of decedent, date of death, name of witnesses, names of jurors (if used), verdict as to cause or manner of death, itemized cost bill, and date of inquest. This is the coroner's report to clerk of courts, chronologically arranged by dates of inquest. No index. 1824-1961, handwritten; 1862—, handwritten on printed forms. Bundles, 3.5 x 3 x 8; Jackets, 3.5 x 4.5 x 9; file boxes (storeroom), 4.5 x 4.5 x 9; file boxes (clerk of courts' office), 10 x 4.5 x 14. 20 bundles and 22 jackets, 1824-1919, Storeroom 3; 8 file boxes, 1899-1917, Storeroom 1; 7 file boxes, 1918—, Clerk of courts' office.

For coroner's records, see entries 326 and 327.

182. FINES COLLECTED

1852—. 8 bundles and 2 file boxes.

Record copies of clerk of courts' annual reports to county commissioners of fines collected in criminal cases showing date of report, number of cases in which fines assessed, total amount of fines, number of cases each type or class of offense, amount of fines collected, amount uncollected, and amount of cost collected. Chronologically arranged by years. No index. Handwritten on printed forms. Bundles, 3 x 3.5 x 8; file boxes, 10 x 4.5 x 14. 8 bundles, 1852-1912, Storeroom 2; 2 file boxes, 1913—, Clerk of courts' office.

183. CONSERVANCY APPRAISAL RECORD

1936—. 1 volume.

Record of assessments against real estate in the taxing of flood control area in Washington County (Muskingum Watershed Conservancy District) showing name of property owner, file number, description of real estate, type of instrument of conveyance, acreage, appraised value for purchase, amount fixed for easement, amount fixed for damages, amount fixed for benefits, amount finally fixed for benefits, amount paid for assessment, and date reported to court under section 30 of conservancy law. Alphabetically arranged by names of owners. No index. Typed on printed forms. 380 pages. 18 x 26 x 2.75. Clerk of courts' office.

The court of common pleas, like many other county institutions, originated in England during the reign of Henry II (George Burton Adams, *Constitutional History of England,* New York, 1921, 109, 134). Established in America during the colonial period, the office was continued by the states following the War of American Independence. The territorial act of 1788, establishing the American colonial policy in the newer west in respect to the judiciary, contained sections authorizing the establishment of a common pleas court to be composed of not less than three nor more than five members. These members, appointed and commissioned by the territorial governor, were given jurisdiction in all civil matters. (Pease, *op. cit.*, 7).

The same act established in every county a primary court called the court of general quarter sessions of the peace to be composed of not more than five or less than three justices of the peace appointed and commissioned by the governor (*ibid.,* 4). This court had limited jurisdiction and criminal matters (*ibid.,* 7). A complete set of the records of this court, which was commonly referred to as the court of common pleas, quarter sessions, is extant in Washington County, from the date of its organization to the end of the territorial period when the court was abolished.

When a constitution was drafted for Ohio in 1802, preparatory to the entrance of the state into the Union, provision was made for a continuation of the territorial court of common pleas (*Ohio Const.* 1802, Art. III. sec. 1). The articles of the constitution, regarding the judiciary, provided for a court of common pleas to be composed of a president and associate judges. The members of the court, appointed by joint ballot of both houses of the general assembly, were to hold court in three judicial districts into which the state was to be divided by legislative action. (*Ibid.,* Art. III, sec. 8).

The court was assigned common law and chancery jurisdiction in all cases as should be provided by law (*ibid.,* Art. III sec. 3). To the court was assigned jurisdiction in probate and testamentary matters and in the appointment of guardians. Moreover, the court of common pleas and supreme court were assigned original cognizance of criminal cases as might be provided by law. (*Ibid.,* Art, XXX, sec. 4). Appeals in civil cases might be made from the county commissioners, justices of the peace, and other inferior courts to the court of common pleas (*ibid.,* Art III, sec. 3). Finally, the court was authorized to appoint a clerk (*ibid.,* Art III, sec. 9).

Since the constitution called for legislative action, an act interpreting the constitutional provisions was passed in 1803. Under this act the court was given original jurisdiction in all cases in law and equity, when the matter in dispute exceeded the jurisdiction of the justices of the peace, and was authorized to take original cognizance of all probate, testamentary, and guardianship matters, and in all criminal matters exceeding the jurisdiction of the justices of the peace, except in cases involving capital punishment (1 O. L. 39-40). A year later, in 1804, the jurisdiction of the court of chancery was restricted in cases where the sum involved more than $500 (2 O. L. 261). In 1807 this restriction was removed, and the court of common pleas was given original jurisdiction in all cases cognizable by a court of chancery, subject to an appeal to the supreme court. (5 O. L. 117).

In 1805 the court was authorized to appoint a county prosecuting attorney (3 O. L. 47). In 1806 the court of common pleas was assigned cognizance of criminal cases, wherein the punishment was capital, if the accused elected to be so tried (4 O. L. 57). The Chancery Act, adopted in 1824, conferred general chancery powers on the court (22 O. L. 75); and, in 1843 it was given concurrent jurisdictions with the supreme court in cases of divorce and alimony (41 O. L. 94).

Significant changes were made in the composition of the court of common pleas and its jurisdiction during the middle of the nineteenth century. Under the constitution of 1851 the judges were made elective for a seven-year term. For the purpose of electing judges the state was divided into nine districts composed of three or more counties. Each district, in turn, was to be subdivided into three parts, in each of which one common pleas judge was to be elected. Court was to be held in every district or county with such jurisdiction that should be fixed by law. (*Ohio Const.* 1851, Art. IV, secs. 3, 4). Provision was made for the removal of judges by a concurrent resolution of two-thirds of the members elected to each house of legislature (*ibid.,* Art. IV, sec. 17).

Interpreting the constitutional provisions the legislature made provisions for judicial districts but left the jurisdiction of the court much the same as it had been in the earlier years of its existence (50 O. L. 70). However, with the re-establishment of the probate court by constitutional provision, the court of common pleas was denied jurisdiction in cases of probate, testamentary, and guardianship matters, but the judgments and final decrees of the probate court could be "reversed, vacated, or modified" on error proceedings by the court of common pleas (51 O. L. 145). A year later, in 1852, the court of common pleas was given original jurisdiction of all crimes and offenses except minor criminal cases the exclusive jurisdiction of which was invested in the justices of the peace or other minor courts (G. C. sec. 13422-5; 51 O. L. 474; 52 O. L. 73). In the same year the court of common pleas was given exclusive jurisdiction and divorce cases (51 O. L. 377).

Since 1906 the court of common pleas has had jurisdiction in naturalization proceedings. In that year the federal statute was amended to limit jurisdiction in the granting of naturalization to the United States district courts and state courts having a clerk, a seal, and jurisdiction in matters of law and equity in which the amount of controversy is unlimited. (*U. S. Statutes at Large,* XXXIV , 596).

At the opening of the twentieth century sweeping changes in the organization of the courts were made. The constitutional amendment of 1912 abolished the divisions and subdivisions provided by the constitution of 1851, and authorized the election of one or more common pleas judges in each county. (*Ohio Const.* Art. IV, sec. 3). Ten years later, the selection of a chief justice of the court of common pleas was authorized. Under an act of March 13, 1923, in counties where there were two or more common pleas judges, they were authorized to designate one of their number as chief justice. The justice so designated by his colleagues was to serve in such a capacity until the expiration of his term, after which time the office of chief justice was to be an elective one. The elective section of the act was nullified by the supreme court on the grounds that the creation of a new elective official was unconstitutional. Accordingly, in 1927, an amendment was passed eliminating the elective provision of the act.

With the increased number of issues presented to the court of common pleas, the problems of judicial administration have become greater. This problem was solved in part by the creation of a chief justice of the court of common pleas who has been given the duties of superintending the business of the court, classifying it, and distributing it among the judges. Besides the duties enumerated, the chief justice annually makes a report to the clerk of courts showing the work performed by the court and by each judge in the proceeding calendar year. Moreover, he reports such other data as the chief justice of the supreme court may require. (G. C. 1558).

In recent years attempts have been made to improve the efficiency of the court by imposing stricter qualifications upon those who seek election to the bench. In 1917 there was passed an act providing that a common pleas judge shall have been admitted to practice as an attorney and counselor-at-law for a period of six years preceding his election (107 O. L. 164).

During the first three decades of Ohio history, the movement for the extension of the popular election of public officers deprived the court of common pleas the privilege of appointing the county recorder (1829), county surveyor (1831), and county prosecutor (1833) (27 O. L. 65; 29 O. L. 399; Salmon P. Chase, *The Statutes of Ohio and of the Northwest Territory*, 1833-1835, III, 1935). The court continued to appoint a clerk of courts until 1851. In recent years, however, as new functions have been added to county government, the court has again been given a limited appointive power. Successive acts in 1886, 1891, 1914, and 1925, authorized the court to appoint a soldiers' and sailors' relief commission, a jury commission, an assignment commissioner, a conservancy district board, and a probation officer (83 O. L. 232; 88 O. L. 200; 103 O. L. 512; 104 O. L. 13-64; 111 O. L. 423). Other appointments, authorized in 1911, are court interpreter and a criminal bailiff (G. C. 1541). Since 1929, the court, in counties having a population in excess of 300,000, has been authorized to appoint one or more psychiatrists, psychologists, or other examiners or investigators who shall hold their offices at the will of the court, and receive such compensation as the judge may determine, not exceeding the amount as may be appropriated by the county commissioners (G. C. 1541; 113 O. L. 467).

The records of the court of common pleas are deposited for safe keeping with the clerk of courts, who is made liable for the destruction of all law reports and books furnished by the state for use of the court and the bar (68 O. L. 109).

Court of General Quarter Sessions of the Peace

184. [ORGANIZATION OF COURT OF QUARTER SESSIONS]
September 1788. In Marriage Record, entry 293.
A record of organization of the court of quarter sessions of the peace showing date of organization, names of justices, and minutes of meeting.

185. CRIMINAL DOCKET
1789-1802. 1 volume.
Docket of criminal causes filed in common pleas court, quarter sessions, showing term of court, name of accused, offense charged, date filed, date bond filed, amount of bond, date of plea, verdict, and sentence. Chronologically arranged by dates of filing. No index. Handwritten. 160 pages. 12 x 8 x 1. Storeroom 2.

186. PROBATE DOCKET

1789-1802. 1 volume.

Record of appointment of administrator or executor in settlement of estates showing name of decedent, date of appointment, date bond filed, amount of bond, names of sureties, date of appraisal, names of appraisers, date inventory and appraisal filed, date of sale of effects of decedent, date sale bill filed, and date of settlement by administrator or executor; also record of appointment of guardian of minors and incompetents showing name of ward, date of appointment, date bond filed, amount of bond, names of sureties, dates of inventory and appraisement, names of appraisers, date inventory filed, and date of settlement of guardians' accounts. Chronologically arranged by dates of appointments. Alphabetically indexed by names of decedents or wards. Handwritten. 190 pages. 14 x 9 x 1. Storeroom 2.

187. JOURNAL AND DOCKET

1791-1802. 9 volumes.

Journal entry record of sessions of territorial common pleas court, quarter sessions, with journal entries in causes filed, appearance docket of cases filed, criminal and civil, showing court term, case number, names of litigants, title of case, names of attorneys, date case filed, date of filing pleas, motions, judgments, executions, verdict of court or jury, itemized cost bill, list of jurors drawn each term of court, and record of fees and cost at each term of court. Chronologically arranged by dates of court terms and by dates of filing. Alphabetically indexed by names of plaintiffs. Handwritten. Average 140 pages. 12 x 8 x .75. Storeroom 2.

188. (Final) RECORD

1795-1802. 2 volumes. Prior records missing.

Record of minutes of sessions of court of common pleas, quarter sessions, showing names of judges in attendance, copy of pleas filed, motions made, petitions filed, record of grand jury panels, copies of reports by public surveyor or on surveys made on order of the court relating to establishing roads, reports giving all survey data with landmarks specified; record of appointments by court, of assessors, constables, supervisors of highways, fence viewers, and overseers of the poor; record of establishing townships, and record of rates established for operating ferries. Chronologically arranged by session dates. For indexes, see entries 205 and 206. Handwritten. Average 400 pages. 14.5 x 9.5 x 2. Storeroom 2.

189. [QUARTER SESSIONS ADMINISTRATION PROCEEDINGS]
November 1788-February 1803. In Marriage Record, entry 293.
Record of proceedings in administration matters before the probate division of the court of general quarter sessions of the peace.

190. [PLAT OF SURVEY OF MARIETTA-ZANESVILLE ROAD]
1802. 1 sheet.
Plat of road from Coal Run on the Muskingum to Zanesville by the Saltworks, surveyed by order of the court of general quarter sessions of the peace, showing plat of road with mile trees indicated for each mile, report and signature of the surveyor, and signatures of the committee. Handwritten. Writing legible; paper faded and fragile, mended. Scale, 1 inch equals 1 mile or 80 chains. Prepared by Elanthan Scofield, surveyor. Diagonal approximately 40 inches. Auditor's office, safe.

191. ORIGINAL RECORDS
1782-1802. 44 bundles.
Original records and documents of territorial court of common pleas and quarter sessions for Washington County, consisting of capias, declarations of particulars, summonses, executive orders, jury venires, judgments, depositions, itemized cost and fee bills, showing term of court, case number, names of litigants, kind of action, date case filed in office of prothonotary, and court or jury verdict. Numerically arranged by case numbers. No index. Handwritten except capias and cost and fee bills which are handwritten on printed forms. The cost and fee bills are imprints and capias are semi-imprints. 6 x 3.25 x 8. Auditor's office, safe.

192. ORIGINAL RECORDS, ADMINISTRATION OF ESTATES AND GUARDIANSHIPS
1790-1802. 27 bundles.
Original records of administration of estates, including letters of authority to administrator or executor, notice of inventory and appraisement, itemized inventory and appraisement record, itemized sale bill, copy of will, bond of administrator or executor, record of settlement by administrator or executor, and itemized cost bill. The record show name of decedent, name of administrator or executor, date appointed, names of appraisers and of sureties on bond, amount of bond, and date of settlement. Guardianship records include letters of authority to guardians, notice of inventory and appraisement, itemized inventory and appraisal of wards assets,

record of settlement, itemized cost bill, guardian's bond, date of appointment, names of guardian, ward, appraisers, and sureties, and amount of bond. All papers of each case banded together. Chronologically arranged by dates of filing. No index. Handwritten. 3 x 3.5 x 8. Storeroom 3.

193. GRAND JURY LIST
1789-1802. 4 bundles.
Original list of freeholders drawn for grand jury duty, common pleas court, quarter sessions, showing court term, names of jurors, and place of residence. Chronologically arranged by dates of courts terms. No index. Handwritten. 3 x 3.5 x 7.5. Storeroom 3.

Dockets

194. APPEARANCE DOCKET
June 1849—. 62 volumes. (22 unnumbered, 1-40).
Docket of causes filed for appearance in common pleas court showing name of litigants, case number, names of attorneys, volume and page numbers of Cash Book, entry 164, Execution Docket, entry 196, and Final Record, entry 204, file box number, title of case, date case filed, dates writs filed, dates of sheriff's returns on writs, date of court order, and journal entries. Numerically arranged by case numbers. Alphabetical index, direct, by names of plaintiffs, and reverse, names of defendants; also separate index, 1873-1878, entry 116. Handwritten on printed forms. 1849-1879, 22 volumes, average 400 pages 14 x 9 x 2; 1879—, 40 volumes, average 630 pages 18 x 12 x 3.75. 22 volumes, 1849-1879, Storeroom 3; 40 volumes, 1879—, Clerk of courts' office.

195. APPEARANCE AND EXECUTION DOCKETS
1841- May 1879. 21 volumes. (A-U). Discontinued.
Docket showing names of litigants, title of case, court term, date case filed, trial date, dates of filing writs and court orders, names of attorneys, itemized cost bill, and date judgment satisfied. Chronologically arranged by dates of filing. Alphabetical index, direct, by names of plaintiffs, and reverse, by names of defendants. Handwritten. Average 560 pages. 14 x 9 x 3. Clerk of courts' office.

196. EXECUTION DOCKET

1803—. 32 volumes (25 unnumbered, 1-7).

Record of executions ordered to satisfy judgments rendered showing names of litigants, case number, date of judgment, date execution ordered, amount of judgment, dates writs issued, sheriff's returns on writs, record of sheriff's sale, and date judgment satisfied; 1879— shows volume and page numbers of Cash Book, entry 164, and of Appearance Docket, entry 194. Chronologically arranged by dates issued. Alphabetical index by names of judgment creditors; also separate indexes 1839-1845, entry 197, 1852—, entries 114 and 115, 1873-1878, entry 116, and 1884—, entry 117. Handwritten 1803-1879, 25 volumes, average 220 pages. 14 x 9 x 1.25; 1879—, 7 volumes, average 600 pages 16 x 11 x 3. 25 volumes, 1803-1879, Storeroom 3; 7 volumes, 1879—, Clerk of courts' office.

197. INDEX TO EXECUTION DOCKET

1839-1845. 1 volume. Discontinued.

Direct and reverse index to Execution Docket, showing names of plaintiff and defendant, volume and page numbers of record, and year. Alphabetically arranged by names of plaintiffs and defendants. Handwritten. 44o pages. 16 x 11 x 2.25. Storeroom 2

198. CRIMINAL DOCKET

1853—. 13 volumes. (1 unnumbered, 1-12). 1857-1876, missing.

Docket of criminal causes filed in common pleas court showing name of accused, case number, defendant's attorney, volume and page numbers of Cash Book, entry 164 and Execution Docket, entry 196, file box number, offense charged, and transcript from magistrate's court filed, date of recognizance, amount of recognizance, names of sureties, date indictment return, date of plea, and verdict of court or sentence. Contains itemized cost bills, 1853-1856. 1853-1856 chronologically arranged by dates of filing; 1857—, numerically arranged by case numbers. Alphabetically indexed by names of defendants in each volume; also separate index, 1884—, entry 117. Handwritten. Average 700 pages. 18 x 12 x 3.5. 1 volume, 1853-1856, Storeroom 3; 12 volumes, 1877—, Clerk of courts' office.

199. CIVIL DOCKET

1877—. 26 volumes. Prior records missing.

Docket of causes filed in common pleas court showing case number, names of attorneys and litigants, file box number, title of case, date filed, dates writs filed and of sheriff's returns on writs, dates of journal entries, and court findings and orders. Numerically arranged by case numbers. 1877-1883, no index; for index, 1884—, see entry 117. Typed on printed forms. Average 430 pages. 7.5 x 11 x 2.25. Clerk of courts' office.

200. COURT DOCKET
1803-1920, 244 volumes. Title varies: 1803-1847, Issue Docket. Discontinued.

Docket of causes filed in common pleas court showing court term, case number, names of litigants and attorneys, title of case, state of suit, and court orders. Chronologically arranged by dates of court terms. No index. Handwritten on printed forms. Average 100 pages. 14 x 11 x 1.5. Storeroom 2.

201. BAR DOCKET
1853-1919. 161 volumes. No prior records. Discontinued.

Docket of causes filed in common pleas court showing court term, case number, names of litigants and attorneys, kind of action, state of suit, and court orders. Chronologically arranged by dates of court terms. No index. Handwritten on printed forms. Average 80 pages. 14 x 10 x .5. Storeroom 2.

202. ADMINISTRATOR, EXECUTOR, AND GUARDIAN DOCKET
1803-1852. 9 volumes.

Record of administration of estates and guardianships showing court term, case number, date filed, name of decedent or ward, name of administrator, executor, or guardian, date appointed, date bond filed, dates of inventory and of appraisement, date of sale, date of settlement, and itemized cost bill. Chronologically arranged by dates of filing. Alphabetically indexed by names of wards or decedents. Handwritten. Average 210 pages. 12 x 8 x 1.25. Storeroom 2.

For subsequent records, see entries 239 and 240.

Journal and Complete Records

203. JOURNAL
1803—. 58 volumes. (1-58).

Record copy of journal entries of cases filed and heard in common pleas court showing court term, case number, names of litigants, and title of case. Entries consist of petitions, bills of particulars, affidavits of information, cross petitions, exceptions, demurrers, court orders, and decrees. Contains: [Returns of Lands for Taxation], 1803-1812, entry 53; [Tavern and Ferry Licenses], 1803-1812, entry 138. Chronologically arranged by dates of court terms and chronologically thereunder by dates of filing. Alphabetically indexed by names of plaintiffs in each volume; also separate indexes, 1852—, entries 114 and 115. 1803-1909, handwritten; 1909—, typed. Average 600 pages. 18 x 12 x 3. Clerk of courts' office.

204. FINAL RECORD
1803—. 144 volumes. (1-144).
Final record of all causes filed and heard in common pleas court showing court term, names of litigants, title of case, case number, date filed, copy of bill of particulars, affidavits of information or transcripts from magistrate's court, copy of petition, cross petition and answer, copy of exceptions or demurrers, and copies of jury's verdict or court findings, also of sentence, 1803-1852, includes testamentary final record. Chronologically arranged by dates of court terms and chronologically thereunder by trial dates. Alphabetically indexed by names of plaintiffs showing names of defendants and page numbers of records; also separate indexes, 1795-1877, entries 205 and 206, and 1852—, entries 114 and 115. 1803-1909, handwritten; 1909—, typed. March 1803-March 1818, average 480 pages 15.5 x 9.5 x 2.5; April 1818—, average 560 pages 18 x 12 x 2.75. Clerk of courts' file room.

205. GENERAL INDEX TO FINAL RECORDS, DIRECT
1795-1877. 1 volume. Discontinued.
Direct index to (Final) Record, entry 188, Final Record, entry 204, and Chancery Record, entry 208, showing names of plaintiff and defendant, also volume and page numbers of record. Numerically arranged by final record volume number and alphabetically thereunder by names of plaintiffs. Handwritten. 490 pages. 13 x 8 x 2.5. Clerk of courts' file room.

206. GENERAL INDEX TO FINAL RECORDS, REVERSE
1795-1877. 1 volume. Discontinued.
Reverse index to (Final) Record, entry 188, Final Record, entry 204, Chancery Records, entry 208, showing names of defendant and plaintiff, also volume and page numbers of record. Numerically arranged by final record volume numbers and

alphabetically thereunder by names of defendants. Handwritten. 490 pages. 13 x 8 x 2.5. Clerk of courts' file room.

207. [RECORD OF COMMON PLEAS COURT]

1805. In Commissioners' Journal, entry 1.

Records of common pleas court showing term of court, names of litigants, title of case, copies of court order and decree, and itemized account of cost taxed. In pamphlet attached under cover of volume 1.

208.CHANCERY RECORD

June 1839-May 1854. 3 volumes. ((1-3). Discontinued.

Complete record copy of proceedings in chancery causes filed in common pleas court showing court term, names of litigants, style of action, date case filed, copy of petition or bill of particulars, all writs issued, affidavits, court order and decree, transcript of testimony and evidence, and copies of dispositions. Chronologically arranged by dates of court terms and chronologically thereunder by dates of hearings. For indexes, see entry 205 and 206. Handwritten. Average 670 pages. 18 x 12 x 3.5. 1 volume, 1839-1845, Storeroom 2; 2 volumes, 1845-1854, Clerk of courts' office.

209. [COMMON PLEAS ADMINISTRATION PROCEEDINGS]

March 1803-April 1810. In Marriage Record, entry 293.

Record of proceedings in administration matters before the probate division of the court of common pleas.

210. DIVORCE RECORDS

1890—. 48 jackets and 9 file boxes. 1803-1889 in Original Records, Civil, entry 211.

Original papers issued in divorce cases filed in common pleas court including petition (affidavit or bill of particulars), cross petition or answer, all writs issued, all journal entries, and itemized cost bill, all names of litigants, case number, date filed, name of attorney, and volume and page numbers of Appearance Docket, entry 194. Chronologically arranged by dates of filing. No index. 1890-1904, handwritten on printed forms; 1904—, typed on printed forms. Jackets, 3.5 x 4.5 x 9; file boxes, 10 x 4.5 x 14. 48 jackets, 1890-1925, Storeroom 2; 1926—, 9 file boxes, Clerk of courts' office.

211. ORIGINAL RECORDS, CIVIL
1803—. 340 bundles, 118 jackets, and 370 file boxes.

Original papers issued in causes filed in common pleas court. Papers include declaration of particulars, all writs issued (Executions, entry 133), court orders and decrees, all journal entries, sheriff's returns on writs, itemized cost bill, and show date of issue, names of litigants, case number, kind of action, date filed, and volume and page numbers of Civil Docket, entry 199. Contains: Praecipes, 1862—, entry 125; Summonses, 1838—, entry 126; Divorce Records, 1803-1889, entry 210; Criminal Records, 1803-1810, entry 212. All papers of each case in the storerooms are banded together, but in the clerk of courts' office all papers of each case are in separate jackets in each file box. Chronologically arranged by dates of filing. For index, see entry 194. 1803-1844, handwritten; 1844-1904, handwritten on printed forms; 1904—, typed on printed forms. Bundles, 5 x 3.5 x 8;Jackets, 3.5 x 4.5 x 9; file boxes (Storeroom), 4.5 x 4.5 x 9; file boxes (Clerk of courts' office), 10 x 4.5 x 14. 61 bundles, 1803-1913, Storeroom 2; 67 file boxes, 1889—, Clerk of courts' office.

212. CRIMINAL RECORDS
1811—. 263 bundles, 91 jackets, and 39 file boxes. 1803-1910 in Original Records, Civil, entry 211.

Original papers issued in criminal cases filed in county courts including summonses, warrants to arrest, affidavits of information, transcripts from magistrate's court, subpoenas and all writs, defendants' pleas, executions for costs, certificates of sentences to penal institution, and itemized cost bills. Papers show court term, name of defendant, offense charge, date issued, case number, volume and page numbers of Criminal Docket, entry 198, and date filed. All records of each case banded together in bundles and jackets, and in file boxes all papers of each case are in separate jackets. Contains: Praecipes, 1862—, entry 125; Summonses, 1838—, entry 126; Indictments, 1897—, entry 214. Chronologically arranged by dates of filing. For index, see entry 194. 1805-1824, handwritten; 1824---, handwritten on printed forms. Bundles, 5 x 3.5 x 8; jackets, 3.5 x 4.5 x 9; file boxes, 10 x 4.5 x 14. 1811-1913, 263 bundles, 91 jackets, Storeroom 2; 1897—, 39 file boxes, Clerk of courts' office.

213. ORIGINAL RECORDS, ADMINISTRATION OF ESTATES AND GUARDIANSHIPS
1803-1850. 419 bundles.

Original records of administration of estates including letters of authority to administrator or executor, notice of inventory and appraisement, itemized inventory and appraisement record, itemized sale bill, copy of will, record of debts and claims filed, bond of administrator or executor, record of settlement by administrator or executor, and itemized cost bill; showing date, name of decedent, name of administrator or executor, names of appraisers and of sureties on bond, and amount of bond. Guardianship records include letters of authority to guardian, notice of inventory and appraisement, itemized inventory and appraisal of ward's assets, guardian's bond, record of settlement, and itemized cost bill; showing date, case number, names of guardian, ward, appraisers, and sureties, amount of bond, and date filed. All papers of each case are banded together. Chronologically arranged by dates of filing. No index. Handwritten. 4 x 3.5 x 8. Storeroom 2.

For subsequent records, see entries 276 and 314.

214. INDICTMENTS
1803-1896. 54 bundles and 20 jackets. 1897— in Criminal Records, entry 212.

Original indictments returned in criminal cases by grand jury showing date of session, name of accused, offense charged, nature of indictment, and date returned. Chronologically arranged by dates returned. No index. 1803-1872, handwritten; 1872-1896, handwritten on printed forms. Bundles, 5 x 3.5 x 8; jackets, 3.5 x 4.5 x 9. Storeroom 3.

215. JOURNAL ENTRIES
1900-1915. 27 file boxes.

Journal entries for recording in cases filed in common pleas court showing case number, names of litigants, title of case, date entry filed, volume and page numbers of Journal, entry 203, volume and page numbers of docket, and name of attorney. Entries consist of affidavit of information, petition, answer to petition, demurrers, and court orders. Chronologically arranged by dates of filing. No index. Typed. 4.5 x 4 x 9.5. Storeroom 1.

Business Administration of Office

216. FEE BOOK, PROBATE DIVISION
1835-1847. 1 volume. Discontinued.

Record of fees taxed in causes coming before probate division of common pleas court showing date case filed, case number, title of case, name of decedent or ward, name of administrator, executor, or guardian, with itemized account of fees taxed and date paid. Chronologically arranged by dates of filing. Alphabetically indexed by names of decedents or wards. Handwritten. 160 pages. 10 x 7 x .75. Storeroom 2.

The constitution under which the state of Ohio operated for the first half century of its existence provided for a supreme court consisting of three judges appointed by a joint ballot of the legislature for a seven-year term. This court was required to hold sessions at least once a year in each county. (*Ohio Const. 1802,* Art. III, sec. 2). The number of judges, according to constitutional provisions, might be increased to four after a period of five years, in which case the judges were permitted to divide the state into two circuits. Accordingly, in 1808, the membership of the court was increased to four and the state was divided into the requisite number of circuits (6 O. L. 32). Two years later, in 1810, the membership of the court was reduced to three (8 O. L. 259); in 1824 it was again increased to four (22 O. L. 50).

By constitutional provision, this court was given original and appellate jurisdiction in "both common law and chancery" cases, and in such cases that should be provided by law. Accordingly, by statutory provision, the court was assigned exclusive cognizance of all cases of divorce and alimony and concurrent jurisdiction of all civil cases both of law and equity where the title to land, or the matter in dispute exceeded $1,000; and appellate jurisdiction from the court of common pleas "in all cases respecting the title of lands, or where the matter in controversy exceeds the value of one thousand dollars, and all cases where the proof or validity of wills or the right of administration shall be in question." (During the first half century of Ohio history the legislature granted decrees of divorce. Although the constitution of 1802 did not prohibit the legislature from exercising such jurisdiction, the supreme court prohibited the practice in 1848 (*Bingham* v, *Miller,* 17 O. L. 445). The constitution of 1851, Art. II, sec. 32, contained a prohibiting clause. Moreover the court was given original cognizance in the trial of capital offense (1 O. L. 36-37). All cases where the title to land or freehold was in question were to be tried and the county where the land was situated. Furthermore the court was given appellate jurisdiction from the court of common pleas in all case in which the court of common pleas had original jurisdiction (14 O. L. 310-354).

In 1831 the supreme court was directed to meet annually in the town of Columbus for the final adjudication of all such questions of law as may have been reserved in any county for decision. This session of the court, known as the court in bank, was required to have its decisions, in each case, reduced to writing, and transmitted to the clerk of the supreme court in each county in which such question was reserved. (29 O. L. 93-94). The clerk was directed to enter such decisions "on the journal of the said court" and such proceedings were to be taken, as if such decisions had been made in the county (29 O. L. 93-94). Six years later, in 1837, an act was passed providing that the final judgment in the supreme court, held within any county within the state, could be re-examined and revised or affirmed in the court in bank upon a writ of error (35 O. L. 60-62).

This judicial arrangement continued until the adoption of the constitution of 1851, which provided a judicial system modeled upon the federal system existing at the time. The supreme court, as established in 1851, became for the first time in Ohio history, a reviewing court of last resort. At the same time the jurisdiction of the supreme court was restricted. In 1852 the court of common pleas, rather than the supreme court, was given original cognizance of all crimes and offenses, except minor criminal cases, the exclusive jurisdiction of which was invested in the justices of the peace and other minor courts. (G. C. sec. 13422-5; 51 O. L. 474; 52 O. L. 72). The supreme court, which, between the years 1803 and 1843, had original cognizance in divorce and alimony cases and after 1843 concurrent jurisdiction with the court of common pleas in such cases, was denied such jurisdiction in 1852 (41 O. L. 49; 51 O. L. 377).

The opinions of the supreme court on circuit and the decisions of the court in bank, as transmitted to the clerk of the supreme court in each county, are in the office of the respective clerks of courts.

217. APPEARANCE DOCKET

1812-1848. 19 volumes. Prior and subsequent records missing.

Appearance docket of causes filed in supreme court showing court term, names of litigants, title of case, date case filed, dates of issuing various writs, dates of court orders and notation of court's orders in case, date of final order and findings, and itemized cost bill. Chronologically arranged by dates of court terms and chronologically thereunder by dates of filing. Alphabetically indexed by names of plaintiffs. Handwritten. Average 200 pages. 10.5 x 8 x 1.25. Storeroom 2.

218. JOURNAL AND DOCKET

1806-1843. 16 volumes. Prior and subsequent records missing.

Journal entry record of sessions of supreme court with journal entries in causes filed in supreme court with docket and causes filed showing term of court, case number, names of litigants, kind of action, date case filed, date pleas and motions were filed, cost bill in case, and list of jurors drawn for each term of court. Chronologically arranged by dates of entries. Alphabetically indexed by names of plaintiffs. Handwritten. Average 130 pages. 12 x 8 x .75. Storeroom 2.

219. (Supreme Court) RECORD
June 1812-1852. 4 volumes. (2-5). Prior records missing.
Record of proceedings in causes filed and heard in county supreme court showing court term, names the litigants, style of case, and date filed. Chronologically arranged by dates of court terms and chronologically thereunder by trial dates. Handwritten. Average 500 pages. 16 x 11 x 3. Clerk of courts' file room.

220. INDEX, SUPREME COURT RECORD, DIRECT AND REVERSE
1803-1852. 1 volume.
Direct and reverse index to (Supreme Court) Record showing names of plaintiffs and defendants, also volume and page numbers of record. Direct index on left-hand page; reverse index on right-hand page. Numerically arranged by record volume numbers and alphabetically thereunder by names of plaintiffs and defendants. Handwritten. 210 pages. 10 x 8.5 x 1.25. Clerk of courts' office.

221. ORIGINAL RECORDS
1803-1852. 172 bundles.
Original papers in cases filed in supreme court of Washington County such as injunctions, judgments, declarations of particulars, divorce petitions, capias, summonses, and transcripts from lower courts; showing case number, court term, names of litigants, kind of action, and itemized account of costs taxed. All records of each case banded together. Chronologically arranged by dates of filing. No index. 1803-1844, handwritten; 1844-1852, handwritten on printed forms. 4.5 x 3.5 x 8. Storeroom 3.

Until 1851 the judicial power of the state of Ohio in matters of both law and equity was invested in the supreme court, the court of common pleas, and the justice courts. During the first fifty years of Ohio history the supreme court served as a court of appeals, holding court in each county annually. When a new constitution was adopted in 1851 the judicial system was extended by the creation of the district courts composed of one supreme court justice and several common pleas judges in the district. These courts were assigned original jurisdiction in the same matters as the supreme court; and such "appellate jurisdiction" as might be provided by law. (*Ohio Const. 1851,* Art. IV, secs. 5-6). Thus by constitutional provision the courts were assigned original cognizance in *quo warranto, mandamus, habeas corpus,* and *procedendo* (*ibid.,* Art. IV, sec. 2). In addition to this, the legislature, in 1852, authorized the courts to issue writs of error, *certiorari, supersedeas, ne exeat,* and all other writs not specifically provided by statute, whenever such writs were necessary for the exercise of its jurisdiction. The same act gave the courts appellate jurisdiction from the court of common pleas in civil cases wherein the latter court had original jurisdiction. (50 O. L. 69).

For the purposes of the district courts the nine common pleas districts were apportioned into five judicial districts. A judge of the supreme court was designated to preside at the sessions of the district courts; in case no judge of the supreme court was present, as was often the case, the judge of the court of common pleas in whose subdivision court was being held was directed to preside. (50 O. L. 69).

The district courts failed to function properly. Evidence seems to indicate that the increasing number of cases coming before the supreme court made it difficult for the justices to attend the meetings of the district courts. Indeed, six years before the creation of the district courts, the supreme court dockets were overcrowded. In 1845 the legislature found it necessary to afford temporary relief by providing appeals from the courts of common pleas to the supreme court (43 O. L. 80). A similar condition of overcrowding existed in the sixties; so that, in 1865, the supreme court justices were relieved of the duty of attending the meetings of the district courts for that particular year (62 O. L. 72). The judicial system had become slow and cumbersome. The courts declined rapidly after 1865 and were finally abolished.

Following the complete collapse of the district courts an amendment to the constitution, adopted in 1883, made provision for circuit courts. "The circuit courts," stated the amendment, "shall be the successor of the district courts, and all cases, judgments, records, and proceedings pending in said district courts, in several counties, of any district, shall be transferred to the circuit courts." (*Ohio Const.* Art. IV, sec. 6). The district courts, however, were to continue to function until the expiration of the terms of office of the district court judges then incumbent but were finally abolished in 1885 (82 O. L. 19). The circuit courts were assigned the same "original jurisdictions with the supreme court, and such appellate jurisdiction as may be provided by law." The composition of the courts and the number of circuits was left to the discretion of the legislature. Accordingly, in 1884, an act was passed dividing the state into seven circuits, and providing for the election of three judges in each circuit (81 O. L. 170).

The circuit courts, in addition to the jurisdiction conferred upon them by the constitution (Art. IV, sec. 6) were authorized by the legislature to issue writs of *supersedeas* in any case, and all other writs not specifically provided by statute when they were necessary for the exercise of its jurisdiction (81 O. L. 170). Moreover, the courts were authorized to make and publish, as they deemed expedient, rules of procedure in their respective circuits, not in conflict with the law or rules of the supreme court. The legislature directed that all cases taken to the circuit courts were to be entered on the docket in the order in which they were commenced, received, or filed, "be taken up and disposed of in the same order." However, cases in which persons were seeking relief from imprisonment or persons who were convicted of a felony; cases involving the validity of any tax levy or assessment; cases involving the constitutionality of a statute; and cases involving public right and proceedings in *quo warranto, mandamus, procedendo,* or *habeas corpus,* could be taken up in advance of their assignment or order of the docket. (81 O. L. 170). In 1913 the circuit courts were superseded by the courts of appeals (*Ohio Const.* Art. IV, sec. 6).

The judicial system of Ohio was again slightly changed in 1913 when, by an amendment to the constitution, the circuit courts were renamed courts of appeals. "The court of appeals," stated the amendment, "shall continue the work of the respective circuit courts and all pending cases and proceedings in the circuit courts shall proceed to judgment and be determined by the respect courts of appeals." (*Ibid.,* Art. IV, sec. 6). The judges of the several circuit courts were designated as judges of the court of appeals, and were directed to perform the duties thereof until the expiration of the term of office. Vacancies caused by the expiration of terms of office of the judges were to be filled by the electors of the respective appellate districts. The term of office was fixed at six years.

The jurisdiction of the court of appeals remain much the same as that of the district court in 1851. However, the court was assigned original cognizance in writs of prohibition and appellate jurisdiction in the trial of chancery cases. (*Ohio Const.* Art. IV, sec 6). Certain restrictions were imposed upon the court: "No judgment of a court of common pleas, a superior court or other court of record" shall be reversed except by "the concurrence of all the judges of the court of appeals" (*ibid.,* Art IV, sec. 6).

At present the court consists of three judges in each of the nine districts into which the state is divided, each of whom shall have been admitted to practice as an attorney-at-law in the state for a period of six years immediately proceeding his election. One court of appeals judge is chosen every two years, and holds office for six years beginning on the ninth day of February next after election. The salary of the court of appeals judge, fixed at $6,000 per year in 1913, was increased to $8,000 in 1920 and so continues. (103 O. L. 418; 108 O. L. pt. ii, 1301). The judges hold at least one session of court annually in each county in the district (G. C. sec. 1514).

District Court

222. BAR CALENDAR

1853-1884. 52 volumes.

Calendar of causes filed in district court showing term of court, case number, trial date, names of litigants, names of attorneys, title of case, state of suit, and how disposed of. Chronologically arranged by dates of court terms and chronologically thereunder by trial dates. No index. Handwritten. Average 80 pages. 14 x 10 x .5. Storeroom 2.

223. APPEARANCE DOCKET

1852-1854. 2 volumes.

Appearance docket of causes filed in district court showing name of litigants, title of case, case number, date appeal filed, date petitions and answers, dates writs issued, date of filing, notation of court orders and decisions in case, itemized cost bill, date costs paid, and by whom paid. Chronologically arranged by dates of filing appeals. Alphabetically indexed by names of plaintiffs. Handwritten. Average 440 pages. 10 x 8 x 2.25. Storeroom 2.

224. COURT DOCKET
1853-1884. 47 volumes.

Docket of causes filed in district court showing term of court, case number, names of litigants, style of cause, and court orders. Chronologically arranged by dates of courts terms. No index. Handwritten. Average 90 pages. 14 x 11 x .5. Storeroom 2.

225. FINAL RECORD
1854-1884. 3 volumes.

Complete record of proceedings in causes filed in district court showing court term, names of litigants, date of filing transcript, copy of transcript, copy of appeal bond, copy of answer, copy of petitions, copy of *demurrers*, copy of motions, copy of amended petitions, and copy of decision of court. Chronologically arranged by dates of court terms. Alphabetically indexed by names of plaintiffs. Handwritten. Average 590 pages. 18 x 12 x 3. Storeroom 2.

226. ORIGINAL RECORDS
1854-1884. 197 bundles.

Original papers issued in cases filed in district court including appeal affidavits, appeal bonds, petitions, answers, *demurrers*, writs, sheriff's returns on writs, depositions, and all journal entries. Papers show names of litigants, nature of case, case number, date filed, volume and page numbers of Appearance Docket, entry 223, and itemized cost bill. Chronologically arranged by dates of filing. No index. Handwritten on printed forms. 4.5 x 3.5 x 8.5. Storeroom 2.

Circuit Court

227. JUDGES' ENTRY BOOK
1887-1912. 13 volumes.

Notations of judges of circuit court and opinions and causes before the court, showing names of litigants, title of case, name of judge, and statement of opinion. Chronologically arranged by dates of court terms. Alphabetically indexed by names of plaintiffs showing names of defendants and page numbers of record. Handwritten. Average 110 pages. 14 x 8 x .5. Storeroom 2.

228. JOURNAL

March 1885—. 2 volumes. (1, 2).

Journal entry record of causes filed and heard in circuit court, 1885- October 1912, court of appeals, January 1913—, showing court term, case number, names of litigants, copy of appeal, and copies of petitions, writs, *mandamus* issued, court orders, decrees, and journal entries. Chronologically arranged by dates of court terms and chronologically thereunder by trial dates. Alphabetically indexed by names of plaintiffs. Handwritten. Average 510 pages. 16 x 11.5 x 2.5. Clerk of courts' office.

229. FINAL RECORD

1884-1913. 3 volumes.

Copy of final record of all cases filed on appeal from lower courts and heard in circuit court showing court term, names of litigants, title of case, case number, dates of filing appeal and transcript from lower court, and copies of transcript, appeal bond, petitions, *demurrers*, answers, motions, amended petitions, decisions, and orders of court. Chronologically arranged by dates of filing appeals. Alphabetically indexed by names of plaintiffs. Handwritten. Average 610 pages. 18 x 12 x 3.25. Clerk of courts' file room.

230. WITNESS BOOK

1885-1912. 1 volume.

Clerk of courts' record of witnesses subpoenaed in circuit court cases showing names of litigants, case number, volume and page numbers of appearance docket, date issued, trial date, and names of plaintiff's and defendant's witnesses with number of days in attendance and mileage. The appearance docket referred to in this record is missing. Chronologically arranged by dates issued. Alphabetically indexed by names of plaintiffs showing names of defendants. Handwritten on printed forms. 200 pages. 17 x 7 x 1.25. Storeroom 2.

231. ORIGINAL RECORDS

1884-1913. 129 jackets.

Original papers issued in cases filed in circuit court including affidavits on appeals, appeal bonds, petitions, answers, *demurrers*, writs, sheriff's returns on writs, depositions, and journal entries, showing names of litigants, nature of case, case number, date filed, volume and page numbers of appearance docket and itemized cost bill. The appearance docket refers to in this record is missing. Chronologically arranged by dates of filing. No index. Handwritten on printed forms. 3.5 x 4.5 x 9. Storeroom 2.

232. APPEARANCE DOCKET
1913—. 1 volume.
Docket of causes filed showing names of litigants, case number, name of attorney, volume and page numbers of Witness Book, Criminal, entry 128, Witness Book, Civil, entry 129, Cash Book, entry 164, and Execution Docket, entry 196, title of case, date case was filed, dates of filing writs and exceptions, dates of court decrees, and mandates. Chronologically arranged by dates of filing. Alphabetically indexed by names of plaintiffs showing names of defendants. Handwritten. 480 pages. 18 x 11.5 x 2.5. Clerk of courts' office.

233. COURT DOCKET
1913—. 4 volumes. (1-4).
Docket of cases filed in court of appeals showing dates for hearing, name of attorney, case number, names of litigants, state of case at close of last term of court, and judge's memoranda. Chronologically arranged by trial dates. Alphabetically indexed by names of plaintiffs showing names of defendants. Handwritten on printed forms. Average 160 pages. 16 x 10 x 1. Clerk of courts' office.

234. RECORD
1913—. 2 volumes. (1, 2).
Final record of all causes filed on appeal from lower courts and heard in court of appeals showing court term, names the litigants, title of case, case number, dates of filing appeal and transcript from lower court, and copies of transcript, appeal bond, petitions, demurrers, answers, motions, amended petition, decisions and orders of court. Chronologically arranged by dates of filing appeals. Alphabetically indexed by names of plaintiffs. Typed. Average 620 pages. 18 x 12 x 3.25. Clerk of courts' office.

235. ORIGINAL RECORDS

1913—. 12 file boxes (labeled by years and by Appeals Court).

Original papers issued in causes filed on appeal from lower courts in court of appeals. Consists of affidavits on appeals, appeal bonds, petitions, amended petitions, answers, *demurrers*, writs, sheriff's returns on writs, depositions, and journal entries; showing names of litigants, nature of case, case number, date issued, volume and page numbers of Appearance Docket, entry 232, and itemized cost bill. All papers of each case in separate jacket. Chronologically arranged by dates issued. No index. Typed on printed forms. 10 x 4.5 x 14. Clerk of courts' office.

The probate court, established by an act of the Northwest Territory on August 30, 1788, consisted of a probate judge with jurisdiction in probate, testamentary, and guardianship matters, and two judges of the court of common pleas, who sat with him and ruled on contested points, defective sentences, and final judgments (Pease, *op. cit.,* 9).

The judicial system established under the first constitution of Ohio in 1802 did not provide for a probate court but vested the court of common pleas with such powers as had been exercised by the court in the territorial period. The constitution of 1851 re-created the probate court and gave it original jurisdiction in "probate and testamentary matters, the appointment of administrators and guardians, the settlement of the accounts of executors, administrators and guardians, the settlement of the account of executives, administrators and guardians, and such jurisdiction in *habeas corpus,* . . . and for the sale of land by executors, administrators and guardians, and such other jurisdiction, . . . as may be provided by law" (*Ohio Const. 1851,* Art. IV, sec. 8). An amendment to the constitution, adopted in 1912, authorized the common pleas judge, when petitioned by ten percent of the qualified voters in the counties having a population less than 60,000, to submit to the voters at any general election the question of combining the probate court and court of common pleas (*Ohio Const.,* Art. IV, sec. 7).

One of the primary functions of the court since its inception has been the settlement of estates. The civil code adopted in 1853 gave the court original jurisdiction in taking proof of wills, and granting letters testamentary and in settling accounts of executors and administrators (51 O. L. 167). Until 1854 the court had jurisdiction and enforcing the pavement of debts and legacies of deceased persons. While the court retains the original jurisdiction regarding estates, new duties have been added in recent years. With the development of inheritance tax laws in 1919 as a new means of taxation, the probate court has been required to determine and assess the tax after the county auditor has appraised the decedent's estate (108 O. L. pt. i. 561).

By constitutional provision the probate court has original jurisdiction in granting marriage licenses (*Ohio Const.,* Art. IV, sec. 8). The court also issues licenses to ministers to solemnize marriages. The former provision was modified by an act in 1931, which requires an elapse of at least five days between the time of application and that of the issuance of marriage licenses (114 O. L. 93). Moreover, the probate courts in certain counties, exclusive of Washington, were given concurrent jurisdiction with the court of common pleas in "divorce, alimony, foreclosure, and partition" cases. Thus in 1894, the legislature conferred such jurisdiction upon the probate court in Allen, Butler, Defiance, Perry, Richland, and Wood Counties (91 O. L. 791; 91 O. L. 799-800). The original act, subject to amendments in 1896, 1900, and 1904, which granted and denied such jurisdiction to the probate courts in certain counties, was repealed in 1911 (92 O. L. 643; 94 O. L. 137-138; 97 O. L. 113-114; 102 O. L. 100). In 1919 concurrent jurisdiction was re-established in Coshocton, Defiance, Henry Licking, Perry, Pickaway, and Richland Counties, and established in Fayette County (108 O. L. pt. i, 625). This jurisdiction was abolished in 1931 (114 O. L. 320).

The jurisdiction of the court extends to the state's unfortunates. The constitution of 1851 gave the court jurisdiction in making inquests respecting lunatics, insane persons, and idiots. The constitutional provision in this respect was interpreted by the civil code of 1853. In 1855 the court was granted jurisdiction in the appointment of guardians for minors, idiots, imbeciles, lunatics, and those incompetent by reasons of advanced age; a year later the court was authorized to commit persons who were mentally incompetent to state institutions maintained for the care of such persons (53 O. L. 81). In recent years the court has been given jurisdiction in trial cases involving neglected, dependent, and delinquent children (see p. 115).

Since the middle of the nineteenth century the probate judge has been required to keep a record of vital statistics. In 1867 the duty of keeping a permanent record of birth and death, which, in 1856, had been conferred upon the clerk of courts, was transferred to the probate judge (64 O. L. 63-64). When, in 1908, a bureau of vital statistics under the direction of the secretary of state was created the probate judge was relieved temporarily of this task (99 O. L. 296-307). In 1921 the act of 1908 was amended so as to require the local registrars to transmit to the district health commissioner, who was directed to serve as a state deputy registrar of vital statistics, all certificates of births and deaths received during the preceding month, and a copy of all such certificates to the probate court. Although the general code still requires the probate judge to keep a permanent record of birth and deaths and an index to such records (G. C. Sec, 10501-15), none has been kept in Washington County since 1908, with the exception of the recording of birth certificates of a few applicants for aid for the aged.

Jurisdiction in naturalization proceedings was exercised by the probate court until 1906 when an amendment to the federal statute vested exclusive jurisdiction in naturalization matters in the United States district courts and all state courts of record having a seal, a clerk, and jurisdiction in actions at law and equity in which the amount in controversy was unlimited (*U. S. Statutes at Large,* XXXIV, pt. ii, 596. See also *State of Ohio* v. *George Metzger and Albert L. Irish,* 10 N. P., h. s., 97ff). The General Code still requires the probate judge to keep a naturalization record and an index to the records, but jurisdiction was transferred to the court of common pleas.

During the early years of its existence the court was given limited criminal jurisdiction in cases in which the sentence did not impose capital punishment or punishment by imprisonment. By the code of civil procedure adopted in 1853 the judgments and final decree of the probate court could be reviewed by the court of common pleas on error (51 O. L. 146). In 1857 the criminal jurisdiction of the probate court was transferred to the court of common pleas (54 O. L. 97 but later acts retain it in certain counties only. Thus the probate court of Washington County was granted concurrent jurisdiction with the court of common pleas in all misdemeanors and all proceedings to prevent crime in 1883 (80 O. L. 48) and continued to exercise such jurisdiction until 1931 when the last vestige of criminal jurisdiction disappeared in all counties with the adoption of the probate code (114 O. L. 475).

Miscellaneous duties, remotely related to probate and testamentary matters, have been added by legislative action. Since 1888 the court has been required to file a certified list of all unknown depositors as furnished by institutions or persons engaged in lending money for profit (85 O. L. 65). In 1896 the probate court was given concurrent jurisdiction with the court of common pleas in the matter of changing the names of persons who desired it (92 O. L. 28) a matter in which the court of common pleas has exclusive cognizance from 1842 to 1896 (40 O. L. 28-29). Since 1896 the probate court has been required to file certificates of doctors and surgeons, and since 1916 the certificates of registered nurses which authorize them to practice their profession in the county (92 O. L. 46; 99 O. L. 499; 106 O. L. 193). Since 1913 the court has been vested with the power to grant injunctions (103 O. L. 427), and since 1915 has had concurrent jurisdiction with the court of common pleas in condemnation proceedings or roads (105 O. L. 583).

In like matter the appointive powers of the probate judge have been expanded. In addition to the authority to appoint administrators and guardians the act of 1861 authorized him to appoint one gauger and inspector of spirits, linseed, lard, and coal oil; one inspector of flour and meal; one inspector of beef, pork, lard, and butter; one inspector of sawyer lumber and shingles; and one inspector of salt

(58 O. L. 105). Then, too, from 1908 to 1913 the probate judge was authorized to appoint a county blind relief commission (see p. 68) comprised of three members each of whom served a three-year term (99 O. L. 57; 103 O. L. 60). Since 1913 he has had authority to appoint members of the county board of visitors (103 O. L. 173-174, 853).

The probate judge, like other county officials, has been required by statute to keep a record of the business of this office. The present system of records, originating for the most part in 1853 and continued by the probate code of 1931, includes a criminal record, administrative docket, guardian's docket, marriage record, record of bonds, naturalization record, and a permanent record of births and deaths (51 O. L. 167; 52 O. L. 103; 72 O. L. 9; 114 O. L. 324).

The probate judge has the care and custody of the files, papers, books, and records belonging to the probate office and is ex officio clerk of the court. The probate code, adopted in 1931, directed the probate judge to preserve for future reference and examination all pleadings, accounts, vouchers, and other papers in each estate, trust, assignment, guardianship, or other proceedings, and such papers to be properly jacketed and tied together; he is required also to make proper entries and indexes omitted by his predecessors. Certificates of marriages, reports of birth, and similar papers not a part of a case or proceeding are to be arranged and preserved separately in the order of dates in which they are filed (114 O. L. 321-322).

At present the probate judge is elected for a four-year term (114 O. L. 320). In recent years there has been an attempt to raise the qualification of those seeking election to this office. Accordingly, an amendment in 1935 to the probate code of 1931 restricted eligibility to the office to a practicing attorney or to a person who "*shall have previously served as a probate judge immediately prior to his election*" (116 O. L. 481).

Calendars and Dockets

236. COURT CALENDAR

1900—. 38 volumes. Prior records missing.

Daily calendar of issues set for hearing showing date, what case, in what matter, and volume and page numbers of Journal, entry 246. Chronologically arranged by daily entries. No index. Handwritten. Average 120 pages. 18 x 12 x .75. Probate court's file room.

237. GENERAL DOCKET

March 1876—. 12 volumes. (A-L).

Docket of all matters, except administration and guardianship, showing names of litigants, style of cause, date filed, dates writs issued, date of trial, file box number of Original Records, entry 314, brief notation of proceedings of trial and court findings, dates of sheriff's returns on writs, itemized cost bill in case. Contains: Assignment Record, April 1927—, entry 248; Transfer and Heirship Record, 1876-1921, entry 266; Record of Feeble-minded Youth, 1876-1905, entry 285; Miscellaneous Record, 1876-1931, entry 315. Chronologically arranged by dates of filing. Alphabetically indexed, direct, by names of plaintiffs, and reverse, by names of defendants. Handwritten. Average 520 pages. 14 x 10 x 2.75. Probate court's office.

238. GENERAL INDEX, ADMINISTRATORS AND EXECUTORS

1867—. 3 volumes. (1-3).

Index showing names of decedent and administrator or executor, volume and page numbers of Administrators' and Executors' Docket, entry 239, Record of Wills, entry 254, Administrators' Bonds and Letters, entry 257, Record of Executors' Bonds and Letters, entry 258, Record of Inventories and Sale Bills, entry 263, Record of Land Sales, entry 265, and Record of Accounts, entry 275; also file box number of Original Records, entry 314. Alphabetically arranged by names of descendants. Handwritten on printed forms. Average 500 pages. 18 x 11.5 x 2.5. Probate court's office.

239. ADMINISTRATORS' AND EXECUTORS' DOCKET

February 1852—. 22 volumes. (A-W, no separate volume for Q).

Docket of administration of estates showing name of decedent, township, date of death, name of administrator or executor, date appointed, amount of bond, names of sureties and appraisers, file box numbers of Original Records, entry 314, dates of filing papers in case, volume and page numbers of Journal entry, entry 246, and Cash Book, entry 307, and itemized cost and fee account, with date of payment of each item. Contains Record of Trustees' Appointments, 1852-1893, entry 261. Chronologically arranged by dates of appointments. Alphabetically indexed by names of descendants; also separate index, 1867—, entry 238. Handwritten on printed forms. Average 600 pages. 14 x 12 x 3. Probate court's office.

For prior records, see entry 202.

240. GUARDIANS' DOCKET

March 1861—. 9 volumes. (A-I). 1852-1860, missing.

Docket of guardianships showing name and age of ward, name of guardian, date of appointment, file box numbers of Original Records, entry 314, amount of guardian's bond, names of sureties on bond, copy of inventory, dates of filing accounts by guardian, and itemized cost bill in case. Chronologically arranged by dates of appointment. Alphabetically indexed by names of wards. Handwritten. Average 590 pages. 14 x 10 x 3. Probate court's office.

For prior records, see entry 202.

241. CRIMINAL DOCKET

April 1883-March 1928. 2 volumes. (1, 2).

Docket of criminal causes filed in probate court showing name of defendant, case number, file box number of Original Records, entry 314, names of attorneys, offense charged, date of transcript from magistrate's court or affidavit of information, amount of bond, names of sureties on bond, dates writs were issued, brief note of progress of case, court findings and sentence, and itemized cost bill. Chronologically arranged by dates of filing. Alphabetically indexed by names of defendants. Handwritten. Average 460 pages. 14 x 10 x 2.5. Probate court's office.

For subsequent records, see entry 242.

242. APPEARANCE DOCKET AND FEE BOOK, CRIMINAL

April 1928-1931. 1 volume. Discontinued.

Docket of criminal cases filed in probate court showing case number, file box number of Original Records, entry 314, amount of bond, date bond filed, volume and page numbers of records, names of defendant and defendant's attorney, offense charged, name of complainant, dates writs were issued, kind of writs issued, itemized account of cost, and amount of fee taxed. Chronologically arranged by dates of filing. Alphabetically indexed by names of defendants. Handwritten on printed forms. 570 pages. 16 x 12 x 2.75. Probate court's office.

For prior records, see entry 241.

243. PRAECIPE DOCKET

February 1928—. 1 volume.

Record copy of writs issued by probate court showing in what matter, date of issue, kind of writ, in whose favor issued, on whom issued, date returnable, name of attorney, and volume and page numbers of docket. Chronologically arranged by dates issued. No index. Handwritten on printed forms. 290 pages. 14 x 9 x 1.75. Probate court's office.

Court Proceedings

244. PROBATE RECORD

December 1789-September 1855. 9 volumes. (1-9). Discontinued.

Complete record of causes and settlement of estates filed and heard in probate division of common pleas court, quarter sessions, 1789-1803, probate division of common pleas court, 1803-1852, showing name of decedent, date filed, in what matter, name of administrator, executor, or trustee, and copies of petitions, cross petitions, answers, court orders and findings, record of appraisements and sales, and accounts filed. Contains record of Wills, December 1789-June 1853, entry 254. This record was transferred from the court of common pleas. Chronologically arranged by dates of filing. Handwritten. Average 620 pages. 18 x 12 x 3.5. Probate court's file room.

245. GENERAL INDEX TO PROBATE RECORDS

1789-1855. 1 volume. Discontinued.

Index to Probate Record showing name of decedent, kind of record, and volume and page numbers of record. Alphabetically arranged by names of decedents. Handwritten on printed forms. 180 pages. 14 x 9 x 1. Probate court's file room.

246. JOURNAL

1852—. 61 volumes. (A-Z, 1-35).

Record copies of journal entries in all cases filed in probate court showing date of entry, names of litigants, title of action, applications for appointment as administrator, executive, guardian, trustee, or assignee, orders for bond, orders to file accounts, legal notices, admit will for probate, petitions to sell real estate, appointment of administrator, executor, guardian, trustee, assignee, and appraisers, orders to take inventory and appraise property, order of sale of property, and all other matters of journal entry. Contains Appeal Bond Record, 1852-1887, 1899—, entry 253. Chronologically arranged by dates of entries. Alphabetically indexed by names of decedents, wards, assigners, or principles. 1852-March 1906, handwritten; April 1906—, typed. Average 600 pages. 18 x 12 x 3.25. Probate court's office.

247. RECORD OF PROCEEDINGS OF THE COMMISSIONER OF INSOLVENTS

1841-September 1853. 1 volume. Discontinued.

Record copy of proceedings in insolvency cases showing date case filed, name of insolvent, copy of application of insolvent for relief as provided by an act for relief of insolvent debtors, schedule of debt and claims, inventory of assets, oath and bond of insolvent debtor, certificate of compliance issued to insolvent debtor by commissioner, and itemized account of fees and costs in case. This record was transferred from the court of common pleas. Chronologically arranged by dates of filing. No index. Handwritten. 210 pages. 14 x 9 x 1.25. Probate court's file room.

248. ASSIGNMENT RECORD

April 1861-March 1927. 11 volumes. (1-11). April 1927— in General Docket, entry 237.

Complete record of proceedings in assignments by insolvent debtors showing date filed, name of assigner, file box number of Original Assignments Records, entry 249, name of assignee, copy of deed of assignment, copies of order to appraise assets, oath of appraiser, inventory and appraisement, schedule of claims against assigner, orders of sale, sale bill, assignee's account on settlement, and cost bill. Chronologically arranged by dates of filing. Alphabetically indexed by names of assigners. 1861-February 1911, handwritten; February 1911-1927, typed. Average 630 pages. 18 x 11.5 x 3.25. Probate court's file room.

249. ORIGINAL ASSIGNMENT RECORDS

1861—. 96 bundles and 22 file boxes. (A-V).

Original papers in assignments including application for appointment of assignee, letter of authority to assignee, assignee's bond, deed of assignment, schedule of debt and liabilities, inventory and appraisement, report of claims, petition to sell property, and settlement record; showing date paper was issued, names of assigner, assignee, appraisers, and sureties on assignee's bond, amount of bond, date filed, and volume and page numbers of Assignment Record, entry 248. 1861-1892, all papers of each case banded together and from ten to fifteen cases in each bundle; 1896— all papers of each case in separate jacket. Chronologically arranged by dates of filing. For index, April 1861-March 1927, see entry 248; 1927—, see entry 237. Handwritten on printed forms. Bundles, 5 x 3.5 x 9; file boxes, 10 x 4.5 x 14. 96 bundles, 1861-1895, Storeroom 1; 22 file boxes, 1896—, Probate file room.

250. WITNESS BOOK

May 1883-October 1931. 3 volumes. (1-3). Discontinued.

Record of witnesses subpoenaed to appear in probate court showing names of plaintiff and defendant, style of cause, trial date, names of plaintiff's and defendant's witnesses, number of days in court, mileage, and total fee. Also contains names of jurors in case of jury trials showing names of litigants, style of case, trial date, number of days in court, mileage, and total fee. Chronologically arranged by trial dates. Alphabetically indexed by names of plaintiffs. Handwritten on printed forms. Average 310 pages. 16 x 11 x 1.75. Probate court's file room.

251. CRIMINAL RECORD

August 1853-November 1931. 3 volumes. (1-3). Discontinued.

Complete record of proceedings in criminal cases filed in probate court showing date filed, case number, file box number of Original Records, Criminal, entry 252, and Original Records, entry 314, name of defendant, offense charged, copy of affidavit of information, copy and testimony and evidence at trial, finding of court, and sentence. Chronologically arranged by dates of filing. Alphabetically indexed by names of defendants. Handwritten. Average 620 pages. 18 x 11.5 x 3.25. Probate court's file room.

252. ORIGINAL RECORDS, CRIMINAL

1853-1896. 79 bundles.

Original papers issued in criminal cases filed in probate court including affidavits of information, transcript from magistrate's court, warrant to arrest, bond, plea of accused, journal entries of verdict of court or jury, sentence, warrant to commit to jail or workhouse, and cost bill; showing names of accused, and of sureties, offense charged, amount of bond, and date filed. Chronologically arranged by dates of filing. For index, see entry 251. Handwritten on printed forms. 5 x 3.5 x 8. Storeroom 1.

For subsequent records, see entry 314.

253. APPEAL BOND RECORD

1888-1898. 1 volume. 1852-1887, 1899— in Journal, entry 246.

Record copy of bonds filed by heirs, administrators, executors, or guardians on appeal of court findings or orders, showing date of bond, names of principal and sureties, amount of bond, in what matter, and date filed. Chronologically arranged by dates of filing. No index. Handwritten. 220 pages. 12 x 9 x 1.25. Probate court's office.

Wills

254. RECORD OF WILLS
July 1853—. 25 volumes. (1-25). December 1789-June 1853 in Probate Record, entry 244.

Record copy of wills probated showing names of testator and witnesses, date of will, date filed for probate, and copy of journal entry approving probation of will. Chronologically arranged by dates filed for probate. Alphabetically indexed by names of testators in each volume; also separate index, 1867—, entry 238. 1853-May 1907, handwritten; June 1907—, typed. Average 630 pages. 18 x 12 x 3.25. Probate court's office.

255. COST BILL RECORD, WILLS
1909-1911. 1 volume. Discontinued.

Record copy of cost bills on probating wills showing name of testator, case number, itemized account of fees taxed, and date filed. Chronologically arranged by dates of filing. Alphabetically indexed by names of testators. Handwritten on printed forms. 490 pages. 14 x 9 x 2.5. Probate court's file room.

Estates

Bonds and Letters

256. ADMINISTRATORS', EXECUTORS', AND GUARDIANS' BONDS
August 1803-May 1867. 2 volumes. (A, B).

Record copies of surety bonds filed by appointed administrators, executors, and guardians, showing name of decedent or ward, name and title or principal, names of sureties, amount of bond, and date filed. Chronologically arranged by dates of filing. No index. Handwritten. Average 640 pages. 18 x 12 x 3.25. Probate court's office.

For subsequent records, see entries 257-259.

257. ADMINISTRATORS' BONDS AND LETTERS
February 1852—. 15 volumes. (A-O).

Record copies of applications for appointments as administrators showing name of decedent, date of death, names and degree of kinship of heirs-at-law, and estimated value of chattel and real property of decedent; copies of letters of administration showing name of decedent, name of appointee, and date of appointment; copies of notices of appointments of administrators; and copies of bonds filed by administrator showing name of administrator, names of sureties, amount of bond, name of decedent, and date filed. Chronologically arranged by dates of applications. Alphabetically indexed by names of decedents in each volume; also separate index, 1867—, entry 238. Handwritten on printed forms. Average 540 pages. 18 x 12 x 2.75. Probate court's file room.

For prior records of bonds, see entry 256; for separate record of notices of appointments 1859-1878, see entry 262.

258. RECORD OF EXECUTORS' BONDS AND LETTERS
July 1867—. 12 volumes. (2-13).

Record copies of applications for appointments as executors showing name of testator, date of death, names and degree of kinship of legatees or devisees, and estimated value of property real and personal; copies of letters testamentary showing name of appointee, name of decedent, and date of appointment; copies of notices of appointments; and copies of bonds filed by executors showing name of executor, names of sureties, amount of bond, name of testator, and date filed. Chronologically arranged by dates of applications. Alphabetically indexed by names of testators in each volume; also separate index, entry 238. Handwritten on printed forms. Average 550 pages. 18 x 12 x 2.75. Probate court's file room.

For prior records of bonds, see entry 256; for separate record of notices of appointment, 1859-1878, see entry 262.

259. RECORD OF GUARDIANS' BONDS AND LETTERS
1865—. 10 volumes. (1-10).

Record copies of applications for appointments as guardians of minors or incompetents showing name of minor or incompetent, if minor, names of parents, name of applicant, age of minor, estimated value of personal estate, of real estate, and names of proposed sureties; copies of orders of appointments of guardians; and copies of bonds filed by guardians showing name of guardian, names of sureties, amount of bond, and name of ward; also copies of letters of guardianship showing name of appointee, name of ward, and date of appointment. Chronologically arranged by dates of applications. Alphabetically indexed by names of wards. Handwritten on printed forms. Average 520 pages. 18 x 12 x 2.75. Probate court's file room.

For prior records of bonds, see entry 256.

260. RECORD OF ADMINISTRATORS' BONDS AND LETTERS, WILLS ANNEXED
1862—. 2 volumes.

Record of appointments of administrators of estates with wills annexed showing name of decedent and case number; copy of application for appointment as administrator showing name of applicant, date of application, names and relationship of heirs-at-law, and estimated value of real and personal property of estate; copy of letter of administration issued by court showing date of appointment, name of appointee, name of decedent, and copy of notice of appointment; and copy of bond filed by administrator showing date of bond, name of appointee, names of sureties, amount of bond, name of decedent, and date approved. Chronologically arranged by dates of filing. Alphabetically indexed by names of decedents. Handwritten on printed forms. Average 580 pages. 18 x 12 x 3. Probate court's file room.

261. RECORD OF TRUSTEES' APPOINTMENTS
1894—. 1 volume. 1852-1893 in Administrators' and Executors' Docket, entry 239.

Record of appointments, bonds, and letters of trustees of estates funds, showing what trusteeship, case number, copy of application for appointment as trustee, copy of journal entry ordering appointment and bond, copy of bond showing names of appointee and sureties, and copy of Journal entry of appointments of trustee. Chronologically arranged by dates of applications. Alphabetically indexed by names of principles. Handwritten on printed forms. 530 pages. 18 x 12 x 1.75. Probate court's office.

262. NOTICES OF APPOINTMENT OF ADMINISTRATORS AND EXECUTORS

1859-1878. 1 volume.

Record copies of notices of appointment of administrators or executors showing date of appointment, name of decedent, name of appointee, and date of notice. Chronologically arranged by dates of notices. Alphabetically indexed by names of decedents. Handwritten. 290 pages. 14 x 9 x 1.5. Probate court's office.

For other records, see entries 257 and 258.

Inventories, Schedule of Debts, Sale Bills, and Transfers

263. RECORD OF INVENTORIES AND SALE BILLS

June 1853—. 49 volumes. (1-3, A, 5-49).

Record copies of inventories of estates of deceased persons and wards showing name of decedent or ward, names of administrator, executor, or guardian, date inventory ordered, names of appraisers, itemized appraisement list, date filed, date sale was ordered, copy of order, date of sale, itemized account of sale of chattels, and date sale account was filed. Chronologically arranged by dates of filing. Alphabetically indexed by names of decedents or wards in each volume; also separate index, 1867—, entry 238. June 1853-December 1906, handwritten; January 1907—, typed. Average 570 pages. 18 x 12 x 2.75. Probate court's office.

264. SCHEDULE OF DEBTS

March 1932—. 1 volume.

Record of debts and claims against estates showing name of decedent, date filed, names the creditors and amount claimed by each, amount allowed on claim, name of administrator or executor, copy of notarization, and volume and page numbers of Journal, entry 246. Chronologically arranged by dates of filing. Alphabetically indexed by names of decedents. Typed. 610 pages. 18 x 12 x 3. Probate court's office.

265. RECORD OF LAND SALES

July 1853—. 32 volumes. (1-32).

Record of sales of real estate by administrators, executors, or guardians, showing date of application for authority to sell, file box number, names of litigants, copies of orders of appraisal and sale, copies of appraisals, account of sale, copies of writs issued by sheriff's return, and copies of notices of sale. Chronologically arranged by dates of applications. 1853-1866, no index; for index, 1867—, see entry 238. July 1853-May 1902, handwritten; June 1902—, typed. Average 560 pages. 18 x 12 x 2.75. Probate court's file room.

266. TRANSFER AND HEIRSHIP RECORD

1922—. 1 volume. March 1876-1921 in General Docket, entry 237.

Record of applications made by administrators or executors for transfer of real estate to lawful heirs by certificate, showing date of application, case number, name of decedent, description of real estate comprising estate, names of heirs-at-law, copy of journal entry authorizing transfer of real estate, and copy of application for transfer showing amount of real estate to be transferred to each heir. Chronologically arranged by dates of applications. Alphabetically indexed by names of decedents. Typed on printed forms. 600 pages. 18 x 12 x 2.75. Probate court's office.

Cost Bills

267. COST BILL RECORD, INVENTORY

1909-1911. 1 volume.

Record copies of cost bills on filing inventory by administrators, executors, and guardians, showing name of decedent or ward, case number, itemized account of fee taxed, and date filed. Chronologically arranged by dates of filing. Alphabetically indexed by names of decedents or wards. Handwritten on printed forms. 190 pages. 14 x 9 x 1.5. Probate court's file room.

For prior and subsequent records, see entry 272.

268. COST BILL RECORD, PETITION TO SELL REAL ESTATE

1909-1911. 1 volume.

Record copies of cost bills on petitions by administrators, executors, and guardians to sell real estate showing name of litigants, case number, itemized account of cost taxed, and date filed. Chronologically arranged by dates of filing. Alphabetically indexed by names of decedents or wards. Handwritten on printed forms. 304 pages. 14 x 9 x 1.5. Probate court's file room.

For prior and subsequent records, see entry 272.

269. COST BILL RECORD, SALE OF PERSONAL PROPERTY
1909-1911. 1 volume.

Copies of cost bills filed on sale of personal property of estates showing name of decedent, case number, itemized account of fees taxed, and date filed. Chronologically arranged by dates of filing. Alphabetically indexed by names of decedents. Handwritten on printed forms. 300 pages. 14 x 9 x 1.5. Probate court's file room.

For prior and subsequent records, see entry 272.

270. COST BILL RECORD, ACCOUNTS
1910-1911. 1 volume.

Record copies of cost bills on filing accounts by administrators, executors, or guardians, showing name of decedent or ward, case number, itemized account of fees taxed, and date filed. Chronological by dates of filing. Alphabetically indexed by names of decedents or wards. Handwritten on printed forms. 490 pages. 14 x 9 x 2.5. Probate court's file room.

For prior and subsequent records, see entry 272.

271. COST BILL RECORD, APPOINTMENT OF ADMINISTRATOR OR EXECUTOR
1899-1911. 1 volume.

Copy of cost bills on appointment of administrators and executors of estates showing name of decedent, case number, itemized account of costs taxed, date filed. Chronologically arranged by dates of filing. Alphabetically indexed by names of decedents. Handwritten on printed forms. 310 pages. 14 9 1.5. Probate court's file room.

For prior and subsequent records, see entry 272.

272. COST BILL RECORD, ESTATES
October 1882—. 5 volumes. (A, 1-4).

Record copies of cost bills and settlement of estates showing name of decedent, name of administrator or executor, itemized account of costs and fees taxed, and date filed. Chronologically arranged by dates of filing. Alphabetically indexed by names of decedents. Handwritten on printed forms. Average 590 pages. 18 x 11.5 x 3. Probate court's file room.

For estate cost bill records, see entries 267-271; for miscellaneous cost bills, see entry 306.

Settlements

273. SETTLEMENT CALENDAR
1876-1899. 2 volumes. Discontinued.

Record of settlement dates for administrators, executors, and guardians, showing names of decedents or ward, names of administrators, executors, and guardians, volume and page numbers of Administrators' and Executors' docket, entry 239, and Guardians' Docket, entry 240, date account due, date notice issued, date account filed, and what account. Alphabetically arranged by names of wards or decedents and chronologically thereunder by dates accounts are due. No index. Handwritten on printed forms. Average 270 pages. 16 x 18 x 1.5. Probate court's office.

274. ROSTER OF SETTLEMENTS
1900-1905. 1 volume. Discontinued.

Record of settlement of accounts by administrators, executors, or guardians, showing name of appointee, title, name of decedent, ward, or assigner, post office address of appointee, volume and page numbers of Administrators' and Executors' Docket, entry 239, or Guardians' Docket, entry 240, inventory and sale bill, for what account, date due, date notice was issued, and date filed. Chronologically arranged by years, alphabetically thereunder by names of appointees, and thereunder by dates due. No index. Handwritten on printed forms. 210 pages. 16 x 15 x 1.25. Probate court's file room.

275. RECORD OF ACCOUNTS
May 1853—. 45 volumes. (1-45).

Record of accounts filed by administrators, executors, trustees, assignees, and guardians, showing date of filing, name of decedent, assigner, or ward, name and title of person filing account, itemized copy of account filed, what account, and date approved by court. Chronologically arranged by dates of filing. Alphabetically indexed by names of decedents, wards, and assigners in each volume; also separate index, 1867—, entry 238. May 1853-1906, handwritten; February 1906—, typed. Average 570 pages. 18 x 12 x 2.75. Probate court's file room.

Original Papers (See also entry 213)

276. GUARDIANSHIP RECORDS, ORIGINAL
1823-1899. 39 bundles.

Original papers issued in guardianships consisting of applications for appointment as guardian, notices of appointment, bonds filed, letters of guardianship, inventories and appraisements, and cost bills. All papers of each case banded together. Chronologically arranged by dates of filing. No index. 1823-1844, handwritten; 1845-1899, handwritten on printed forms. 4.5 x 3.5 x 8. Storeroom 1.

For subsequent records, see entry 314.

277. GUARDIANS' BONDS AND LETTERS, ORIGINAL
1853—. 18 file boxes.

Original bonds filed and letters of guardianship issued. Bonds show date of bond, name of appointee, names of sureties, amount of bond, and date filed; letters show date of appointment, name of appointee, ward, deceased parent, and date filed. Chronologically arranged by dates of filing. No index. Handwritten on printed forms. 10 x 4.5 x 14. Probate court's file room.

278. ORIGINAL RECORDS, ESTATES
1805-1897. 716 bundles.

Original papers of administration of estates consisting of applications for appointment as administrator or executor, notices of appointment, bonds filed, letters of administration or testamentary, and letters of guardianship; inventories and sale bills, accounts filed, final settlements, and cost bills. Bills show date, name of decedent, name of administrator or executor; bonds show, in addition, names of sureties, amount of bond, and date filed. Chronologically arranged by dates of filing. No index. 1805-1944, handwritten; 1843-1897, handwritten on printed forms. 4.5 x 3.5 x 8. 707 bundles, 1805-1897, storeroom 1; 9 bundles, 1867-1881, storeroom 3.

For subsequent records, see entry 314.

Inheritance Taxes
(See also entries 363-366, 441-448)

279. INHERITANCE TAX RECORD
1906-1917. 1 volume.

Record of estates subject to inheritance tax assessments showing name of decedent, names of heirs, devisees, or legatees, names of administrator, executor, or trustee, kind of inheritance, value of estate, legal exemption, net value for taxation, date of certificate issued to county auditor, costs taxed, amount tax due, and date paid. Chronologically arranged by dates of certification to auditor. Alphabetically indexed by names of decedents. Handwritten on printed forms. 100 pages. 16 x 11 x .75. Probate court's file room.

For other records, see entry 280 and 281.

280. INHERITANCE TAX RECORD
1919—. 2 volumes. (1, 2).

Record of inheritance taxes assessed on estates showing volume and page numbers of Administrators' and Executors' Docket, entry 239, case number, name of decedent, date of death, name of administrator or executor, estimated value of property, value as fixed by court, total indebtedness, cost of administration, net value of estate, names and relationship of heirs-at-law, names of legatees or devisees, value of each share of estate, tax assessed on each share, tax, district, date tax accrued, and date tax paid. Chronologically arranged by dates of filing. Alphabetically indexed by names of decedents. Handwritten on printed forms. Average 590 pages. 18 x 11.5 x 3. Probate court's file room.

For other records, see entry 279 and 281.

281. INHERITANCE TAX, ESTATES NOT SUBJECT TO TAX
1919—. 1 volume.

Record of estates settled by probate court, the value of which are within the legal inheritance tax exemptions, showing case number, name of decedent, date of death, name of administrator or executor, volume and page numbers of Journal, entry 246, estimated value of property, inventory value, value as fixed by court, total legal exemptions, and date filed. Chronologically arranged by dates of filing. No index. Handwritten on printed forms. 300 pages. 18 x 11.5 x 1.5. Probate court's file room.

For other records, see entries 279 and 280.

Dependents

282. LUNACY RECORD

1855—. 10 volumes. (2 volumes, 1855-1890, unnumbered; 1-8).

Record of proceedings on lunacy affidavits showing date of filing charges, name of person filing affidavit, copies of: warrant to arrest, medical certificate filed by physician making examination of alleged lunatic, proceedings at inquest hearing, application for admission to state institution, warrants to convey to institution, sheriff's returns on writs with cost bill, record of discharge of patient from institution, and file box numbers of Original Records, entry 314. Contains Epileptic Record, 1855-1892, entry 284. Chronologically arranged by dates of filing affidavits. Alphabetically indexed by names of principles. 1855-1891, handwritten; 1891-1914, handwritten on printed forms; 1915—, typed on printed forms. Average 500 pages. 18 x 12 x 2.5. Probate court's office.

283. LUNACY RECORDS, ORIGINAL

1854-1895. 9 bundles.

Original papers issued in lunacy proceedings consisting of affidavits of complaint, applications for admission to state institution, warrants to arrest, medical certificates, inquest proceedings, journal entry of commitments to institution, warrants to convey to institution, sheriff's returns on writs, and cost bills; showing name of alleged incompetent or lunatic, name of person filing complaint, name of physician, and date filed. Chronologically arranged by dates of filing. No index. Handwritten on printed forms. 4 x 3.5 x 8. Storeroom 1.

For subsequent records, see entry 314.

284. EPILEPSY RECORD

1893—. 1 volume. 1855-1892 in Lunacy Record, entry 282.

Record of proceedings in epileptic cases showing name of afflicted person, case number, copy of application for admission to state institution, names of nearest relatives, copy of warrants to arrest, copy of medical certificate by physician, copy of order to commit to institution, copy of warrant to convey to institution, and copies of sheriff's returns on writs with cost bill. Chronologically arranged by dates of application for admission to institution. Alphabetical index by names of principals. Handwritten on printed forms. 310 pages. 18 x 12 x 1.75. Probate court's office.

285. RECORD OF FEEBLE-MINDED YOUTH

1906—. 1 volume. March 1876-1905 in General Docket, entry 237.

Record copies of applications for admission of feeble-minded youth to state institution, showing warrant to arrest, medical certificate, affidavit of information, copy of inquest proceedings, warrants to convey to institution. Each record entry shows name of alleged feeble-minded youth, name of parent, guardian, or next friend, name of physician, and sheriff's return on writs. Chronologically arranged by dates of filing. Alphabetically indexed by names of youths. Handwritten on printed forms. 300 pages. 18 x 12 x 2.25. Probate court's office.

Naturalization

286. NATURALIZATION RECORD, FIRST PAPERS

1859-1899. 1 volume. 1900-1906, missing.

Record copies of declarations of aliens to become naturalized citizens of the United States, showing date, name of alien, nativity, date of entry into the United States, and date recorded. Chronologically arranged by dates of filing. Alphabetically indexed by names of aliens. Handwritten on printed forms. 500 pages. 14 x 9 x 2.5. Probate court's office.

For subsequent records, see entry 157.

287. NATURALIZATION RECORD

September 1859-1902. 3 volumes. (1-3). 1903-1906, missing.

Record of naturalization of aliens showing date of issue, name of alien, nativity, date of first papers, names of witnesses to residence in the United States, copy of affidavit and oath of allegiance to the United States by applicant, and date filed. Chronologically arranged by dates of filing. Alphabetically indexed by names of applicants. Average 440 pages. 14 x 9 x 2.5. Probate court's office.

Vital Statistics

Births and Deaths (See also entries 592-595).

288. BIRTH RECORD

July 1867-March 1908. 4 volumes. (1-4). Discontinued.

Record of births as filed for record showing date recorded, consecutive number of birth, date of birth, place of birth, sex and color of child, name of father, maiden name of mother, and residence of parents. Birth dates are still recorded, especially since 1935 in connection with aid for the aged pensions. A total of 37 recordings since March 1908, of births dating May 1852-April 1916. Chronologically arranged by dates reported and numerically by consecutive record numbers. Alphabetically indexed by family names showing consecutive record number. Handwritten. Average 520 pages. 18 x 12 x 2.5. Probate court's file room.

289. INDEX TO BIRTH RECORDS

July 1867-March 1908. 1 volume.

Index to Birth Record showing christian name of child, consecutive record number, and volume and page numbers of record. Alphabetically arranged by names of families. No index. Handwritten. 320 pages. 18 x 12 x 1.75. Probate court's office.

290. REPORTS OF BIRTHS

1867-1908. 41 bundles. Discontinued.

Original quarterly reports by physicians and midwives of birth, showing date of report, christian name of child, date of birth, place of birth, sex, color, name of father, maiden name of mother, residence of parents, and by whom reported. Chronologically arranged by dates of reports. No index. Handwritten on printed forms. 5 x 3.5 x 9. Storeroom 2.

291. RECORD OF DEATHS

March 1867-February 1908. 2 volumes. (1, 2). Discontinued.

Record of deaths as reported to probate court by physicians or morticians, showing date reported, consecutive record number, name of decedent, date of death, marital status, age, place of death, place of birth, occupation, names of parents, color, cause of death, late residence, and name of person reporting. Chronologically arranged by dates reported and numerically by consecutive record numbers. Alphabetically indexed by names of decedent showing consecutive record number. Handwritten on printed of forms. Average 820 pages. 18 x 11.5 x 4.25. Probate court's file room.

292. REPORT OF DEATHS

1868-1908. 34 bundles. Discontinued.

Original quarterly reports by physicians and undertakers of deaths, showing date of report, name of decedent, place of death, age, date of birth, place of birth, date of death, sex, color, names of parents, cause of death, last residence, name of person reporting, and date filed. Chronologically arranged by dates of filing. No index. Handwritten on printed forms. 4.5 x 3.5 x 9. Storeroom 2.

Marriages

293. MARRIAGE RECORD
October 1788—. 26 volumes. (1-26).
Record of marriage licenses issued by Washington County probate court and reported by person solemnizing marriage, showing names of contracting parties, residence, date married, name of magistrate or ordained minister solemnizing the marriage, and date filed in clerk of courts' office, 1802-1852, and probate court, 1852—. Volume 1, 1788-1841, contains: [Religious Societies], 1820-1830, entry 99; [Miscellaneous Permits], 1802-1812, entry 138; [Registration of Negroes], 1805-1809, entry 173; [Distribution of Status Books], 1788-1841, entry 178; [Organization of Court of Quarter Sessions], September 1788, entry 184; [Quarter Sessions Administration Proceedings], November 1788- February 1883, entry 189; [Common Pleas Administration Proceedings], March 1803-April 1810, entry 209; Marriage Record Affidavits, 1881—, entry 296; Ministers' License Record, 1817-December 1864, entry 300. Chronologically arranged by dates of entries. For index, October 1788- December 1864, see entry 294; January 1865—, alphabetically indexed in each volume, direct, by names of grooms, and reverse, by names of brides. October 1788- December 1864, handwritten; January 1865—, handwritten on printed forms. Average 600 pages. 17 x 11.5 x 3. Probate court's file room.

294. MARRIAGE RECORD, INDEX
1788-December 1864. 1 volume. Discontinued.
Index to Marriage Record, volume 1-3, showing names of brides and grooms, and volume and page numbers of record. Alphabetically arranged by names of grooms. Handwritten. 440 pages. 13 x 9 x 2.25. Probate court's file room.

295. MARRIAGE RETURNS
1790—. 66 bundles and 7 file boxes.
Original certificates filed under clerk of courts, 1790-1852, and probate court 1852—, by ministers and magistrates certifying to the solemnizing of marriage showing date, place of ceremony, names of contracting parties, signature of minister

or magistrate, and date filed. Chronologically arranged by dates of filing. No index. 1790-1852, handwritten; 1852—, handwritten on printed forms. Bundles, 4 x 2 x 7.5; file boxes, 10 x 4.5 x 14. 40 bundles, 1790-1870, Storeroom 2; 26 bundles, 1871-1906, Storeroom 1; 7 file boxes, 1907—, Probate court's file room.

296. MARRIAGE RECORD AFFIDAVITS

1843-1880. 9 volumes. Prior records missing 1881— in Marriage Record, entry 293.

Affidavits by applicants for marriage licenses declaring themselves to be of legal age, to have no wife or husband living, and not first cousins or near of kin, showing date, names of applicants, consecutive number, signatures of applicants, and name of probate judge. Numerically arranged by consecutive numbers. No index. Handwritten on printed forms. Average 300 pages. 12 x 8 x 1.5. Probate court's office.

297. MARRIAGE LICENSE APPLICATIONS

1906-1931. 25 file boxes.

Original applications for marriage licenses showing names of applicants, date of application, residence, age, place of birth, names of parents, occupation of each applicant, and name of magistrate or minister solemnizing marriage. Chronologically arranged by dates of applications. No index. Handwritten on printed forms. 10 x 4.5 x 14. Probate court's file room.

298. MARRIAGE CONSENTS

1870—. 8 jackets and 2 file boxes.

Original written consents to marriage of minors by parents, guardians, or next friend, showing date, name of applicant for marriage license, name of person or persons giving consent, with relationship to applicant. Chronologically arranged by dates of consent. No index. Handwritten. Jackets, 4.5 x 9 x 1.5; file boxes, 10 x 4.5 x 14. 8 jackets, 1870-1900, Storeroom 2; 2 file boxes, 1901—, Probate court's file room.

299. MARRIAGE RECORD, JOURNAL

1931—. 1 volume.

Request for waiver of time limit before marriage license is issued showing reason for request, dates, consecutive number, names of contracting parties, and copy of journal entry granting request. Chronologically arranged by dates of request. Alphabetically indexed by names of grooms. Handwritten on printed forms. 510 pages. 18 x 12 x 2.75. Probate court's file room.

Licenses

300. MINISTERS' LICENSE RECORD

1853—. 4 volumes. 1817-December 1864 in Marriage Record, entry 293. Record copies of licenses issued to ordained ministers to solemnize marriages, showing date, name of minister, church denomination, and date recorded. Chronologically arranged by dates of recording. Alphabetically indexed by names of ministers. Handwritten on printed forms. Average 410 pages. 14 x 9 x 2.25. Probate court's file room.

301. NURSES' AND LIMITED PRACTITIONERS' RECORD

1916—. 1 volume.

Record copies of certificates issued by state medical board to graduate nurses on passing examinations, showing certificate number, name of licensee, date of diploma, graduate of what training school for nurses, date of certificate, date recorded; also record copies of certificates issued by state medical board to applicants for limited practice (prohibited from prescribing drugs or performing major surgery, or to treat infections, contagious, or venereal disease), showing certificate number, name of license, what branch license is for, date of certificate, and date recorded. Chronologically arranged by dates of recording. Alphabetically indexed by names of licensees. Handwritten on printed forms. 100 pages. 16 x 10 x 1.25. Probate court's office.

302. RECORD OF MEDICAL CERTIFICATES

April 1896—. 1 volume.

Record copies of certificates issued by state board of medical examiners to applicants, on examination, to practice medicine and surgery, showing name of applicant, graduate of what medical school, date of graduation, date of certificate, and date recorded. Chronologically arranged by dates of recording. Alphabetically indexed by names of physicians. Handwritten on printed forms. 400 pages. 16 x 10 x 2. Probate court's office.

303. RECORD OF WATERCRAFT LICENSES

1860—. 2 volumes.

Record copies of licenses issued to operate watercraft on Ohio and Muskingum Rivers, showing name of applicant, name of watercraft, kind of craft, date of application, and date recorded. Chronologically arranged by dates issued. Alphabetically indexed by names of licensees. Handwritten on printed forms. Average 300 pages. 16 x 11 x 1.75. Probate court's office.

Business Administration of Office

304. RECORD OF COSTS PAID

1887-1899. 1 volume. Discontinued.

Record of cost and fees paid, showing date paid, in what matter, by whom paid, amount, and to whom due. Chronologically arranged by dates received. No index. Handwritten on printed forms. 270 pages. 14 x 9 x 1.5. Probate court's office.

305. RECORD OF ACCRUED FEES

January 1907-September 1925. 2 volumes. (1, 2). Discontinued.

Record of fees accrued showing date accrued, case number, in what matter, to whom charged, total fee, civil causes, criminal causes, due from county, juvenile court, transcripts and copies, sundries, and date paid. Chronologically arranged by dates of accrual. No index. Handwritten on printed forms. Average 220 pages. 18 x 12 x 1.25. Probate court's file room.

306. COST BILL RECORD, MISCELLANEOUS

December 1882—. 7 volumes. (A, 1-6).

Record of cost and fees taxed in miscellaneous matters as claims of administrators or executors, petitions, applications, citations, admissions to bail, *habeas corpus*, lunacy inquest, commitments to boys' or girls' industrial school, proceedings in aid of execution, adoption, appropriation proceedings, and other jury cases, showing name of decedent, ward, defendant, administrator, executive, or guardian, nature of cause, itemized account of cost and fees taxed, and date filed. Chronologically arranged by dates of filing. Alphabetically indexed by names of decedents, wards, children, defendants, or plaintiffs. Handwritten on printed forms. Average 220 pages. 18 x 11.5 x 2.25. Probate court's file room.

For cost bills in estates, see entries 267-272.

307. CASH BOOK

1889—. 9 volumes .(1-9).

Record of cash receipts and disbursements showing date received, from whom received, title of case, volume and page numbers of docket in which case is recorded, amount received, to whom paid, date paid out, signature of payee, amount paid, and judges fee. Chronologically arranged by dates of receipts. No index. Handwritten on printed forms. Average 280 pages. 18 x 14 x 1.5. Probate court's file room.

308. RECORD OF UNCLAIMED COSTS AND FEES

1907—. 1 volume.

Record of unclaimed costs and fees paid into county treasury showing to whom money is due, amount, volume and page numbers of docket in which case is recorded, case number, date paid in, date certificate for recovery was issued, and certificate number. Alphabetically arranged by names of payees. No index. Handwritten on printed forms. 180 pages. 15 x 10 x 1. Probate court's office.

Miscellaneous

309. [TREASURY EXAMINERS' REPORT]

1874. In record of bonds(Official), entry 379.

Copy of report of treasury examiners to the probate court on the condition of the county treasury at the inspection of 1874.

For subsequent records, see entry 310.

310. RECORD OF TREASURY EXAMINATIONS

1886-1914. 2 volumes. Discontinued.

Record copy of treasury examinations as filed with probate judge by treasury examiners, showing date of examination, balance to credit of each fund, total receipts into treasury of each fund account, total disbursement of each fund, grand total disbursements, total overpayments, total balance, county auditor's attest to report, examiners' names, and date filed. Chronologically arranged by dates of filing. No index. Handwritten on printed forms. Average 140 pages. 18 x 12 x .75. Storeroom 1.

For prior records, see entry 309.

311. RECORD OF UNCLAIMED DEPOSITS
1888—. 2 volumes.

Record of unclaimed deposits as reported by bank officials to probate court, showing date of report, name of bank, name of bank official making report, name of depositor, amount to credit of account, and date of last credit or debit to account. Chronologically arranged by dates of reports. No index. 1888-1896, handwritten; 1897—, handwritten on printed forms. 1888-1896, 1 volume, 190 pages. 12 x 8 x 1; 1897—, 1 volume, 420 pages. 16 x 11 x 2.25. 1 volume, 1888-1896, Storeroom 1; 1 volume, 1897—, Probate court's office.

312. RECEIPT FOR PAPERS REMOVED
1925—. 1 volume.

Record of court papers removed from files showing case number, title of case, date removed, name of person removing papers, and date returned. Chronologically arranged by dates removed. No index. Handwritten on printed forms. 160 pages. 16 x 10 x 1. Probate court's office.

313. DAY BOOK
1876-1877. 1 volume. Discontinued.

Probate judges daily record of causes set for hearing, record of licenses issued, and fees received. Chronologically arranged. Handwritten. 220 pages. 12 x 8 x 1.25. Storeroom 2.

314. ORIGINAL RECORDS
1895—. 560 file boxes. (608-1168).

Original papers issued in matters filed in probate court concerning administration of estates, guardianships, criminal cases, juvenile cases, and all cases of dependents and incompetents. Records of administration of estates include applications for appointments as administrator or executor, notices of appointment, bonds, inventories and sale bills, accounts filed, cost bills, and various other documents; guardianship records include applications for appointment as guardian, notices of appointment, bonds, letters of guardianship, inventories and appraisements, accounts filed, final settlements, cost bills, and various documents; criminal records include affidavits of information, warrants to arrest, transcripts from magistrates' courts, bonds, pleas of accused, journal entries of court or jury verdicts, sentences, warrants to commit to jail or workhouse, cost bills, and various other documents;

juvenile records include affidavits of complaint or delinquency, warrants to arrest, reports of juvenile or probation officer in case, journal entries of court findings, sentences, and warrants to convey to institution; records of dependents and incompetence including affidavits of complaint, applications for admission to state institution, warrants to arrest, medical certificates, inquest proceedings, journal entries to commitments to institution, warrants to convey to institution, sheriff's returns on writs, and cost bills. All records of each case are together in a jacket on which the title of the case, name of the decedent, ward, or defendant, and date case filed are written. Chronologically arranged by dates of filing. For indexes, see entries 237-241, 251, 282, and 316. 1895-1906, handwritten on printed forms; 1907—, typed on printed forms. 10 x 4.5 x 14. 228 file boxes, 608-745, 1035-1124, Probate court's office; 332 file boxes, 746-1034. 1125-1167, Probate court's file room.

For prior original papers, see entries 213, 252, 276, 278, 283, and 317.

315. MISCELLANEOUS RECORD

1932—. 1 volume. March 1876-1931 in General Docket, entry 237. Record of miscellaneous items of origin and foreign probate courts, as copies of election of surviving spouse under provisions of a will, applications for transfer of real estate, petitions to file transcript; showing date, name of decedent, administrator, or executor, county, and state. Chronologically arranged by dates of filing. Alphabetically indexed by names of decedents. Typed. 420 pages. 18 x 12 x 2.25. Probate court's office.

The juvenile court, though of uncertain origin, has been generally recognized as an American contribution to the administration of social justice. The establishment of such courts was the logical outcome of the practical philosophy of enlightened public men that child offenders against the law, or conventional social standards; should not be treated as criminals, but as unfortunate needing the help, supervision, and protection of the state (Miriam Van Waters, *Youth in Conflict,* N. Y., 1925, 147, 159, 161). Although the idea of a separate court for the trial of juvenile offenders was an institution of gradual growth, the first court of this kind in the United States was established in 1899, in Chicago, Cook County, Illinois, by an act of the legislature of that state. The Illinois experiment gave an impetus to the children's movement in the middle west. (Edwin H. Sutherland, *Principles of Criminology,* Chicago, 1934, 270-272.

The Ohio legislature was not slow in seeing the advantage of the Illinois experiment, and accordingly, in 1902, an act passed creating the juvenile court in Cuyahoga County. Under this act all counties having a population of over 380,000 and an insolvency court were authorized, under an extension of the jurisdiction of this court, to establish children's courts. The stipulations of this act excluded Washington County. It gave the court jurisdiction of the trial of cases involving delinquent and neglected children; defined the terms "delinquent, dependent, and neglected"; authorize the appointment of a probation officer, and made it his duty to investigate the facts of cases coming before the court, and to take charge of the offender before and after trial. The clerk of the juvenile court was directed to keep a journal in which was to be recorded the minutes of the cases. The judge was to serve for a period of five years. (95 O. L. 785). The term remained at five years until 1935 when it was extended to six years.

Two years after the establishment of the Cuyahoga County juvenile court, the assembly provided by statute for the establishment of juvenile courts in the rural counties of the state which, because of their lack of population, were unable to create the newer agencies under the provisions of the act of 1902. Under the act of 1904 the judges of the court of common pleas, probate court, and where established, the insolvency courts, wherein three or more judges held court concurrently, were authorized to appoint one of their members as "juvenile judge." The court was given original jurisdiction in all cases involving neglected, dependent, and delinquent children under the age of sixteen years; and all children, who had been scheduled in the past for trial in a justice of the peace or police court were in the future to be tried before a juvenile judge. As under the act of 1902, the judge was authorized to appoint a probation officer, and the clerk of courts was directed to keep a journal of the minutes of each case. (97 O. L. 561). In 1908 the court was given jurisdiction in cases involving minors under seventeen years of age, and such children as were brought before the juvenile judge were to become wards of the court until they had attained the age of twenty-one years. The county commissioners were authorized to provide by lease or purchase, a "detention home" where neglected or dependent children might be detained pending the final disposition of their cases. The clerk of courts was directed to keep not only a journal, but also an appearance docket containing all orders, judgments, and findings of the court. It provided also for case studies to be made by the probation officer. (99 O. L. 196). The age jurisdiction of the court was increased to eighteen in 1913 (193 O. L. 877).

While provisions were being made for the establishment of juvenile courts, the legislature gave the court jurisdiction in cases involving adults who committed crimes against children or contributed to the delinquency of dependent children. Thus in 1906 it was made a misdemeanor to contribute to the delinquency of a child under seventeen years of age (98 O. L. 314). Two years later the "lack of parental care" was defined and it was made a misdemeanor to fail to support a minor, or to cause him to engage in begging (99 O. L. 196). In 1913, "proper parental care" was defined by statute (103 O. L. 870).

Marked progress has been made in the medical treatment of juveniles. While the act of 1913 authorized the juvenile judge to submit any child sentenced to an institution for correction to a mental test, the act of 1929 authorized him to submit any child coming before the court to a mental and physical test to be made by a physician or psychiatrist (103 O. L. 872; 113 O. L. 471). To further the scientific handling of children, the county commissioners were authorized, in the same year, to lease or construct a separate building to be known as the "juvenile court" which should be appropriately constructed, arranged, furnished, and maintained for the convenience and the effective transaction of the business of the court, including adequate facilities to be used as laboratories, dispensaries, or clinics for the scientific use of specialist attached to the court (113 O. L. 470).

One of the guiding principles of the court has been to make its "custody and discipline" of children approximate as possible that which should be given by their parents. In cases involving neglected or dependent children, not sentenced to state institutions, it has been the policy of judges to assign children to private homes, and make arrangements for their adoption. Many other functions have been taken over by the juvenile court such as administering mothers' pensions (103 O. L. 877).

The juvenile court of Cuyahoga County is the only independent juvenile court in the state. There are seven other juvenile courts in Ohio attached to the court of domestic relations. In Washington County, as in all counties where there is no independent juvenile court or no court of domestic relations, the probate judge serves as judge of the juvenile court (G. C. Sec. 1639-7).

316. JUVENILE DOCKET AND RECORD
August 1906—. 5 volumes. (1-5).
Docket of cases filed in juvenile division showing case number, name of juvenile, age, color, residence, school and teacher, name, residence, nativity and occupation of parents, guardian, or next friend, date of filing case, name of person filing affidavit of delinquency, dates of filing or issuing all writs with brief notation of each step in proceedings of case, and file box number of Original Records, entry 314. Chronologically arranged by dates of filing. Alphabetically indexed by names of juveniles. Handwritten on printed forms. Average 260 pages. 16 x 11 x 1.5. Probate court's office.

317. COMMITMENTS, BOYS' AND GIRLS' INDUSTRIAL SCHOOLS
1887-1897. 2 file boxes.
Original papers issued in commitment of delinquent boys to Boys' Industrial School at Lancaster and of delinquent girls to Girls' Industrial School at Delaware, showing name of delinquent, offense charged, age, and name of parent or guardian. Chronologically arranged by dates of filing. No index. Handwritten on printed forms. 10 x 4.5 x 14. Probate court's office.

For subsequent records, see entry 314.

318. RECORD, MOTHERS' PENSIONS
February 1914-June 1936. 3 volumes. Discontinued.
Record of mothers' pensions showing name of applicant, address, names and dates of birth of dependent children, date application filed, copy of report on investigation of application, copy of journal entry approving or rejecting application, amount of award, and record of payments. Chronologically arranged by dates of application filed. Alphabetically indexed by names of applicants. 1914-1917, handwritten on printed forms; 1917-June 1936, typed on printed of forms. Average 440 pages.

16 x 11 x 2.25. Probate court's file room.

For subsequent records of aid to dependent children, see entries 655-659; for other records, see entry 36, 319, 320.

319. MOTHERS' PENSIONS, REJECTED AND CLOSED CASES

1915-June 1936. 1 file box.

Original papers issued in rejection of application for mothers' pensions or in closed cases when dependent children reach sixteen years of age or are placed in an institution. Chronologically arranged by dates of filing. No index. Handwritten on printed forms. 10 x 4.25 x 14. Probate court's office.

For subsequent records of aid to dependent children, see entries 655-659; for other records, see entries 36, 318, 320.

320. APPLICATIONS, MOTHERS' PENSIONS

1914-June 1936. 7 file boxes.

Original applications by mothers of dependent children for pensions showing date, name of applicant, residence, names and ages of dependent children, and date filed. Chronologically arranged by dates of filing. Handwritten on printed forms. 10 x 4.25 x 14. Probate court's office.

For subsequent records of aid to dependent children, see entries 655-659; for other records, see entries 36, 318, 320.

321. ADOPTION RECORDS, ORIGINAL

1861—. 3 file boxes.

Original papers issued in adoption proceedings showing names of applicants, name of child, names of child's parents, age of child, report of investigation of application, and journal entry approving application. Chronologically arranged by dates of filing. No index. 1861-1907, handwritten on printed forms; 1909—, typed on printed forms. 10 x 4.25 x 14. Probate court's office.

In 1891 the judges of the court of common pleas in counties having a population not less than 33,000 nor more than 50,000 were authorized to appoint four residents of the county to serve as a jury commission for a term of one year. Washington County came within the limitations of the act. It was the duty of this commission to determine the qualifications and fitness of persons to be selected as jurors. (88 O. L. 200). Three years later, in 1894, the provisions of the act were extended to all other counties in the state except Cuyahoga, Franklin, Hamilton, Lucas, Montgomery, and Mahoning (91 O. L. 176). In 1902 the statute was amended to include all counties (96 O. L. 3). In 1913 the number of jury commissioners in each county was reduced to two (103 O. L. 513; 105 O. L. 106).

The jury code, which became effective August 2, 1931, provided for a jury commission of the same number and same qualifications previously provided for, to hold office at the pleasure of the court, and to meet and select prospective jurors both grand and petit, for the ensuing year from a list provided by the board of elections (114 O. L. 193-213). At the beginning of each jury year, the commissioners are required to make a new and complete jury list, known as the annual jury list, arranged alphabetically by precincts, districts, and townships, recording the name, occupation, business address, and residence of each prospective juror, and to prepare an index to this list. A duplicate list is certified by the commissioners and filed in the office of the clerk of court of common pleas. (114 O. L. 205).

The jury commissioners select prospective jurors for civil and criminal cases as well as for the grand jury. It selects jurors for the probate court, juvenile court, and other minor courts.

322. JOURNAL

1931—. 1 volume.

Record of minutes of meetings of jury commission with record of exemptions for jury duty for cause, showing name of elector excused, reason for excusing, and date recorded. Chronologically arranged by dates of entries. No index. Typed. 300 pages. 14 x 10 x 1.5. Clerk of courts' office.

323. JURY LISTS

1861—. 21 jackets and 12 file boxes.

Lists of grand and petit jurors drawn for jury duty for each court term, also special venires, petit jurors, showing term of court, date drawn, name, township, city ward, address, and date subpoenaed; petit jury list also shows what case and trial date. Chronologically arranged by dates of court terms. No index. Handwritten on printed forms. Jackets, 3.5 x 4.5 x 9; 5 file boxes, 4.5 x 4.5 x 9.5; 7 file boxes, 10 x 4.5 x 14. 21 jackets, 1870-1919, Storeroom 2; 5 file boxes, 1861-1885, Storeroom 1; 7 file boxes, 1920—, Clerk of courts' office.

The grand jury, sometimes called the palladium of English liberty, has as its function the preliminary examination of persons charged with a capital or other infamous crime. The inherent right, guaranteed by the federal constitution, is recognized in the provisions of the Ohio constitution of 1802 and 1851 and in the amendments of 1912.

Under the present system, which does not differ in detail from that inaugurated in the early days of the state's history, the grand jury is composed of fifteen members, resident electors of the county having "the qualifications of jurors" (G. C. sec. 13436-2). It is the duty of the grand jury "to inquire of and present all offenses committed in the county in and for which it was empaneled and sworn" (G. C. sec. 13436-5). The proceedings of the grand jury are secret and each juror is required to take an oath to preserve such secrecy. Moreover, no grand juror may be required to reveal the way he or other grand jurors voted. (G. C. sec. 13436-16).

The grand jurors are aided in their investigations by the county prosecuting attorney who since 1869 has been authorized by statute to present evidence before this body and compelled the attendance of witnesses against whom he may institute contempt proceedings if they refuse to testify. (See p. 127). The prosecuting attorney must leave the room before the jurors begin the expression of their views or before a poll is taken. The courts have decreed, however, that the mere presence of the prosecuting attorney in the room during the deliberations is "not sufficient to sustain a plea of abatement" (see *State* v. *Stichtenoth,* 8 N. P., n. s., 297-338). Since 1902 the official court stenographer of the county, may take shorthand notes of testimony, and furnish a transcript to the prosecuting attorney, at his request. This reporter, like to prosecuting attorney and his assistants, is required to retire from the jury room before the grand jury begins its deliberations. (G. C. sec, 13436-8).

At least twelve of the fifteen jurors must concur in finding an indictment (G. C. 13436-17). Indictments found by the grand jury are presented by the foreman to the court and are filed with the clerk of courts (G. C. sec. 13436-21). No grand juror or officer of the court is permitted to disclose that a person has been indicted before such indictment is filed and the case docketed (G. C. Sec. 13436-15). Any incarcerated person charged with an indictable offense who has not been indicted during the term of court at which he is held to answer is discharged (G. C. sec. 13436-23).

Since 1869 it has been the duty of the grand jury to visit the county jail once at each term of court at which they may be in attendance, examine its state and condition and inquire into the discipline and treatment of prisoners, and return a written report to the court (G. C. sec. 13436-20).

The majority of contemporary opinion holds that the grand jury, although still defended as a safeguard against needless oppressive prosecution, seems to be of little usefulness in the administration of modern criminal justice. It is argued that the grand jury not only delays the prosecution of criminal offenses but makes it impossible to place responsibility for neglect of duty, and is, in many instances, a rubber stamp for the opinion of the county prosecuting attorney.

The grand jury keeps no permanent records. For records in other offices, see entries 193, 212, and 214.

The petit jury, likes the grand jury, had its origin in England during the reign of Henry II (George Burton Adams, *Constitutional History of England,* N. Y., 1921, 116). The right of trial by jury, guaranteed by the federal constitution, was included in each of the Ohio constitutions. At any trial, in any court, for the violation of a statute of the state of Ohio, or any ordinance of any municipality, except in cases where the penalty involved does not exceed a fine of fifty dollars, the accused is entitled to a trial by jury (G. C. sec. 13443).

Except in the method of selecting prospective jurors, the petit jury has remained unchanged for over 134 years. At each session of the court the jury commission (see p. 125) selects not less than fifty or more then seventy-five names of jury service. A venire is issued to the county sheriff for the persons whose names are so drawn to appear on a day fixed for the trial (G. C. sec. 13443-1). From the person so summoned a jury of twelve is empaneled. The county prosecuting attorney and the defense council may, in capital cases, peremptorily challenge six of the jurors. In other cases, four peremptory challenges are allowed. (G. C. secs. 13443-4, 13443-6). Other challenges, alternatively made, may be made for reasons prescribed by statute (G. C. Sec. 13443-8).

When the case is submitted, the jury may decide to question before it in court, or retire to deliberate. Upon retiring the jury members, in charge of an officer at a convenient place, must be kept together until they agree upon a verdict or are discharged by the court. The court may permit them to separate at night. (G. C. Sec. 11420-3). If the jurors disagree as to testimony, or desire to be further instructed on the law in the case, they may request the officer in charge to conduct them to the court for additional information (G. C. sec. 11420-6). In civil actions a jury renders a verdict upon the concurrence of three-fourths or more of its members. This verdict, in writing, is signed by each juror concurring therein. (G. C. sec. 11420-9).

Under the criminal code adopted in 1929 the accused may waiver his right to a jury trial I favor of a trial by a judge. This procedure, although criticized by some, is considered by others to be a logical step in the administration of criminal justice in a modern state.

No separate records are kept by the petit jury.

The office of county prosecuting attorney, unlike the sheriff and coroner, is relatively one of the newer agencies in the administration of criminal justice. Established in America by the English during the colonial period, it offers a striking difference in the development of American criminal procedures as contrasted with English procedure where criminal prosecutions were usually instituted by private persons. As developed in recent years, the office of prosecutor has become one of the state's most important agencies in its defense against modern crime.

The acts of the Northwest Territory placed the responsibility for criminal prosecutions upon the attorney general, who, in turn, appointed and commissioned persons to prosecute cases in their respective counties.

While the acts of the Northwest Territory outlined the local institutions for the newer states, the constitution of Ohio contained no provision for a prosecutor, leaving its creation to the discretion of the legislature. In 1803, during the first session of the legislature, an act was passed authorizing the supreme court to appoint in each county an attorney to prosecute cases on behalf of the state (1 O. L. 50). Two years later, the appointing power was vested in the court of common pleas (3 O. L. 47). The office remained an appointive one until 1833 when the electorate of the county was directed to choose a prosecutor in each county for a two-year term (3 O. L. 13-14; Chase *op. cit.*, III, 1935). The act of 1852 left the office elective and the term unchanged, but in 1881 the term of office was set at three years, and in 1906 it was reduced to two years (78 O. L. 260; 98 O. L. 271-272).

Under the present system the prosecutor is elected for a four-year term. He is required to give bond of not less than $1000 conditioned for the faithful performance of the duties of his office. If the office becomes vacant the court of common pleas is authorized to appoint a successor. (G. C. sec. 2912).

The county prosecuting attorney is authorized to appoint clerks, assistants, and stenographers and to fix their salaries subject to the approval of the county commissioners. Since 1911 he has been authorized to appoint a secret service agent or officer whose duty it is to aid him in the collection of evidence to be used in the trial of criminal cases and in matters of a criminal nature. The compensation of such an officer is determined by the court of common pleas. (G. C. secs, 2914, 2915-1).

Most important among the duties of the prosecuting attorney are those connected with criminal prosecutions. Differing little from those of the early days of the office, these duties include the prosecution on behalf of the state of all complaints, suits, and controversies in which the state is a party, and such other suits, matters, and controversies as he is directed by law to prosecute within or without his county, in the probate court, common pleas court, and court of appeals. In conjunction with the attorney general, he prosecutes cases in the supreme court which originated in his county. G. C. sec. 2916).

In felony cases, when a complaint is made to the prosecutor, he is required to examine the evidence and determine if it is sufficient for prosecution. If he decides in the affirmative, he prepares the evidence for presentation to the grand jury (See p. 123). If this body returns an indictment, the prosecutor prepares to present the evidence and trial court. The court of common pleas may appoint an attorney to assist the prosecutor in criminal cases. (G. C. sec. 2918). In the case of conviction, the prosecutor causes execution to be issued for the fines or cost and pays into the county treasury all money so received (G. C. sec. 2916). Without reference to the grand jury, the county prosecutor may initiate prosecutions in misdemeanor cases in the court of common pleas by information (G. C. sec. 13437-34). After prosecution is inaugurated, he may eliminate the case without trial by means of *nolle prosequi*. Although he is prohibited from enlisting the *nolle prosequi* without leave of the court on good cause shown, his requests are usually granted. (G. C. sec. 13437-32). After prosecution has begun, it remains with the prosecuting attorney whether the case shall be pressed and steps taken that will lead to conviction.

Besides prosecution in criminal cases, the prosecuting attorney also acts in civil matters. He may bring suit in the name of the state when he is convinced that public money is being misapplied or is being illegally withheld or withdrawn from the county treasury. Moreover, he may bring suit against persons violating the obligations of contracts of which the county is a party, or when county property is being sued or occupied illegally. (G. C. sec. 2921).

In addition to these, other duties have been prescribed by statute. On the request of the judge having jurisdiction over juvenile cases, he must prosecute individuals for committing crimes against children (G. C. sec. 1664). Furthermore, when directed by the court of common pleas, he must prosecute persons for keeping a house of prostitution (G. C. secs. 6212-5, 6212-7). At the instigation of the secretary of state, he must prosecute any officer who refuses to furnish gratuitously statistical information for the use of that office (G. C. sec, 174).

The prosecuting attorney has also served in an advisory capacity since 1906 (98 O. L. 160-161). He acts as an advisor to all county boards and officials and to township officers who may require his opinion in writing on matters connected with their official duties (G. C. sec, 2917). In addition to this, he prepares official bonds for all county officers (G. C. sec. 2920).

The prosecuting attorney is required to make annually a report to the county commissioners stating the number of criminal prosecutions completed, the name or names of the party or parties to each, and the amount collected in fines, and cost, and the amount forfeited (G. C. sec. 2926). Moreover, on the demand of the attorney general he must make an annual report on forms provided by the state on all criminal actions prosecuted by indictment in his county (G. C. sec. 2925; 78 O. L. 120; 90 O. L. 225).

324. PROBATION RECORDS

1931—. 1 file drawer. Prior records missing.

Record of reports by offenders placed on probation by county courts showing name of offender, offense, date placed on probation, term of probation, conditions of probation, and record of reports made by probationer. Alphabetically arranged by names of probationers. No index. Typed on printed forms. 12 x 12 x 24. First National Bank Building, Prosecuting attorneys' private office.

325. ANNUAL REPORTS

1931—. 1 file drawer.

Duplicate copy of annual reports by prosecutor to county commissioners on number of cases prosecuted in county courts and amount of fines and costs assessed showing date of report, total number of cases prosecuted in common pleas court, number of first degree murders, number of murders of lesser degrees, number of other cases against persons, number of cases against property, number of cases against public morals, total amount of fines and costs assessed, amount of fines and costs assessed each class or type of offense, and amount allowed for aid in prosecuting state cases. Chronologically arranged by dates of reports. No index. Typed on printed forms. 12 x 12 x 24. National Bank Building, Prosecuting attorneys' private office.

The office of coroner, next to that of sheriff the oldest county office in America, had its inception in England during the latter part of the twelfth century when the coroner kept a record of activities in the county, especially regarding criminal justice. At the end of the thirteenth century it was his duty to make inquests whenever there was a sudden death in the shire, and the results were recorded in the coroner's rolls and presented to the justices when they made their eyre. (Sir Frederick Pollock and Frederic William Maitland, *The History of English Law Before the Time of Edward I,* Cambridge, 1895, I, 519, 571; II, 588, 641).

This office, transplanted in America during the colonial period, was continued by the states, and was adopted by the territory of which the state of Ohio was then a part. An ordinance of the Northwest Territory published in 1788 authorized the governor to appoint a coroner in each county within the territory. This act, together with a supplementary act of 1795 adopted from the Massachusetts code, fixed the power and duties of the coroner. He was empowered to do any act which, by previous legislation had been delegated to the sheriff; and was given the ancient duty of English coroners in holding preliminary investigations over the bodies of all persons found within his county, who were believed to have died by violence or casualty. (Pease, *op. cit.,* I, 24-25, 272-275).

The Ohio Constitution of 1802 continued the historic office, making it elective for a two-year term (*Ohio Const. 1802,* Art. VI, sec. 1). A statute of 1805 defined the duties and authority of the coroner which, in the main, were comparable with those prescribed in the territorial code, except that he was denied the privilege of concurrent jurisdiction with the sheriff (3 O. L. 156-161). The act further provided that the coroner should receive his remuneration from fees; and that if the office of sheriff were to become vacant, the coroner was to execute temporarily the duties of the sheriff (3 O. L. 158-161). The latter provision remained active until its abrogation in 1887 (84 O. L. 208-210).

The constitution of 1851 and the constitutional amendment of 1912 left the duties of the coroner unchanged and it was not until recent years when he became an aid in the scientific detection of crime that laws have been passed which materially affected his office. By the legislative act of 1921 and all counties having a population of 100,000 or more only licensed physicians were eligible to the office, and at the same time the coroner was made official custodian of the morgue (109 O. L. 43-44). In 1927 an act was passed, apparently designed to attract more highly trained physicians, which set the salary of the coroner at $6,000 per year in all counties having a population of 400,000 or more, and authorize him to appoint one stenographer, a secretary, and three assistant custodians of the morgue (112 O. L. 204-205). Two years later, in counties having a population of 400,000 or more, the coroner was empowered to appoint a pathologist to serve as deputy coroner whose duties are to make chemical tests and conduct autopsies (113 O. L. 497).

In 1936 the tenure of office of the coroner was extended from two to four years (G. C. sec. 2823).

(For other records, see entry 181)

326. CORONER'S INQUEST RECORD

1848—. 4 volumes. (1-4).

Coroner's record of inquest held in homicidal, accidental, or sudden deaths, showing name of decedent, date and cause of death, sex and color of decedent, date of inquest, nativity, names of witnesses, names of jurors if jury is empaneled in case, itemized cost bill, and inventory of personal effects found on body. Chronologically arranged by dates of inquest. Alphabetically indexed by names of decedents. Handwritten. Average 200 pages. 16 x 10 x 1.25. 3 volumes, 1848-July 1923, Storeroom 3; 1 volume August 1923—, Clerk of courts' office.

327. CORONER'S INQUEST

1794-1817. 2 bundles.

Original records of coroner's inquests held in cases of homicidal, accidental, or sudden deaths, showing date of inquest hearing, name of decedent, place of death, transcript of hearing, verdict of coroner or jury, names of witnesses, names of jurors if used, itemized cost bill, record of effects found on body of decedent, and date filed. Chronologically arranged by dates of filing. No index. Handwritten. 4 x 3.5 x 8. Storeroom 3.

The office of county sheriff, one of the oldest elective offices in America, had its inception in the Anglo-Saxon period of English history (Adams, *op cit.,* 17-19; W. A. Morris, "The Office of Sheriff in the Anglo-Saxon period," *English Historical Review,* XXXI, 19-40). This ancient institution was introduced into the American colonies in modified form and continued by the states created after independence. (For a comparative study of the sheriff in England and Chesapeake colonies, see Harreld Kerraker, *The Seventeenth-Century Sheriff,* Chapel Hill, 1930). The office assumed a new significance in the latter part of the eighteenth century when a flood of colonists swept across the Alleghenies to establish homes in the Northwest Territory organized by congress in 1787. In the remoter west the pioneers, far removed from the orderly legal processes in courts of the east, were subjected to the machinations of the lawless element evidenced in every new community. In 1792 the governor and judges of the territory adopted an act which provided for the appointment by the governor of a sheriff in each county, and defining his duties; to keep and preserve the peace, and suppress affrays, routs, riots, unlawful assemblies, and insurrections; to apprehend, and confine in jail all felons and traitors; to return persons who, having committed a crime in his county, and have taken refuge in another; to attend upon the court of common pleas and court of appeals during their sessions, and to execute all warrants, writs, and processes directed to him by the proper and lawful authority. (Pease, *op. cit.,* I, 8).

When Ohio entered the union as a state in 1803 the office of sheriff was continued by constitutional provision, and was made elective for a two-year term (*Ohio Const. 1802,* Art. V, sec, 1). Although it did not specifically provide for the office, the constitution of 1851 stated that no person shall be eligible to the office for more than four in any period of six years (*Ohio Const. 1851,* Art. X, sec. 3). This provision was repealed by an amendment in 1933 authorizing any county to adopt a charter form of government. The term of office remained at two years until 1936, when it was extended to four years. (116 O. L. pt. ii, 1st. Sec. H. 603). The sheriff received his remuneration from fees until 1906 when a definite salary was specified by the legislature (3 O. L. 49-51; 33 O. L. 18; 35 O. L. 53; 52 O. L. 86). The salary for each sheriff was based on the population of his county according to the last federal census next proceeding his election (98 O. L. 86).

The duties of the sheriff were and are prescribed by statute. During the legislative session of 1805 the general assembly passed an act defining the duties of the sheriff, which was in all respects, similar to the provision inherited from the territorial code (3 O. L. 156-158). In the same year the sheriff was designated as the county's executioner, and was bound to carry out sentences of death when imposed by the courts upon those convicted of murder. Hanging was the legal method for the infliction of the death penalty (Chase, *op. cit.,* I, 97-101, 442-443). Public executions, the general rule during the earlier years, were abolished in 1844 (42 O. L. 71). In 1886 the sheriff's duties in this respect were delegated to the warden of the Ohio Penitentiary (83 O. L. 145).

As in England the sheriff, during the earlier years of his office, was required to notify the electors of his county of the time and place of holding elections. He was required to furnish the ballot boxes at the expense of the county, hold special elections when so directed by the governor, and deliver the poll books to the secretary of state (2 O. L. 88-89; 3 O. L. 331-332). Since 1892 these duties have been taken over by the board of elections (see p. 258).

An act of 1831, repealing the act of 1805, redefined the duties of the sheriff as a conservator of the peace in his county and as an executive agent of the courts (29 O. L. 112). The present duties of the sheriff in this respect are survivals from the provisions of this act (29 O. L. 112-113; 82 O. L. 26). In the execution of his duties, as prescribed by law, he was again empowered to summon to his aid such persons as he deemed necessary to perform his lawful duty and the apprehension of criminals (29 O. L. 112-113). Thus the *posse comitatus* was at his disposal as it is today. In 1818 the sheriff had been authorized to appoint, with the consent of the court of common pleas, one or more deputies who, like himself, were required to give bond for the faithful performance of the duties of their office. The sheriff was made responsible for their neglect of duty or misconduct in office. (29 O. L. 410).

Not only was the sheriff charged with the duty of apprehending law violators, but he was made responsible for their safe keeping. As early as 1803 he also was made the official custodian of the county jail (3 O. L. 157). Although the early statues directed the county commissioners to provide dungeons for the incarceration of prisoners, the act of 1847 directed the sheriff to exercise reasonable care for the preservation of the life, health, and welfare of those committed to his care. He was and is authorized to transport prisoners to other counties for safekeeping (3 O. L. 157; 29 O. L. 112-113; 93 O. L. 131). In 1910 provision was made for the removal of the sheriff by the governor if he were proved guilty of negligence in not affording a prisoner adequate protection from mob violence (101 O. L. 109).

Although the sheriff is still regarded as the chief peace officer in the county, many of his earlier duties in this respect have been absorbed by the development of other agencies of law enforcement, notably the state highway patrol. On the other hand, the powers of the sheriff to suppress affrays, riots, and unlawful assemblies became especially important in times of strikes or threatened riots. On a properly issued warrant he may arrest any person charged with the probability of doing injury to another person or the property of another (G. C. sec. 13463). Moreover, since 1921 the sheriff has forwarded to the bureau of criminal identification all fingerprints of persons arrested for a felony (110 O. L. 5; 109 O. L. 585), and since 1913 has been authorized to arrest any prisoner violating his parole (103 O. L. 405).

As an executive agent of the court the sheriff still executes all writs, warrants, and other processes directed to him by lawful authority; he attends the court of common pleas and court of appeals during their sessions, and, when required, the probate court (29 O. L. 112, 316; 82 O. L. 26). Although the jury commission has supplanted the clerk of courts in the matter of selecting names of prospective jurors from the jury wheel, the sheriff's duties in this respect remain much as they were in the earlier years of his office.

The sheriff was and is required by law to keep a record of the business of his office. The present practice of keeping a foreign execution docket began in 1838. (36 O. L. 18; 57 O. L. 6; 84 O. L. 208-209). Since 1842 the sheriff has kept a cash book (40 O. L. 25; 65 O. L. 115; 84 O. L. 208; 86 O. L. 239), and since 1843 a jail register (41 O. L. 74). Indexes, direct and reverse, to the foreign execution docket were prescribed by the legislature in 1925 (111 O. L. 31). Since 1843 he has been required annually to submit the jail register, in certified copies, to the clerk of courts, the county auditor, and the secretary of state (41 O. L. 74). Since 1850 he has been required, on the first day of September in each year, to submit to the county commissioners a certified statement of all fines and costs collected during the year and the amount of fees collected and paid to the clerk of courts of common pleas (G. C. Sec, 2504; 48 O. L. 66).

The sheriff's records are public property and open to the inspection of the public. They are transferred, together with all effects appertaining to the office, to his successor.

All records are located in the sheriff's office unless otherwise indicated.

Dockets and Court Orders

328. FOREIGN SUMMONS DOCKET

1878—. 3 volumes. (1-3). Prior records missing.

Sheriff's record of summonses issued by courts other than Washington County on residents of Washington County, showing what county, what court, names of litigants, case number, name of attorney, date writ received, date served, dates returned, copy of sheriff's costs and fee bills, and copy of sheriff's return on writ. Chronologically arranged by dates received. Alphabetically indexed by names of plaintiffs. Handwritten on printed forms. Average 460 pages. 16 x 11 x 2.5.

329. FOREIGN EXECUTION DOCKET

1842—. 7 volumes. (2 volumes, 1842-1860, unnumbered; 1-5).

Record of executions ordered by courts other than Washington County courts on property located in Washington County to satisfy judgments rendered, showing names of litigants, from what court, execution number, case number, date writ received, date returnable, name of attorney, copy of order of sale, itemized cost bill, and record of sheriff's sale. Chronologically arranged by dates writs received. 1842-1852, no index; 1852-1884, alphabetically indexed by names of plaintiffs; 1885—, alphabetically indexed, direct, by names of plaintiffs, and reverse, by names of defendants. Handwritten on printed forms. 1842-1852, 1 volume 300 pages. 14 x 10 x 1.5; 1853—, 6 volumes. Average 440 pages. 16 x 11 x 2.25.

330. PARTITION RECORD

1871—. 3 volumes. (1-3).

Sheriff's record of sale of real estate in partition proceedings showing execution docket and page numbers, names of litigants, date order of appraisement and sale filed, record of sale of property, record of distribution of proceeds of sale with distributees, and copy of sheriff's cost and fees. Chronologically arranged by dates of orders to sell. Alphabetically indexed by names of plaintiffs. Handwritten. Average 440 pages. 16 x 11 x 2.5.

331. DESK BLOTTER

1935—. 1 volume. Record initiated 1935.

Record of complaints reported and filed with sheriff's department showing date, name of complainant or person reporting, nature of complaint and date on same, and report of officer investigating complaint or report. Chronologically arranged by dates of filing. No index. Handwritten. 599 pages. 16 x 11 x 3.5.

332. LEDGER, COMMON PLEAS COURT

1901-1925. 3 volumes. Discontinued.

Sheriff's record of writs received, served, and returned, showing date received, names of litigants, kind of writ or writs, date served and returned, and fee. Chronologically arranged by dates of writs. Alphabetically indexed by names of plaintiffs. Handwritten. Average 470 pages. 14 x 9 x 2.5.

333. REGISTER FOR THE INSANE

1890—. 1 volume.

Sheriff's register of insane persons conveyed to state institution showing commitment number, name of person, place of nativity, date of commitment, date discharged, by what authority, what institution committed to, number of days in county jail, and sheriff's fees. Chronologically arranged by dates committed. No index. Handwritten on printed forms. 310 pages. 16 x 11 x 1.75.

334. RECORD OF LEGAL NOTICES

1883—. 6 volumes. Prior records missing.

Clipped copies of legal notices and advertisements showing what newspaper, names of litigants, title of case or purpose of notice, contents of advertisements and notices, sale of property on foreclosure and partition proceedings, all execution orders on sale of property; also record of sale showing to whom sold, amount of sale, and sheriff's costs and fees. Chronologically arranged by dates of entries. No index. Advertisements printed; records of sales handwritten. Average 180 pages. 13 x 8.5 x 1.5.

Jail Records

335. JAIL REGISTER

1860—. 7 volumes. Prior records missing.

Register of commitments to county jail showing commitment number, name of prisoner, nativity, offense, date of commitment, date of discharge, by whose authority committed, number of days in jail, number of days in dungeon, and sheriff's fees. Chronologically arranged by dates of commitments. No index. Handwritten on printed forms. Average 390 pages. 18 x 12 x 2.25.

336. REPORTS, BOARDING PRISONERS

1887—. 3 file boxes.

Record copies of monthly reports by sheriff to county commissioners on cost of feeding prisoners confined in county jail, showing date of reports, number of meals served for period of report, cost per meal, and number of prisoners confined in jail for period of report. Chronologically arranged by dates of reports. No index. Handwritten on printed forms. 8 x 8 x 16.

For commissioners copies, see entry 6.

337. SHERIFF'S CASH BOOK

1869—. 6 volumes. (1-6). Prior records missing.

Sheriff's record of cash receipts and disbursements showing date received, case number, names of litigants, nature of suit, amount, manner of payment, to whom paid, date paid out, and amount. Chronologically arranged by dates of entries. Alphabetically indexed by names of debtors. Handwritten on printed forms. Average 290 pages. 16 x 11 x 1.75.

338. RECORD OF ACCRUED FEES

1907—. 6 volumes.

Sheriff's record of fees accrued showing date accrued, case number, in what matter, to whom charged, total fee in civil and in criminal cases, also amount due for county and foreign writs, from probate and juvenile cases, and from sundries, and date of payment. Chronologically arranged by dates accrued. Alphabetically indexed by names of debtors. Handwritten on printed forms. Average 320 pages. 18 x 14 x 1.75.

339. RECORD OF PAYMENTS INTO COUNTY TREASURY

1907-1909. 1 volume. Discontinued.

Sheriff's record of payments of cost and fees into county treasury, showing dates, names of litigants, title of case or service rendered, amount, and volume and page numbers of Sheriff's Cash Book, entry 337. Chronologically arranged by dates of entries. No index. Handwritten on printed forms. 210 pages. 14 x 9 x 1.25.

340. RECEIPT BOOK

1861—. 4 volumes, Prior records missing.

Receipts to sheriff by payees on settlement of judgments, executions, and foreclosures, showing names of litigants, style of case, date, name of sheriff, amount of settlement, and signature of payee. Chronologically arranged by dates of entries. No index. Handwritten on printed forms. Average 400 pages. 18 x 12 x 3.

Miscellaneous

341. WANTED FILE

Current. 3 file drawers.

Description of suspects wanted by federal bureau of investigation, police and sheriff's departments, showing name and aliases of suspect, physical description with fingerprint classification if on file, date, place, and description of crime committed. As the suspects are apprehended, the cards are removed from the files. Alphabetically arranged by names of suspects. No index. Typed on printed forms. 5 x 8 x 8.

342. RECORD OF ESCAPES

Current. 1 file drawer.

Description of convicts who have escaped from penal institutions showing name and aliases of convict, date of escape, from what institution, what crime, description of prisoner with fingerprint classifications, and nativity of convict. As convicts are apprehended, the cards are removed from the file. Alphabetically arranged by names of convicts. No index. Typed on printed forms. 5 x 8 x 18.

343. REPORTS, FINES AND FEES

1861—. 9 bundles and 2 file boxes.

Record copies of sheriff's reports to county commissioners of fines and fees collected showing date of report, name of payer, in what matter, amount of fine, amount of cost, total collected, and date reported to clerk of courts. Chronologically arranged by dates of reports. No index. Handwritten on printed forms. Bundles, 3 x 3.5 x 8; file boxes, 8 x 8 x 16. 9 bundles, 1861-1899, Storeroom 3; 2 file boxes, 1900—, Sheriff's office.

344. ATLAS OF WASHINGTON COUNTY

1875. 1 volume.

Political maps of county showing townships, highways, streams, railroads, cities, towns and villages, section lines, and range lines and numbers; maps of each township of the county showing section and range lines, boundary lines of land tracts, with names of owners of each tract, roads, streams, and towns and villages; plat map of towns and villages showing boundary lines of community and corporation, lot boundary lines, streets and alleys, lot numbers, street names, and location of public buildings; also county directory giving summary of industrial pursuits of each township and town with short biography of prominent citizens. From surveys by D. J. Lake, county engineer. Published by Titus, Simmons, and Titus, 31 South Street, Philadelphia, Pennsylvania. Alphabetically arranged by names of townships and towns. Alphabetical table of contents. Printed, engraved, and lithographed. Scales vary. 93 pages. 16 x 14 x 1.

The office of county treasurer was established by an act of the Northwest Territory in 1792 and continued by the state of Ohio (Pease, *op. cit.,* 68-69). Although the constitution of 1802 made no provision for the office of county treasurer, it was created by the legislative act of 1803 (1 O. L. 98). The treasurer, appointed by the associate judges in 1803 and by the county commissioners in 1804, was required to take an oath and give bond for the faithful performance of the duties of his office, and was subject to removal by the appointing power (1 O. L. 98; 2 O. L. 154). The treasurer remained an appointive official until 1827 when the office became an elective one by popular vote in the county (25 O. L. 25-32). Although it did not specifically create the office the constitution of 1851 stated that no person shall hold the office of treasurer for more than four years in any six (*Ohio Const. 1851,* Art. X, sec. 3). This provision was repealed in 1933 by an amendment authorizing any county to adopt a charter form of government. Interpreting the constitutional provision the legislature fixed the term of office at two years in 1859 (65 O. L. 105). The term of office continued at two years until 1935 when it was extended to four years (116 O. L. pt. ii, 1st s. sess, H. 603). Until 1906 the county treasurer received his remuneration from fees; since that date his salary has been determined by law according to the population of the county.

The duties of the treasurer were defined by statute in the earlier period and specified in detail by the acts of 1827 and 1831 repealing previous acts. The provisions of the latter act, although subject to amendment and repeal, furnished the basis for subsequent legislation and laid the basis for present duties of the treasurer, which do not differ greatly from those prescribed by the earlier statutes.

In 1803 the treasurer was given his present duty of giving public notice of the tax duplicate. On receiving from the county auditor a duplicate of the taxes assessed upon the property of the county, the treasurer prepares and post notices in three places in each township including the place in which elections are held; and inserts the notice for six consecutive weeks in the newspaper having the greatest circulation in the county (1 O. L. 98; 29 O. L. 29; 52 O. L. 124). He receives money and payment of taxes levied for the county, for the state, and for other purposes, and gives the payer a receipt (G. C. sec. 2650; 29 O. L. 292; 76 O. L. 71; 85 O. L. 327). In the earlier years of the office the treasurer was required to give announcement of the time he would be in the respective townships of the county and in his office at the seat of justice to receive tax collections. Since 1858 the treasurer has been authorized to prescribe the semiannual payment of taxes or assessments levied upon real estate or upon delinquent real estate taxes or assignments (55 O. L. 62; 55 O.

L. 101). Moreover, since 1908, the commissioners have been authorized to extend the time of paying taxes for not more than thirty days after the time fixed by law (99 O. L. 435; 114 O. L. 730; 115 O. L. pt. ii, 226).

After each semiannual collection of taxes, the treasurer is required to report to the auditor showing the amount of taxes received in each taxing district in the county since the last settlement. Since 1904 the semiannual settlements have been made under the heads of liquor, cigarette, inheritance, delinquent personal, road, and general taxes. The treasurer keeps his accounts in books which enable him to compile such reports. (G. C. sec. 2643; 29 O. L. 296; 97 O. L. 458).

After the taxes are collected and immediately after each settlement with the county auditor, the county treasurer, upon the presentation of the proper warrant from the auditor, pays to the township treasurer, city or village treasurer, the treasurer of school district, or treasurer of any "legally constituted board authorized by law to receive the funds or proceeds of any special tax levy," or other officer delegated with authority to receive such funds, all money in the county belonging to such boards and subdivisions. (G. C. sec. 2689; R. S. 1122; 56 O. L. 101). In addition, after the treasurer has made each settlement with the county auditor, he is required to pay to the state treasurer, on warrant from the state auditor, "the full amount of all sums" found by the latter to belong to the state (56 O. L. 101; 114 O. L. 732).

Another function of the county treasurer, which had its inception in the earlier years of the office, is the collection of delinquent taxes. It was and is his duty to assess a penalty on the tax duplicate for nonpayment of taxes – which penalty when collected, is paid to the treasurer's fund. If the treasurer is unable to collect the delinquent taxes, he is authorized to apply to the clerk of court of common pleas who serves notice to show cause why such taxes were not paid. The court may enter a rule against the delinquent taxpayer for the payment and cost and enforce it by attachment. (G. C. sec. 2660; 56 O. L. 175; 99 O. L. 435).

During the last decade provision has been made whereby delinquent taxes, assessment, and penalties charged on the tax duplicate against any entry of real estate maybe paid in installments during the five consecutive semiannual taxpaying periods, "whether such real estate has been certified as delinquent or not" (G. C. sec. 2672; 114 O. L. 827). The Wittemore Act, passed as an emergency measure in 1933, provided for the collection by installments, without interest or penalty, of delinquent real estate taxes and assessments, personal property, and classified property taxes. Anyone electing to pay such delinquent real property taxes and assessments in installments pursuant to this act may, at any installment period, pay the entire unpaid balance of the principal sum of such delinquent taxes and assessments, in which event no interest shall be charged or collected on the amount so paid. (115 O. L. 161-164; 116 O. L. pt. ii, 14-21; 116 O. L. 261-267). In some counties more populous than Washington the treasurer maintains a separate bureau for the collection of delinquent taxes.

The county treasurer has charge by the funds collected by taxes, and also other funds belonging to the county. Although other acts made provision for storage vaults in the county treasury for county deposits, the commissioners have been authorized, since 1894, to receive sealed bids for deposits of county funds; and the banks of trust companies offering the highest rates of interest are selected as the county depositories. (91 O. L. 403; 102 O. L. 60; 115 O. L. pt. ii, 215).

The treasurer is required to keep an account current with the county auditor – a practice which originated in 1831. Each day the treasurer makes a statement to the county auditor for the previous day's business showing amount of taxes received on auditor's drafts, the amount received from other sources, together with the amount of money deposited in the depository, the total amount paid out by check and by cash, and the balance in the treasury. (G. C. sec. 2642; 97 O. L. 458).

The treasurer, as well as the sheriff, prosecuting attorney, and clerk of courts, is required to report annually to the county commissioners (G. C. sec. 2504). Since 1874 the county auditor and county commissioners have been required to make a thorough examination of all books, vouchers, accounts, moneys, bonds, securities, and other property in the treasury at least every six months (G. C. sec. 2699; R. S. 1129; 71 O. L. 137). Besides being under the supervision of the county commissioners and county auditor, the treasurer is subject to the supervision of the state auditor. In 1902 an act was passed providing for a uniform system of accounting and auditing for all public offices in the state, under the direction of a bureau of inspection in the office of the state auditor, and for the annual examination of the finances of all public offices. (G. C. sec. 2641; 114 O. L. 728; R. S. 1084).

The treasurer is a member of the budget commission, the county board of revision, and serves as a trustee of the sinking fund (G. C. sec. 5625-19; G. C. sec. 5580; see also pp. 204, 207, and 208). Since the inception of the office the treasurer has been the official custodian of the bonds furnished to the state by the county auditor, county commissioners, and county sheriff. Since 1869 he has been required to record and preserve a record of the deputies appointed and removed by the county auditor (G. C. sec. 2563; 66 O. L. 35).

Like other county officials, the treasurer is required at the expiration of his term to turn over to his successor all books, papers, moneys, and records appertaining to his office (G. C. sec. 2693).

Tax Records
(See also entries 396, 398-448)

Tax Duplicates

345. TREASURER'S TAX DUPLICATE

1825—. 302 volumes. No prior records.

Duplicate of annual, 1825-1858, and semiannual, 1859—, taxes assessed, showing tax district, name of landowner, range, township, section, and lot numbers, acreage, description of tract, number of acres taxed, valuation of land and buildings, amount of tax, amount of delinquencies and penalties, and total due. Contains Personal Duplicates, 1825-1881, entry 347. Alphabetically arranged by names of tax districts and alphabetically thereunder by names of property owners. No index. 1825-1909, handwritten on printed forms; 1910—, typed. Average 400 pages. 18 x 12.5 x 2.5. Auditor's office.

346. DUPLICATE ASSESSMENTS

1897—. 3 volumes. 1902-1927, missing.

Duplicate of special assessments for public improvements such as street paving, sidewalks, improved highways, and sewers, showing what improvement, tax district, name of property owner, range, township, and section numbers, acreage, lot number, description of tract, feet frontage, property value, amount of assessments, amount of annual installments, delinquencies, and total due. Alphabetically arranged by names of tax districts, thereunder by names of improvement projects, and thereunder by names of property owners. No index. 1897-1901, handwritten; 1928—, typed. 500 pages. 17 x 14 x 2.5. Treasurer's office.

347. PERSONAL DUPLICATE

1898-1916. 38 volumes. 1825-1881 in Treasurer's Tax Duplicate, entry 345; 1917-1931, missing.

Duplicate of taxes assessed on personal or chattel property showing name of tax district, name of owner, property value, amount of tax, delinquencies, penalties, and total due. Alphabetically arranged by names of tax districts and alphabetically thereunder by names of property owners. No index. Handwritten on printed forms. Average 480 pages. 18 x 12 x 2.25. Storeroom 3.

For subsequent records, see entry 348.

348. TREASURER'S GENERAL PERSONAL TAX DUPLICATE

1932—. 6 volumes.

Record showing assessment certificate number, tax district, tax rate, name of taxpayer, address, property value, total tax assessed, amount of advance payment, balance due, and delinquency. Alphabetically arranged by names of tax districts and alphabetically thereunder by names of taxpayers. No index. Typed on printed forms. Average 300 pages. 16 x 16 x 2.5. Storeroom 3.

For prior records, see entry 347.

349. TREASURER'S CLASSIFIED DUPLICATE

1932—. 6 volumes,

Record showing tax district, assessment certificate number, name of taxpayer, address, value of unproductive investments, and tax assessed; also deposits and tax assessed, credits and tax assessed, moneys and other intangibles and tax assessed, total tax assessed, amount of advanced payments, balance due, and taxes unpaid. Alphabetically arranged by names of tax districts and alphabetically thereunder by names of taxpayers. No index. Typed on printed forms. Average 250 pages. 14 x 18 x 1.25. Treasurer's office.

350. TREASURER'S LIQUOR TRAFFIC TAX DUPLICATE

1886-1919. 4 volumes. Discontinued.

Liquor tax duplicate showing year, name of licensee, location of business, name of owner of real estate, description of real estate, amount delinquent, date commencing business, amount of assessed, amount due June 20, amount to be accounted for after June settlement, and date payment made. Chronologically arranged by years and alphabetically thereunder by names of licensees. No index. Handwritten on printed forms. Average 152 pages. 18 x 14 x 1. Three volumes, 1886-1915, Storeroom 3; 1 volume, 1916-1919, Treasurer's office.

351. TREASURER'S CIGARETTE TRAFFIC TAX DUPLICATE
1903—. 3 volumes.

Duplicate of cigarette traffic tax assessment showing name of licensee, business address, name of owner of real estate, description of real estate, date license issued, date assessment paid, and amount of tax. Chronologically arranged by years and chronologically thereunder by dates licenses issued. No index. Handwritten on printed forms. Average 180 pages. 18 x 14 x 1. 1 volume, 1903-1915, Storeroom 3; 2 volumes, 1916—, Treasurer's office.

352. ADDITIONS AND DEDUCTIONS DUPLICATE
1909—. 4 volumes.

Record of additions to or deductions from the regular tax duplicate by reason of omissions on previous duplicate, new buildings, improvements, buildings destroyed, or revision by board of equalization, showing tax district, year, name of property owner, range, township, section, and lots of numbers, reason for revision, acreage, value, and amount of addition or deduction. Alphabetically arranged by names of tax districts and alphabetically thereunder by names the taxpayers. No index. Handwritten on printed forms. Average 480 pages. 18 x 16 x 2.5. Treasurer's office.

For auditor's record of additions and deductions, see entries 429-432.

Delinquent Taxes

353. TAX LIST, DELINQUENT PERSONAL
1898—. 11 volumes.

Tax list of delinquent personal tax showing tax district, name of taxpayer, address, property value, amount of tax assessed, years delinquent, total delinquencies and penalties, and total amount due. Alphabetically arranged by names of tax districts and alphabetically thereunder by names of taxpayers. No index. 1898-1921; handwritten; 1922—, typed. Average 420 pages. 17 x 11 x 2.25. Treasurer's office.

354. DELINQUENT RETURNS
1859—. 19 volumes. 1913-1926, missing.
Record of delinquent lands showing tax district, name of owner, range, township, and section numbers, acreage, lot number, description of tract, number of acres taxed, value, taxes and penalties due, and treasurer's reason or not collecting. Alphabetically arranged by names of tax districts and alphabetically thereunder by names of owners. No index. Handwritten on printed forms. Average 700 pages. 18 x 12 x 3.5. 16 volumes, 1859-1912, Storeroom 3; 3 volumes, 1927—, Treasurer's office.

Tax Collections and Receipts

355. RECORD OF TAX COLLECTIONS
1904—. 34 volumes.
Record showing tax district, date of collection, name of taxpayer, receipt number, dog tax, road tax, special assessments, all other tax collections, and total collected. Contains Personal and Classified Tax Payment Record, 1904-1931 entry 356. Alphabetically arranged by names of tax districts and alphabetically thereunder by names of taxpayers. No index. Handwritten on printed forms. Average 540 pages. 18 x 11.5 x 2.75. Treasurer's office.

356. PERSONAL AND CLASSIFIED TAX PAYMENT RECORD
1932—. 12 file boxes. 1904-1931 in Record of Tax Collections, entry 355.
Personal and classified assessment certificate stubs showing certificate number, year, name of taxpayer, address, property value, amount of tax, amount of advanced payment, balance due, and date paid. Chronologically arranged by dates paid. No index. Typed on printed forms. 7 x 9 x 24. Treasurer's office.

357. RECORD OF INSTALLMENT PAYMENTS (Whittemore Plan)
1932-1937. 2 volumes. Discontinued.
Record of undertakings by county treasurer to collect delinquent real taxes in six or ten annual installments showing tax district, name of taxpayer, description and location of real estate, property value, total amount delinquent, amount of each annual installment, and record of payments. Alphabetically arranged by names of tax districts and chronologically thereunder by dates of entries. No index. Typed on printed form. Average 520 pages. 18 x 14 x 2.25. Treasurer's office.

358. LIQUOR ASSESSMENT RECEIPT STUBS
1918-1919. 1 volume.
Receipt stubs showing date, from whom received, amount, business address, and name of dispenser. Numerically arranged by stub numbers. No index. Handwritten on printed forms. 19 x 9 x .75. Treasurer's office, vault.

359. TAX RECEIPTS [STUBS]
1898—. 566 volumes and 53 file boxes. 1917-1928, missing.
Receipt stubs of taxes paid showing consecutive receipt number, name of taxpayer, tax district, date paid, and amount paid. Alphabetically arranged by names of tax districts and alphabetically thereunder by names of taxpayers. No index. Handwritten on printed forms. Volumes average 80 pages. 16 x 11 x .5; file boxes, 5 x 6 x 20. 566 volumes, 1898-1916, Storeroom 3; 53 file boxes, 1929—, Treasurer's office.

Tax Stamps

360. INVENTORY AND SALE RECORD, SALES TAX STAMPS
1935—. 5 volumes.
Daily inventory of record of sales tax stamps showing number on hand, number received, and numbers sold of each denomination; also record of sales showing dates, name of vendor, license number, number of each denomination sold, total amount of sale less vendor discount, and total collected. Chronologically arranged by dates of entries. No index. Handwritten on printed forms. Average 540 pages. 14 x 12 x 2.75. Treasurer's office.

361. RECORD OF BEVERAGE AND MALT DEALERS
1933-1936. 2 volumes. Discontinued.
Record of sales of beverage and malt excise stamps and bottle caps, showing name of dealer, address, kind of business, date, number of stamps sold, and date of license. Chronologically arranged by dates of licenses and sales. No index. Handwritten on printed forms. Average 390 pages. 11 x 14 x 2. Treasurer's office.

362. COSMETIC LICENSE TAX AND STAMP SALES
1933-1934. 1 volume. Discontinued.

Record showing name of licensee, address, kind of business, date of license, and license fee; also record of excise stamps showing date of sale, number, and denomination. Chronologically arranged by dates of licenses and sales. No index. Handwritten on printed forms. 370 pages. 12 x 14 x 2. Treasurer's office.

Inheritance Taxes (See also entries 279-281)

363. TREASURER'S INHERITANCE TAX CHARGES
1932—. 1 volume.

Record showing date certified, name of decedent, to whom charged, value of estate, amount taxable, amount of tax assessed, tax district, and date paid. Chronologically arranged by date certified. No index. Typed. 300 pages. 12 x 12 x 1.5. Treasurer's office.

364. COLLATERAL INHERITANCE TAX DUPLICATE
1915-1920. 1 volume.

Records showing tax district, name of decedent, names of heirs to estate, date certified, amount of estate, amount taxable, amount of tax, and date paid. Chronologically arranged by dates certified. No index. Handwritten on printed forms. 220 pages. 14 x 16 x 1.25. Treasurer's office.

365. INHERITANCE TAX RECEIPTS
1899—. 2 volumes. 1925-1930, missing.

Receipt stubs of collateral inheritance tax payments showing receipt number, date, amount of tax, by whom paid, and name of decedent. Numerically arranged by consecutive receipt numbers. No index. Handwritten on printed forms. Average 240 pages. 9 x 8 x 1.25. Treasurer's office.

366. PAY-IN ORDERS
1931. 3 volumes. Prior records missing.

Record of orders issued by the auditor for money to be paid into the county treasury by the executor or administrator of estate of the decedent to be placed to the credit of the undivided inheritance tax fund, showing names of executor and decedent, amount of tax as fixed by court, discount allowed, amount collected, and names of township and county treasurer. Chronologically arranged by dates of filing. No index. Typed on printed forms. Average 300 pages. 10 x 5 x 1.5. Treasurer's office, vault.

Business Administration of Office

Ledgers and Cash Books

367. (Fund) LEDGER
1862-1868. 3 volumes.

Treasurer's fund ledger showing date, amount, and source of cash receipts credited to each fund; also debit to each fund showing date, for what, and amount; also balance to each fund each thirty day period. Chronologically arranged by dates of entries. No index. Handwritten on printed forms. Average 350 pages. 14 x 9 x 1.5. Storeroom 3.

368. (Collection) LEDGER
1875—. 11 volumes. 5 unnumbered, 1-6).

Treasurer's record of collections debited to county treasurer and credited to account of each tax district, showing each tax collection and settlement period. Chronologically arranged by semiannual settlement periods (August and February). Alphabetically indexed by names that tax districts. Handwritten on printed forms. Average 500 pages. 18 x 12 x 3. 5 volumes, 1875-1904 , Storeroom 3; 6 volumes, 1904—, Treasurer's office.

369. RECEIPTS AND DISBURSEMENTS
1920—. 1 volume.

Record of receipts of pay-in orders from depository general tax, cigarette tax, inheritance tax; showing date, total receipts, and balance in treasury, total disbursements, general warrants, court warrants, receipts and deposits, drafts, balance in depository, and total balance in treasury and depositories. Numerically arranged by dates of entries. No index. Handwritten on printed forms. 450 pages. 18 x 12.5 x 21. Treasurer's office vault.

370. APPORTIONMENT RECORD

1871—. 5 volumes. 1903-1925, missing.

Record of cash receipts and credit to each fund and each tax district, showing name of tax or school district, date of settlement with tax or school district, itemized account of cash receipts, total amount credited to district, and auditors order number on county treasurer with semiannual settlement with districts. Chronologically arranged by dates of settlements. No index. Handwritten on printed forms. Average 320 pages. 15 x 10 x .5. 3 volumes, 1871-1920, Storeroom 3; 2 volumes, 1926—, Treasurer's office.

371. JOURNAL

1869-1908. 9 volumes.

Treasurer's daily record of cash receipts and disbursements showing cash received, date, pay-in order number, and amount; sundry receipts showing from what source, amount of tax collections, and total each month; also expenditures showing dates, warrant or order number, amount paid out, and total for month. Chronologically arranged by dates received or paid out. No index. Handwritten on printed forms. Average 500 pages. 14 x 10 x 2. Storeroom 3.

For subsequent records, see entry 372.

372. TREASURER'S DAILY BALANCE

1904—. 8 volumes.

Treasurer's daily record of itemized cash receipts from all sources, disbursements classified, total receipts, total disbursements, and balance. Chronologically arranged by daily entries. No index. Handwritten on printed forms. Average 380 pages. 17 x 12 x 2. Treasurer's office.

For prior records, see entry 371.

373. DAY BOOK

1850-1895. 8 volumes. No prior or subsequent records.

Treasurer's daily record of cash receipts showing date, source of receipts, amount of each item, and daily total. Chronologically arranged by consecutive dates. No index. Handwritten on printed forms. Average 380 pages. 14 x 9 x 2. Storeroom 2.

Vouchers and Warrants

374. RECORD OF ORDERS REDEEMED
1809-August 1904. 17 volumes.

Record of orders redeemed showing, 1809-1826, date redeemed, name of payee, order number, and amount; 1827-1904, date redeemed, order number, name of payee, what fund, for what, and amount. Chronologically arranged by dates paid. No index. Handwritten on printed forms. 1 volume, 1809-1926, 300 pages. 16 x 7 x 2.25; 1827-1904, average 430 pages. 16 x 11 x 2.25. Storeroom 3.

For subsequent records, see entry 375.

375. TREASURER'S JOURNAL OF WARRANTS REDEEMED AND PAYMENTS INTO TREASURY
September 1904—. 16 volumes. (1-16).

Treasurer's record of auditor's warrants redeemed showing date, name of payee, for what, warrant number, credit to treasurer, and debit to what fund; record of payments into treasury showing date, name of payee, for what, pay-in order number, debit to treasurer, and credit to what fund. Chronologically arranged by dates entered. No index. Handwritten on printed forms. Average 480 pages. 18 x 12 x 2.5. Treasurer's office.

For prior records, see entry 374.

376. TREASURER'S RECORD OF COURT WARRANTS REDEEMED
1904—. 2 volumes.

Records showing date, name, warrant number, and purpose, such as paying petit jurors, grand jurors, grand jury witnesses, criminal case witnesses, lunacy, minor, and coroner's court witnesses. Chronologically arranged by dates of entries and numerically thereunder by warrant numbers. No index. Handwritten on printed forms. Average 400 pages. 18 x 13 x 2. Treasurer's office, vault.

377. RECORD OF AUDITOR'S WARRANTS (Pay-in)
July 1858-December 1896. 9 volumes. Subsequent records missing.

Treasurer's record of auditor's pay-in warrants showing warrant number, date of warrant, name of payer, for what, amount of warrant, and date filed. Chronologically arranged by dates paid in. No index. Handwritten on printed forms. Average 340 pages. 12 x 8 x 1.5. Storeroom 3.

378. VOUCHERS PAID
1803-1820. 9 bundles.

Vouchers issued by county commissioners for payment from county funds of bills and claims, showing date, name of payee, for what, amount and date paid; vouchers issued by clerk of courts and approved by judges of common pleas court for payment of witnesses and juror fees, showing date, name of payee, for what service, amount, and date paid. Chronologically arranged by dates paid. No index. Handwritten. 5 x 3 x 7. Treasurer's office, vault.

Bonds

Official Bonds (See also entries 171, 524-527)

379. RECORD OF BONDS (Official)
1834—. 2 volumes.

Record copies of bonds filed by elected county officials showing date of bond, name of principal, to what office, names of sureties, amount of bond, and date filed; also record copies of licensed auctioneers' bonds showing date of bond, name of principal, names of sureties, amount of bond, and date filed. Contains [Treasury Examiner's Report], 1874, entry 309. Chronologically arranged by dates of filing. No index. Handwritten. Average 450 pages. 15 x 10 x 2. 1 volume, 1834-1910, Storeroom 3; 1 volume, 1911—, Treasurer's office.

380. RECORD OF ADDITIONAL BOND, COUNTY RECORDER
1896. 1 volume.

Record copy of additional surety bond filed by county recorder under provision of an act by general assembly passed in 1896, which act required recorders to register land titles. Copy shows name of principal, names of sureties, amount of additional bond, date of bond, date approved by judge of common pleas court, and date filed with county treasurer. Chronologically arranged by dates of filing. Alphabetically indexed by names of principles. Handwritten on printed forms. 100 pages. 18 x 12 x .75. Storeroom 3.

381. TOWNSHIP CLERK, BOND RECORD
1923—. 2 volumes.
Record copies of surety bonds filed by township clerks showing name of official, names of sureties, amount of bond, date of bond, dates approved by township trustees, date recorded, and copy of clerk's oath. Chronologically arranged by dates of filing. Alphabetically indexed by names of officials. Handwritten on printed forms. Average 300 pages. 16 x 11 x 1.5. Treasurer's office.

Debenture Bonds (She also entries 23, 24, 528-537)

382. EMERGENCY AND CASUALTY BRIDGE BONDS
1913-1920. 1 volume. Discontinued.
Record showing sales of bridge bonds giving number of bond, amount of bond, date of sale, when and where payable, by whom purchased, place of residence, when and by whom payable, rate of interest. Chronologically arranged by dates of sales and numerically thereunder by bond numbers. No index. Handwritten on printed forms. 50 pages. 18 x 12 x .5. Treasurer's office.

Reports

383. SEMIANNUAL STATEMENT OF TREASURER
1871-1881. 1 volume. No prior or subsequent records.
Copy of semiannual statement by county treasurer to county commissioners showing date, receipts into various funds, amounts transferred from one fund to another, balance on hand at beginning of period, amounts of orders redeemed, amounts of treasurer's fees, amount paid to state treasurer, total disbursements, amounts of overdraft, and balance of each fund. Commissioners' copies of these reports not located. Chronologically arranged by semiannual dates. No index. Handwritten on printed forms. 280 pages. 18 x 12 x 1.75. Storeroom 3.

384. FINANCIAL REPORT
1857—. 5 volumes.
Treasurer's record copy of detailed annual report to county commissioners showing total receipts from tax collections and total receipts from all other sources; also detailed account of expenditures showing amount expended from each fund and department and recapitalization showing balance or deficit of each fund.

Chronologically arranged by years and alphabetically thereunder by names of funds or departments. No index. Handwritten on printed forms. Average 750 pages. 14 x 17 x 4. 4 volumes, 1857-1927, Storeroom 2; 1 volume, 1928—, Treasurer's office.

For Commissioners' copies, see entry 6.

385. TREASURER'S ACCOUNTS

1831—. 2 bundles and 1 file box.

Record of annual examination of treasurer's accounts by county auditor showing itemized account of amount debited treasurer from all sources, itemized account of payments to auditor's order crediting treasurer, and balance. Chronologically arranged by years. No index. Handwritten on printed forms. Bundles, 4 x 3.5 x 8; file box, 5 x 6 x 20. 2 bundles, 1831-1911, Storeroom 3; 1 file box, 1912—. Treasurer's office.

386. DEPOSITORY BIDS

1925—. 1 file box. Prior records missing.

Original bids submitted by banking institutions for deposits of county funds showing name of bank, date, amount of interest on active funds, amount of interest on inactive funds, and date filed. Chronologically arranged by dates of filing. No index. Typed on printed forms. 5 x 6 x 20. Treasurer's office.

387. [TREASURER'S FUND ACCOUNT]

1787-1825. In Road Record (First series), entry 679.

Copy of treasurer's annual statement of fund account showing amount collected and credited to each fund and itemized account of annual expenditures of each fund.

388. TREASURER'S LEDGER

1910—. 22 volumes. Prior records missing. Title varies: 1910-1935, Transfer Ledger.

Record of transfer of county funds by the auditor from one fund to another showing what fund, to what fund, and amount transferred. Alphabetically arranged under tabs by names of funds and chronologically thereunder by dates of entries. Handwritten on printed forms. 21 volumes, average 400 pages. 14 x 9.5 x 2; 1 volume, 300 pages. 18 x 19 x 2.5. 21 volumes, 1919-1935, Store room 3; 1 volume, 1936—, Treasurer's office, vault.

The first Ohio constitution, in 1802, did not provide for the office of a county auditor and it was not until 1820 that the general assembly by joint resolution appointed an auditor in each county for a one-year term (18 O. L. 70). In 1821 the office became elective and the term was fixed at one year (19 O. L. 116). In 1831 the term was set at two years, in 1877 at three years, in 1906 reduced to two years, and in 1919 extended to four years (29 O. L. 280; 74 O. L. 381).

The county auditor is required to take oath and give bond for faithful performance of the duties of his office; to preserve all copies of entries, surveys, extracts, and other documents transmitted to his office from the state auditor; and to transfer to his successor all books, records, maps, and other papers pertaining to his office (19 O. L. 116; R. S. 1033; G. C. secs. 2559, 2582). With the approval of the county commissioners he is authorized to appoint deputies, for whose official acts he and his sureties are held liable; a record of these appointments has been filed with the county treasurer since 1869 (55 O. L. 20; 66 O. L. 35; G. C. sec. 2563). If the office of county auditor falls vacant the county commissioners are authorized to appoint a successor (29 O. L. 280-291; 67 O. L. 103).

The first auditor in each county was required to list all lands in his county subject to taxation. From this list and one submitted to him by the county commissioners and the state auditor the county auditor was directed to make a tax duplicate to keep in a book for that purpose, and to give a copy of the list to the tax collector. (18 O. L. 70). The auditor was directed to compile from the treasurer's duplicate a list of lands on which taxes were delinquent, and if such lands were sold for taxes to grant a deed to the purchaser (18 O. L. 70; 19 O. L. 116).

Subsequent legislation expanded and itemized the duties of the auditor regarding taxation; with modifications to meet modern requirements these duties have continued much as they were doing the earlier years of his office. During the 1840s the office of county assessor was abolished and provision was made for township assessors whose duty it was made for township assessors whose duty it was to list all taxable property and make a return to the auditor (39 O. L. 22-25). Since 1874 the auditor is required by statute to keep a book in which he lists additions to and deductions from the amount of the tax assessment (71 O. L. 30). In 1915 he was made chief assessing officer of the county (106 O. L. 246).

The county auditor has served as a member and the secretary of the county budget commission since its beginning in 1911, his duties including keeping full and accurate record of the proceedings of that body. For the purpose of adjusting the tax rate and fixing the amount to be levied each year the commissioners are governed by the amount of taxable property as shown on the auditor's tax list for the current year. He submits to the commissioners the annual tax budget given by him each taxing authority of each subdivision, together with an estimate of any state levy prepared by the state auditor, and such other information as a budget commission may request or the state tax commission require. (G. C. sec. 5625-19; 112 O. L. 339).

Tax settlements had been made annually until 1859 when the auditor was required to make semiannual settlement with the treasurer to ascertain the amount of taxes the treasurer is to stand charged (G. C. sec. 2596; 56 O. L. 132; 78 O. L. 226). Since 1904 liquor, cigarette, and inheritance taxes have constituted separate funds. All other taxes are credited to the general fund. (97 O. L. 457).

Since 1831 the county auditor has kept an account current with the county treasurer showing the payments of moneys into the treasury, listing the date, by whom paid, and on what fund. On receiving the treasurer's daily statement the auditor enters on his account current the amount shown as a charge to the treasurer. (29 O. L. 280-291; 67 O. L. 103). Another important function of the county auditor is the approval before payment of bills and other claims against the county. Since 1831 he is authorized to issue, on presentation of proper voucher, all warrants on the county treasurer for moneys payable from the county treasury; and to preserve all warrants, showing the number, date of issue, amount for which drawn, in whose favor, and from what fund (G. C. sec. 2570; R. S. 1024; 29 O. L. 280-291; 67 O. L. 103). County money due the state is paid on warrant of the state auditor. Since 1904 a bill or voucher for payment from any fund controlled by the county commissioners or board of county infirmary directors is filed with the county auditor and entered in a book for that purpose at least five days before its approval for payment by the commissioners, and when approved the date is entered opposite the claim (97 O. L. 25; 108 O. L. pt. i, 272).

Besides approving bills and claims against the county, the auditor in 1835 was given the duty of certifying all moneys, except collections on the tax duplicate, into the county treasury, specifying by whom paid and the fund to which such payment is credited. Such moneys he charges to the treasurer and keeps a duplicate copy of the statement in his office. Since 1835 all costs collected in penitentiary cases which have been or are to be paid by the state have been certified into the treasury as belonging to the state. (33 O. L. 44; 67 O. L. 103).

In 1902 the legislature provided for a system of uniform accounting and auditing of all public offices, and for the annual examination of their finances, under the director of a bureau of inspection in the office of state auditor (95 O. L. 511-515). Since 1904 the county auditor is required to report to the commissioners on county finances; on the first business day of each month he prepares in duplicate a statement of the county finances for the proceeding month, compares it with the treasurer's balance, and submits it to the commissioners who post one copy of it in the auditor's office for thirty days for public inspection. (67 O. L. 13; 97 O. L. 457).

During the development of the office additional duties in great diversity have been delegated to the county auditor. Since 1833 he has been authorized to discharge prisoners jailed for nonpayment of fine or amercement due the county when in his opinion payment is not collectible G. C. sec.2576; 31 O. L. 18; 67 O. L. 103). In 1838 an act was passed making him county superintendent of schools. He was relieved of this duty in 1848 when a county superintendent of schools was authorized in each county (see p. 211). Since 1846 he has served as the sealer of weights and measures, is responsible for the preservation of copies of the original standards delivered to his office, and enforces in his county all state laws regulating weights and measures (G. C. sec. 2615; 44 O. L. 55; 58 O. L. 78; 101 O. L. 234). In 1861 he was authorized to report to the state auditor statistics concerning the deaf, dumb, blind, insane, and idiots in his county, with the names and addresses of their parents or guardians (58 O. L. 40). Eight years later, in 1869, he was authorized to report to the same officer statistics concerning livestock in his county as returned to his office by assessors, and an abstract of the funded indebtedness of his county, and of each township, city, village, and school district (G. C. sec. 2604). In 1862 he was authorized to each issue peddlers' licenses to persons who filed a statement of stock in trade in conformity with the law requiring the listing of such stock for taxation, and since 1917 he issues dog licenses (59 O. L. 67; 79 O. L. 96; 107 O. L. 535).

Since 1824 the county auditor has served as clerk to the county commissioners, his duties including keeping an accurate record of their proceedings and preserving all documents, books, records, maps, and papers which might be required to be filed in his office (G. C. sec. 2566; 22 O. L. 269). Since 1850 he has been official custodian of the reports submitted to the commissioners by the prosecuting attorney, the clerk of courts, the sheriff, and the treasurer; these reports are recorded by the auditor in books kept especially for the purpose (G. C. sec. 2504; R. S. 886; 48 O. L. 66).

The county auditor is a member of the board of revision established 1825, and serves as a trustee and the secretary of the board of the sinking fund trustees established 1919 (see pp. 206 and 208).

In recent years there has been increasing criticism of the office of county auditor. The chief complaint is the duplication of the work of the office of county treasurer, the daily registers of the two offices being similar in all respects.

Property Transfers

389. TRANSFER LISTS

1824-1837. 3 bundles. No prior records.

Auditor's record of real estate transfers showing names of grantor and grantee, date of transfer, consideration, kind of deed, original proprietor, and description of tract. Chronologically arranged by years and chronologically thereunder by dates of transfer. Handwritten 3.5 x 4 x 11. Storeroom 3.

For subsequent records, see entry 390.

390. TRANSFER RECORD

1838—. 21 volumes. (1-21).

Auditor's record of real estate transfers showing date, names of grantor and grantee, range, township, section, and lot numbers, acreage, description tract, date of transfer, and consideration. Alphabetically arranged by names of taxing district and alphabetically thereunder by names of grantors. No index. 1838-1913, 1916—, handwritten; 1914-1915, typed. Average 220 pages. 18 x 14 x 1.25. Auditor's office.

For prior records, see entry 389.

391. RECORD OF DEEDS, DELINQUENT LAND SALES

1811-1836. 3 bundles.

Record of deeds to land sold for delinquent taxes, showing name of owner, township or town, amount of delinquent tax and penalty, description of tract, value, date sold, amount sold for, cost of sale, name of purchaser, and date deed furnished. Chronologically arranged by years. No index. Handwritten. 3 x 4 x 10. Storeroom 3.

For subsequent records, see entry 392.

392. RECORD OF AUDITOR'S DEEDS

1837—. 1 volume.

Record of deeds or land sold for delinquent taxes showing tax district, name of original owner, date of sale, name of purchaser, range, township, and sectional numbers, acreage, description of tract, quantity sold, amount of sale, to whom deed was made, date of deed, and signature county auditor. Chronologically arranged by dates deeds issued. No index. Handwritten on printed forms. 530 pages. 18 x 12 x 2.75. Auditor's office.

For prior records, see entry 391.

Plats and Maps

393. PLATS

1853. 2 volumes.

Plats of lands, town lots, and buildings in the various townships in Washington County made out in conformity with an act of the general assembly of the state of Ohio, passed April 13, 1852, showing name of owner, range, township, lot, and section numbers, number of acres taxed, acreage of plow, meadow, and wood land, value of land and buildings, and description. Prepared by county surveyor. No systematic arrangement. Alphabetically indexed by names of landowners. Handwritten and hand sketched. Average 200 pages. 16 x 11 x 2.5. Auditor's office.

394. PLAT MAPS

1800, 1890, 1900, 1909, 1913. 124 volumes. (labeled by names of subdivisions).

Plat maps of tax district subdivisions of Washington County showing townships by sections, with boundary lines of sections and townships, boundary lines of land tracts with name of owner of each tract, acreage, roads, railroads and streams; also villages, towns, and city wards, showing streets, alleys, streams, railroads, lot lines, and dimensions. Prepared by county surveyor's department for county auditor's office. 1913 maps corrected to 1924. No systematic arrangement. No index. 1880, 1890, 1900, and 1909, hand sketched black and white maps; 1913, blueprints. Scales vary: 1 inch equals 100 feet to 1 inch equals 1/4 mile. 1880, 1890, 1900, 1909, average 32 pages. 20 x 23 x 1; 1913 average 14 pages. 25 x 20 x .5. Storeroom 3.

395. PLAT MAPS
1924. 26 volumes. (corrected to date).
Plat maps of tax district subdivisions showing township, special school district, corporation boundary lines, farm tract and out-let boundary lines, name of owner, and area of tract; town lot lines with lots of dimensions and lot numbers; range and section lines with range and section numbers; township, county, and state highways with their numbers; streets and alleys with names; additions, allotments, and subdivisions to corporations with name and boundary lines; also streams and railroads. Each tax district bound separately. Prepared by county surveyor's department for auditor. No systematic arrangement. No index. Blueprint. Scales vary: 1 inch equals 100 feet to 1 inch equals 80 rods. Average 40 pages. 26 x 20 x .75. Auditor's office.

Tax Records
(See also entries 345-366)

Levies, Appraisements, and Assessments

396. REQUEST FOR TAX LEVY
1828-1862. 35 bundles.
Copies of resolutions passed by trustees of the various townships of the county asking for county auditor to levy the stated amount of taxes in the township to provide necessary township funds. Chronologically arranged by dates filed. No index. Handwritten. 4 x 6 x 7. Storeroom 3.

397. GENERAL INDEX TO FILE BOXES
1882—. 1 volume.
Index to file boxes in auditor's inner office. There are a total of 234 file boxes; 9 horizontal rows, each row numbered 1-9; vertical rows, each row lettered A-Z. Index shows earliest date of record in file box and file box number. Alphabetically arranged by record titles. Typed. 200 pages. 11.5 x 10 x 1. Auditor's inner office.

398. PETITIONS
1888. 1 file box (C6).
Record of petition by directors of school districts praying for a levy on taxpayers of said district for the repair and maintenance of the district school building

showing date and names of local directors. Chronologically arranged by dates of petitions. For index, see entry 397. Handwritten. 13 x 5 x 10. Auditors inner office.

399. REAPPRAISEMENT RECORD, QUADRENNIAL
1914—. 176 volumes.
Auditor's record of quadrennial reappraisements of real estate showing tax district, name and address of owner, range, township, section, and lot numbers, acreage, land value, building value, total value, and value as revised by board of revision. Alphabetically arranged by names of tax districts and alphabetically thereunder.

400. RECORD, RAILWAY APPRAISALS
1891-1902. 1 volume.
Auditor's record of appraisal or property of Marietta, Columbus, and Cleveland Railroad Company for tax purposes as returned by the board of assessors and appraisers, showing date of appraisement and amount. Chronologically arranged by dates of returns. No index. Handwritten. 100 pages. 14 x 9 x .5. Storeroom 3.

401. MILITARY COMMUTATION ASSESSMENTS
1863-1865. 3 volumes.
Record of assessments of Washington County residents of military age, for the benefit of families of Union soldiers, showing name, township or town, amount due, penalty, total due, and total paid. Alphabetically arranged by names of residents. No index. Handwritten on printed forms. Average 110 pages. 14 x 9 x .75. Storeroom 3.

402. ASSESSMENTS, REAL PROPERTY, DECENNIAL
1870-1910. 135 volumes.
Auditor's record of tax assessments on real estate showing name of owner, tax district, description of lot or tract, land value, building value, total land and buildings, amount added or deducted by county board of equalization, and amount added or deducted by state board of equalization. Alphabetically arranged by names of tax districts and alphabetically thereunder by names of landowners. No index. Average 40 pages. 16 x 11 x 1.5. Storeroom 3.

403. AUDITOR'S SPECIAL ASSESSMENTS
1909—. 3 volumes.

Auditor's record of special assessments levied on real estate for public improvements as highways, streets, and sewers, showing name of improvement, tax district, name of owner, description of property, number of acres or foot frontage, value, amount of assessment, amount each annual installment, years delinquent, amount delinquent, and penalty. Alphabetically arranged by names of tax districts and alphabetically thereunder by names of owners. No index. 1909-1920, handwritten on printed forms; 1921—,typed on printed forms. Average 1200 pages. 16 x 11 x 6. 2 volumes, 1909-1920, Store room 3; 1 volume, 1921—, Auditor's office.

404. DUPLICATE SPECIAL ASSESSMENTS
1887-1916. 1 volume.

Duplicate of special assessments for sewer construction in city of Marietta, showing what sewer district, street, name of property owner, number and description of lot, foot frontage, amount of assessment, amount of annual installments, due date of annual installments, and date each paid. Numerically arranged by sewer district numbers and alphabetically thereunder by names of property owners. No index. Handwritten on printed forms. 330 pages. 18 x 12 x 1.75. Storeroom 3.

405. ABSTRACT OF REAL PROPERTY
1910-1914. 11 volumes. No prior records; discontinued.

Auditor's list of real estate subject to taxation showing in whose name assessed, address, tax district, description tract or lot, acreage, acreage available, meadow and uncultivated lands, acreage of oil and mineral lands, land value, building value, and total value. Alphabetically arranged by names of landowners. No index. 1910-1913, handwritten on printed forms; 1914, typed on printed forms. Average 80 pages. 18 x 14 x .5. Storeroom 3.

406. PERSONAL TAX CERTIFICATES
1932—. 32 bundles and 5 file boxes. Title varies: 1932-1934, 32 bundles, Assessment Certificates, Personal.

Certificates of assessments on personal property showing certificate number, name of taxpayer, tax district, value of property, amount of assessment, amount of advanced payment, and balance due. 1932-1934, also shows year, amount in arrears of penalty, and total due; also value of classified personal property, amount in arrears and penalty, tax due, total due, and grand total. 1932-1934, numerically arranged by certificate numbers; 1935, alphabetically arranged by names of taxing districts and numerically thereunder by certificate numbers. No index. Typed on printed forms. Bundles, 5 x 5.5 x 8.5; file boxes, 8 x 18 x 24. 32 bundles, 1932-1934, Storeroom 1; 5 file boxes, 1935—, Auditor's office.

407. JOURNAL

1910. 1 volume. No prior records; discontinued.

Record copy of minutes of meeting of board of realty assessors with list of valuations on real property what taxation purposes. Chronologically arranged by dates of meetings. No index. Handwritten. 460 pages. 14 x 10 x 2.25. Storeroom 3.

Tax Duplicates and Lists

408. TAX DUPLICATE

Dates cannot be determined but are prior to 1839, 2 volumes.

Auditor's duplicate of real property showing tax district, name of owner, range, township, section, and lot numbers, acreage in tract, acreage of meadow, plow, and wood lands, total acres taxed, land building value, and description of tract; the duplicate is entered on the left-hand pages and on the right-hand pages are the plat maps of lands showing boundary lines and area of each tract, name of owner, courses of roads, and courses of streams. Alphabetically arranged by names of tax districts. No index. Handwritten on printed forms; plat maps, hand sketched. Condition of binding, poor. Average 500 pages. 18 x 12 x 3.5. Storeroom 3.

For subsequent records, see entry 409; for other records, see entries 51 and 52.

409. TAX DUPLICATE

1839-1909. 175 volumes.

Auditor's annual, 1839-1958, and semiannual, 1859-1909, tax duplicate of real property, showing tax district, name of owner, acreage and tract, range, township, section, and lots of numbers, value of land and buildings, description of tracts; also number of acres taxed, and amount of state, county, and township road taxes, 1839-1866. Contains duplicate record of delinquent taxes and penalties, 1859-1909, plat maps in back of volume of each tax district showing boundary lines of each tract or lot with name and address of owner, roads, streets, alleys, and streams, 1870-1898; record of amount added or deducted by county board of equalization and amount added or deducted by the state board of equalization. Contains: Tax List Real Property, entry 410; Personal Tax List, entry 413. Alphabetically arranged by names of tax districts and alphabetically thereunder by names of owners. No index. Handwritten on printed forms. Average 760 pages. 18 x 12 x 3.25. Storeroom 3.

For prior records, see entry 408.

410. TAX LIST REAL PROPERTY

1910-1928. 19 bundles. 1839-1909 in Tax Duplicate, entry 409. Subsequent records destroyed at end of current tax year.

Auditor's record of tax assessments on real property showing tax district, name of owner, year, description of property, acreage, lot number, value, value as equalized by board of revision and tax commission, amount assessed, special assessments, and delinquent taxes, penalties, and total due. Contains Auditor's Tax List, Real (Property), entry 411. Alphabetically arranged by names of tax districts and alphabetically thereunder by names of owners. No index. Typed on printed forms. Average 850 pages. 17 x 14 x 4.5. Storeroom 1.

411. AUDITOR'S TAX LIST REAL (Property)

Current. 3 volumes. 1910-1928 in Tax List Real Property, entry 410. Subsequent records destroyed at end of current tax year.

Record showing tax district, name of owner, range, township, section, and lot numbers, acreage, description of tract, land and building value, and total value for taxation. Alphabetically arranged by names of tax districts and alphabetically thereunder by names of owners. No index. Typed on printed forms. Average 580 pages. 16 x 12 x 2.25. Auditor's office.

412. OMITTED TAX DUPLICATE

1887-1908. 1 volume. No prior or subsequent records.

Duplicate of taxes omitted from regular duplicate showing name of owner, tax district, years omitted, property value, amount of tax, penalty, total due, tax rate, and date paid. Alphabetically arranged by names of property owners and chronologically thereunder by years. No index. Handwritten on printed forms. 180 pages. 18 x 11 x 1. Auditor's office.

413. PERSONAL TAX LIST

1910—. 28 volumes. Title varies: 1910-1931, Personal Tax Duplicate. 1839-1909 in Tax Duplicate, entry 409.

Duplicate taxes assessed on personal property showing tax district, name and address of property owner, taxable value, amount of assessment, and amount delinquent. 1932— also shows certificate number, amount of advance payment, balance due, and date to pay. Alphabetically arranged by names of tax districts and alphabetically thereunder by names of property owners. No index. 1910-1914, handwritten on printed forms: 1915—, typed on printed forms. Average 490 pages. 18 x 13 x 2.5. 22 volumes, 1910-1931, Storeroom 3; 6 volumes, 1932—, Auditor's office.

414. AUDITOR'S CLASSIFIED TAX LIST

1932—. 3 volumes.

Record shows assessment certificate number, name and address of taxpayer, amount of productive investments, unproductive investments, credits, moneys, and other taxable intangibles, total tax for year, advance payment, tax due, date paid, and amount of unpaid taxes for year. Chronologically arranged by tax years and alphabetically thereunder by names of taxpayers. No index. Typed on printed forms. Average 500 pages. 18.5 x 17 x 2.5. Auditor's office.

415. TAX LIST, PUBLIC UTILITIES

1914-1922. 1 volume. Discontinued.

Auditor's tax list of taxable property of public utilities showing name of company, tax district, and property value. Alphabetically arranged by names of utilities. No index. Typed. 280 pages. 14 x 9 x 1.5. Storeroom 3.

416. AUDITOR'S CIGARETTE TRAFFIC TAX DUPLICATE

1903-1931. 11 volumes.

Auditor's cigarette tax assessment duplicate showing name of licensee, business address, name of owner of real estate, description of real estate, date license issued, date tax paid, and amount of tax. Chronologically arranged by years and chronologically thereunder by dates of licenses. No index. Handwritten on printed forms. Average 200 pages. 18 x 14 x 1.25. Storeroom 3.

417. AUDITOR'S LIQUOR TRAFFIC TAX DUPLICATE
1883-December 1919. 3 volumes. Discontinued.

Auditor's liquor tax assessment duplicate showing name of licensee, location of business, owner of real estate, description of real estate, amount delinquent, date commencing business, and amount assessed. Alphabetically arranged by names of licensees and chronologically thereunder by date issued. No index. Handwritten on printed forms. Average 200 pages. 18 x 14 x 1.25. Storeroom 3.

418. DUPLICATE OF TAXES ON DOGS
1878-1882. 2 volumes. No prior or subsequent records.

Auditor's duplicate tax levied on dogs showing year, tax district, name of owner, number of dogs, amount of tax, and date paid. Alphabetically arranged by names of tax districts and alphabetically thereunder by names of owners. No index. Handwritten on printed forms. Average 290 pages. 16 x 11 x 1.5. Storeroom 3.

419. COUNTY AUDITOR'S WORK SHEET
1922—. 7 bundles and 1 volume.

Record of general taxes and penalties certified delinquent showing name of owner, description of tract, range, township, section, and lot numbers, acreage, foot frontage, tax district, and valuation. Alphabetically arranged by names of tax districts and alphabetically thereunder by names of owners. No index. Typed on printed forms. Volume, 2847 pages. 13.56 x 12 x 14.5; bundles, 1,100 sheets, 13.5 x 12 x 5. 7 bundles, 1922-1934, Storeroom 1; 1 volume, 1835—, Auditor's inner office.

Tax Returns

420. MERCHANTS' CAPITAL
1811-1847. 3 bundles. Discontinued.

List of merchants in Washington County showing location (town) of business and amount of capital invested as returned by district assessors to county auditor and attested by clerk of courts. Chronologically arranged by years. No index. Handwritten. 3 x 3.5 x 8. Storeroom 3.

421. PERSONAL PROPERTY RETURNS

1922-1931. 451 binders.

Returns of personal property for taxation by individuals showing tax district, year, name and address of owner, itemized list of chattels and value of each item; also agricultural statistics by farmers, total value of chattels and credits as listed by owner, value as revised by auditor, value as revised by county board of equalization and value as revised by state tax commission. Alphabetically arranged by names of tax districts and alphabetically thereunder by names of owners. No index. Handwritten on printed forms. Average 150 pages. 14 x 9 x 1.5. to 1000 pages. 14 x 9 x 5. Storeroom 1.

For subsequent records, see entry 422.

422. INDIVIDUAL RETURN ON TAXABLE PROPERTY

1932—. 20 file boxes (labeled by names of tax districts).

Original individual returns of taxable property giving name and address of property owner, item of taxable property, total listed value, tax rate, and amount of tax. Alphabetically arranged by names to tax districts and alphabetically thereunder by names of property owners. No index. Handwritten on printed forms. 12 x 16 x 23. Auditor's office.

For prior records, see entry 421.

423. RETURN OF OIL AND GAS PROPERTY

1905-1926. 3 volumes.

Property valuation on returns by operating companies for taxation showing name of company, address, names of owners of real estate under lease, acreage, number of producing wells, amount of rental paid on each well, total value of leasehold, and taxable value as fixed by auditor. Alphabetically arranged by names of operating companies. No index. 1905-1914, handwritten on printed forms; 1915-1926, typed on printed forms. Average 300 pages. 14 x 9 x 1.5. Storeroom 3.

For subsequent records, see entry 424.

424. OIL AND GAS RETURNS

1927—. 17 file boxes (labeled Oil Returns).

Record of returns of oil and gas properties giving date, tax district, name and address of person, firm, or corporation operating property, acreage leased, owner of royalty, and gross monthly production and number of barrels of oil and cubic feet of gas. Chronologically arranged by dates of returns. No index. Handwritten on printed forms. 18 x 5 x 12. Auditor's office.

For prior records, see entry 423.

425. BANK RETURNS

1918—. 1 file box.

Record of tax notices to state banks or banking associations, organized under the laws of the state of Ohio, requiring cashier of said bank to make report, under oath, giving in detail the resources and liabilities of said bank or banking association. Chronologically arranged by years. No index. Handwritten on printed forms. 18 x 5 x 12. Auditor's office.

426. TAX RETURNS, CORPORATIONS

1870-1910. 12 file boxes.

Original returns of personal and chattel property for taxation by corporations showing name of corporation, date, itemized statement of personal property owned with value of each item, total amount returned, and name of person making return. Chronologically arranged by years. No index. Handwritten on printed forms. 4.5 x 4.5 x 10. Storeroom 3.

For subsequent records, see entries 427 and 428.

427. TAX STATEMENT

1911-1913. 1 file box (E1).

Tax statements of incorporated companies showing date, name of corporation, amount of surplus and undivided profits, amount of capital, stock, amount of bonded indebtedness, assessed value of real estate, amount of fire insurance carried on buildings, amount of money on hand or in bank, amount of accounts receivable, amount of accounts and bills payable, and amount of real and personal property at last inventory. Chronologically arranged by dates of filing. For index, see entry 397. Typed on printed forms. 13 x 5 x 10. Auditor's inner office.

For prior records, see entry 426; for subsequent records see entry 428.

428. INCORPORATED COMPANIES' TAX RETURN

1914—. 4 file boxes (labeled Incorporated Companies).

Personal property tax returns of incorporated companies showing date, name and address of company, kind of business, authorized capital stock subscribed and outstanding, all moneys in possession or on deposit, credits, debits, excess credits, materials, merchandise, autos, livestock, and other personal property. Chronologically arranged by dates of filing. No index. Typed on printed forms. 18 x 5 x 12. Auditor's office.

For prior records, see entries 426 and 427.

Additions and Deductions (See also entry 352)

429. ADDITIONS AND DEDUCTIONS, DUPLICATE
1874—. 8 volumes. ((1-8).
Auditor's duplicate of additions to or deductions from tax duplicate showing tax district, year, name of owner, range, township, section, and lot numbers, description of tract, value of real estate and personal property, amount added or deducted, and reason for revision. Alphabetically arranged by names of tax districts and alphabetically thereunder by names of property owners. No index. Handwritten on printed forms. Average 430 pages. 16 x 11 x 1.25. 3 volumes, 1874-1908, Storeroom 3; 5 volumes, 1909—, Auditor's office.

430. ADDITION ORDERS
1874—. 4 volumes.
Stubs of auditor's orders to county treasurer to add the stated amount to the current tax duplicate showing consecutive order number, date, name of property owner, amount added, and reason. Numerically arranged by consecutive order numbers. No index. Handwritten on printed forms. Average 180 pages. 14 x 4.5 x 1. 2 volumes, 1874-1912, Storeroom 3; 2 volumes, 1912—, Auditor's office.

431. DEDUCTION ORDERS
December 1874—. 5 volumes.
Stubs of auditor's orders for deductions of stated amount from tax duplicate showing consecutive order number, date, what tax duplicate, reason for deduction, amount of deduction, and name of taxpayer. Numerically arranged by consecutive order numbers and chronologically by dates issued. No index. Handwritten on printed forms. Average 180 pages. 14 x 4.5 x 1. 2 volumes, 1874-1906, Storeroom 3; 3 volumes, 1907—, Auditor's office.

432. PERSONAL PROPERTY ADDITIONS
1912-1917. 1 file box (E6). Discontinued.
Record of additional taxes on personal property including moneys and credits subject to taxation showing name of owner, name of township, and by whom listed. Chronologically arranged by dates of returns. For index, see entry 397. Handwritten on printed forms. 13 x 5 x 10. Auditor's inner office.

Exemptions

433. APPLICATIONS FOR EXEMPTION
1933—. 1 file box (G8).
Applications to county auditor for tax exemption for schools, churches, cemeteries, armories, and public buildings, giving name of taxing district, subdivision or addition, location and total value of land and buildings. Chronologically arranged by dates of filing. For index, see entry 397. Handwritten and typed on printed forms. 13 x 5 x 10. Auditor's inner office.

434. AUDITOR'S EXEMPT LIST
1854—. 2 volumes.
List of properties tax exempt including churches, schools, county and municipal lands and buildings, charitable institutions, and libraries, showing tax district, what buildings and lands, description of tract or lot, owner, land value, and building value. Alphabetically arranged by names of tax districts and alphabetically thereunder by names of owners. No index. Handwritten on printed forms. Average 380 pages. 12 x 14 x 2. 1 volume, 1854-1916, Storeroom 3; 1 volume, 1917—, Auditor's office.

Delinquent Taxes

435. DELINQUENT RETURNS
1821-1895. 9 volumes.
Auditor's record of unpaid taxes showing tax receipt number, tax district, name of property owner, range, township, section, and lot numbers, acreage, description of tract, property value, taxes and penalty due, and treasurer's reason for not collecting. Contains Delinquent Personal Tax List, entry 440. Alphabetically arranged by names of tax districts and alphabetically thereunder by names of

property owners. No index. Handwritten on printed forms. Average 480 pages. 16 x 11 x 2.5. Store room 3.

For subsequent records, see entry 436.

436. RECORD OF DELINQUENT REAL ESTATE

1896—. 9 volumes. (1-9).

Record showing tax district, name of owner, range, township, section, and lot numbers, acreage, description of tract, acreage taxed, value, years delinquent, total tax, and penalty due. Chronologically arranged by years, alphabetically thereunder by tax districts, and alphabetically thereunder by names of landowners. No index. Handwritten on printed forms. Average 570 pages. 18 x 11.5 x 3. 3 volumes, 1896-1912, Storeroom 3; 6 volumes, 1913—, Auditor's office.

For prior records, see entry 435.

437. DELINQUENT LANDS AND RECORD OF SALE

1823—. 4 volumes. (1 volume, 1823-1841, unnumbered, 1-3).

List of lands on which taxes are delinquent showing name of owner, acreage, range, township, section, and lot numbers, acreage taxed, value, description of tract, amount tax due, penalty, interest, and total due; also copy of advertisement offering lands for sale for taxes, penalties, and interest due. Record of sales showing name of owner, acreage, range, township, section, and lot numbers, acreage taxed, value, description, amount due, quantity sold, amounts sold for, name of purchaser, date redeemed, and by whom redeemed. Chronologically arranged by years and alphabetically thereunder the names of landowners. No index. Handwritten on printed forms. Average 590 pages. 18 x 12 x 3. 3 volumes, 1823-1841, 1866—, Auditor's office; 1 volume, 1842-1965, Storeroom 3.

438. DELINQUENT LANDS, NONRESIDENT OWNERS

1820-1846. 3 volumes. No prior or subsequent records.

List of lands returned delinquent by treasurer and certified as such to state auditor, the lands being ordered sold for taxes, penalties, and interest due, showing name of owner, address, township or town, acreage, range, township, section, and lot numbers, acreage taxed, tax rate, original proprietor, account of taxes, penalty, and interest, total due, copy of advertisement for sale of lands as published in the *American Friend* and Marietta *Gazette;* record of sale of lands showing name of purchaser, amount sold for, and date of sale. Chronologically arranged by years. No index. Handwritten. Average 270 pages. 12 x 10 x 1.5. Storeroom 3.

439. CERTIFICATE OF REDEMPTION

1878-1931. 7 volumes. No prior records.

Auditor's duplicate copy of certificates of redemption showing date issued, certificate number, date certificate delinquent, tax district, name of owner, lot number, amount of delinquent tax, penalty, interest, auditor's fee, total due, and date paid. Numerically arranged by certificate numbers. No index. Handwritten on printed forms. Average 200 pages. 6.5 x 9 x 1. Storeroom 1.

440. DELINQUENT PERSONAL TAX LIST

1877-1932. 5 volumes. 1821-1895 also in Delinquent Returns, entry 435; discontinued. Title varies: 1877-1916, 4 volumes, Delinquent Duplicate, Personal.

Auditor's duplicate of delinquent personal taxes showing tax district, name of owner, property value, amount of tax, years delinquent, penalty, and total due. Includes unpaid dog and road taxes, penalty, and totals, 1917-1932. Chronologically arranged by years, alphabetically thereunder by names of tax districts, and alphabetically thereunder by names of taxpayers. No index. Handwritten on printed forms. Average 260 pages. 16 x 11 x 1.75. 4 volumes, 1877-1916, Storeroom 3; 1 volume, 1917-1932, Auditor's inner office.

Inheritance Taxes (See also entries 279-281)

441. PRELIMINARY NOTICE

1912–21—. 1 file box (F6).

Preliminary notice from probate court in matters of inheritance tax showing date, name of decedent, date of death, residence and place of death, name of administrator or executor, description, and value of property, and copy of notarization. Chronologically arranged by dates of filing. For index, see entry 397. Handwritten on printed forms. 13 x 5 x 10. Auditor's inner office.

442. JOURNAL ENTRY DETERMINING TAX WITHOUT AUDITOR'S APPRAISAL

1926—, 1 file box (G6).

Record of determination of inheritance tax showing dates, name of decedent, tax district, gross value of estate, value of personal property and real estate, allowances of cost of administration, names of successors and their relationship to decedent, value of succession as found by the court, amount of exemption, balance subject to tax, amount of tax, date of accrual of tax, person assessed, name of the executor or administrator, and signature of probate judge. Chronologically arranged by dates of filing. For index, see entry 397. Handwritten on printed forms. 13 x 5 x 10. Auditor's inner office.

443. ENTRY FIXING INHERITANCE TAX

1918—. 2 file boxes (E6, I1).

Copy of probate court journal entry fixing the amounts of inheritance tax, showing date, name of decedent, state and county, name of executor or administrator, late residence of decedent, amount of taxes fixed by the court, names and age of beneficiary, relationship, kind of legacy, value of legacy, amount taxable, and total amount of tax. Chronologically arranged by dates of filing. For index, see entry 397. Handwritten on printed forms. 13 x 5 x 10. Auditor's inner office.

444. DISCOUNT MEMORANDUM

1933—. 1 file box (D9).

Affidavits from the probate court to the county auditor certified that the determination for inheritance tax has been fixed in the matter of the decedent and that there is no tax found due. Chronologically arranged by dates issued. For index, see entry 397. Typed. 13 x 5 x 10. Auditor's inner office.

445. DUPLICATE, INHERITANCE TAX CHARGES

1919—. 2 volumes.

Auditor's duplicate of inheritance tax charges as certified by probate court showing case number, date certified, name of decedent, amount, tax assessed, name of person to whom tax charged, amount charged, and date paid. Chronologically arranged by dates certified. No index. Typed on printed forms. Average 570 pages. 11 x 11 x 3. 1 volume, 1919-1929, Storeroom 1; 1 volume, 1930—, Auditor's office.

446. AUDITOR'S INHERITANCE TAX RECORD
1899-1901. 1 volume. Discontinued.
Auditor's record of inheritance tax charges showing name of decedent, name of administrator or executor, case number, amount of direct and collateral tax, value of property subject to tax, probate court cost and fees, total tax, and fees. Chronologically arranged by dates of filing. No index. Handwritten on printed forms. 150 pages. 16 x 11 x 1. Storeroom 3.

447. PAY-IN ORDERS, INHERITANCE TAX (Collateral)
1897-1924. 1 volume.
Duplicate copy of pay-in orders showing date, amount to be paid, name of payer, name of decedent, and tax district. Chronologically arranged by dates of orders. No index. Handwritten on printed forms. 190 pages. 8 x 5 x 1. Auditor's office.

448. INHERITANCE RECEIPTS FROM TREASURER
1915—. 2 file boxes (D6, G6).
Receipts for inheritance tax paid to county treasurer showing name of executor or administrator, name of decedent, amount of taxes fixed by court with interest added, total amount collected to be placed to the credit of the undivided inheritance tax fund, name of township, and signature of county treasurer. Chronologically arranged by dates of filing. For index, see entry 397. Handwritten on printed forms. 13 x 5 x 10. Auditor's inner office.

Business Administration of Office

Apportionments (See also entries 455-458)

449. APPORTIONMENT RECORD
1852-1912. 5 volumes. (1-5).
Auditor's record of annual, 1852-1858, or semiannual, 1859-1912, apportionment of funds collected by taxation to subdivisions showing year, name of subdivision, amount to school, township, and corporation funds, and amount due each tax district subdivision, number of order on county treasurer for total amount due each subdivision, and signature of subdivision finance officer acknowledging settlement. Chronologically arranged by years and alphabetically thereunder by names of

subdivisions. No index. Handwritten on printed forms. Average 540 pages. 14 x 10 x 2.75. 4 volumes, 1852-1900, Storeroom 3; 1 volume, 1901-1912, Auditor's office.

450. APPORTIONMENT OF TAXES

1809-1829. 2 bundles. Discontinued.

Auditor's record of apportionment of taxes by county commissioners showing net amount of land tax collected for resident and nonresident owners, amount of tax collections due state, amount due county, and amount due each township and town. Chronologically arranged by years. No index. Handwritten. 3 x 3.5 x 7. Storeroom 3.

For subsequent records, see entry 451.

451. APPORTIONMENT, TOWNSHIP TAX

1826-1892. 66 bundles.

Auditor's annual record of apportionment of township tax funds to the various townships showing township, amount tax levied, amount delinquent, treasurer's fee, net amount, date paid to township treasurer, and order number. Alphabetically arranged by names of townships. No index. Handwritten. 4.5 x 3.5 x 8. Storeroom 3.

For prior records, see entry 450.

452. ROAD TAX APPORTIONMENT

1825-1902. 53 bundles. No prior or subsequent records.

Auditor's annual record of apportionment of road tax funds to the various tax districts showing tax district, amount of tax levied, amount delinquent, treasurer's fee, net amount, date paid to treasurer of tax district, and order number. Alphabetically arranged by names of tax districts. No index. Handwritten. 4.5 x 3.5 x 8. Storeroom 3.

Budgets

453. APPROPRIATION LEDGER

1901—. 7 volumes.

Auditor's record of appropriations to each fund or department by county commissioners and expenditures from each fund, showing fund or department, amount credited to fund or department, amount debited to each fund or department, date, name of payee or vendor, for what, warrant number, amount of warrant, appropriation or authorization, debit, credit, and unencumbered balance. Alphabetically arranged by names of funds or departments and chronologically thereunder by entry dates. No index. Handwritten on printed forms. Average 800 pages. 12 x 15 x 4. 2 volumes, 1901-1911, Storeroom 3; 5 volumes, 1912—, Auditor's office.

454. BUDGETS
1913—. 22 file boxes.
Auditor's copy of budget for each subdivision each year showing amount allowed to each fund and total for subdivision for year. Chronologically arranged by years. Handwritten on printed forms. 1913-1931, no index; 1932—, see entry 397. 4.5 x 4.5 x 10. 18 file boxes, 1913-1931, Storeroom 3; 4 file boxes, 1932—, Auditor's inner office.

Settlements (See also entries 449-451)

455. DISTRIBUTION OF MOTOR VEHICLE LICENSE FEES
1925-1932. 2 bundles. Discontinued.
Record of distribution of motor vehicle license fees to subdivisions by auditor showing date, number of vehicles registered each subdivision, amount of fees, total fees, amount to county, and amount to each township and corporation. Chronologically arranged by dates of distribution. No index. Handwritten on printed forms. 5 x 4 x 11. Storeroom 1.

456. SETTLEMENT RECORD
1822—. 17 bundles and 11 volumes.
Auditor's detailed statement, annual 1822-1858, semiannual, 1859—, of receipts from all sources and expenditures showing amount of real and chattel duplicate, amount of tax collected, amount of income from other sources, amount credited to county, township, town or corporation, and school funds; also total expenditures in each tax district, total expenditures in county, amount of special assessments and for what purpose, total balance or deficit each tax district and county on annual settlement. Chronologically arranged by years. No index. Handwritten on printed forms. 7 bundles, 1822-1858, 3 x 4.5 x 12; 10 bundles, 1859-1900, 3.5 x 6 x 13; 11

volumes, 1901—, 170 pages 26 x 18 x 1.25. 17 bundles, 1822-1900, Storeroom 3; 11 volumes, 1901—, Auditor's office.

457. ANNUAL SETTLEMENTS, SCHOOL FUNDS

1913—. 5 volumes.

Auditor's record of annual settlements of school funds showing township or special school district; auditor's statement of distribution of February settlement on annual settlement (August 31), showing balance on hand at beginning of year, amount of February settlement, amount of August settlement, amount from other sources, expenditures of each fund, balance of each fund, and total balance or deficit. Chronologically arranged by years and alphabetically thereunder by names of townships or special districts. No index. Handwritten on printed forms. Average 470 pages. 16 x 11 x 2.5. Auditor's office.

For prior records, see entry 449.

458. ANNUAL SETTLEMENTS, TOWNSHIPS AND MUNICIPALITIES

1913—. 4 volumes.

Auditor's record of annual settlements of township in municipal funds showing name of township or municipality; statement of distribution of February settlement; statement of distribution of August settlement; statement of annual settlement (August 31); showing balance on hand at beginning of year, amount of February settlement, amount of August settlement, amount from other sources, total for year; expenditures of each fund, balance of each fund, and total balance or deficit. Chronologically arranged by years and alphabetically thereunder by names of townships or municipalities. No index. Handwritten on printed forms. Average 480 pages. 16 x 11 x 2.5. Auditor's office.

For prior records, see entry 449.

Bills

459. INVOICES

1891—. 11 bundles and 1 file box (D7).

Invoices from Gallipolis state institution for epileptics for care and maintenance of inmates committed from Washington County, showing date of invoice, itemized statement of charges, and date filed. Chronologically arranged by dates of filing. 1891-1831, no index; for index, 1932—, see entry 397. Handwritten on printed forms. Bundles, 3.5 x 4.5 x 9; file box, 10 x 4.5 x 14. 11 bundles, 1891-1931, Storeroom 3; 1 file box, 1932—, Auditor's inner office.

460. INVOICES

1891—. 14 bundles and 2 file boxes (J7, J8).

Invoices from Athens state hospital for insane for care and maintenance of inmates committed to institution from Washington County, showing date of invoice, itemized statement of charges, and date filed. Chronologically arranged by dates of filing. 1891-1928, no index; for index, 1929—, see entry 397. Handwritten on printed forms. Bundles, 5 x 3.5 x 8; file boxes, 10 x 4.5 x 14. 14 bundles, 1891-1928, Storeroom 3; 2 file boxes, 1929—, Auditor's inner office.

461. ANIMAL CLAIM RECORD

1917—. 6 volumes. (1-6).

Record copy of claims filed for compensation for animals killed or injured by dogs showing date filed with township trustees, name and address of claimant, number of animals killed, number of animals injured, kind of animals, value, amount of claim, affidavit on claimed, testimony of supporting witnesses, date filed with county commissioners, amount of claim, amount of witness fees and mileage, total amount of claim, and date claim was approved by commissioners. Chronologically arranged by dates of filing. Alphabetically indexed by names of claimants. 1917-1936 handwritten on printed forms; 1937—, typed on printed forms. Average 400 pages. 16 x 11 x 2. Auditor's office.

For other records, see entry 46.

462. AUDITOR'S DOCKET, BILLS FILED, COMMISSIONERS'

1904—. 6 volumes. (1-6).

Auditor's record of bills filed with commissioners by creditors for payment from funds showing date of bill, consecutive number, name of creditor, for what, amount of bill, date filed, date approved, amount approved, date paid, and warrant number. Chronologically arranged by dates of filing. No index. Handwritten on printed forms. Average 650 pages. 18 x 12 x 3.5. Auditor's office.

For prior records, see entry 3.

463. GENERAL INDEX OF INFIRMARY AND CHILDREN'S HOME BILLS

1922-1932. 1 volume. Discontinued.

Auditor's index to infirmary and children's home bills as entered in Commissioners' Journal, entry 1, showing name of payee, volume and page numbers of Commissioners' Journal, date paid, warrant number, amount, and for what. Alphabetically arranged by names of payees and chronologically thereunder by dates paid. Handwritten on printed forms. 560 pages. 18 x 12 x 2.75. Auditor's office.

464. AUDITOR'S DOCKET, BILLS FILED, INFIRMARY

1913—. 2 volumes. (1, 2).

Auditor's record of bills filed with county commissioners' infirmary account, showing date of bill, consecutive number, name of creditor, for what, amount of bill, date filed, date approved, amount approved, date paid, and warrant number. Chronologically arranged by dates of filing. No index. Handwritten on printed forms. Average 400 pages. 18 x 12 x 2. Auditor's office.

465. AUDITOR'S DOCKET, BILLS FILED, CHILDREN'S HOME

1913—. 2 volumes.

Record of bills filed with county commissioners, children's home account, showing date of bill, number of bill, name of creditor, for what, amount, date filed, date approved, amount approved, date paid, and warrant number. Numerically arranged by consecutive bill numbers. No index. Handwritten on printed forms. Average 430 pages. 18 x 11.5 x 2.25. Auditor's office.

466. CRIMINAL COST BILLS

1843—. 240 file boxes.

Original cost bills in criminal cases showing what court, name of defendant, offense charge, date of bill, and itemized account of cost and fees taxed. Chronologically arranged by dates of filing. 1843-1929, no index; for index, 1930—, see entry 397. Handwritten on printed forms. 1843-1929, 4.5 x 4.5 x 10; 1930—, 10 x 4.5 x 14. 234 file boxes, 1843-1929, Storeroom 3; 5 file boxes, 1930—, Auditor's inner office.

Vouchers and Warrants

467. CHILDREN'S HOME REPORTS AND VOUCHERS

1869-1912. 99 file boxes. 1913— in Vouchers, Commissioners', entry 471. Vouchers issued by superintendent or directors of children's home for payment of bills, showing date, voucher number, name of creditor, for what, and date filed. Contains [Children's Home Reports], 1877-1812, entry 14. Chronologically arranged by dates are filing. No index. Handwritten on printed forms. 4.5 x 4.5 x 10. Storeroom 3.

468. VOUCHERS, INFIRMARY

1841—. 262 bundles, 47 jackets, and 10 file boxes. No prior records. Infirmary vouchers issued by clerk of board of infirmary directors, 1857-1912, and by commissioners, 1913—, for payment of bills and claims against county infirmary, showing date issued, voucher number, name of creditor, for want, amount, and date paid. Chronologically arranged by dates paid. 1841-1932, no index; for index, 1933—, see entry 397. Handwritten on printed forms. Bundles, 4 x 3.5 x 6; jackets, 3.5 x 4.5 x 8; file boxes, 10 x 4.5 x 14. 262 bundles, 47 jackets and 3 file boxes, 1841-1932, Storeroom 3; 7 file boxes, 1933—, Auditor's inner office.

469. VOUCHERS, GENERAL

1923—. 71 bundles, 217 jackets, and 12 file boxes.
Vouchers issued by county commissioners and various county officials for payment of bills and claims against county from county funds, showing date issued, voucher number, name of creditor, for what, amount, and date paid. Chronologically arranged by dates paid. 1823-1928, no index; for index, 1929—, see entry 397. Handwritten on printed forms. Bundles, 4 x 3 x 4; jackets, 3.5 x 4.5 x 9; file boxes, 10 x 4.5 x 14. 71 bundles, and 217 jackets, 1823-1928, Storeroom 3; 12 file boxes, 1929—, Auditor's inner office.

470. INDEX OF AUDITOR'S VOUCHERS

1924-1934. 2 volumes. (1, 2). Discontinued.
Index record of auditor's pay-in vouchers showing date of issue, voucher number, amount, and for what. Alphabetically arranged by names of payers. Handwritten on printed forms. Average 400 pages. 18 x 12 x 2. Auditor's office.

471. VOUCHERS, COMMISSIONERS'
1804—, 1,216 bundles, 1,401 jackets and 54 file boxes.

Vouchers issued by county commissioners to creditors of county for payment of bills and claims allowed, showing date issued, voucher number, name of creditor, for what, what fund, amount of voucher, and date paid. Contains Children's Home Reports and Vouchers, 1913—, entry 467. Chronologically arranged by dates paid. 1804-1931, no index; for index, 1931—, see entry 397. Handwritten on printed forms. Bundles, 4 x 3.5 x 6; jackets, 3.5 x 4.5 x 9; file boxes, 10 x 4.5 x 14. 1,216 bundles and 1,401 jackets, 1804-1931, Storeroom 3; 54 file boxes, 1931—, Auditor's inner office.

472. COMMISSIONERS' VOUCHERS, RELIEF
1933-1936. 32 jackets.

Vouchers issued by commissioners authorizing pavement of bills and claims for relief purposes, showing voucher number, name of creditor or payee, date of bill, amount, for what, name of relief client, date paid, and warrant number. Chronologically arranged by dates approved. No index. Typed on printed forms. 4.5 x 4 x 9. Storeroom 1.

473. RECORD OF VOUCHERS, SINKING FUND
1919—. 2 volumes. No prior records.

Record of vouchers issued by sinking fund trustees for payment of bond principal and interest, showing voucher number, amount, date, what issue, payment of bond, number or numbers, amount of interest, and names of sinking fund trustees. Chronologically arranged by dates issued. No index. Handwritten on printed forms. Average 300 pages. 9 x 12 x 1.5. Auditor's office

474. JOURNAL OF WARRANTS ISSUED AND PAYMENTS INTO COUNTY TREASURY
1904—. 18 volumes. (1-18).

Auditor's records of warrants issued on county treasurer for payment from county funds showing date, names of payee, for what, warrant number, amount credited to treasurer, and amount debited each county fund; also record of payments into county treasury showing date, by whom paid, for what, pay-in order number, amount debited to treasurer, and amount credited to each fund. Chronologically arranged by dates of entries. No index. Handwritten on printed forms. Average 440 pages. 18 x 12 x 2.5. 3 volumes, 1904-1915, Storeroom 3; 15 volumes, 1915—, Auditor's office.

475. AUDITOR'S COURT WARRANTS
1904—. 2 volumes.

Record of court warrants issued for jury and witness fees showing date, name of payee, and warrant number for common pleas court petit jury, grand jury, also, grand and Jury witnesses, and witnesses in criminal cases; for probate court jury, criminal witnesses, and witnesses in lunacy and epilepsy cases; also for witnesses in minor courts, coroner's witnesses, and jurors. Chronologically arranged by dates of warrants. No index. Handwritten on printed forms. Average 300 pages. 16 x 11 x 1.5. Auditor's office.

476. GENERAL WARRANTS, REDEEMED
1873—. 461 bundles, 185 jackets, and 39 file boxes (W1-9 and 3-7, O 1-8, M 4-8, H 1-9, Z 2-4). No prior records.

Auditor's warrant on county treasury for payments of bills and claims authorized by county commissioners or other county executives by voucher, showing warrant number, date, name of payee, amount, for what, what fund, and date cancelled. Chronologically arranged by dates cancelled. 1873-1972, no index; for index, 1932—, see entry 397. Handwritten on printed forms. Bundles and 185 jackets, 1873-1931, Storeroom 3; 39 file boxes, 1932—, Auditor's inner office.

477. COURT WARRANTS REDEEMED
1897—. 68 jackets and 4 file boxes (J4, H4, J7, B5).

Cancelled warrants issued for payment of witnesses and jurors including mileage fees, in common pleas and probate courts, giving name of witnesses or juror, date of appearance, nature of case, and amount of fee paid. Numerically arranged by certificate numbers. 1897-1932, no index; for index, 1933—, see entry 397. Handwritten on printed forms. Jackets, 9 x 4.5 x 3.5; file boxes, 10 x 4.5 x 14. 68 jackets, 1897-1932, Storeroom 3; 4 file boxes, 1933—, Auditor's inner office.

478. WARRANT RECEIPTS (Stubs)
1879—. 65 volumes. No prior records.

Auditor's receipt stubs for warrants issued on county treasury showing warrants number, date, amount of warrants, what fund, voucher authority, for what, and signature of payee. Numerically arranged by consecutive warrant numbers. No index. Handwritten on printed forms. Average 500 pages. 17 x 5.5 x 2.5. 55 volumes, 1879-1931, Storeroom 3; 10 volumes, 1932—, Auditor's office.

General Accounts

479. JOURNAL
1838—. 11 volumes.
Auditor's record of receipts and expenditures of county funds showing amount debit to county treasurer and itemized account of expenditures each fund; also total debt and credit to treasurer each thirty day period. Chronologically arranged by dates of entries. No index. Handwritten on printed forms. Average 490 pages. 16 x 11 x 2.5. 8 volumes, 1838-1914, Storeroom 3; 3 volumes, 1915—, Auditor's office.

480. (Fund) LEDGER
1850—. 9 volumes.
Auditor's fund account ledger: fund credits showing date credited, what source, pay-in order number, and amount; also total credit and debit each thirty day period. Alphabetically arranged by names of funds and chronologically thereunder by dates of credits or debits. No index. Handwritten on printed forms. Average 700 pages. 14 x 10 x 3.5. 6 volumes, 1850-1915, Storeroom 3; 3 volumes, 1916—, Auditor's office.

481. DUPLICATE PAY-IN ORDERS
July 1858—. 27 volumes.
Duplicate copies of pay-in orders issued by auditor directing payment to county treasury showing consecutive order number, date, name of payer, amount and for what. Numerically arranged by order numbers. No index. Handwritten on printed forms. Average 230 pages. 10 x 7 x 1.25. 24 volumes, 1858-1927, Storeroom 3; 3 volumes, 1928—, Auditor's office.

482. JOURNAL
1870-1880. 1 volume. No prior or subsequent records.
Auditor's record of court costs in criminal causes showing name of defendant, term of court, case number, names of jurors (grand or petit), with amount per diem and

mileage due, order number, sheriff's cost and fees, and clerk's fees. Chronologically arranged by dates of court terms. No index. 604 pages. 16 x 11 x 3. Storeroom 3.

483. CASH BOOK
1867-1906. 2 volumes.
Record of fees collected by auditor's office showing date, by whom paid, for what service, and amount. Chronologically arranged by dates of entries. No index. Handwritten on printed forms. Average 390 pages. 14 x 9 x 2. Storeroom 3.
For subsequent records, see entry 484.

484. RECORD OF FEES AND PEDDLERS' LICENSES
1907—. 1 volume.
Record of peddler's licenses showing date issued, name of licensee, amount of fee, and license number. Record of fees show date, by whom paid, amount, and for what service. Record of fees in back of volume; record of peddlers' licenses in front of volume. Chronologically arranged by dates issued or entries. No index. Handwritten on printed forms. 530 pages. 14 x 10 x 2.75. Auditor's office.
For prior record of fees, see entry 483; for prior records of peddlers' licenses, see entry 494.

485. CERTIFICATES, FEES
1801—. 254 bundles, 133 jackets, and 11 file boxes.
Certificates issued by clerk of courts and probate court to witnesses and jurors for fees, showing date of certificate, name of witness or jury, case number, names of litigants, days in court, mileage, total fee due, date filed with auditor, and date paid. Chronologically arranged by dates paid. 1801-1932, no index; for index, 1933—, see entry 397. Handwritten on printed forms. Bundles, 5 x 3.5 x 7; jackets, 3.5 x 4.5 x 9; file boxes, 1933—, Auditor's inner office.

Special Accounts

486. RECORD OF EXPENDITURES, INFIRMARY
1913—. 3 volumes.
Record of expenditures of county home funds showing date, name of payee, warrant number, amount, for what, and what fund. Chronologically arranged by dates of

entries. No index. Handwritten on printed forms. Average 370 pages. 16 x 11 x 2. 2 volumes, 1913-1928, Storeroom 3; 1 volume, 1928—, Auditor's office.

487. RECEIPTS AND EXPENDITURES, CLASSIFIED
1913—. 2 volumes. (1, 2).
Record of receipts of children's home funds showing date, source, from whom, and amount; also record of expenditures showing dates, to whom, warrant number, amount, and for what. Chronologically arranged by dates received or disbursed. No index. Handwritten on printed forms. Average 400 pages. 18 x 12 x 2. Auditor's office.

488. RECORD OF SOLDIERS' RELIEF PAYMENTS
1910—. 1 volume. No prior records.
Record showing name of recipient, address, amount of monthly payment, warrant number for each payment, and date of payment. Alphabetically arranged by names of townships and chronologically thereunder by dates of payments. No index. Handwritten on printed forms. 320 pages. 12 x 18 x 1.5. Auditor's office.

489. BLIND PENSION RECORD
1904-June 1936. 2 volumes. (1, 2). Discontinued.
Record of blind beneficiaries showing name and address of recipient, amount of quarterly benefits, date payment authorized, warrant number, and date paid. Chronologically arranged by dates paid. No index. Handwritten on printed forms. Average 180 pages. 14 x 9 x 1. Auditor's office.

490. RECORD OF PAYMENTS OF MOTHERS' PENSIONS
1915-June 1926. 1 volume. Discontinued.
Auditor's record of payments from mothers' pension fund showing name of payee, address, monthly benefit, date authorized, warrant number, and date paid. Chronologically arranged by dates page. Alphabetically indexed by names of payees. Handwritten on printed forms. 300 pages. 14 x 9 x 1.5. Auditor's office.

491. COUNTY POOR RECORD
1901-1913. 1 volume. No prior records. Discontinued.
Record of relief benefits to indigents outside of county infirmary, showing name, age, color, and legal residence of client, place of birth, how long a resident of

county, present physical and mental condition, habits, marital status, and reason for relief; record of payments or commodities furnished showing date and order number for commodity or aid. Chronologically arranged by dates of aid. No index. Handwritten on printed forms. 295 pages. 14 x 9 x 1.5. Auditor's office.

492. LEDGER

1837-1855. 1 volume. Discontinued.

Fund commissioners' account of surplus revenues showing date of item entries, amount of surplus funds, what fund, and how and where invested. Chronologically arranged by dates of entries. No index. Handwritten. 500 pages. 14 x 9 x 2.5. Storeroom 3.

493. COMPENSATION AND DAMAGES

1915-1924. 1 file box. (C3).

Auditor's records of the amounts paid for compensation and damages to various landowners necessitated by the construction of roads, showing date, name of landowner, amount paid, and signature of county surveyor. Chronologically arranged by dates of entries. For index, see entry 397. Typed on printed forms. 13 x 5 x 10. Auditor's inner office.

Licenses and Permits

494. LICENSE RECORD

1862-1906. 1 volume.

Auditor's record of licenses issued to ferry operators and to peddlers, joint date of issue, name and address of licensee, kind of license, license number, and fee. Chronologically arranged by dates issued. No index. Handwritten on printed forms. 430 pages. 14 x 10 x 2.25. Storeroom 3.

For subsequent records of peddlers' licenses, see entry 484.

495. CIGARETTE DEALERS' LICENSE RECORD

1931—. 1 volume.

Record of licenses and issued to traffic in sale of cigarettes, showing receipt number, name of person, firm, or corporation licensed, address, date license issued, and amount of tax. Chronologically arranged by years and chronologically thereunder by dates issued. No index. Handwritten on printed forms. 280 pages. 11 x 14 x 1.5. Auditor's office.

For prior records, see entry 416.

496. CIGARETTE DEALERS' LICENSE, DUPLICATE COPY
1931—. 8 volumes.

Duplicate copies of licenses issued to traffic in cigarettes, showing date issued, license number, name of licensee, business address, and expiration date. Numerically arranged by license number. No index. Handwritten on printed forms. 220 pages. 11 x 15 x 1.25. 6 volumes, 1931-1935, Storeroom 1; 2 volumes, 1936—, Auditor's office.

497. APPLICATION FOR CIGARETTE DEALERS' LICENSE
1909—. 5 bundles and 2 file boxes (A6, E8).

Original applications showing date, name of applicant, business address, name of city, village, or township, and street or rural route address. Chronologically arranged by dates of applications. 1909-1930, no index; for index, 1931—, see entry 397. Handwritten on printed forms. Bundles, 4 x 3.5 x 10.5; file boxes, 10 x 4.5 x 14. 5 bundles, 1909-1930, Storeroom 3; 2 file boxes, 1931—, Auditor's inner office.

498. COSMETIC DEALERS' LICENSE APPLICATIONS
1933-1934. 1 file box (E8).

Applications for cosmetic dealers' licenses showing date, name and address of dealer, date of the ending of the current twelve months period, and the name of city, village, or township. Chronologically arranged by dates of applications. For index, see entry 397. Handwritten on printed forms. 13 x 5 x 10. Auditor's inner office.

499. APPLICATION FOR BEVERAGE DEALER'S LICENSE
1933-1935. 1 file box (S6).

Applications to the auditor of Washington County for licenses to retail beverage dealers as provided by law, showing dates, name and address of applicant, city, village, or township, and date current period ends. Chronologically arranged by dates of applications. For index, see entry 397. Handwritten on printed forms. 13 x 5 x 10. Auditor's inner office.

500. MALT DEALER'S LICENSE APPLICATION
1933-1935. 2 file boxes (A8, A9).

Applications to county auditor for malt dealers' licenses showing date file, name of applicant, business address, date beginning sale, and date ending twelve month period. Chronologically arranged by dates of applications. For index, see entry 397. Handwritten on printed forms. 13 x 5 x 10. Auditor's inner office.

501. VENDOR'S LICENSE APPLICATION
1935—. 2 file boxes (F5, F6).

Original applications for vendor's license under sales tax laws showing date of application, name of applicant, business address, kind of business, and date issued. Chronologically arranged by dates of applications. For index, see entry 397. Handwritten on printed forms. 10 x 4.5 x 14. Auditor's inner office.

502. DOG TAG APPLICATIONS
1918-1935. 47 jackets.

Original applications by dog owners for dog tags showing application number, date, age of dog, description of dog, address of owner, tag number, and signature of applicants. Chronologically arranged by dates of applications. No index. Handwritten on printed forms. 3.5 X 4.5 X 9. Storeroom 3.

For subsequent records, see entry 503.

503. APPLICATIONS FOR THE REGISTRATION OF DOGS
1936—. 29 volumes.

Record showing date, age, sex, color, and breed of dog, if known, amount of fee paid, penalty if any, number of tag, and signature of applicant. Chronologically arranged by dates issued. No index. Handwritten on printed forms. Average 200 pages. 9 x 4 x 1. Auditor's inner office.

For prior records, see entry 502.

504. DOG AND KENNEL REGISTER
1918—. 3 volumes.

Register of dog tag applications showing application number, application date, name of applicant, number of dogs kept, registration fee, address where dog is kept, tag number, date of registration certificate, date duplicate tag issued, and tag number. Alphabetically arranged by names of applicants and chronologically thereunder by dates of applications. Numerically indexed by tag numbers showing initial letters of surnames of owners and pages and lines of record. Handwritten on printed forms. Average 510 pages. 18 x 15 x 2.75. 2 volumes, 1918-1932, Storeroom 3; 1 volume, 1933—, Auditor's office.

Reports and Statements

505. JUSTICES' REPORTS
1843—. 75 bundles and 4 file boxes (J6-J9).
Original annual reports by justices of peace to county auditors showing township, name of justice, itemized account of fines and costs assessed in criminal cases, and date filed. Chronologically arranged by years. 1843-1919, no index; for index, 1920—, see entry 397. 1843-1961, handwritten; 1862—, handwritten on printed forms. Bundles, 4 x 3.5 x 8; file boxes, 10 x 4.5 x 14. 75 bundles, 1843-1919, Storeroom 3; 4 file boxes, 1920—, Auditor's inner office.

506. CLERK OF COURTS' REPORTS, UNDER GARBER LAW
1893-1897. 5 bundles. Discontinued.
Monthly report by clerk of courts to county auditor showing amount of fees, commission and allowances, and percentage collected for service rendered. Chronologically arranged by dates of filing. No index. Handwritten on printed forms. 3.5 x 3.5 x 8. Storeroom 3.

507. CENSUS ENUMERATION REPORT
1880. 3 volumes.
Enumeration list of inhabitants of Washington County as returned to auditor by district enumerators of decennial United States census, showing name, color, sex, and age. Alphabetically arranged by names of inhabitants. No index. Handwritten on printed forms. Average 320 pages. 14 x 9 x 1.5. Storeroom 3.

508. RECORD ENUMERATION OF YOUTH
1858-1864. 2 volumes.
Enumeration list of school age unmarried youths between six and twenty-one years of age, showing name of parent, names and ages of children, number of males, number of females, township, district, and returns made by district assessors.

Alphabetically arranged by family names. No index. Handwritten on printed forms. Average 180 pages. 14 x 10 x 1. Storeroom 3.

509. ENUMERATION REPORTS

1832—. 88 bundles and 3 file boxes.

Original reports to county auditor by district enumerators on unmarried youths between five and twenty-one years of age, showing township or town school district number, name of parent, and names and ages of children. Chronologically arranged by years. No index. 1832-1871, handwritten; 1872—, handwritten on printed forms. Bundles, 4.5 x 3.5 x 8; file boxes, 10 x 4.5 x 14. 88 bundles, 1832-1929, Storeroom 3; 3 file boxes, 1930, Auditor's office.

510. REPORTS, DEAF, DUMB, INSANE, AND IDIOTIC PERSONS

1867—. 5 bundles and 2 file boxes.

Duplicate copies of auditor's report to state auditor on number of deaf, dumb, insane, and idiotic persons cared for by public funds, showing dates, names of persons under each classification, how each is cared for, and amount of public funds contributed toward care of persons reported. Chronologically arranged by dates of reports. No index. Handwritten on printed forms. Bundles, 3 x 4 x 9; file boxes, 10 x 4.5 x 14. 5 bundles, 1867-1922, Storeroom 3; 2 file boxes, 1923—, Auditor's office.

511. (School) REPORTS

1839-1913. 75 bundles.

Annual reports by town, township, and village clerks to county auditor on school statistics, showing number of elementary schools in subdivision, value of school property, number of teachers employed, average monthly wage of teachers, number of weeks school in session, number of pupils in each school, total number of puples for each subdivision, average monthly enrollment, average daily attendance, and date filed. Chronologically arranged by years. No index. 1839-1844, handwritten; 1845-1913, handwritten on printed forms. 5.5 x 3.5 x 8. Storeroom 3.

For subsequent records, see entry 512.

512. REPORTS, BOARD OF EDUCATION

1914—. 11 file boxes.

Original annual reports by village, township, and special district boards of education, to county auditor, showing school district, number of subdistricts, school buildings, and schoolrooms, value of school property, number of teachers and superintendents, average monthly wage of teachers, number of weeks of school, number of pupils in district, number of boys, number of girls, average monthly enrollment, and average daily attendance. Chronologically arranged by years. No index. Handwritten on printed forms. File boxes, 1914-1928, 4.5 x 4.5 x 10; 1929—, 10 x 4.5 x 14. 8 file boxes, 1914-1928, Storeroom 3; 3 file boxes, 1929—, Auditor's office.

For prior records, see entry 511.

513. REPORTS OF EXAMINATIONS OF TOWNSHIP SCHOOL DISTRICTS

1902-1911. 1 file box (H1). Discontinued.

Record showing amount of state common school funds, local school funds, property valuation, amount of treasurer's and clerk's bonds, amount of deposits in bank, balance in hands of treasurer, amount expended as per orders, and total balance on hand. Chronologically arranged by dates of filing. For index, see entry 397. Typed on printed forms. 13 x 5 x 10. Auditor's inner office.

514. RECORD OF TREASURY EXAMINATIONS

1886-1903. 1 volume.

Record copy of treasury examiners' reports to probate judge which is filed with county auditor, showing date of examination, balance to credit of each fund, overpayments from each fund, total balance, total overpayments, net cash balance, date filed, and examiners signatures. Chronologically arranged by dates of filing. No index. Handwritten on printed forms. 80 pages. 18 x 12 x .5. Storeroom 3.

For subsequent records, see entry 515.

515. REPORTS, EXAMINATION OF WASHINGTON COUNTY TREASURY

1904-1914. 1 file box (A7). Discontinued.

Record copies of reports to the probate judge on examinations of the treasury of Washington County, showing balances in the treasury as filed with county auditor. Chronologically arranged by dates of examinations. For index, see entry 397. Handwritten on printed forms. 13 x 5 x 10. Auditor's inner office.

For prior records, see entry 514.

516. ANNUAL REPORT, COUNTY OFFICIALS
1883—. 3 volumes, (1-3).

Auditor's record copies of annual reports to county commissioners by county prosecutor, clerk of courts, sheriff, and county treasurer, showing county prosecutor's criminal prosecutions, name of accused, fine assessed, recognizance forfeited, and amount collected; clerk of courts' showing fines assessed, name of accused, amount assessed, amount collected, sources of funds paid into county treasury, and amount paid in; sheriff's criminal cases showing name of defendant, amount collected, date paid to clerk of courts, and amount paid over to clerk; and treasurer's report showing source of fee and amount of each item. Arranged under tabs by names of offices and chronologically thereunder by dates of annual reports. No index. Handwritten on printed forms. Average 400 pages. 18 x 12 x 2. 1 volume, 1883-1904, Storeroom 3; 2 volumes, 1905—, Auditor's office.

517. REPORT, DELINQUENT LANDS
1825—. 27 bundles and 2 file boxes (C4, G7).

Duplicate copy of county auditor's report to state auditor of lands on which taxes are delinquent, showing year, name of landowner, range, township, section, and lot numbers, acreage, description tract, value, amount of delinquent tax, penalty, and total due. Chronologically arranged by years. 1825-1923, no index; for index, 1924—, see entry 397. Handwritten. Bundles, 4 x 3.5 x 8; file boxes, 10 x 4.5 x 14. 27 bundles, 1825-1923, Storeroom 3; 2 file boxes, 1924—, Auditor's inner office.

518. DEBT REPORTS ON BONDS AND NOTES IN VILLAGE, TOWNSHIP, AND SCHOOL DISTRICTS
1932—. 1 file box (P8).

Records of village, township, and school indebtedness, showing outstanding debts, bonds redeemed, balances outstanding, new issues outstanding, rate of interest, and date of maturity. School district records shows general outstanding debts, bonds redeemed, balance outstanding, new issues during previous month, total outstanding, rate of interest, and date and maturity. Chronologically arranged by dates of filing. For index, see entry 397. Handwritten on printed forms. 10 x 4.5 x 14. Auditor's inner office.

519. DEPOSITORIES

1915-1928. 1 file box (A5).

Original reports to county auditor of deposit of township funds by the various township clerks, showing date, name and address of depository, and amount of bond. Chronologically arranged by dates of reports. For index, see entry 397. Handwritten and typed on printed forms. 10 x 4.5 x 14. Auditor's inner office.

520. DEPOSITORIES' MONTHLY STATEMENTS

1915—. 6 file boxes (G8, C8, F7, A6, B2, A3).

Depositories' monthly statement to the county auditor, showing date of deposit, name of bank, interest credited for past month, balance now on deposit to the credit of the county, amount on hand, deposits, withdrawals if any, and daily balance. Chronologically arranged by dates of deposits. For index, see entry 397. Handwritten on printed forms. 13 x 5 x 10. Auditor's office.

521. FINANCIAL STATEMENTS, MONTHLY AND ANNUAL

1905—. 27 bundles and 3 file boxes (S6-S8).

Record copies of auditor's monthly and annual financial statements to county commissioners showing date and itemized account of cash receipts from all sources credited to county funds; also itemized general account of expenditures showing debt to each fund and balance or deficit of each fund. Chronologically arranged by dates of statements. 1905-1932, no index; for index, 1933—, see entry 397. Handwritten on printed forms. 27 bundles, 1905-1932, Storeroom 1; 3 file boxes, 1933—, Auditor's inner office.

For other records, see entry 6.

522. RECORD OF INDEBTEDNESS, TOWNSHIPS AND SCHOOL DISTRICTS

1872—. 84 bundles and 2 file boxes.

Annual indebtedness record of subdivisions, except municipalities, showing name of subdivision or school district, date of report, amount of refunded debt, amount of unfunded debt, provision to pay the debt, amount of cash on hand applicable to debt payment, amount anticipated income applicable to debt payment as reported by district assessors 1872-1894, and by clerks of subdivisions 1895—. Chronologically arranged by dates of reports. No index. Handwritten on printed forms. Bundles, 5 x 4 x 10; file boxes, 10 x 4.5 x 14. 84 bundles, 1872-1930, Storeroom 3; 2 file boxes, 1931—, Auditor's inner office.

523. STATEMENT OF THE AMOUNT OF FEES AND SALARIES
1916—. 1 file box (C2).

Record of fees and salaries received by or due to the county officers of Washington County for the fiscal year, showing name of office, salary of officer, assistants, deputies, and clerks. Chronologically arranged by dates of reports. For index, see entry 397. Typed on printed forms. 10 x 4.5 x 14. Auditor's inner office.

Bonds

Official Bonds (See also entries 171 and 379-381)

524. COUNTY OFFICERS' BOND RECORD
1831—. 3 volumes. 1902-1903, missing. Title varies: 1831-1886, Record of Bonds; 1887-1902, Record of Official Bonds.

Record copies of surety bonds filed with the county auditor by the county treasurer, sheriff, coroner, prosecuting attorney, clerk of courts, and probate judge, showing names of principal and of sureties, what office, date of bond, date filed, and copy of oath of office. Contains bonds of assessors, free turnpike commissioners, and master commissioner, 1831-1886. Chronologically arranged by dates of filing. 1831-1886, handwritten; 1887—, handwritten on printed forms. Average 300 pages. 16 x 11 x 1.75. 2 volumes, 1831-1902, Storeroom 3; 1 volume, 1904—, Auditor's office.

525. OFFICIAL BONDS
1882—. 1 file box (B2).

Original official bonds which were filed by county treasurer, sheriff, and coroner, showing date, name of officer and title of office to which he is bonded, names of sureties, amount of bond given, certification of approval by prosecuting attorney at signatures of bondsmen, copy of oath of officials administered by the clerk of courts, and signatures of both the official and the clerk of courts. Chronologically arranged by dates of applications. For index, see entry 397. Handwritten on printed forms. 10 x 4.5 x 14. Auditor's inner office.

526. BONDS OF ASSESSORS

1915-1924. 1 file box (B3).

Original bonds of assessors and deputy assessors in the county, township, districts, villages, and corporations, showing date, names of bondsmen, amount of bond, the territory which assessor shall cover, date bond filed, approval of bond, and seal and signatures of attorney general of Ohio and of the prosecuting attorney of Washington County. Chronologically arranged by dates of filing. For index, see entry 397. Handwritten on printed forms. 10 x 4.5 x 14. Auditor's inner office.

527. BONDS OF SCHOOL OFFICERS

1922—. 1 file box (E4).

Certified copies of bonds of clerk-treasurers of school funds, clerks of board of education, and township clerks, giving name of clerk, names of sureties, amount of bond, signatures of the president and of the clerk of the board of education. Chronologically arranged by dates of filing. For index, see entry 397. Handwritten on printed forms. 10 x 4.5 x 14. Auditor's inner office.

Debenture Bonds (See also entries 23, 24, and 382)

528. RECORD OF BONDS

1852-1872. 1 volume.

Record of bonds issued in favor of the Marietta and Cincinnati Railway Company, showing number and amount of each bond, due date, amount of semiannual interest, and interest due date. Chronologically arranged by dates issued. No index. Handwritten on printed forms. 80 pages. 20 x 13 x .5. Storeroom 3.

529. BOND REGISTER

1871—. 2 volumes. (1, 2).

Register of bonds authorized and issued by county commissioners for highways, county buildings, poor relief, and refunding purposes, showing for what purpose issued, names of county commissioners and of county auditor authorizing issue, amount of issue, date of issue, date of sale, to whom sold, numbers of bonds, denominations, rate of interest, maturity dates, record of redemption, and interest payments. Chronologically arranged by dates issued. No index. Handwritten on printed forms. Average 300 pages. 18 x 14 x 1.5. Auditor's office.

530. FUNDING BONDS
1923-1928. 1 file box (G5).
Resolutions to provide for the funding of existing indebtedness of the board of education, showing township, date, names of school board members, amount of net floating indebtedness, total funded and unfunded debt, and total of outstanding indebtedness. Chronologically arranged by dates of meetings. For index, see entry 397. Handwritten on printed forms. 10 x 4.5 x 14. Auditor's inner office.

531. BONDS AND INTEREST COUPONS
1925—. 2 file boxes (P7, W6).
Original road improvement bonds showing date of issue and date of maturity, rate of interest to be paid, name and number of road to be improved, total cost, and authorization and signatures of the county commissioners and county auditor. Chronologically arranged by dates issued and numerically thereunder by bond numbers. For index, see entry 397. Handwritten on printed forms. 10 x 4.5 x 14. Auditor's inner office.

532. BONDS AND INTEREST COUPONS
1932—. 1 file box (W6).
Original bonds for poor relief showing date of issue, date of maturity, amount of bond, rate of interest to be paid, the full amount of the bond issued, as authorized and signed by the board of county commissioners and by the auditor. Chronologically arranged by dates issued and numerically thereunder by bond numbers. For index, see entry 397. Handwritten on printed forms. 10 x 4..5 x 14. Auditor's inner office.

533. BOND ORDINANCES
1926—. 1 file box (C7).
Record copies of city (Marietta) ordinances providing for the issuance and sale of bonds to pay the cities share of the costs and expense of improving the city streets to the corporation line and certified by the auditor, showing the date, name of street, and kind of improvement. Chronologically arranged by dates of filing. For index, see entry 397. Typed. 10 x 4.5 x 14. Auditor's inner office.

534. BOND RESOLUTIONS

1928—. 1 file box (B7).

Resolutions to issue bonds, after submission to the electors by the board of education in the different school districts in Washington County, for the erection of new schools, building additions, and improving and enlarging of school buildings, showing name of school and of district, amounts of bonds, total amount, interest, and date of maturity. Chronologically arranged by issues. For index, see entry 397. Typed on printed forms. 10 x 4.5 x 14. Auditor's inner office.

535. CERTIFICATE OF COUNTY AUDITOR

August 27, 1935. 1 file box (C7).

Record of certificate of county auditor, certifying the average levy throughout the life of the bonds which will be required to pay the interest on and retire the bonds proposed to be issued by the board of education of the Little Hocking rural school district in the sum of $16,500, for the purpose of constructing a fireproof elementary school building in conjunction with the United States government. Sealed and signed by the county auditor. Chronologically arranged by dates of filing. For index, see entry 397. Typed. 10 x 4.5 x 14. Auditor's inner office.

536. ROAD BONDS REDEEMED

1909—. 14 file boxes.

Road bonds redeemed by Washington County; issued and sold to provide funds for the building and improvement of highways as authorized by the county board of commissioners, showing date issued, bond number, amount of bond, rate of interest, and date redeemed. Chronologically arranged by date issued and numerically thereunder by bond numbers. 1909-1928, no index; 1929—, see entry 397. Typed and handwritten on printed forms. 10 file boxes, 4.5 x 4.5 x 10; 4 file boxes, 10 x x 5 x 14. 10 file boxes, 1909-1928, Storeroom 1; 4 file boxes, 1929—, Auditor's inner office.

537. BONDS REDEEMED

1921-1923. 1 file box (X3).

These are county five percent experiment farm bonds and are payable on date of maturity with interest payable semiannually, showing date of maturity, rate of interest, signatures of county commissioners and of county auditor, and seal.

Chronologically arranged by dates of filing and numerically thereunder by bond numbers. For index, see entry 397. Printed. 10 x 4.5 x 14. Auditor's inner office.

Recognizance Bonds

538. FORFEITED RECOGNIZANCE RECORD

1877-1904. 1 volume. No prior or subsequent records.

Record of bail bond recognizance forfeited, showing in what court, case number, names of defendant and sureties, date of bond, description of real estate or other property posted for the security of the bond, amount of bond, and date certified forfeited to county prosecutor by the county auditor. Chronologically arranged by dates forfeited. No index. Handwritten on printed forms. 160 pages. 14 x 9 x .75. Storeroom 2.

Registers and Rosters

539. RECORD OF DEPUTIES

1870-1900. 1 volume. Discontinued.

Auditor's record copies of appointment of deputy auditors with copy of oath of office by deputy appointed, showing date of appointment and name of appointee; also record copy of annual report to county treasury examiners showing date report filed, total amount debited treasurer, expenditures from each fund, balance or deficit of each fund, and total balance, 1871-1880. Chronologically arranged by dates of filing. No index. Handwritten. 120 pages. 14 x 10 x .75. Storeroom 3.

540. APPOINTMENTS OF DEPUTIES

1901—. 11 file boxes (D6-D9, L3-L8, C6).

Record copies of certificates, with the approval of the judge of the court of common pleas, in the manner of the appointments of deputy recorders, law librarians, court bailiffs, deputy treasurers, deputy clerks of the courts, and court stenographers, showing date certificate filed, name of appointee, office appointed to, date appointment is effective, oaths of appointees, and signatures of appointee and of clerk of courts. Chronologically arranged by dates of appointments. For index, see entry 397. Handwritten on printed forms. 10 x 4.5 x 14. Auditor's inner office.

541. SCHOOL BOARD
1914—. 1 file box (D7).
List of names of members of schools' boards and officers showing dates, name of school districts, name of board members, their addresses, and dates of the expiration of terms. Chronologically arranged by dates of filing. For index, see entry 397. Typed on printed forms. 10 x 4.5 x 14. Auditor's inner office.

542. NAMES OF TOWNSHIP OFFICERS
1914—. 1 file box (B5).
Records from the township clerk to the county auditor certifying the names of the township officers and justices of the peace of said township in office, with the post office address, commencement and expiration of term, showing name of officer, political party to which each officer is affiliated, name of office, and signature of clerk. Chronologically arranged by dates of entries. For index, see entry 397. Handwritten on printed forms. 10 x 4.5 x 14. Auditor's inner office.

543. CORPORATION OFFICERS
1917—. 1 file box (B5).
Certificates of election of municipal officials issued by clerks of municipal corporations to the county auditor, showing date certificate was issued, name and office of official, and signatures of officer and corporation clerk. Chronologically arranged by dates of entries. For index, see entry 397. Handwritten on printed forms. 10 x 4.5 x 14. Auditor's inner office.

Ministerial Land and School Records

544. RECORD OF MINISTERIAL AND SCHOOL LANDS
1828-1911. 1 volume. Discontinued.
Record sale of ministerial (section 29 of each township, Ohio Land Company's grant reserved for support of religion) and the school lands (section 16 of each township set aside for support of education of youth), showing name of purchaser, name of original lessor, lot number, acreage, date of surrender, date of sale, range, township, and section numbers, description of tract, appraised valuation, amount sold for, terms of payments, dates deferred payments due, anticipated interest, and total amount. Chronologically arranged by dates of surrenders and sales. No index.

Handwritten on printed forms. 230 pages. 16 x 11 x 1.25. Auditor's office.

For other records of school lands, see entry 545.

545. RECORD OF SCHOOL LANDS

October 1853-April 1896. 1 volume.

Record of sale or lands in section 16 of each township (known as school lands under the provisions of the congressional ordinance of 1785 which reserved lot number 16 of every township for the purpose of providing education for the youth of the Northwest Territory), showing the result of elections held to vote on the sale of these lands and record of the sale of lands. It shows date of sale, name of purchaser, acreage to each purchaser, amount each tract sold for, and terms of sale. Chronologically arranged by dates of entries. No index. Handwritten. Condition poor. 210 pages. 14 x 10 x 1.25. Storeroom 3.

For prior and subsequent records of sales, see entry 544.

546. RECORD (Free School Library)

1854-1855. 1 volume.

Auditor's record of books supplied to each school district showing name or number of school district, titles of books, number of volumes of each title, price debited to school district for each volume, and total debit for each district. Chronologically arranged by debits to districts. No index. Handwritten on printed forms. Condition poor. 120 pages. 12 x 8 x .75. Storeroom 3.

547. RESOLUTIONS FOR THE REASSIGNMENT OF SCHOOL DISTRICTS BY THE BOARD OF EDUCATION

1905-1926. 1 file box (C6). No prior or subsequent records.

Record copies of resolutions for the reassignment of rural school districts, according to the best interest of the communities, and under the provisions of the general code of the state of Ohio, with plat maps showing districts to be transferred, boundary lines of new districts established, and name of real estate owners in the new districts set up. Chronologically arranged by dates issued. For index, see entry 397. Typed. 10 x 4.5 x 14. Auditor's inner office.

548. RESOLUTIONS

1932—. 1 file box (B7).

Resolutions of board of education accepting the amounts and rates as determined by the budget commission, and authorizing the necessary tax levies and certifying them to the county auditor; showing the date of resolution, name of school district, and signature of county auditor. Chronologically arranged by dates of meetings. For index, see entry 397. Handwritten on printed forms. 10 x 4.5 x 14. Auditor's inner office.

Weights and Measures

549. RECORD OF SEALER OF WEIGHTS-MEASURES

1908—. 3 volumes. Prior records missing.

Record showing date of inspection, name of firm, individual, or corporation, address, kind of business, types of weighing and measuring devices tested, kinds of commodities reweighed or remeasured, number found correct, number found incorrect and whether under or over; also record of orders issued to owners of weighing and measuring devices. Chronologically arranged by dates of entries. No index. Handwritten on printed forms. Average 270 pages. 26 x 16.5 x 1.5. 2 volumes, 1908-December 1936, Storeroom 3; 1 volume, January 1937—, Commissioners office.

550. [INSPECTION] RECORD

1914—. 5 bundles and 2 file boxes. No prior records.

Record of inspections made by deputy sealer of weights and measures showing date, inspection number, name of owner of weighing and measuring device, address, kind of business, type of weighing device, type of measuring device, findings, and orders of deputy sealer of weights and measure. Numerically arranged by inspection numbers. No index. Handwritten on printed forms. Bundles, 16 x 24 x 1.5; file boxes, 10 x 4.5 x 14. 5 bundles, 1914-1932, Storeroom 1; 2 file boxes, 1933—, Auditor's office.

Miscellaneous

551. ADVANCE DRAWS

1920—. 2 file boxes (F8, R9).

Record of requests for advance of funds, from the trustees of the various townships to the county auditor, showing date, name of township, amount requested, warrant number, amount issued, and date filed. Chronologically arranged by dates of request. For index, see entry 397. Handwritten on printed forms. 10 x 4.5 x 14. Auditor's inner office.

552. UNCLAIMED COST AND BANK DEPOSITS
1917—. 1 volume.

Record of cost and fees unclaimed and paid into county treasury by county officials, showing date paid in, by what official, to whom due, case number, volume and page numbers of cash book, amount, date warrant was issued by auditor for recovery, and warrant number. Also unclaimed bank deposits showing date paid into county treasury, by orders of what court, name of depositor, date of last credit or debit entry, name of bank paying into treasury, amount, date warrant was issued by auditor for recovery, and warrant number. Alphabetically arranged by names of payees or depositors and chronologically thereunder by dates paid in. No index. Handwritten on printed forms. 190 pages. 16 x 14 x 1.75. Auditor's office.

553. OBJECTIONS TO SPECIAL ASSESSMENTS
1920-1928. 1 file box (Q4).

Records of objections to special assessments on property for the building of roads, giving reason of property owners' protest and calling for an investigation by the commissioners or a committee appointed for such investigations, showing names of property owners, location, and description of each tract or lot. Chronologically arranged by dates of filing. For index, see entry 397. Handwritten. 10 x 4.5 x 14. Auditor's inner office.

554. SURVEYOR'S CERTIFICATE OF CORRECTION
1916—. 1 file box (F9).

Record copies of resurveys of land by county surveyor, correcting a prior one, showing date, name of landowner, name of previous owner, name of township, range, township, section, and lot numbers, and description of plat map tract surveyed, with boundary lines and dimensions tracts shown. Chronologically arranged by dates of filing. For index, see entry 397. Handwritten on printed forms. 10 x 4.5 x 14. Auditor's inner office.

555. CERTIFICATES OF AGREED DIVISION OF VALUATION
1927—. 1 file box (B8).

Certificates of agreed division of valuation in transfers of lands and lots to the auditor of Washington County, showing date, names of grantor and grantee, lot number, subdivision or addition, acreage, value of land and a buildings, total valuation, and signature of grantor and grantee. Chronologically arranged by dates of filing. For index, see entry 397. Handwritten on printed forms. 10 x 4.5 x 14. Auditor's inner office.

556. BUILDING NOTICES
1919—. 9 file boxes (F9, N5-N9, R3-R5).
Notices to the county auditor of the erection or construction of buildings or improvements outside the city of Marietta, giving dimensions and estimated cost, location, lot number, description the tract or lot as given by on the tax duplicate, and signature and post-office address of owner. Chronologically arranged by dates of filing. For index, see entry 397. Handwritten on printed forms. 10 x 4.5 x 14. Auditor's inner office.

557. INSURANCE RECORD
1871—. 1 volume.
Record of insurance carried by the county commissioners on county structures such as courthouse, children's home, and infirmary buildings, fairground buildings, bridges, and motor equipment, showing name of insurance company, policy number, date issued, amount insured, on what, amount of premium, date of expiration of policy, description of property, and name of agent writing risk. Chronologically arranged by dates issued. No index. Handwritten on printed forms. 270 pages. 16 x 11 x 1.5. Auditor's office.

558. RECORD OF ESTIMATES, BRIDGES
1870-1923. 1 volume. Discontinued.
Auditor's record of estimates made by county surveyor on material cost for the construction and repair of bridges, showing what bridge, date estimate was made, itemized list of material and cost, total amount estimated, and date filed. Chronologically arranged by dates of filing. No index. Handwritten. 180 pages. 14 x 10 x 1. Storeroom 3.

559. POLL LIST AND TALLY SHEET
1832-1859. 27 bundles.

Township poll and tally sheets of elections held in the several townships for land appraisers and district tax assessors; poll list showing name of electors casting ballots in each election, and tally sheets showing number of votes received by each candidate as land appraiser or tax assessor. No systematic arrangement. No index. Handwritten. 1.5 x 3.5 x 8. Storeroom 3.

A budget commission was established in Washington County in 1911 under the act of that year which made provision for the establishment of a budget commission in each county to be composed of the county auditor, the mayor of the largest municipality, and the prosecuting attorney (102 O. L. 266). It was not until after the World War, when county expenditures steadily increased that the importance of improved methods of finances were forcibly brought to the attention of the legislature. This new need was met, in 1927, by the establishment of a budget commission in each county. This commission, consisting of the auditor, treasurer, and prosecuting attorney, receives and examines the annual budget of the county, municipal, township, and school authorities, with an estimate of the amount to be raised for state purposes in each subdivision (112 O. L. 399). If the total amount exceeds the sum authorized to be raised, the commission adjusts the amount to be raised and may change and revise the estimates. The commission may reduce all items in the budget, but it is prohibited from increasing the total of any budget or any item.

The adjusted budget is certified to the taxing authority in each subdivision. If the work of the commission is satisfactory, each taxing authority by ordinance or resolution authorizes the necessary tax levies and certifies them to the county auditor. (G. C. sec. 5625-25). On the other hand, the taxing authority in any subdivision may appeal, through its fiscal officer, from the decision of the budget commission to the state tax commission of Ohio, which is empowered to adjust the estimates of revenues and balances in fixing the tax rates (G. C. sec. 5625-28).

The county auditor, as secretary to the commission, is required to keep a full and accurate record of the proceedings of the commission.

560. [BUDGET COMMISSIONS MINUTES]

1911-1913 in (Board of Revision) Journal, entry 563.

Record copy of minutes of meetings of the budget commission showing property valuation for each tax district, anticipated operating expenses for each district, and tax rate for each district.

For subsequent records, see entry 561.

561. JOURNAL

1914—. 1 volume.

Record of minutes of meetings of budget commission showing total property valuation, real and personal, for each tax district, anticipated operating expenses for each tax district, commission's budget for each fund for each district, and tax rate for each district. Chronologically arranged by dates of meetings. No index. Typed. 340 pages. 14 x 10 x 1.75. Auditor's office.

For prior records, see entry 560.

The county board of revision, the object of which was to correct some of the defects and inequities of assessments, was established by the legislature in 1825. The first board of revision, or equalization as it was sometimes called, was composed of the county commissioners, the county auditor, and the assessor. The board was authorized to meet at the seat of justice on the first Monday in June annually "to hear and determine the complaint of any owner of property listed and valued by the assessor . . . and shall correct any list valuations made by the assessor, either by adding to or deducting from his valuation." (23 O. L. 66). The act of 1831, repealing the act of 1825, left the duties and personnel of the board unchanged. (29 O. L. 278).

In 1859 the legislature made for provision for two county boards of equalization. One board, composed of the auditor and commissioners, was directed to meet annually for the purpose of equalizing real and personal property, and moneys and credit in the county. The other board, composed of the auditor, surveyor, and commissioners, was authorized to meet sexennially for the same purpose. (56 O. L. 57, 60).

The act of 1863, amending the act of 1859, left the personnel and duties of the annual county board unchanged. The second county board, although continuing without alteration and composition or duties, was directed to meet decennially, rather than sexennially. (60 O. L. 57, 69). The legislative act of 1868, amending the act of 1863, left the membership of the annual and special boards, as well as their duties, practically unchanged (65 O. L. 160-170).

The annual and special boards of equalization were abolished, when, in 1913, the state tax commission of Ohio was given the task of supervising the assessment of real and personal property in the state. Under this arrangement each county constituted a district. In each district containing less than 60, 000 inhabitants by which stipulation Washington County was included, there was to be appointed by the governor one state tax commissioner. In all other districts there was appointed, in the same matter, two state deputy tax commissioners. In each district there was appointed a district board of complaints. This board, appointed by the state tax commission with the consent of the governor, took over the duties and powers formerly vested in the boards of equalization. The county auditor, made secretary to the board of complaints, was required to be present at each meeting in person or by deputy, and keeps an accurate record of their proceedings to be kept in a book for that purpose. (103 O. L. 491). Moreover, the board was directed to take full minutes of all evidence given before it and might have such evidence taken in shorthand and extended into typewritten form. The auditor was required to preserve in his office separate records of all minutes and documentary evidence offered in each complaint. (103 O. L. 791).

The arrangement, after being in operation for two years, was abrogated by the legislature in 1915. In that year the county auditor, under the supervision of the tax commission of Ohio, became the chief assessing officer in the county. The treasurer, prosecutor, probate judge, and the president of the county commissioners were to constitute a board for the purpose of appointing three members to constitute a board of revision. Again the county auditor was made secretary to the board and was directed to keep a record of their proceedings and to preserve in his office a separate record of all minutes and documentary evidence offered in each complaint. (105 O. L. 257-258),

Under the present system, inaugurated in 1917, the treasurer, auditor, and the president of the commissioners constitute a board of revision. This board organizes annually, on the second Monday in June, by electing a chairman for the ensuing year. The county auditor serves as secretary to the board. (G. C. secs. 5537, 5592). The county board of revision may, with the consent and approval of the tax commission of Ohio, employee experts, clerks, and other employees (G. C. sec. 5587).

The duties of the board, not differing in detail from those prescribed in 1825, include the hearing of all complaints relating to valuation or assessments of real property as it appears upon the tax duplicate of the "then current year." The board is authorized to investigate all complaints and may increase or decrease any valuation or correct any assessment complained of, or may order a reassessment by the original assessing official. (G. C. sec. 5597). However, no valuation is increased without giving notice to the person in whose name the property affected is listed (G. C, sec. 5599). The board of revision, in all respects, is governed by the laws respecting the valuation of real property and makes no change of any valuation "except in accordance with such laws" (G. C. sec. 5596).

On the second Monday in June, annually, the county auditor lays before the board of revision the returns of assessments of any real property for the current year, and the board proceeds to review the assessment. The board of revision certifies its action to the county auditor, who corrects the tax list and duplicate according to the additions and deductions ordered by the board. The auditor is prohibited, by statute, from making up his tax list and duplicate, until the board has completed its work and has returned to him all the returns laid before it with revisions. (G. C. sec. 5605). But in the event the tax duplicate has been delivered to the county treasurer, the auditor is required to certify such corrections to him and enter such corrections in his tax duplicate (G. C. sec. 5602).

In its investigations the board may examine, under oath, persons as to their or others' real property. In the event witnesses fail to appear or refuse to testify, the board by its chairman is authorized to make a complete in writing to the probate judge, who, by statute, is directed to institute proceedings against them. (G. C. sec, 5596). The decision of the board are subject to appeal, within thirty days after a decision is served, to the tax commission of Ohio. (G. C. sec. 5610).

The secretary of the board is required to keep "an accurate record of the proceedings of the board in a book to be kept for that purpose" (G. C. sec. 5592). The county auditor, as in 1913, is required to preserve in his office separate records of all minutes and documentary evidence offered in each complaint (G. C. sec. 5603). The records of the board are open to the inspection of the public (G. C. sec. 5591).

562. (Board of Equalization) JOURNAL
1870-1903. 2 volumes. No prior records.

Record of minutes of meetings of county board of equalization with record copy of revision of real and personal property valuations for taxation, showing name of owner, tax district, description of property, amount added to or deducted from original valuation, and reason for revision. Chronologically arranged by dates of sessions. No index. Handwritten. Average 490 pages. 18 x 12 x 2.5. Storeroom 3.

For subsequent records, see entry 563.

563. (Board of Revision) JOURNAL
1904-1912. 1 volume.

Record copy of minutes of meetings of board of revision showing date, order of business, record of adjustment made on taxation values of real and personal property, with name of property owner, tax district, and amount of revision. Contains [Budget Commission Minutes], 1911-1913, entry 560. Chronologically arranged by dates of meetings. No index. Handwritten. 480 pages. 18 x 12 x 2.5. Auditor's office.

For prior records, see entry 562; for subsequent records, see entry 564.

564. (Board of Complaints) JOURNAL
1913—. 1 volume.

Record copy of minutes of meetings of board of complaints with record of complaints filed on property values for taxation by owners, showing name of complainant, tax district, nature of complaint, and revision of assessments recommended. Chronologically arranged by dates of meetings. No index. Typed. 420 pages. 16 x 11 x 2.25. Auditor's office.

For prior records, see entries 562 and 563.

SINKING FUND TRUSTEES

The board of sinking fund trustees, composed of the prosecuting attorney, auditor, and treasurer, was organized in 1919 in Washington County and in each county owing a bonded debt. The county prosecuting attorney serves as president of the board and the auditor as secretary. It is a duty of the trustees to provide for the payment of all bonds issued by the county and the interest maturing thereon.

All bonds issued by the county must be recorded in the office of the trustees of the sinking fund, bear a stamp containing the words "Recorded in the office of the sinking fund trustees," and signed by the secretary before they become valid in the hands of the purchaser. Since 1922, in the event the secretary is unable to act, by reason of absence or disability, such recording and authenticating is performed by the county treasurer. (G. C. Sec. 2976-25).

On or before the first Monday in May of each year, the trustees certify to the county commissioners the rate of tax necessary to provide a sinking fund both for the payment and maturity of bonds heretofore issued by the county and for the payment of interest on the bonded indebtedness. The amount certified by the trustees is set forth without diminution in the annual budget of the commissioners. (G. C. sec. 2976-26). Then, after each semiannual settlement of taxes and assessments, the county auditor reports to the trustees the amount of money in the treasury of the county charged to the credit of the sinking fund. Money drawn from the county treasury for investment or disbursement is by the issuance of a voucher signed by all the members of the board and directed to the county auditor. The trustees are directed, by statute, to invest all moneys subject to their control in United States bonds, Ohio bonds, or bonds of a municipal corporation, school district, township, or county in the state.

The board members are required to keep "a full and complete record of their transactions, a complete record of the funded debt of the county specifying the dates, purposes, amounts, numbers, maturities, and rates and maturities of interest and installments thereof, and where payable, and an account exhibiting the amount held in the sinking fund for the payment thereof." (G. C. sec. 2976-24).

The meeting of the trustees are open to the public. All questions relating to the purchase or sale of securities or the payment of bonds or interest are decided by a yea and nay vote, which is recorded in their journal.

565. SINKING FUND JOURNAL

1919—. 1 volume.

Record copy of minutes of meetings of sinking fund trustees showing date, order of business, record of bonds issued or sold, maturity dates of issues, bond numbers of each issue, and interest coupon due dates. Chronologically arranged by dates of meetings. No index. Typed. 270 pages. 14 x 10 x 1.5. Auditor's office.

The county board of education, a modern administrative and supervisory agency developed during the last two decades, supplanted the smaller educational units, which, established during the early period of Ohio history, became inefficient and unable to meet the moderate requirements as demanded by rural communities.

During the earlier period of Ohio history educational administration, because of the newness of the state, the sparseness of the population, and the undeveloped means of transportation was, by necessity, local in character. For fourteen years after the accession of Ohio to statehood, though the constitution stated that means of education should be encouraged by the general assembly no legislation was enacted for public schools (*Ohio Const. 1820,* Art. VIII sec. 3, 25, 27). It was not until 1817 that the legislature authorized six or more people in the townships to form associations to build school houses and to be incorporated for educational purposes (15 O. L. 407). This was a beginning, but as yet the values of an educational system were not readily perceived by those engaged in subduing a stubborn wilderness.

The first permanent law for the organization of schools in Ohio was passed in 1821. Under the provisions of this act, the electors of the township were authorized to vote on the proposition of dividing the townships into school districts. If the proposal carried, there were to be elected three school commissioners, who, in turn, were authorized to select a clerk and a collector who should act as a treasurer. They were instructed also, to levy taxes for the support of schools and to hire teachers. (19 O. L. 54).

As education began to advance in the early years of the nineteenth century, some kind of state control was needed. Accordingly, in 1837, the office of state superintendent of schools was established. A year later an act was passed making the county auditor also the county superintendent of schools; and in each township the clerk became superintendent of the smaller unit. The county superintendent was made responsible to the state superintendent in all educational affairs. In the same year each incorporated city, town, or borough not regulated by a charter was made a separate school district. The voters in each division were authorized to elect three directors. (31 O. L. 21). The effectiveness of this organization, however, was destroyed in 1840, when the legislature abolished the office of state superintendent and the secretary of state took over his functions of tabulating and transmitting school statistics (38 O. L. 130). Seven years later, twenty-five counties exclusive of Washington were allowed to have county superintendents (45 O. L. 32), and in 1848 the provisions of the previous act were extended to all other counties in the state (46 O. L. 86).

Although marked changes were made in the curriculum of the schools, the history of education and Ohio from 1850 to the early part of the twentieth century was largely one of the gradual transference of powers from districts to townships, and from townships to county in the interest of a better system of education. It was not, however, until within the last three decades that the county became the unit for educational administration (70 O. L. 195, 204; 97 O. L. 354).

Although the county superintendent was known as early as 1838, the first permanent law for the establishment of a county board of education was enacted in 1914. Under this act the school districts were classified, and provision was made for a county school district, exclusively of the territory embraced in any city or village desiring exemption. The county district was to be under the supervision of five board members elected by the presidents of the village and rural school boards. The members were to hold office for one, two, three, four, and five years respectively, and each year one member was to be selected.

The county board of education was authorized to change school district lines; afford transportation for children living more than two miles from a schoolhouse; appoint a county superintendent; and certify annually to the county auditor the number of teachers and superintendents employed, their salaries, and the amount apportioned for each school district. The county superintendent, acting as secretary of the board, was required to keep in a book provided for that purpose a full record of the proceedings of the board properly indexed. Each motion, together with the name of the person making it and the vote thereon, was to be entered on the record. (104 O. L. 133; 108 O. L. pt. i, 704).

The county was divided into administrative divisions containing one or more villages or rural school districts. Each district was to be under the supervision of a district superintendent, who was required to visit the schools in his charge, direct and assist teachers in the performance of their duties, and classify and control promotions of pupils. Moreover, he was required to report annually to the county superintendent on matters under his charge, and assemble teachers for the purpose of conferring on curricular matters, discipline, and school management. (104 O. L. 133-145).

Significant changes were made by the act of 1920, under which the county board members became elective. They were authorized to appoint one or more assistant county superintendents for a term of three years. Washington County, however, has no assistant. The board was authorized to publish, with the advice and consent of the county superintendent, a minimum course of study to serve as a guide to local board members. The same act abolished the office of district superintendent. (G. C. secs. 4728-1, 4729; 108 O. L. pt. i, 704).

The county organization has placed the rural schools on a plane of equality with the city schools. The consolidation of the smaller units has eliminated the small, ill-equipped schools, and provides under one roof facilities and instruction suited to the needs of the rural children under the supervision of educational specialist.

Records are located in the main office of the board of education unless otherwise specified.

Journals and Reports

566. MINUTES
1914—. 3 volumes.
Record copy of minutes of meetings, regular and special, of county board of education, showing date, order of business, and copy of all resolutions passed; also itemized list of bills and claims allowed, showing date of bill, name of creditor, for what, amount of bill, and payment voucher number. Chronologically arranged by dates of meetings. No index. Typed. Average 250 pages. 14 x 10 x 1.5.

567. COUNTY RECORD OF BOARDS
1924—. 1 file box.
Record of meetings and minutes of district boards of education. Alphabetically arranged by names of boards and chronologically thereunder. No index. Handwritten. 12 x 16 x 30.

568. FINANCIAL REPORT
1914—. 3 file boxes.
Record copy of county superintendent's annual financial report to state department of education, showing cash receipts from all sources for school purposes, total amount to tuition fund, total amount to contingent fund, and amount of state aid; also itemized account of expenditures, showing total for teaching and for supervision, total for transportation of pupils, total for janitors and other contingent expenses, amount of indebtedness (bonds and interest) paid off, and total unpaid

and indebtedness. Chronologically arranged by years. No index. Typed on printed forms. 10 x 8 x 16.

569. STATISTICAL REPORT

1914—. 6 file boxes.

Record copy of school superintendent's annual report to state department of education on school statistics, showing number of schools in county under supervision, number school rooms, number of consolidated schools, number of high schools, number of teachers, number of principals, number of pupils in county, number of elementary pupils, number of high school pupils, and number of weeks of school. Chronologically arranged by years. No index. Typed. 10 x 8 x 16.

Record of Pupils

570. SCHOOL ENUMERATION

1915—. 23 bundles.

Enumeration of the youths of Washington County between the age of five and eighteen years, giving name, address, age, sex, and name of parent or guardian. Chronologically arranged by years and alphabetically thereunder by names of youths. No index. Handwritten. 3 x 8 x 14. 13 bundles, 1915-1927, Storeroom 1; 10 bundles, 1927—, Board of education main office.

571. SCHOOL RECORD

1914-1924. 11 volumes.

Attendance, promotion, and home record of pupils of township and village schools showing what school, name of teacher, name of pupil, grade, age, number of days attended school each month, record of examinations showing grade received in each study, record of promotion; also home record showing name of pupil, date of birth, date entered school, name of parent or guardian, and residents. This report is made by teacher to county superintendent of schools. Alphabetically arranged by names of schools and alphabetically thereunder by names of pupils. No index. Handwritten on printed forms. Average 600 pages. 14 x 12 x 3.5. Storeroom 1.

For subsequent records, see entry 572.

572. PRACTICAL REGISTER AND COMPLETE RECORD BOOK

1925—. 970 volumes.

Record of attendance and grades as kept by teachers for each room in all school districts in Washington County, except cities of Marietta and Belpre. Annual statistical report is made from this record showing name, age, and grade of pupil, promotion record, and name of teacher. Alphabetically arranged by names of pupils. No index. Handwritten on printed forms. Average 35 pages. 15 x 12 x .25. 270 volumes, 1925-1930, Storeroom 1; 700 volumes, 1931—, Board of education main office safe file, south wall.

For prior records, see entry 571.

573. ATTENDANCE RECORD

1926—. 1 file box. No prior records found.

Records of school attendance in county kept by attendance officer. Alphabetically arranged by names of pupils. No index. Handwritten on printed forms. 12 x 16 x 30. Filing cabinets, north wall.

574. PUPILS' RECORD CARDS ACTIVE

1924—. 5 file boxes.

Individual advancement cards of students in school together with record of their grades. Alphabetically arranged by names of pupils. No index. Handwritten on printed forms. 5 x 5 x 20. Filing cabinet, north wall.

575. PUPILS' RECORD CARD INACTIVE

1924—. 4 file boxes.

Record of students who have finished school or were forced to leave county schools. Alphabetically arranged by names of pupils. No index. Handwritten on printed forms. 5 x 5 x 20. Filing cabinet, north wall.

576. WORKING CERTIFICATES

1930—. 4 file boxes.

Record of pupils under compulsory age limit leaving school for employment, showing name and age of pupil, name of parent or guardian, and name of employer. Alphabetically arranged by names of pupils. No index. Handwritten on printed forms. 6 x 10 x 20. Filing cabinet, north wall.

577. RELIEF

1931-1932. 1 file box. Discontinued.

Record of clients receiving school relief from county. Alphabetically arranged by names of townships and alphabetically thereunder by names of recipients. No index. Handwritten on printed forms. 4 x 5 x 20. Filing cabinet, north wall.

Records of Teachers

578. RECORDS OF TEACHERS' EXAMINATIONS

1890—. 4 volumes.

Records names of teachers and their grades made in examinations for teaching certificates; also type and term of certificate. Alphabetically arranged by names of teachers. No index. Handwritten. Average 200 pages. 10 x 16 x 2. Safe file, south wall.

579. SEMESTER HOURS, TEACHERS' CREDITS

1924—. 1 file box.

Record of credits of employed teachers, expired credit certificates, and record of semester hours. Alphabetically arranged by names of teachers. No index. Handwritten on printed forms. 14 x 18 x 20. Filing cabinet, north wall.

580. WASHINGTON COUNTY NORMAL

1922-1925. 1 volume. Discontinued.

Record of county normal schools at Lowell and Waterford, Ohio. Registration and attendance records showing name of registrant, address, age, teaching experience, and normal school credits. Alphabetically arranged by names of students. No index. Handwritten. 250 pages. 10 x 16 x 2. South wall.

Miscellaneous

581. MAPS, SCHOOL DISTRICTS

1936—. 22 maps.

Plat map of each township showing boundary lines of each school district, area, name of owner of each tract of land, location of school building, and school bus routes. Prepared by county engineer. Alphabetically arranged by names of townships. No index. Hand drawn, black and white. No scale shown. 30 x 28 x .75.

582. BUDGET

1926—. 2 bundles.

Record of appropriations by county board of education and of operating expenses of board showing total receipts from all sources and total expenditures itemized by funds. Chronologically arranged. No index. Handwritten. 8 x 12 x 2. Safe file, south wall.

583. GENERAL CORRESPONDENCE

1933—. 2 file boxes.

Records include miscellaneous monthly reports, teachers' certificates, and general correspondence. Alphabetically arranged by names of schools. No index. Handwritten and typed. 14 x 18 x 30. Filing cabinet, north wall.

584. INACTIVE GENERAL CORRESPONDENCE

1934—. 1 file box.

Correspondence which has been completed by office and is considered as dead. Alphabetically arranged by names of schools and correspondence. No index. Handwritten and typed. 12 x 16 x 30. Filing cabinet, north wall.

585. MISCELLANEOUS FILE

1926—. 1 file box.

Miscellaneous correspondence and office reports on attendance in county. Alphabetically arranged by names of schools. No index. Handwritten and typed. 12 x 16 x 30. Filing cabinet, north wall.

The general health district, or county health department, is one of the recent developments in county health administration. An act of legislature in 1919 provided that townships and municipalities in each county, exclusive of any city with 25,000 or more population, should constitute a general health district; cities with 25,000 or more population, municipal health district; and municipalities of not less than 10,000 or more than 35,000 population, and maintaining a board of health meeting the qualifications of the legislative act, were authorized after examination by the state health department to continue operation as separate health districts. (108 O. L. pt. i, 238).

An amendment in December 1919 made each city a health district; the townships and villages in each county were combined into a general health district; and a city and general health district might combine for administrative purposes (108 O. L. pt. ii, 1085). The mayor of each municipality not constituting a city health district, and the chairman of the trustees of each township, are authorized to meet at the seat of justice and by selecting a chairman and a secretary organize a district advisory council which selects and appoints a district board of health composed of five members one of whom must be a physician, who serve without compensation (108 O. L. pt. ii, 1085).

Within thirty days after their appointment the members of the district board of health–the county board of health–organized by appointing one of their members president and other president *pro tempore.* The board is authorized to appoint as district health commissioner a licensed physician who is designated deputy state registrar of vital statistics and is required to report monthly to the state registrar of vital statistics, and who serves as secretary to the board (G. C. sec. 1261-32; 108 O. L. pt. i, 242).

On recommendation of the district health commissioner the board appoints a whole-time public nurse, a clerk, and such additional public health nurses, physicians and others as maybe necessary for the proper conduct of its work. The board studies the prevalence of disease, especially communicable diseases, provides treatment of venereal diseases, and is authorized to make any and all regulations it deems necessary for the prevention or restriction of disease, and the prevention, abolition or suppression of nuisances. It provides for inspection of public charitable, benevolent, correctional and penal institutions; and may provide inspection of dairies, stores, restaurants, hotels and other places where food is manufactured, handled, stored, sold or offered for sale. The board is authorized to carry on necessary laboratory tests by establishing a laboratory or contracting with existing laboratories, and all state institutions supported in the whole or in part by public funds must furnish such laboratory service to a county board of health under the terms agreed upon (108 O. L. Pt. ii, 1088-89).

The health department is financed by public taxation. The district board of health annually estimates in itemized form the amount needed for the fiscal year, and these estimates are certified by the county auditor and submitted to the county budget commissioner who may reduce any item but cannot increase any item or the aggregate of all items. The total amount fixed by the budget commissioners is apportioned by the county health department on the basis of taxable valuations in the townships and municipalities composing the district. (108 O. L. pt. ii, 1091).

All records of the board of health are located in the main office of the board.

Journals and Reports

586. MINUTE BOOKS
1820—. 2 volumes.
Record of minutes and proceedings of the county board of health, including all financial transactions. Chronologically arranged. No index. Handwritten. 300 pages. 14 x 8 x 2.

587. DAILY NOTEBOOK
1920—. 2 volumes.
Record of the daily business transactions by the county board of health, including a register of visitors to the office. Chronologically arranged. No index. Handwritten. Average 300 pages. 14 x 8 x 2.

588. NURSING VISITS
1936. 1 file box.
Reports by the visiting nurses of visits and treatments of patients in various parts of the county, showing name and address of patient and detailed report. Alphabetically arranged by names of townships and alphabetically thereunder by names of patients. No index. Handwritten on printed forms. 3 x 10 x 14.

589. REPORT OF WATER ANALYSIS
1920—. 1 file box.
Reports of the analysis of drinking water taken in the various parts of the county and findings of sanitarian in charge. Alphabetically arranged by names of applicants for analysis. No index. Handwritten on printed forms. 4 x 10 x 24.

590. SANITARIAN'S RECORDS
April 1936—. 1 file box.
Reports of the findings of the sanitarian regarding sanitary investigations of conditions in Washington County. Alphabetically arranged by names of township. No index. Handwritten on printed forms. 4 x 10 x 24.

591. MISCELLANEOUS FILE
1920—. 2 file boxes.
Copies of the annual and monthly reports to the state board of health concerning the activities of the county board of health. Chronologically arranged. No index. Handwritten. 12 x 18 x 24.

Vital Statistics
(See also entries 288-292)

592. BIRTHS
1920—. 2 file boxes.
Copies of birth certificates showing name of infant, name and address of parents, date and place of birth, and signature of attending physician. Alphabetically arranged by names of townships and alphabetically thereunder by names of infants. No index. Handwritten on printed forms. 12 x 18 x 24.

593. DEATHS
1920—. 2 file boxes.
Copies of death certificates showing name of decedent, age, and place and cause of death. Alphabetically arranged by names of townships and alphabetically thereunder by names of decedents. No index. Handwritten on printed forms. 12 x 18 x 24.

594. BIRTHS AND DEATHS

Current year. 1 file box.

Record of births and deaths for the current year only showing name of infants or decedents, and dates of births or deaths. Alphabetically arranged by names of townships and alphabetically thereunder by names of infants or decedents. No index. Handwritten on printed forms. 12 x 18 x 24.

595. RECORD OF BIRTHS AND DEATHS

1920-1935. 2 volumes. Discontinued.

Register of births and deaths in Washington County, excepting the city of Marietta, showing names of infants or decedents, places of births or deaths, and causes of death. Alphabetically arranged by names of townships and alphabetically thereunder by names of infants or decedents. No index. Handwritten. Average 300 pages. 18 x 12 x 3.

Immunizations and Communicable Diseases

596. DIPHTHERIA IMMUNIZATION

1920—. 4 file boxes.

Record of diphtheria immunizations made in Washington County showing name of patient, date, and consent of parent or guardian in cases of minors. Alphabetically arranged by names of townships and alphabetically thereunder by names of patients. No index. Handwritten on printed forms. 12 x 18 x 24.

597. TYPHOID IMMUNIZATION

1920—. 1 file box.

Record of typhoid immunizations made in Washington County showing names of patient, dates, and consents of parents or guardians in cases of minors. Alphabetically arranged by names of townships and alphabetically thereunder by names of patients. No index. Handwritten on printed forms. 12 x 18 x 24.

598. COMMUNICABLE DISEASE RECORD

1920—. 2 file boxes.

Record of required reportable communicable diseases showing what disease, name of patient, and report of case. Alphabetically arranged by names of townships, and alphabetically thereunder by names of patients. No index. Handwritten on printed forms. 6 x 18 x 24.

Business Administration of Office

599. CASH BOOK

1920—. 2 volumes.

Record of receipts from all sources and expenditures of this office showing date and nature of receipt or disbursement. Chronologically arranged. No index. Handwritten. 300 pages. 18 x 14 x 2.

600. ORDERS FOR WARRANTS

1920—. 3 volumes.

Orders for warrants for salaries of employees and expenses of the board of health office. Chronologically arranged. No index. Handwritten. Average 500 pages. 15 x 8 x 3.

Miscellaneous

601. FAMILY RECORD

1920—. 2 file boxes.

Record of blind and tubercular patients in Washington County showing names and addresses of patients and case histories. Alphabetically arranged by names of townships and alphabetically thereunder by names of patients. No index. Handwritten on printed forms. 6 x 10 x 18.

602. SCHOOL RECORDS

1920—. 3 file boxes.

Record cards of reports of physical examinations of school children showing name of children, what school, and report of findings. Alphabetically arranged by names of schools and alphabetically thereunder by names of pupils. No index. Handwritten on printed forms. 4 x 10 x 14.

603. PRESCHOOL CLINIC RECORDS
1920—. 1 file box.

Record of activities of clinics held for children of preschool age. Alphabetically arranged by names of children. No index. Handwritten on printed forms. 4 x 10 x 14.

604. MATERNAL AND INFANT WELFARE
1920—. 2 file boxes.

Record of activities of clinics held for infant and maternal welfare. Alphabetically arranged by names of clients. No index. Handwritten on printed forms. 4 x 4 x 14.

The Washington County poorhouse, now called the county home, was established in 1840 under the provisions of the legislative act of 1816, which authorized the county commissioners to purchase land and construct poorhouses in which to care for the county's indigent (14 O. L. 248-249). By the same act the commissioners were authorized to appoint annually a board of directors of seven which was authorized to make rules and regulations for the management of the institution and to appoint a superintendent. Accordingly in 1835 the county commissioners purchased a tract of land to be used as a poor farm, but before the buildings were erected petitions were circulated for a change of location, and as a consequence the first tract was sold and the commissioners bought a tract of 198 acres east of Marietta. Thereafter suitable buildings were erected and formally opened in 1840. The buildings of brick now in use were erected on the same site in 1884 and were remodeled in 1908.

The board of directors was empowered to make all rules and regulations necessary for the management of the institution. Paupers not having residence requirements to obtain institutional care could be removed to their legal place of residence by the directors. Furthermore, the directors, or a committee of the body, were required to visit the institution monthly and report to the commissioners on such matters as the treatment of inmates, the clothing, and food. Each year the board was required to report to the commissioners on the state of the institution together with a full and accurate account of their proceedings including accounts and disbursements. (14 O. L. 449).

By the legislative act of 1831, the membership of the board was reduced to three. This board, like its predecessor, was authorized to appoint a superintendent. It was his duty, upon the order of the board, to discharge from the poorhouse any person who had been admitted because of illness when he had sufficiently recovered. Moreover the directors were authorized to remove paupers to their legal place of residence. (29 O. L. 319). Besides this, any "pauper" rejected by the board of directors could be turned over to the township overseers to be cared for by contracting with the lowest bidder (29 O. L. 321-322).

In 1850 the name county poorhouse was changed to that of county infirmary. Fifteen years later, in 1865, the board of infirmary directors, consisting of three resident electors, were to be elected by the voters of the county for a three-year term. This board was still authorized to appoint a superintendent, and was still required to make inspection visits, and report their findings to the county commissioners. (62 O. L. 24-25).

Although reports had been recorded in previous years, it was not until the decade of the seventies that the legislature enacted measures looking forward to some business-like management of this ancient institution. Accordingly, in 1872, an act was passed which required each infirmary director, as well as the superintendent, to give bond conditioned for the faithful performance of the duties of his office (69 O. L. 120-121). Under this act the directors were required to report semiannually to the county commissioners the condition of the infirmary, the number of inmates, and such other information as the county commissioners believed proper. Furthermore, the board of directors was required to file a full account "of all moneys received and paid out, together with the vouchers . . . from whence received, to whom and for what paid out" with the county commissioners, who, after examining it, entered the report in the minutes of their proceedings. This report, as well as the vouchers, were filed in the auditor's office, and was to be "safely preserved" by that officer. (69 O. L. 121-122).

The county infirmary served also as a place for the confinement of children, the mentally ill, and persons afflicted with epilepsy. Although the state assumed responsibility for the mentally ill in the early years of the nineteenth century, it was not until 1900 that it was made unlawful to confine the insane and epileptics in the county home. (93 O. L. 274). In the meantime, in 1884, the legislature prohibited the housing of children in the county infirmary who were eligible to a county children's home or to some other charitable institution. However exceptions were made in the case of insane, idiotic, and epileptic children. (103 O. L. 890). The latter provision is still effective in Ohio.

By an act of May 31, 1911 effective January 1, 1913, the board of infirmary directors was abolished and the powers formally exercised by this body were transferred to the county commissioners and the infirmary superintendent (102 O. L. 433). The superintendent is still required to keep a record of the inmates, as prescribed by statute, and to report annually to the county commissioners. This report, the acceptance of which is evidenced by an entry in the minutes of the commissioners' journal, is filed with the county auditor and by him preserved. (G. C. sec. 2535). In 1919 the name county infirmary was changed to that of county home (108 O. L. pt. i, 68).

The county commissioners still make provision for the establishment and maintenance of the county home, appoint a superintendent, and make regular inspection visits. Since June 1, 1932 the superintendent has been appointed from the list of names of persons eligible under civil service regulations. Moreover, since

1882, they have been authorized to appoint an infirmary physician, who, like the superintendent, is required by statute to report to the county commissioners. This report, made quarterly, includes such information as the nature and extent of medical services rendered, to whom, and the character of the disease treated. (G. C. sec. 2546; 73 O. L. 90; 102 O. L. 436; 108 O. L. pt. i, 269).

Since 1929 the commissioners have been authorized, whenever the buildings of the county home become unsuitable for habitation or whenever the population is too small for economical operation, to abandon the county home and provide for the care of inmates and others afterwards accepted as a county charge by boarding them with another county home (G. C. Sec. 2557).

Although corrective measures have been passed, the county home has remained one of the most unprogressive institutions of the county. There is no uniform system of administration of indigent relief. The state department of public welfare is authorized to inspect the county home, but is powerless to enforce its recommendations.

All records of this office are located at the institution in the office of the superintendent unless otherwise indicated.

Case Records and Reports

605. JOURNAL

1865-1912. 5 volumes. 1935— in Commissioners' Journal, entry 1. Prior records missing.

Record of minutes of meetings of the board of infirmary directors with record of bills and claims filed and approved showing consecutive bill number, date of bill, name of creditor, for what, and amount of bill approved. Contains copies of directors annual reports to county commissioners showing date of report, for what period, itemized account of funds received, itemize account of expenditures, number of inmates cared for, number admitted since last report, number discharged, number died, and number registered at time of report. Contains: Infirmary Journal, entry 5; Record of Outside Relief, 1910-1912, entry 614. Chronologically arranged by dates of entries. 1865-1909, no index; 1910-December 31, 1912, alphabetically indexed by names of creditors, outside clients, or principles. Handwritten. Average 436 pages. 16 x 11 x 2.25. 3 volumes, 1865-1897, Superintendent's office; 1 volume, 1897-1909, County courthouse storeroom 2; 1 volume, 1910-1912, County courthouse, Auditor's office.

606. REGISTER, ADMISSIONS

1836-1917. 4 volumes.

Record of admissions to county infirmary showing date admitted, name, age, sex, nativity, physical and mental condition, from what township, town and county admitted, date of birth, place of birth, date of discharge or death, and date apprenticed or absconded. Chronologically arranged by dates of admissions. No index. Handwritten on printed forms. Average 260 pages. 18 x 11 x 1.5.

For subsequent records, see entry 607; for other records of discharges and deaths, entry 609.

607. INDEX FILE, "REGISTER"

1910—. 1 file box divided into 3 compartments (Register, Deaths, Discharges).

Register of admissions showing date of admission, name, sex, age, color, nativity, admitted from what township, town, and county, and physical and mental condition; in case of death the information is added to card showing date of death, cause, place of burial, and card removed to compartment labeled death; in case of discharge or inmate leaving institution the information is added to card showing date of discharge, destination of inmate, reason for discharge, and if case of a run away it is so noted and card removed to compartment labeled Discharges. Alphabetically arranged by names of inmates. No index. Handwritten on printed forms. File box, 6 x 24 x 16; each compartment, 6 x 8 x 16.

For prior records, see entry 606; for other records of discharges and deaths, see entry 609.

608. REGISTER OF CHILDREN

1881-1882. 1 volume. Only separate records found.

Register of children in county infirmary showing date admitted or born, name, consecutive number, date and place of birth, date indentured or placed out on trial, and name of person taking child. Chronologically arranged by dates admitted. No index. Handwritten. 170 pages. 14 x 10 x 1. County courthouse storeroom 3.

609. DISCHARGES

1864-1931. 3 volumes. Discontinued as a separate record.

Record of discharges from institution and record of death showing date of discharge or death, reason for discharge, destination of inmate discharged, name of person assuming responsibility of inmate discharged, date of death, cause the death, known relatives, and place of burial. Chronologically arranged by dates of discharges or deaths. No index. Handwritten on printed forms. Average 220 pages. 16 x 10 x 1.25.

For prior records, see entry 606; for separate records, see entry 607.

610. INDENTURES

1843-1887. 2 volumes. Discontinued.

Record of indentures of inmates by the board of infirmary directors showing name of inmate, date, name of person taking inmate, and copy of indenture agreement between the directors and persons taking inmate. Chronologically arranged by dates of indentures. No index. Handwritten. Average 190 pages. 16 x 9 x 1.

611. DAILY MOVEMENT OF INMATES AND ANNUAL REPORTS TO DIVISION OF CHARITIES

1912—. 25 volumes.

Daily record of admissions, discharges, and deaths, showing names of inmates registered. This becomes the record copy of the superintendent's annual report to the state division of charities on statistics of inmates. Chronologically arranged by daily entries with annual entry at end of each year. No index. Handwritten on printed forms. Average 80 pages. 16 x 9 x .5.

Business Administration of Office

612. ACCOUNT BOOK

1878-1908. 2 volumes.

Superintendent's record of sale of produce for institution farm showing date sold, what, and amount. Chronologically arranged by dates of sales. No index. Handwritten. 180 pages. 16 x 10 x 1.

For subsequent records, see entries 613.

613. RECORD RECEIPTS AND EXPENDITURES

1878—. 3 volumes.

Record of cash receipts from all sources including sale of farm produce, and itemized account of expenditures and operation of institution showing date, to whom, and for what. Chronologically arranged by dates of entries. No index.

Handwritten on printed forms. Average 520 pages. 18 x 12 x 2.75.

For other records of sale of farm produce, see entry 612.

614. RECORD OF OUTSIDE RELIEF

1887-1897. 1 volume. 1910-1912 in Journal, entry 605.

Record of aid to indigents by infirmary directors showing dates, order number, name of recipient, kind of aid, and amount of order. Chronologically arranged by dates of orders. No index. Handwritten on printed forms. 390 pages. 16 x 11 x 2.

Miscellaneous

615. VISITOR'S REGISTER

1881-1915. 1 volume. Discontinued.

Register of visitors at institution showing dates, names, addresses, and remarks. Chronologically arranged by dates of visits. No index. Handwritten on printed forms. 490 pages. 14 x 10 x 2.5.

616. INVENTORY

1906—. 2 volumes.

Record copy of annual inventory of equipment and institution furnishings by superintendent to infirmary director, 1906-1912, to commissioners 1913—, showing itemized list and estimated value of each item. Chronologically arranged by years, no index. Handwritten on printed forms. Average 280 pages. 16 x 10 x 1.5.

The home of orphan children established in Washington County in 1858 was the first such institution to be founded in Ohio. This home was in operation before provision was made for institutional care of children outside the county infirmary. From her earnings as a teacher, Miss C. A. Fay (later Mrs. Ewing) purchased twelve acres of land twenty miles southeast of Marietta and built a small house with the plan in view of caring for unfortunate children. In the operation of her home she received aid from charitable citizens and an allowance from the county, which however never exceeded $1.20 a week for each child. She took nine children to begin her venture and in a few years was caring for as many as thirty at one time. During the ten years that she conducted the home she cared for a total of 101 children, most of whom she placed in private homes, many by adoption. (*Williams, History of Washington County,* 117-118).

Although the legislature made provision for the institutional care of the county's indigent as early as 1816, it was not until after the middle of the nineteenth century, when hundreds of Ohio children were left homeless by the scourge of civil war, that the legislature enacted measures for the care of dependent children. Previous to this time the Ohio statute relative to the care of children had been taken from the territorial code which authorized the overseers of the poor, and later the trustees of the "poor house" to apprentice the children of the indigent, boys under eighteen and girls under twenty-one years of age (Pease, *op. cit.,* 219; 3 O. L. 276; 8 O. L. 223-224; 29 O. L. 318). The fact that this system was not only inhuman, but entirely unsatisfactory, is evidenced by the innumerable advertisements for run-away apprentices appearing in the press.

In 1865 the legislature authorized the county commissioners to receive request for orphans' asylums, and, when funds accumulated in sufficient quantities, to construct such a home, and appoint a board of directors consisting of six persons who were given the task of managing the institution, subject to the rules and regulations of the county commissioners. This board, electing a president and a treasurer from its own number, was required annually to make a report of the receipts and disbursements of the asylum, together with a number of orphans received into and discharged from the institution. This report was to be published by the commissioners in a newspaper having a general circulation. (62 O. L. 97).

A year later, in 1866, the commissioners were authorized, when in their judgment the best interest of the wards of the county would be served, to establish children's homes, and to provide by means of taxation, funds to be used for the purchase of a site, to construct buildings, and to maintain such charitable institutions (63 O. L. 46). Consequently in 1867 the county commissioners purchased one hundred acres of land, just north of Marietta and immediately erected suitable buildings. The home was opened in 1868, the first in the state under the new law. (Williams, *op cit.,* 117-118). The brick buildings now in use were erected in 1907-1908. Then, in 1876, an act, repealing all previous legislation was passed, which established the present-day duties of the county commissioners, trustees, superintendent, and matron in respect to children's home. The act authorized the county commissioners to appoint a board of trustees and a superintendent of each children's home. (73 O. L. 64). Since February 7, 1930 the superintendent has been appointed from a list of names of persons eligible under civil service regulations.

The board of trustees consists of five members appointed for a five-year term. The trustees, besides appointing a superintendent, hold annual meetings at which time they examine all accounts presented for payment, examine into the condition of the property and the manner and care offered to the wards. Annually, or oftener, they are required to file with the state board of charities a detailed account giving the where-abouts of each child and the physical condition of each ward under their care. (G. C. sec. 3082-1).

The superintendent, operating under the rules and regulations of the trustees, has entire charge and control of the home and its inmates. He may appoint a matron, assistant matron, and other necessary employees, subject to the approval of the board of trustees. It is the duty of such employees to care for the inmates in the home, direct their employment and give suitable physical, mental and moral training. Under the direction of the superintendent, the matron has general management and supervision of the household duties of the home. The matron, like other employees, receives such salaries as the trustees made direct and may be removed by the superintendent or at the pleasure of a majority of the trustees. (G. C. sec. 3085).

The county children's home serves as an asylum for children under eighteen years of age who have resided in the county one year and who are, in the opinion of the trustees, eligible to admission by reason of orphanage, abandonment, or neglect by parents, or the inability of parents to provide for them (G. C. sec. 3089). Children are admitted to the home on order of the juvenile court or upon the order of a majority of the board of trustees. Since 1876 each child committed to the children's home must be accompanied by a statement of the facts setting forth his name, his age, his birthplace, and his condition. These facts, recorded by the superintendent in the book kept for that purpose, are confidential and open to inspection at the discretion of the board of trustees only. (G. C. sec. 3098; 73 O. L. 64; 83 O. L. 196; 99 O. L. 187; 103 O. L. 864). All wards of the children's home who have been committed to the institution because of abandonment, neglect, or dependency by the juvenile court or who have been voluntarily surrounded by the parents or under the exclusive jurisdiction, guardianship, and control of the trustees until they have become of lawful age (G. C. sec. 3093).

The county commissioners may, subject to the approval of the board of state charities, after an opportunity has been given to the electorate to demand a referendum on the proposition, abandon the children's home. If the home is discontinued, they may sell the site and buildings and use the funds as they deem expedient, providing that the wards in the children's home who are placed in foster homes and those who are under the guardianship of the trustees are legally committed to the guardianship of the board of state charities (109 O. L. 533). If any county where there is no children's home established, the commissioners may enter into contracts for the care of its dependent and neglected children with another children's home or with any institution or association in a state which has as its object the care of such children, subject to the confirmation of the board of state charities (G. C. Sec. 3092).

All records of this office are located in the superintendent's office, north wall.

Case Records

617. MINUTES

1866—. 3 volumes.

Record of proceedings of the board of trustees of home showing dates of meetings, names that trustees present, and business transacted. Chronologically arranged by dates of meetings. No index. Handwritten. Average 500 pages. 16 x 10 x 3.

618. ROSTER

1866—. 1 volume.

List of all children living at the children's home and names of townships from which entered. Alphabetically arranged by names of children. No index. Handwritten. 500 pages. 16 x 10 x 3.

619. REGISTER OF ADMISSIONS, PLACEMENTS
1866—. 1 volume.
Record of children taken into home showing date, age, and from what township entered; also placements made from home into private homes. Chronologically arranged by dates of admissions. No index. Handwritten. 240 pages. 20 x 14 x 4.

620. CHILDREN DISCHARGED
1905—. 2 file boxes.
Card file showing discharge record of each child, court orders, and date of discharge or commitment to some state institution. Alphabetically arranged by names of children. No index. Handwritten. 8 x 12 x 14.

621. DAILY REPORTS
1929—. 1 file box.
Daily record of children in Washington County home showing number of children beginning each day, number of admissions, number of discharges, and total for the day. This becomes the superintendent's copy of the report to state division of charities. Chronologically arranged. No index. Handwritten on printed forms. 8 x 12 x 14.

622. YEARLY SCHOOL RECORDS
1935—. 1 file box.
Record of progress of children in school, as kept by the superintendent, showing the number of boys and girls in each grade. Alphabetically arranged by names of children. No index. Handwritten on printed forms. 8 x 12 x 14.

Business Administration of Office

623. CONTINGENT RECORD
1894—. 1 volume.
An itemized account of expenditures from fund allowed for emergencies showing receipts and disbursements. Chronologically arranged by dates of entries. No index. Handwritten. 500 pages. 16 x 10 x 2.

624. RECEIPTS AND EXPENDITURES
1866—. 3 volumes.
Superintendent's record of all receipts and expenditures of children's home, showing date, name of payee or payer, from what source received or for what purpose paid. Chronologically arranged by dates of entries. No index. Handwritten. Average 120 pages. 20 x 14 x 4.

Miscellaneous

625. CORRESPONDENCE RECORDS
1929—. 2 file boxes.
Record of all correspondence directed to superintendent in connection with affairs pertaining to the Washington County children's home. Chronologically arranged. No index. Handwritten on printed forms. 8 x 12 x 14.

626. MISCELLANEOUS
1921—. 8 file boxes.
Miscellaneous records consisting of weight records of children, insurance policy on county home property, and payroll of children's home employees. Alphabetically arranged by names of children or subjects. No index. Handwritten on printed forms. 8 x 12 x 14.

The board of county visitors, an agency for the examination and inspection of county institutions supported wholly or in part by county or municipal taxation, was created by an act of the general assembly in 1882. Under this act, the judge of the court of common pleas was authorized to appoint five persons, three of whom were to be women, who were to visit periodically such county institutions as the county infirmary, county jail, municipal prisoners, and children's home, and file annually a report of their proceedings and recommendations for changes with the clerk of courts, and to forward a copy to the state board of charities. The members, appointed for an indefinite period, were to serve without compensation. (79 O. L. 107).

By the act of 1892 the personnel of the board was increased to six persons, three of whom were to be women, and not more than three to have the same political affiliations. Furthermore the act made it the duty of the probate judge, whenever proceedings were instituted in his court to commit a child under sixteen years of age to the boys' industrial home or to the girls' industrial home, to have notice given to the board of such proceedings; and it was made the duty of the board of visitors to attend the meetings of the court, as a body or as a committee, to protect the interests of the child (89 O. L. 161).

While the provisions of the act of 1892 were redefined by the acts of 1898 and 1900, these acts did not, in the main, affect the duties of the board (93 O. L. 57; 94 O. L. 70). The latter act, however, made the board a continuous body with two members serving for one year, two members serving for two years, and two members serving for three years. In addition to this, the board was allowed a minimum expense schedule for the service. (94 O. L. 70). Six years later the board was authorized to recommend to the county commissioners measures for the more economical administration of county institutions. Their report, together with their recommendations, was to be filed each year with the judge of the probate court and with the county prosecuting attorney. (98 O. L. 28).

In 1913 the power of appointment of board members was transferred to the probate judge. Under this act the juvenile judge, like the probate judge under the act of 1892 was authorized to notify the visitors when any proceedings were instituted in his court for the commitment of any child to a state institution of correction. The act continued the practice of annually filing the reports of the board with the probate judge, prosecuting attorney and state board of charities. (103 O. L. 173-174, 888).

No permanent records are kept by the board of county visitors.

County relief for the indigent, one of the most pressing problems of the twentieth century, was met in frontier Ohio. As early as 1805 there was passed an act, modeled from the territorial law, which was similar in all respects to the poor laws of seventeenth century England (3 O. L. 272). Under the early enactments the township trustees were authorized to appoint overseers of the poor. In 1816 the county commissioners were authorized to construct "poor houses" for the care of the county's indigent. As the system developed in succeeding decades the county was made responsible for those who have become permanently disabled, and for paupers who could not be satisfactorly cared for except at the county infirmary, now called the county home. The township trustees and officials of municipal corporations were made responsible for providing temporary relief to needy residents of the state, or the county, township, or city. In the event any person became chargeable to the township in which he had not gained legal residence, it was the duty of the overseers, later the township trustees, to remove him to the township where he was legally settled. With slight alterations, the principles of the system continued until the twentieth century. (For an excellent study, but biting criticism of the administration of relief in Ohio prior to 1934 see Aileen Elizabeth Kennedy, *The Poor Law and its Administration,* Sophonisba P. Breckinridge, ed., *Social Service Monographs*, no. 22, University of Chicago Press, Chicago, 1934).

The unprecedented depression in the third decade of the twentieth century proved the antiquated, uncentralized system was entirely inadequate. As a result of the abnormal employment and the crop failures following the drought of 1930, many local subdivisions of the county charged by law to administer support and medical relief to the indigent were unable to discharge their obligations. Accordingly, in 1931, the legislature passed an emergency act authorized the county, township, and municipal taxing authorities to borrow money and issue bonds for poor relief, providing the state commission found that no other funds were available (114 O. L. 11-12).

During the early months of 1932 the governor, aware of the wide-spread suffering in the state, called the legislature into special session (see message of the governor to the Eighty-ninth General Assembly in 114 O. L. pt. ii, 6-8). At this session the legislature authorized him to appoint a state relief commission composed of five members to study the relief situation. This commission was permitted to cooperate with the national, state, or local relief commission, which, in many counties, had been established and was already functioning. Since the county and township treasuries were depleted, on account of the excessive drain caused by the mounting relief load and a steady decline of tax collections, the legislature authorized an excise tax on utilities, for the years 1932-1937, to be used for relief purposes. This state tax was to be allocated to the counties on the basis of population, the tax duplicate, and the value of the utilities property in the county as of 1930. (114 O. L. pt. ii, 19-20). The funds allocated to each county under this act were to be credited to the "county poor relief excise fund."

The county commissioners were authorized to borrow money for emergency relief and evidence such indebtedness by the issuance of negotiable bonds and notes. Upon submission of such a resolution to the state tax commission, the commission was directed to establish the amount which would probably be allocated to the county from the public utility excise taxes, and was directed to calculate the total amount of bonds, the principal and interest on which might be paid out of such estimated allocation. The date of maximum maturity of such bonds was to be on or before March 15, 1938. If, in the year 1932, additional funds were needed for poor relief, the county commissioners were authorized, after the state tax commission found that no other funds were available, to issue additional bonds in the amount not exceeding one-tenth of one percent of the general tax list and duplicate of the county. The maturity date of such additional bonds was to be on or before September 15, 1940. (114 O. L. pt. ii, 20).

The proceeds of such sale of such bonds were to be placed in a special fund, denominated the "emergency relief fund." No expenditures were to be made from this fund except in accordance with the method and under the uniform regulations prescribed by the state relief commission, and in no case after December 31, 1933. The county commissioners were authorized to distribute, prior to the first of March 1933, portions of the fund to the political subdivisions of the county, according to the needs for poor relief determined by the county and set forth in such an approved budget. The money distributed to the subdivisions was to be expended in them for poor relief, including the renting of lands and the purchase of seeds for gardening by the unemployed. (114 O. L. pt, ii, 22). County poor relief included mothers' pensions, soldiers' relief, temporary assistance to nonresidents, maintenance of a county and children's home, and work and direct relief. In the townships and municipalities relief was interpreted to be the support of the poor and burial of the indigent dead. Each subdivision administering funds under this act was expected to require labor in exchange for relief given to any family where there resided an able-bodied wage earner. (114 O. L. pt. ii, 17).

In February 1933, the tenure of the state relief commission was extended to March 1, 1935 (115 O. L. 22). In the same year, the legislature levied an additional stamp tax on the sale of bottled and bulk beer, malt, cosmetics, and toilet preparations to furnish additional funds for emergency relief (115 O. L. 642-646; 649; 115 O. L. pt, ii, 33, 83, 247, 5, 177, 200, 256). The state treasurer was authorized to appoint the county treasurer as his deputy for the purpose of selling tax stamps to be affixed to such articles (115 O. L. 642-646).

When, in 1935, the state relief commission ceased to exist by reason of the term of the acts creating it, the legislature passed a measure designed to coordinate and correlate all emergency poor relief work, activities, and administration with the federal emergency relief administration which was authorized to administer and direct the distribution and expenditure of federal funds for relief in the state. Accordingly, all powers previously vested in the state relief commission were transferred to the county commissioners. Whenever in their discretion such action was necessary in order to continue the coordination and correlation of state, local, and federal funds they were authorized to appoint, with the approval of the director of finance of the state of Ohio, a representative or representatives of such emergency poor relief. If such an officer was appointed, the representative succeeded to all powers and functions, which, under the act, were delegated to the county commissioners. This representative, however, was subject to such terms and conditions in respect to auditing, examinations, and reports as were directed by the county commissioners and such a federal agency. The county commissioners were directed to conduct relief activities outside limits of municipal corporations through the township trustees, insofar as practicable, and were to be guided by the recommendations of the township trustees with respect to relief need in such political subdivisions. Again, as in 1932, the commissioners were authorized, if the state tax commission found that no other means existed to provide funds, to borrow money, and issue bonds in the year 1935-1936. The maximum maturity date of such bonds was to be on or before March 1, 1944. (116 O. L. 571). Other bonds, in addition to those secured by the county's share of the excise tax, might be issued not to exceed one-fifth of one percent of the general tax list of the county (116 O. L. 575). If the county was unable to issue bonds by reason of the limitations imposed by the constitution (Art. XII, sec, 2), The taxing authority of each subdivision was authorized to submit the question of issuing bonds to the electorate either at a general or special election (116 O. L. 578).

The year 1936 saw the re-creation of the state relief commission. Consisting of four members appointed by the governor, this body was organized to serve until January 31, 1937. Again, as in 1932, the commission was directed to study problems of relief, to receive advice from federal, state, and local governmental departments, to cooperate with agencies of the national and local governments and private agencies engaged in the administration or financial support of direct or indirect relief, to administer moneys appropriated to the commission for poor relief, to examine the conduct of local governmental agencies and administering relief, and to order the distribution and payment of moneys from the state treasury.

The county commissioners were authorized to administer all advances by the state to the relief commission and were directed to operate through duly authorized agencies of townships, municipalities, and school districts. Within the appropriations made by the commissioners and subject to the rules and regulations of the state relief commission, the commissioners were instructed to appoint assistants and other employees as were necessary.

The county commissioners, like the state relief commission, were directed to cooperate with all agencies of the federal, state, and county governments, and with the private agencies which were engaged in administering relief or financial support to the needy. It was made the duty of all county, township, and municipal governments administering relief or assistance to dependents to report to the county commissioners, at its request, the name and address of all persons to whom they were providing aid and the amount and character of aid given. (116 O. L. pt. ii, 133-148).

The principle of issuing bonds and securing them by the county share of the utility taxes was continued. Moreover, there was appropriated to the state relief commission from the general revenue fund the sum of $3,000,000 which was designated as the "state relief rotary fund." The various counties of the state which had not issued bonds and were not authorized to do so without the consent of the people, were empowered to obtain an advance from the state relief rotary fund in an amount equal to that of bonds which were permitted to be issued. If the county failed to repay the total of all advances and interest at two percent before June 1936, the state relief commission was directed to refuse to make further allocations or distributions to the county. (116 O. L. pt. ii, 133-148).

In the early months of 1937 the legislature authorized the state relief commission to serve until April 1937. Under this act the county commissioners were authorized to give temporary support and medical relief to nonresidents and to all needy persons possessing a legal residence in the county. Funds may be expended for both direct and work relief. However, all persons on relief able and competent to perform labor who refuse to accept private employment under prevailing conditions and prevailing wages, may be dropped from the relief roles. This ruling does not apply, however, to areas where strikes are prevalent. On the other hand, any person receiving relief in the county is permitted to engage in any business without losing his relief status. During the period of such employment, he is required to forfeit the pro rate amount of relief received by him, and is eligible to his former relief status upon the conclusion of such employment.

The county commissioners are required to file with the state relief commission a budget and a detailed statement and plan showing how the funds to be received are to be expended, the purpose for which they are to be used, the nature and kind of works to be carried on, and the number of persons to be aided by such relief. Besides this, the county commissioners must file a complete analysis of their proposed expenditures, together with an estimate of all available resources, including the unencumbered proceeds of any bonds heretofore issued and the amount of bonds which the county commissioners have a right to issue without a vote of the people on the approval of the state tax commission of Ohio as authorized in 1935.

Of the funds allocated to the county by the state relief commission for direct relief, the commissioners may, when they believe that the cost of administration may be reduced, reallocate the funds on a percentage basis, of relief requirements of the various subdivisions (*Page's Ohio Cumulative Code Service,* Cincinnati, 1937, no. 20, 65-67).

The emergency relief measures passed during the period 1932-1937 gave the counties for the first time a centralized relief administration.

All records are located and the relief administration office.

627. MASTER FILE

1933— 5 file boxes.

Card index file to case records, entry 628-630, active, closed, and direct relief, showing name of client, case number, address, date of application, and number of dependents. There are two file boxes to active case records, two file boxes to closed cases, and one file box to direct relief cases. Alphabetically arranged by names of clients. Typed. 6 x 9 x 12.

628. CASE RECORDS, ACTIVE
1933—. 12 file boxes.

Complete record of active cases showing name and address of each applicant for relief, case number, marital status, age, nativity, number of dependents, investigator's report on the application, and itemized record of aid furnished. Numerically arranged by case numbers. For index, see entry 627. Handwritten on printed forms. 13 x 15 x 24.

629. CASE RECORDS, CLOSED
1934—. 9 file boxes.

Complete record of closed cases showing name and address of each applicant for relief, case number, marital status, age, nativity, number of dependents, investigator's report on the application, and itemized record of aid furnished. Numerically arranged by case numbers. For index, see entry 627. Typed on printed forms. 13 x 15 x 24.

630. CASE RECORDS, DIRECT RELIEF
1936—. 3 file boxes.

Complete record of direct relief cases showing name and address of each applicant for relief, case number, marital status, age, nativity, number of dependents, investigator's report on the application, and itemized record of aid furnished. Numerically arranged by case numbers. For index, see entry 627. Typed on printed forms. 13 x 15 x 24.

631. CCC RECORDS
1933—. 4 file drawers.

Case records of CCC enrollees, including application, showing dates, name of applicant, address, age, number and names of dependents, name of proposed allottee, medical certificate, investigation report on application, and enrollment certificates. All records of each case in folder, 10 x 12. Numerically arranged by case numbers. Typed on printed forms. 12 x 12 x 26.

632. INDEX, CCC RECORDS

1933—. 2 file drawers.

Index to CCC Records showing date of application, case number, date enrolled, to what camp assigned, name and address of allottee, and date discharged. Alphabetically arranged by names of applicants. Typed on printed forms. 4.5 x 6 x 15.

633. ASSIGNMENT RECORD

1935—. 12 file boxes.

Record of assignments of persons to WPA projects in Washington County. Alphabetically arranged by towns and townships and alphabetically thereunder by names of persons assigned. No index. Handwritten on printed forms. 6 x 9 x 12.

634. FINANCIAL STATEMENTS

1936—. 1 file box.

Original financial statements filed by WPA employees. Chronologically arranged. No index. Handwritten on printed forms. 11 x 16 x 25.

635. CORRESPONDENCE

1936—. 2 file boxes.

Letters from persons desiring information regarding work and relief. Chronologically arranged. No index. Handwritten and typed. 11 x 15 x 18.

SOLDIERS' RELIEF COMMISSION, SOLDIERS' BURIAL COMMISSION

The soldiers' relief commission was established by an act of the legislature passed May 19, 1886, entitled "an act to provide for the relief of the indigent Union soldiers, sailors, and marines, and the indigent wives, widows and minor children of indigent or deceased Union soldiers, sailors, and marines." Under provisions of this act the commissioners of each county were authorized to levy a specified tax for the purpose of creating a fund for the relief of such beneficiaries; and the judge of the court of common pleas was authorized to appoint three county residents, at least two of whom are honorably discharged Union soldiers, to serve for a term of three years as members of the commission, which was organized by the selection of a chairman and a secretary and was known as the soldiers' relief commission. (83 O. L. 232).

An act in 1887, provided that councilmen of city wards, as well as the board of trustees of the townships, certify to the soldiers' relief commission the names of those requiring and entitled to aid under the act (84 O. L. 100).

By act of the legislature, passed April 28, 1890, the soldiers' relief commission was required to appoint annually a committee of three in each township and a committee of three in each ward in any city in the county, whose duty it was to receive all applications for aid and to certify them to the soldiers' relief commission (87 O. L. 352).

Sections 2930 and 2933-4 of the General Code were amended, March 6, 1917, to provide for the appointment to each county commission of one member who is the wife or widow of an honorably discharged soldier, sailor, or marine of the Civil War or of the Spanish-American War, the other two members to be honorably discharged soldiers, sailors, or marines of the United States; and for the appointment to each township and ward committee of a wife or widow of a soldier, sailor, or marine of the United States. (107 O. L. 27). Two years later, in 1919, the provisions of the act were extended to include indigent veterans of the World War or to indigent parents, wives, widows, or minor children of such veterans (108 O. L. pt. i, 633).

On April 6, 1929, sections 2930 and 2934 of the General Code were amended to provide for the appointment by the court of common pleas in each county of a soldiers' relief commission, to consist of three members, one to be the wife, widow, son or daughter of an honorably discharged soldier, sailor, or marines of the Civil War, of the Spanish-American War, or of the World War, the other two members to be honestly discharged soldiers, sailors, or marines of the United

States– one of whom, whenever possible, to be a member of the Spanish-American War Veterans, the other a member of the American Legion. (113 O. L. 466).

636. JOURNAL OF SOLDIERS' RELIEF COMMISSION
1886—. 2 volumes. (1, 2).
Record copy of minutes of soldiers' relief commission with record of applications by soldiers, sailors, or marines for relief showing record of approval or rejection, amount of relief awarded each applicant, copy of report by commission to county auditor giving list of applicants recommended for relief payments, and amount recommended. Chronologically arranged by dates of meetings and dates of reports to auditor. No index. 1886-June 1930, handwritten; July 1930—, typed. Average 280 pages. 16 x 11 x 1.5. Auditor's office.

For other records, see entries 7, 37, 637.

637. APPLICATIONS, SOLDIERS' RELIEF
1887—. 204 bundles.
Original applications for relief by ex-soldiers, sailors, and marines, their widows, mothers, and dependent children showing name of applicant, age, member of what company, regiment or vessel, length of service, number of dependents, occupation, physical condition, and date filed. Chronologically arranged by dates of filing. No index. Handwritten on printed forms. 6 x 3.5 x 8. 185 bundles, 1887-1934, storeroom 3; 19 bundles, 1935—, Auditor's office.

For other records, see entries 7, 37, 636.

SOLDIERS' BURIAL COMMISSION

In 1884 the legislature made provision for a soldiers' burial commission in each county, to consist of three persons in each township appointed by the county commissioners, was directed to defray the expense incurred in the interment of any honorable discharged Union soldier, sailor, or marine who died in poverty. The commission, serving at the pleasure of this appointing power, was required to report to the county commissioners the name, rank, and command of the decedent which report was transcribed by the county commissioners in a book kept for that purpose. (81 O. L. 146-147). The original act, amended in 1891, extended the provisions of the act to include the interment of the wives or widow of Union soldiers (88 O. L.

330-331). In 1893 the act was again amended to provide for the interment of mothers of Union soldiers, sailors and marines, and army nurses (90 O. L. 177). In 1908 the personnel of the commission was reduced to two.

Under the present law which became effective in 1921 the county commissioners are authorized to appoint two suitable persons in each township and ward in the county, who are directed with the approval of the family or friends of the deceased, to contract with an undertaker and directs the burial in a respectable manner of the body of any honorably discharged soldier, sailor, or marine having at any time served in the army of the United States, or the mother, wife or widow of any soldier, sailor, or marine, or that of any war nurse who served at any time in the army of the United States who died in poverty (G. C. sec. 2950; 108 O. L. pt, i, 211-212; 109 O. L. 212).

The burial commission is instructed to enforce all laws relative to the burial of indigent veterans, investigate the financial status of the decedent's family, and report its findings to the county commissioners, together with the name, rank, and command to which the deceased belonged, date of death, place a burial, occupation while living, and an itemized statement of the cost of burial (99 O. L. 100).

Upon receiving this report of the burial commission, the county commissioners transcribe the information in a book kept for that purpose, and certify the expense to the county auditor who draws his warrant for payment to the person or persons specified by the county commissioners (99 O. L. 101).

The amount contributed by the county of the burial of an indigent veteran set by legislature at $35 in 1884 was increased to $75 in 1908, to $100 in 1921 (81 O. L. 146-147; 99 O. L. 99; 109 O. L. 212; G. C . sec. 2951). Since 1908, each member of the burial commission has been allowed $1 for each service performed (99 O. L. 99; G. C. sec. 2951).

The soldiers' burial commission keeps no permanent records. For the report of the commission to county commissioners, see entry 50.

Provision for the relief of the indigent was made in 1805, but it was not until 1898 that the legislature provided separate relief for the indigent blind. The act authorized the township trustees to certify to the county commissioners an amount not to exceed $100 per person per annum for such relief, the certification to be made a record listing the name of the beneficiary and the amount required; and directed the county commissioners to levy on the townships the amount certified, this amount to be paid into the county treasury and thence to the township treasurer to be used for blind relief (93 O. L. 270).

Six years later in 1904, certification authority was transferred from the township trustees to the probate judge, who was required to register the name and address of beneficiaries and to issue to each a certificate giving his name, address, and the amount to be drawn. Persons eligible for relief were blind males over 21 and blind females over 18 years of age, without property or other means of support. Not less than two county citizens, one a physician selected by the court, was required to testify that the applicant has been a resident of the state for five years and a resident of the county for one year immediately preceding the filing of an application for relief. (97 O. L. 392-394).

The act of 1904 was declared unconstitutional for the reason that it required spending for a private purpose public funds raised by taxation (*Auditor of Lucas County* v *The State,* 75 O. S. 114-137). Hence, in 1908, an act was passed authorizing the county commissioners to levy a stipulated tax to create a fund for relief for the needy blind, the maximum benefits not to exceed $150 per person per annum to be paid quarterly; and authorizing the probate judge to appoint a blind relief commission consisting of three members for a three-year term, directed to meet annually in the office of the county commissioners to examine applications recorded in order of their receipt in a book furnished by the county commissioners (99 O. L. 56-58).

The blind relief commission was abolished by the legislature in 1913 and its powers and duties were transferred to the county commissioners who were authorized, on evidence furnished by a registered physician or surgeon that the applicant for blind relief might have such disability benefitted or removed by medical or surgical treatment, and with the written consent of the patient, to expand all or part of a year's relief allowance for this purpose (103 O. L. 60).

Six years later, in 1919, this allowance for blind relief was raised to $200 per person for annum, and the county commissioners were authorized to appoint such clerks as they might deem necessary to investigate applications and to serve at the pleasure of the county commissioners (108 O. L. pt. i, 421-422).

In 1927 the maximum benefit for blind relief was increased to $400 per person per annum, but in the event of a husband and wife both being blind and both applying for relief, the total maximum benefit for the two was fixed at $600 per annum (112 O. L. 109).

In April 1936 the state accepted the provision of the Social Security Act approved August 14, 1935, providing federal grants for state aid to the blind, and the legislature designated the Ohio commission for the blind the administration agency in the state, and the county commissioners were made the administration agency in the county. The county commissioners were directed to appropriate from the general fund of the county a sum sufficient when supplemented by federal and state grants to provide for the blind a subsistence "comparable with decency and health," and if they failed to make such appropriations the attorney general was directed to bring *mandamus* proceedings against them.

The act of 1936 provides that those entitled to blind relief are persons not less than eighteen nor more than sixty-five years old, who have lost their sight while residents of the state, and who have resided in the state for a period of five years in the nine years immediately preceding application, the last year of which period shall have been continuous. Applications for blind relief are filed with the county commissioners who are required by statute to list such claims in their order of application in books kept for that purpose. At least ten days prior to action on a claim the applicant files a duly certified statement, including a certificate from a registered physician "skilled in disease of the eye" stating to what extent the applicant's vision is impaired, and written evidence from two reputable citizens that they know the applicant to be blind and that "he has the qualifications to entitle him to the relief asked." The county commissioners may allow the examining physician a fee not to exceed three dollars, and may employ an additional physician to examine the applicant. If after such inquiry the county commissioners are satisfied that the applicant is entitled to relief, they are directed by statute to issue an order for such sum as the board finds necessary, not to exceed the maximum fixed in 1927, such sum to be paid monthly from the fund created for that purpose. The ruling of 1913 concerning medical and surgical treatment for applicants remains in effect. Persons whose applications are denied by the county commissioners may appeal to the state commission for the blind which on its own motion may revise any decision of the county commissioners. Both the Ohio commission for blind relief and the county commissioners have power to issue subpoenas, compel presentation of papers and examine witnesses.

At least once a year, oftener if directed by the Ohio commission for the blind, the county commissioners must examine the qualifications, disabilities and needs of all persons on the list of the blind, and may increase or decrease the amount of relief according to the budgetary requirements within the limits fixed by law. If the county commissioners remove a name from the list of the blind they are required to notify the county auditor and the Ohio commission for the blind as to their action.

Records of blind relief are open to public inspection.

Journal and Case Records
(See also entry 39)

638. (Blind Relief) RECORD

May 1908-November 1912. 1 volume. December 1912-May 1936 in Commissioners' Journal, entry 1.

Records of minutes of meetings of blind relief commission; record of applications for blind relief filed with commission showing application number, date filed, name of applicant, address, date application approved or rejected, amount awarded; and record of payments of relief awards. Record of minutes, chronologically arranged by dates of meetings; applications and awards, chronologically arranged by dates of filing. No index. Handwritten. 280 pages. 16 x 11 x 1.75. Storeroom 3.

For subsequent record of applications, see entry 640.

639. APPLICATION FOR BLIND RELIEF

June 1936—. 1 file box.

Applications for blind aid made out in the blind relief office, witnessed by two reliable residents of the county, and notarized; also physicians' certificates as to condition of applicants' eyes. Arranged in sections by titles of actions taken and alphabetically thereunder by names of applicants. No index. Typed. 20 x 18 x 30. Commissioners' office, south wall.

640. BLIND RELIEF REGISTER

June 1936—. 1 volume.

Case record of blind relief applications including action taken, grants, rejections, denials, withdrawals, and changes as status, as revisions and terminations; contains examining physicians' report on the condition of applicants' eyes. There is an alphabetical list of applicants for blind pensions in the back of this volume. Arranged in sections by titles of action taken and alphabetically thereunder by names of applicants. No index. Typed on printed forms. 200 pages. 12 x 18 x 2. Commissioners' office, south wall.

For prior record of applications, see entry 638.

641. INDIVIDUALS ACCEPTED FOR AID TO BLIND
June 1936—. 1 file box.

Record of open and closed cases of applicants for blind relief. The case record includes applications, certificates of actions taken, running records, correspondence, and rejections. Arranged in sections by titles of actions taken and alphabetically thereunder by names of applicants. No index. Typed. 20 x 18 x 30. Commissioners' office, south wall.

Reports

642. STATEMENT OF RECEIPTS AND EXPENDITURES
June 1936—. 1 file box.

Copy of county auditor's monthly statements to the state auditor, division of public assistance, of balance on hand, funds received from state and federal government, expenditures for blind aid, and administration costs. Chronologically arranged by dates of statements. No index. 20 x 18 x 30. Commissioners' office, south wall.

643. VOUCHERS - MONTHLY PAYMENTS
June 1936—. 1 file box.

Statement of money paid out for blind relief showing name and address of recipient and amount of award. Chronologically arranged by dates of payments. No index. Typed. 20 x 18 x 30. Commissioners' office, south wall.

644. MONTHLY STATISTICAL REPORTS
June 1936—. 1 file box.

Copies of monthly reports to county commissioners showing new applications, total grants, rejections, reinstatements, and pending cases; also money payments including any medical and hospital expenses involved. Chronologically arranged by dates of reports. No index. Handwritten on printed forms. 20 x 18 x 30. Commissioners' office, south wall.

645. QUARTERLY REPORTS
June 1936—. 1 file box.

Copies of quarterly reports to state auditor of estimated expenditures for approaching quarter showing number of applicants who were granted blind relief aid during the past quarter. Chronologically arranged by dates are reports. No index. Handwritten and typed on printed forms. 20 x 18 x 30. Commissioners' office, south wall.

Old age pensions although well known in Europe at the end of the nineteenth and beginning of the twentieth century and in a few American states during the same period, were not provided for an Ohio until recently (Arthur Lyon Cross, *A Shorter history of England and Greater Britain,* N. Y., 1925, 746-747; J. Salwyn Schapiro, *Modern and Contemporary European History 1815-1925,* N. Y., 1923, 295). During the depression years the sight of thousands of aged persons who had lost their homes and savings, and as a result of such losses faced starvation, touch the sensibilities of Ohioans. Accordingly, in 1933, an "Old Age Pension" law, proposed by initiative petition, was voted upon at the general election that year, providing for the granting of aid to the aged in Ohio under certain conditions. The law was adopted by a majority of the electors voting thereon (115 O. L. pt. ii, 431-439). The act as amended in 1936, provides, among other things, that any person 65 years of age or upward (unless confined at any penal or corrective institution or the state hospital) who is a citizen of the United States, who has resided in Ohio not less than five years during the nine prior to making application for aid, and who has resided for one year in the county wherein application for aid is made is eligible to receive a pension, providing his income from all and every source does not exceed $360 per year (116 O. L. pt. ii, 1st s. sess, H. 605; 116 O. L. pt. ii, 1st s. sess. H. 558). Moreover the applicant must be able to support himself, and have no husband, wife, child, or other person who is legally responsible for his support. In addition to this, the net value of all real and personal property of the unmarried applicant, less all encumbrances and liens, must not exceed $3,000; if the applicant is married the net value of the property of husband or wife shall not exceed $4,000. It may be required that such property, as a condition precedent to payment of aid, be transferred to the division of aid for the aged in trust. This provision does not, however, prohibit the applicant or his wife from occupying such property during their lifetime. (115 O. L. pt. ii, 431-439). An amendment to the act in 1937 eliminated the transfer of property as a possible condition precedent to granting aid, leaving the transfer optional. The amended act further states that any property, either real or personal, which had heretofore been conveyed to the division and trust could be reconveyed to the grantor by the division (Amended G. C. sec. 1359-6).

For the purpose of administering the old age pension law that was created in 1933 in the state department of public welfare of division of aid for the aged. The chief of the division of aid for the aged, appointed by the director of public welfare with the approval of the governor, is authorized to appoint all necessary assistants, clerks, stenographers, and other employees and fix their salaries, subject to the approval of the director of public welfare (115 O. L. pt. ii, 431-439).

In each county the commissioners constitute a board for administering the act. However, if the commissioners by a majority vote decline to serve in such capacity, the chief of the division of aid for the aged is authorized, with the consent of the director of public welfare, to appoint a board consisting of three to five members, who, like the county commissioners, serve without compensation. The local boards are required to keep such reports as the division may prescribe, and are also authorized to employ, subject to the approval of the division, such investigators, clerks, and other employees as are necessary for performance of their duties. (115 P. L. pt. ii, 431-439).

In 1937 the chief of the division was directed to appoint an advisory board in each county consisting of five citizens of such county. The members of the board, appointed for two years, are required to take an oath of office before entering upon their duties (G. C. sec. 1359-12).

Applications for relief were made annually to the local board but an act of the legislature in 1937, reorganizing the division of aid for the aged, omitted the provision for annual reapplication. Each applicant is thoroughly investigated. In its investigations the local board is not bound by common law or statutory rules of evidence, but is authorized to make inquiries in such a matter as seems "best calculated to conform to substantial justice." For the purpose of its investigations, each county board has the power to compel the attendance and testimony of witnesses. Decisions of the local boards may be appealed to the division. (115 O. L. pt. ii, 431-439).

After the applicants have been investigated by the local board, "certificates of aid" are granted to persons entitled to relief in conformity with the provisions of the law. Each certificate bearing the applicant's name and the pension allowed, as well as the records pertaining to the investigation, is forwarded to the division, which may approve, modify, or reject the certificate and findings of the board. (115 O. L. pt. ii, 435).

Under the provisions of this act the state became the general guardian of public and private welfare. The pension system relieves the increasing burden placed upon county homes, which, even under the most favorable conditions, are a poor substitute for homes. Although $2,625,000 was appropriated by the legislature for old age pensions in the early part of 1935, the cost to the public, in the long run, should not be much greater than that of the antiquated system of support in charitable institutions (116 O. L. 510).

All the records of this office are located in aid for the aged office, second floor.

646. REGISTER

1934—. 1 volume.

Record of all persons applying for or granted aid giving name and address; also liability of relatives and case number. Alphabetically arranged by names of clients. No index. Handwritten on printed forms. 250 pages. 18 x 12 x 2. Front desk, file drawer.

647. DAILY REPORT ACTIVITY

1934—. 1 file box.

Applications received daily for aid listing name, address, names of relatives, insurance, and property owned. Alphabetically arranged by names of applicants. No index. Handwritten on printed forms. 14 x 2 x 12. Filing cabinet, west wall.

648. INDEX

1934—. 3 file drawers.

Index to Case Record, [Pending] Cases, entry 649, Case Records, Active Cases, entry 650, Case Records, Closed Cases, entry 651, and Reallocated Cases, entry 652, showing name of recipient or applicant, case number, address, date of application, date approved or rejected, and amount of grant. Alphabetically arranged by names of applicants or recipients. Typed on printed forms. 4.5 x 6 x 18.

649. CASE RECORDS [Pending] CASES

1936—. 1 file box.

Record of cases pending approval at Columbus, Ohio, listing name and address of applicant. Numerically arranged by case numbers. For index, see entry 648. Handwritten on printed forms. 18 x 14 x 14. Filing cabinet, east wall.

650. CASE RECORDS, ACTIVE CASES

1934—. 5 file boxes.

Record of cases in the county receiving aid at the present time listing name, address, and amount of grant. Numerically arranged by case numbers. For index, see entry 648. Handwritten on printed forms. 22 x 13 x 15.

Filing cabinet west and south walls.

651. CASE RECORDS, CLOSED CASES
1934—. 2 file boxes.
Record of cases of persons denied aid, cases withdrawn, and cases of deceased persons, listing name, address, and reason for closing case. Numerically arranged by case numbers. For index, see entry 648. Handwritten on printed forms. 14 x 14 x 18. Filing cabinet, west wall.

652. REALLOCATED CASES
1936—. 1 file box.
Record of increases in amount of aid; also reinstatement of closed cases listing name, address, reason for increase or reinstatement, and case number. Numerically arranged by case numbers. For index, see entry 648. Handwritten on printed forms. 16 x 14 x 24. Filing cabinet, west wall.

653. RECEIPTS
1934—. 1 file box.
Record of change of insurance beneficiary, property records, and rejected applications, listing names, addresses, and remarks. Alphabetically arranged by names of clients and applicants. No index. Handwritten on printed forms. 14 x 2 x 12. Filing cabinet, west wall.

654. LETTERS
1934—. 1 file box.
Letters relative to business of the office. Alphabetically arranged by names that correspondence. No index. Handwritten and typed. 14 x 30 x 8. Front desk, file drawer.

Aid to dependent children, although provided by the Ohio legislature in 1913 in the form of mothers' pensions, assumed a new significance, when in April 1936, the Ohio legislature accepted the provisions of the Social Security Act. With the acceptance of the act, the sections of the General Code (1683-2 - 1683-10) relative to mothers' pensions were repealed.

The administration of the act in the state is delegated to the department of public welfare through the division of charities. In the administration of the act, the department was authorized to prescribe forms, certificates, reports, records, and accounts to be kept by the local departments.

The administration of the act in the counties is delegated to the juvenile judge or to judge of the court of domestic relations, excepting in counties in which by charter or by law the powers were vested in or imposed upon "a county department, board or commission, or officer other than the juvenile judge." In Washington County the juvenile judge performs this function. When he serves in the capacity of county administrator, the juvenile judge is directed to utilize the services of the employees of the court exercising juvenile jurisdiction. In the performance of his duties the judge is authorized to compel the attendance of witnesses and the production of books, and may institute contempt proceedings against persons refusing to testify. Except for this, power is conferred upon a judge or administrative powers only.

Those entitled to aid under the act include, among others, a child residing in the state less than sixteen years of age who has been deprived of parental support or care by reason of death, continued absence of a parent, or mental or physical incapacity of a parent. However, a child more than sixteen but less than eighteen years of age may receive aid at the discretion of the county administration.

Application for aid is made to the juvenile court by the parent or a relative, with whom the child must be living. Before aid is granted, a careful examination of the home is made by the employees of the juvenile court. If a child is found to be eligible, the court may grant such amount as is deemed proper. The amount of aid payable to any child is determined on the basis of actual needs "and shall be sufficient to provide support and care requisite for health and decency." In the event aid is granted, the home of such a child must be visited four times during each year. Each month the county auditor issues warrants upon the county treasurer for the payment of the warrants certified by the court. The decisions of the juvenile judge are subject to abrogation or modification by the department of public welfare. Any person attempting to receive aid on behalf of any child entitled to such aid is deemed guilty of a misdemeanor and upon conviction may be punished by fine or imprisonment or both.

The provisions of the act are financed by federal, state, and local funds. The county commissioners are required to include in the annual tax budget an amount not less than that computed to yield a levy of fifteen one-hundredths of one mill on each dollar of the general tax list of the county. If the commissioners failed to comply with the provisions of the act relative to appropriations, the state department of public welfare is directed to request the attorney general to institute *mandamus* proceedings against them. (G. C. sec. 1359-31 - 1359-45; 116 O. L. pt. ii, 188-95).

All records of this office are located in the probate court file room.

Case Records
(See also entries 36, 318-320)

655. REGISTER
July 1, 1936—. 1 volume.

Register of applications received, applications denied or withdrawn, reason for action taken, and register of grants, listing name, address, number of children coverage by budget, and monthly amount of grant. Alphabetically arranged by names of clients. No index. Handwritten on printed forms. 100 pages. 15 x 24 x 1.

656. CASE RECORDS, ACTIVE CASES
July, 1936—. 3 file boxes.

Record of applications and verifications of birth, death, disability, marriage, divorce, and social history of cases receiving aid, showing name of applicant, residence, and names and ages of dependent children. Alphabetically arranged by names of clients. No index. Handwritten on printed forms. 18 x 20 x 30.

657. CASE RECORDS, PENDING CASES
July, 1936—. 1 file drawer.

Cases that have been investigated, history compiled, and are awaiting action by the bureau of public assistance board. Alphabetically arranged by names of clients. No index. Handwritten on printed forms. 18 x 20 x 30.

658. CASE RECORDS, CLOSED CASES
July 1936—. 1 file box.

Record of cases closed by reason of death of dependent child, reaching maximum age, admitted to institution, or relative able to support. Alphabetically arranged by names of clients. No index. Handwritten on printed forms. 18 x 20 x 30.

659. REJECTED CASES
July 1936—. 1 file box.

Record of cases rejected because of failure to qualify. Alphabetically arranged by names of clients. No index. Handwritten on printed forms. 18 x 20 x 30.

(State Deputy Supervisors of Elections)

The responsibility for supervising and conducting elections in the county is delegated to state deputy supervisors of elections, the county board of elections. This board, created by the legislature in 1892 and consisting of four qualified voters in the county, is appointed for a four-year term by the secretary of state, who, by virtue of his office, is the chief election official of the state. (89 O. L. 455). On the first Monday in March in the even-numbered years, the secretary of state appoints two board members, one of whom is from the political party which casts the highest number of votes in the state for the office of governor at the last preceding state election, and the other from the political party which cast the next highest vote at such election. (G. C. sec. 4785-8). For the method of appointment when the term of each of the four members of the board expires on the same date see (G. C. sec. 4785-8a). The board members may be removed by the secretary of state for the neglect of duty, malfeasance, misfeasance in office; for willful violation of the election laws; or for other good and sufficient causes (G. C. sec. 4785-11). The compensation of the members is determined by the basis of population of the county and is paid by the county (G. C. sec. 4758-18). Similarly the expenses of the county board are paid from the county treasury, "in pursuance of appropriation by the county commissioners," in the same manner as other expenses are paid (G. C. sec. 4785-20).

The persons so appointed by the secretary, meeting five days after their appointment, select one of their members as chairman and a resident elector of the county as clerk who is not a member of the board (G. C. Sec. 4785-10). The board is vested with authority to establish, define, and provide election precincts; fix places of registration; provide for the purchase, preservation, and maintenance of voting booths, ballot boxes, books, maps, flags, blanks, cards of instruction, and other equipment used in registration and to issue rules, regulations, and instructions not inconsistent with the law or contrary to the rules and regulations as established by the chief election official (G. C. Sec. 4785-13).

Besides providing places of voting and equipment, the board is authorized to appoint clerks and other officers of elections. On or before the first day of September before each November election the board by a majority vote is authorized, after careful examination and investigation as to the qualifications, to appoint for each precinct six " competent persons, four as judges and two as clerks, who shall constitute the election officers of such precincts." Not more than two of the judges and one of the clerks, states the law, "shall be members of the same political party." Precinct election officers, appointed for a one-year term, may be removed by the board for neglect of duty, malfeasance, or misconduct in office. (G. C. sec. 4785-25).

The county board of elections is authorized to receive and examine and certify the sufficiency and validity of nominating petitions. They receive the election returns, canvas the returns, then make abstracts therefrom and transmit them to the proper authorities. They issue certificates of elections on forms prescribed by the secretary of state and report annually to the same official, on forms prescribed by him, the number of voters registered, the elections held, and such other information as the secretary of state may require. Moreover, the board prepares and submits to the proper authorities a budget estimating the cost of elections for the ensuring year. (G. C. sec. 4785-13).

Finally, the board is empowered to investigate irregularities, nonperformance of duty or violation of election laws by election officials. For the purpose of conducting investigations they may administer oaths, issue subpoenas, summon witnesses, and compel the presentation of books, papers, and records in connection with any investigation and report the facts to the prosecuting attorney. (G. C. sec. 4785-13).

The secretary of state, in 1930, ruled that members of the various board of elections were to be considered as state officers. This had reference to appointments made under sec. 4785-8a of the General Code. (See George C. Trautwein, *Supplement to Page's Annotated General Code 1926 to 1935,* ed. Cincinnati, 1935, note on page 688).

All the records are located and the office of H. S. Dyar in the First National Bank Building, Room 526.

660. MINUTES OF BOARD OF ELECTION

1930—. 3 volumes.

Record of all business transactions, financial reports, and appointments of officers of the board of elections. Chronologically arranged by dates of entries. No index. Handwritten. Average 150 pages. 12 x 15 x 1.5. East wall.

661. POLL BOOK TALLY SHEETS
1935-1936. 196 volumes.
List of registered voters of the precincts giving name and address, also signature of voter. Tally sheets give total votes received by each candidate in precinct. Alphabetically arranged by precincts. No index. Handwritten on printed forms. Average 25 pages. 20 x 12 x .5. East wall.

662. ABSTRACT OF VOTES
1924—. 1 bundle.
Record of total votes taken from poll book and tally sheets showing total number of votes for each candidate or proposal voted on. Chronologically arranged by years. No index. Handwritten on printed forms. 24 x 16 x 24. Southwest corner.

663. DECLARATION OF CANDIDATES
4 file boxes.
Original petitions as required of candidates before they are eligible to run for office. Chronologically arranged. No index. Handwritten on printed forms. 4 x 3 x 8. Northeast corner.

664. CASH BOOK
1922—. 3 volumes. 1925-1929 missing.
Record of fees paid by candidate listing names, office candidate desires, and amount of fee. Chronologically arranged. No index. Handwritten on printed forms. Average 100 pages. 12 x 14 x 1. Northeast corner.

665. RECEIPT FOR FEE
1926—. 2 volumes.
Duplicate receipts or fees collected from all candidates listing name, office, and amount. Chronologically arranged by dates of receipts. No index. Handwritten on printed forms. Average 200 pages. 10 x 14.5 x 1.5. Southwest corner.

666. ORDERS FOR WARRANTS

1902—. 3 volumes.

Complete record of bills paid for heat, light, and salaries. Chronologically arranged by dates of entries. No index. Handwritten on printed forms. 200 pages. 10 x 15 x 1.5. Southwest corner.

667. MISCELLANEOUS

1936—. 11 file boxes.

Miscellaneous records consisting of oaths of the election officials, acceptance of appointments, name and addresses of city and county clerks and judges, and petitions for local option. Chronologically arranged by dates. No index. Handwritten on printed forms. 4 x 5 x 12. Southwest corner.

The office of county surveyor, another English institution transplanted to America during the colonial period, became an important office in frontier Ohio where land title and boundary lines were often in dispute. The office is purely a creature of statute, there being no constitutional provision for its establishment.

The first act of the general assembly pertaining to the surveyor was passed during the first legislative session of 1803. Under this act the court of common pleas was authorized to appoint a person well qualified to act as county surveyor. He received his commission from the governor, was required to give bond conditioned for the faithful performance of the duties of his office, and was directed to survey all lands which were sold or were to be sold for taxes. The surveyor was authorized to appoint chainmen or markers whose function it was to establish corners. The surveys made by the surveyor or his deputies were the only ones to be accepted as legal evidence in any court of law or equity. For remuneration, the surveyor was permitted to retain all fees collected by him in the operation of his office. (1 O. L. 90-93).

Although it made no fundamental change in the duties of the surveyor, the act of 1816 fixed his term of office at five years; authorized him to appoint deputies, and made him responsible for their official acts. Moreover he was made liable to removal by the court for negligence or incompetency, and was made liable to a suit by persons believing themselves damaged by his negligence or that of his deputies. (14 O. L. 424-425). A year later, in 1817, provision was made for the appointment of a successor in the event the office became vacant because of death, resignation, or removal (15 O. L. 65).

The act of 1831 consolidated the previous acts, redefined the duties of the surveyor, increased the amount of his bond, and authorized him, when directed by the county commissioners, to procure from the surveyor general's office "a certified plat, together with the field notes of corners, and bearing trees to each section, quarter section, lot, or original survey in his county, and cause the same to be preserved in a book by him provided for that purpose; which shall be deposited in the county auditor's office, for the use of the landholders in the county." It provided further, that the surveyor should keep "a fair and accurate record of all official surveys made by himself or by his deputies," in a suitable book to be kept by him for that purpose, and that he should number his surveys progressively. (29 O. L. 402). More significant, however, was the fact that the office was made elective for a three-year term by the act of 1831. The term remained at three years until 1906 when it was reduced to two-year period. (29 O. L. 399; 98 O. L. 245-247).

During the years of the development of the office other duties have been delegated to the surveyor. In 1842 he was given the duty of ascertaining and reporting trespassing on public lands (40 O. L. 57). Ten years later, he was given the same powers as the justice of the peace to take and certify deeds, mortgages, powers of attorney, and other instruments affecting real estate, to administer oaths, and to take and certify affidavits (52 O. L. 70). In 1867 he was given authority, when directed by the county commissioners, to transcribe any and all dilapidated maps, records of plats, and field notes of surveys in other counties (64 O. L. 216-217; 78 O. L. 258). Similarly, in 1881, he was authorized to procure from any office in the state a certified plat together with the field notes of corners, quarter sections, lots, or original surveys and place them in a book provided for that purpose. Certified copies from his book were to be taken as *prima facie* evidence. (29 O. L. 399; 78 O. L. 285).

With the increase in modern means of transportation, there developed a growing need for more efficient methods of road construction and maintenance. Accordingly, in 1906, the surveyor was directed to act, whenever the services of an engineer were required, in the capacity of an engineer was with respect to roads, turnpikes, bridges, or ditches, except in cities of the first grade (98 O. L. 245-247). He was directed by statute to perform all duties in his county which would be done by a civil engineer or surveyor, to prepare all plans, specifications, and estimates of cost, and to submit forms for contracts for the construction and repair of all bridges, culverts, roads, draws, ditches, and other public improvements (except building) over which the county commissioners had authority. At the same time, he was made responsible for the inspection of all public improvements, and was directed to keep a complete list of all estimates and bids received for such work, as well as of contracts awarded for improvements. (95 O. L. 245-247).

Similarly, another measure enacted in 1919 increased the duties of the surveyor regarding road construction and road maintenance. Under this act the surveyor was authorized to designate one of his deputies as maintenance engineer. This engineer, under the direction of the surveyor, was to have charge of all "road maintenance and repair work" in his county. Furthermore, when authorized by the county commissioners, the surveyor was to appoint a maintenance supervisor or supervisors to have charge of the maintenance of improved highways within a district or districts established by the commissioners or surveyors, and containing not less than ten miles of improved country roads. (108 O. L. pt. 9, 497).

In 1923 the surveyor was delegated to assist the county planning commission whenever such commission was established (110 O. L. 312).

Thus the general responsibility of planning and directing county road construction is vested, by statute, in the county surveyor. Because of this increased responsibility placed on this office there has been an attempt to raise the general qualifications of those seeking election to it. Accordingly, in 1935, an act was passed changing the title of the office to that of "county engineer,' and eligibility to the office was restricted to "professional and registered surveyors listed to practice in the state of Ohio" (116 O. L. 283). This act was amended in 1936 to permit the incumbent to continue in office upon re-election, regardless of a lack of those qualifications (116 O. L. pt. ii, 152).

Plats, Surveys, and Maps

668. RECORD OF SURVEYS

1805—. 22 volumes. (1-22).

Record of surveys of land tracts made by county surveyors showing date of survey, survey number, description of tract surveyed, and name of owner of tract; also plat sketch of surveyed tract showing boundary lines, length of each boundary line, area of tract, streams, roads, and location of landmarks. Numerically arranged by survey numbers. 1805-1934, handwritten; 1934—, typed. Plats hand drawn. Average 380 pages. 16 x 12 x 3. Engineer's office.

669. INDEX TO SURVEYS

1805—. 2 volumes. (1, 2).

Index to Record of Surveys showing range, township, section, and survey numbers; with sketch of tract surveyed showing boundary lines, area, boundary landmarks, description of tract, and volume and page numbers of record. Numerically arranged by township, sections, and survey numbers. Handwritten and hand sketched. Average 350 pages. 16 x 12 x 2.75. Engineer's office.

670. SURVEYOR'S ROAD PLATS

1877-1895. 1 volume.

Copy of road plats showing name of road, sketch of route of road with elevation and grades noted, streams, bridges, names of abutting landowners, length of each section of road, with total length, name of surveyor, and date recorded. Prepared by county surveyors. Chronologically arranged by dates of recording. No index. Handwritten and hand sketched. 310 pages. 16 x 12 x 2.5. Engineer's office.

671. PLAT SURVEYS

1920—. 29 volumes. (labeled by names of subdivisions).

Blueprint plat maps of townships, corporations, and city wards of Marietta, showing boundary lines of subdivision, lot lines, boundary lines of out-lots and township tracts, lot number, area of out-lots and township tracts, roads, highways, streets and alleys, with names of streets and alleys and highway numbers, streams, bridges, and railroads. Kept up-to-date by revisions. Prepared by county engineer's department. No arrangement. No index. Blueprints. Scales vary from 1 inch equals 100 feet to 1inch equals 1,000 feet. Average 60 pages. 22 x 16 x .75. Engineer's office.

672. FIELD BOOKS, LAND SURVEYS

1909—. 34 volumes. (labeled by years).

Survey data and field notes of surveys of lands showing date of survey, name of owner of tract, location of tract, notes of landmarks on boundary lines, bearing of boundary lines, area of tract, and name of surveyor. Chronologically arranged by dates of recording. Alphabetically indexed by names of landowners. Handwritten. Average 90 pages. 7 x 4.5 x .5. Engineer's work room.

673. FIELD BOOKS, ROAD SURVEYS

1900—. 202 volumes. (1-202).

Record of surveyor's field notes on road surveys giving survey data, such as, curve degree, elevation, grade cubic yards of excavation or fill, and name of surveyor. Chronologically arranged by dates of recording. No index. Handwritten. Average 90 pages. 7 x 4.5 x .5. Engineer's work room.

674. ATLAS OF WASHINGTON COUNTY

1875. 1 volume.

Political maps of county showing townships, corporations with roads, streets, alleys, railroads, streams, section and range lines, section and range numbers and boundary lines of land tracts with area and name of owner; corporations or hamlets showing boundary lines of corporation or hamlet, lot lines with lot numbers, street names, and location of public buildings; also county directory giving brief summary of industrial pursuits of each township and town with short biography of prominent citizens. From surveys by D. J. Lake, county engineer. Published by Titus, Simmons and Titus, 31 South Street, Philadelphia, Pennsylvania. Alphabetically arranged by names of townships and towns. Alphabetical table of contents. Printed, engraved, and lithographed. 93 pages. 16 x 14 x 1. Engineer's office.

675. MISCELLANEOUS PLAT MAPS
1892-1934. 137 maps (each map tagged with name of survey or farm owner).
Blueprint plats of tracts showing boundary lines, section lines, names of owners of tracts, and area of tract. These maps were prepared and connection with oil and gas leases for companies having the land under lease. Name of company, date of survey, and name of surveyor shown. Prepared and published by county engineering department. No systematic arrangement. No index. Blueprints. Scales vary from 1 inch equals 40 rods to 1 inch equals 100 rods. 20 x 20. Engineer's work room.

676. PLAT MAP, MARIETTA TOWNSHIP AND MARIETTA CITY
1902. 1 volume.
Map showing township, section, corporation lines, boundary lines of land tracts and lots, roads, streets, and ally names, names of owners of township tracks and out-lots, in-lot numbers, location and names of public buildings, names of allotments, subdivisions and additions, in-lot dimensions and areas of out-lots and township tracts, streams, railroads, and Marietta ward boundaries. Read from surveys by Fred B. Roe, county engineer. Published by George F. Cramm and Company, 130 Fulton Street, New York City, 1902. No systematic arrangement. Alphabetically indexed by names of allotments, subdivisions, additions, and city wards. Printed and lithographed. Scale, 1 inch equals 1,000 feet. 50 pages. 18 x 16 x 1. Engineer's work room.

Roads and Bridges
(See also entries 19-25)

677. COMMISSIONERS' RECORD OF ROADS
1875-1915. 2 volumes. (1, 2).
Record copy of petition presented to county commissioners to establish and extend roads and highways showing name of person presenting petition, name of proposed road, description of route of proposed road, names of petitioners, copy of notice of

petition filed, copy of affidavit of posting notice, copy of bond filed by petitioners, copy of report of viewers to commissioners recommending or rejecting establishment of road, copy of surveyor's report on survey of proposed road with sketches of route and survey data on elevation and grade, and copy of commissioners' approval or rejection of petition. Chronologically arranged by dates of petitions. Alphabetically indexed by names of persons presenting petition; also separate index, entry 678. Handwritten on printed forms. Average 600 pages. 18 x 12 x 3.5. Engineer's office.

For other records, see entries 20 and 21.

678. INDEX TO COMMISSIONERS' ROAD RECORD
1875-1915. 1 volume.

Index to commissioners' record of roads, showing township, name of road, name of freeholder presenting petition, title of petition, date, section number through which the road runs, and volume and page numbers of record. Alphabetically arranged by names of townships. Handwritten. 230 pages. 14 x 10 x 1.5. Engineer's office.

679. ROAD RECORD (First Series)
1793-1902. 4 volumes. (1-4).

Record surveys of proposed routes for roads and highways showing sketch of route, surveyor's data on elevation, grades, fords, bridges, and description of route. Beginning with volume 2, 1925, record shows length of each section of road with estimate of cost, and name of surveyor. Volume 1, 1793-1825, contains: [Clerk of Courts Report], entry 8; [Treasury Receipts], entry 43; [Tax Collector's Accounts}, entry 175, and [Treasurer's Fund Account], entry 387. Chronologically arranged by dates of recording. Handwritten. Average 350 pages. 16 x 12 x 2.5. Engineer's office.

For subsequent records, see entries 681.

680. INDEX ROAD RECORD (First Series)
1793-1902. 1 volume.

Index to Road Records (First Series) showing date of survey, name of road, and volume number and page numbers of record. Chronologically arranged by dates of surveys. Handwritten. 410 pages. 16 x 11 x 2.2. Engineer's office.

681. ROAD RECORD (Second Series)

1903—. 3 volumes. (1-3).

Surveyor's record of county and township roads showing township, name or number of road, section numbers through which road runs, road width, date surveyed, length of road, date road granted, name of surveyor, and field book number and page; also sketch of road route as surveyed showing name of abutting landowners; and survey date showing curve degree, elevation, and grade. Alphabetically arranged by names of townships and chronologically thereunder by date surveyed. No index. Handwritten and hand sketched. Average 500 pages. 18 x 12 x 3.25. Engineer's office.

For prior records, see entry 679.

682. SPECIFICATIONS AND ESTIMATES

1891—. 3 file drawers. Prior records missing.

Record copy of specifications and estimates furnished by surveyor to commissioners covering proposed construction or repair of county roads and bridges. All papers of each proposal banded together. Shows name of proposed construction or repair, specifications for construction of same, with estimate of cost of labor and material, damages to abutting landowners, and date filed. Chronologically arranged by dates of filing. No index. Handwritten on printed forms. 12 x 12 x 26. Engineer's office.

683. SURVEYOR'S CONTRACT RECORD

1901—. 6 volumes. (1-6). Prior records missing.

Record copies of commissioners' resolutions authorizing the improvement or repair of county roads and bridges, copy of advertisement for bids, record of bids received, and copy of contract entered into by surveyor with the approved bidder, giving date, name or number of road or bridge, specifications of contract, amount of contract, date contract to be completed, and record of payments to contractor on account. Chronologically arranged by dates of contracts. Alphabetically indexed by names of contractors. 1901-1927, handwritten; 1928—, typed. Average 280 pages. 20 x 14 x 1.75. Engineer's work room.

Business Administration of Office

684. APPROPRIATION LEDGER

1920—. 5 volumes. Prior records missing.

Record of funds appropriated annually by county commissioners to surveyor's department, showing amount allocated to road maintenance, equipment, bridge, surveyor's general funds, and miscellaneous; also itemized account of expenditures of each fund, showing date, to whom paid, and amount. Alphabetically arranged by names of funds. No index. Handwritten on printed forms. Average 420 pages. 15 x 20 x 2.75. Engineer's office.

685. FEE RECORD

1872—. 3 volumes.

Record of fees for surveying services in surveys of land tracts for individuals or on court order showing date of service, to whom charged, amount, what survey, and date paid. Chronologically arranged by dates of entries. No index. Handwritten on printed forms. Average 290 pages. 16 x 11 x 1.5. Engineer's work room.

686. REPORTS

1922—. 2 file drawers. Prior records missing.

Duplicate copy of monthly reports by county surveyor to county commissioners showing what roads, highways, and bridges inspected, what work done, with type of repair or new construction on roads and bridges. Chronologically arranged by dates of reports. No index. Typed on printed forms. 10 x 4.5 x 22. Engineer's office.

687. INVENTORIES, TOWNSHIP EQUIPMENT

1927—. 1 file drawer. Prior records missing.

Surveyor's record copy of road maintenance equipment owned by each township showing date of inventory, township, itemized list of equipment with value, and date filed with county commissioners. Chronologically arranged by dates of inventories. No index. Handwritten on printed forms. 12 x 12 x 26. Engineer's office.

688. MISCELLANEOUS RECORDS

1926—. 1 file drawer. Prior records missing.

Original bills, contracts, and assessments for county highway improvement showing date of bill, date filed, name of creditor, for what, and amount, contracts entered into by county surveyor by authority of county commissioners with individuals or firms for construction or repair of county roads and bridges; also record of assessments on abutting landowners for their share of highway improvements, showing township, name of road, name of landowner, and amount of assessment. Arranged by titles or subjects and chronologically thereunder by dates of filing. No index. Handwritten and typed. 12 x 12 x 26. Engineer's office.

The legislature at its 1914 session, following the disastrous floods of the previous year, made provision for the establishment of conservancy districts in Ohio the objects of which were to prevent floods, to protect cities, villages, farms, and highways from inundation. This act, authorized by the constitutional amendment of 1912 (Art. II, sec. 3), was upheld by the courts as a valid exercise of the police power of the state (*County of Miami* v. *Dayton,* 92 O. S. 223-224, 236). The conservancy districts, according to the act, may be established not only to prevent floods but to regulate streams, reclaim overflowed lands, provide irrigation, regulate the flow of streams, or divert water courses.

The court of common pleas of any county in the state or any judge in vacation is authorized, after a petition signed either by five hundred freeholders or by a majority of freeholders has been filed with the clerk of courts, to establish a conservancy district which might be within or without the county where the court is located. The court, after conducting hearings on the petition as to the purpose of the district, may declare the district organized and give it a corporate name. The clerk of courts, within thirty days after the district has been declared a corporation by the court, transmits to the secretary of state, and to the county recorder in each county having lands in the district, copies of the findings and the decree of the court incorporating the district which, according to statue, is considered a political subdivision.

Within thirty days after the decree of incorporation the court is authorized to appoint three persons, at least two of whom are freeholders in the district, to serve as a board of directors to serve three, five, and seven years respectively. After the expiration of their term the tenure of office is five years. The board of directors, after taking an oath that they "will not be interested directly or indirectly in any contract let by the district," organized by selecting one of their members as president and some person, not a member of the board as secretary. The board is authorized to employ a chief engineer who may be an individual, copartnership, or corporation; an attorney; and such other engineers and attorneys as may be necessary for carrying on the work. The board may provide for their compensation, which, with all other necessary expenditures, shall be taken as a part of the cost of improvement. While the chief engineer prepares plans and specifications of work, all contracts which exceed $1,000 are let by competitive bidding.

The board, or its agents, is authorized to enter upon lands within or without the conservancy district for the purpose of making surveys. They are authorized to exercise the right to eminent domain; condemn property, after appraisal, for the use of the district; make regulations to protect their work by prescribing the method of building roads, bridges, or fences; to remove bridges, cemeteries, or other structures impeding their work; and to cooperate with the federal government, with persons, railways, corporations, the state government of Ohio or other states, for assistance for drainage, conservancy, or other improvements.

To finance such improvements the board is authorized to levy upon the property of the district a tax not to exceed three-tenths of a mill on the assessed valuation. This tax is certified to the county auditor, and to the various treasurers of the counties within the district and is used to pay the expenses of organization, surveys, and plans. The commission is authorized further to borrow money at a rate not to exceed six percent per annum and levy assessments for a bond fund. (104 O. L. 13-64).

The board is required to "keep in a well-bound book a record of all its proceedings, minutes of meetings, certificates, contracts, bonds given by employees, and all corporate acts, which shall be open to the inspection of all owners of property in the district, as well as to all other interested parties." The secretary, who may serve also as treasurer, is designated as the "custodian of the records of the district and its corporate seal." (104 O. L. 18).

Washington County is in the Muskingum conservancy district, and the records of its board are housed at New Philadelphia.

The agricultural and mechanical society of Washington County, Ohio, and Wood County, Virginia, was organized April 28, 1819, and held an exhibition at Marietta, October 18, 1826. The organization was a predecessor of the Washington County agricultural society which was organized on June 24, 1846 and held a fair at Marietta on the 15th of the following October. This society was organized according to the provisions of the law of February 28, 1846, which authorized the formation of county societies and made provision for their aid by the counties (*Report of the Ohio Department of Agriculture,* 1936; 44 O. L. 70). On February 15, 1853, the legislature declared such societies to be bodies corporate and politic, capable of suing and being sued, and of holding in fee simple such real estate as they might purchase for sites whereon to hold fairs, to be paid for by the county commissioners (51 O. L. 333).

By act of the legislature passed February 20, 1861, county agricultural societies were required to report annually to the state board of agriculture, and to meet with the state board at Columbus once each year (58 O. L. 22). In 1883 the legislature provided for the organization of district or county agricultural societies. The act making this provision stipulated that when thirty or more persons, residents of any county or district embracing two counties, organized themselves into an agricultural society, under the rules and regulations of the state board of agriculture, the county might aid such societies of the grant not to exceed $400 per year. (80 O. L. 142). By act of April 21, 1896, provision was made for representation in county society of thirty or more residents of any county or district embracing two or more counties (92 O. L. 205). In 1900 the legislature extended the amount of county aid to $800 per year (94 O. L. 395). Later, on May 6, 1902, the legislature passed an act authorizing thirty or more residents of a county or of a district embracing one or more counties, to organize themselves into an agricultural society (95 O. L. 403).

On April 17, 1919, the legislature provided for the organization of county and independent agricultural societies, the payment of class premiums; defined the duties of persons competing for premiums; prescribed the publication of treasurers' accounts and the list of awards by societies; designated conditions of membership in a county agricultural society; authorized the society to elect a board of directors consisting of eight members, and prescribed their term of office and the matter of their election. The act further stipulated how such societies might obtain state aid, and authorized the county commissioners to insure all buildings belonging to agricultural societies. (108 O. L. pt. I, 381-385).

The legislature in 1921 passed an act stipulating that the total amount of county aid to county agricultural societies should not exceed one hundred percent of the amount paid by the society in regular class premiums (109 O. L. 240). By Act of March 27, 1925, the county commissioners were authorized to purchase or to lease, for a term not less than twenty years, real estate whereon to hold fairs under the management of the county agricultural society and to erect thereon suitable buildings (111 O. L. 238). On March 10, 1927, the legislature authorized the county commissioners to appropriate annually on the request of the agricultural society a sum not less than $1,500 or more than $2,000 from the general fund for the purpose of "encouraging agricultural fairs" (112 O. L. 84).

The most recent legislation affecting agricultural societies was that of March 19, 1935. This act provides that where no duly organized county agricultural society existed, and when no fair was held by a duly organized county agricultural society which had held an annual exposition for three years previous to January 1, 1933, the county commissioner should, on the request of the independent society, appropriate annually from the general fund a sum not more than $2,000 or less than $500 for the encouragement of independent agricultural fairs (115 O. L. 47).

No separate records of the agricultural society in Washington County were located. The proceedings of the county commissioners regarding county fairs are recorded in the Commissioners' Journal, entry 1.

In 1914 the federal government passed an act providing for cooperative agricultural extension between the state agricultural college and the United States department of agriculture. The purpose of the extension service was to give instruction and practical demonstrations in agriculture and home economics to persons not attending college, and to give such information through field demonstrations, publications and other means. The funds for such work were to be supplied in part by the federal government and part by the state. (*U. S. Statutes at Large,* XXXVIII, pt. I, 372-374).

A year following the federal legislation, the Ohio legislature accepted the provisions of the act by providing that when twenty or more residents of the county organized themselves into a "farmers' institute society for the purpose of teaching better methods of farming, stock raising, fruit culture and business connected with agriculture," accepted a constitution and bylaws conforming to the rules and regulations prescribed by the trustees of the Ohio State University, and elected proper officers, the institute should be a corporate body. The Ohio State University was required to furnish speakers for their annual meeting. At the close of the session trustees were authorized to publish the lectures in pamphlet or book form.

Besides maintaining an institute, the society was authorized to maintain a county experiment farm. Furthermore the county commissioners were authorized to select a county agent subject to the approval of the dean of the college of agriculture of the Ohio State University. The first agent of Washington County was appointed in 1914. It is the duty of the agent to inspect and study the agricultural conditions in his county, distribute agriculture literature, cooperate with the United States Department of Agriculture and the college of agriculture of the Ohio State University. In the event the commissioners failed to make such an appointment, the electorate could require them to do so on a referendum vote. (106 O. L. 356-359).

In 1929 the original legislation was amended so as to authorize the trustees of the Ohio State University to employ home demonstration agents and boys' and girls' club agents. The county extension agent was given the additional duty of carrying the teachings of the college of agriculture of the Ohio State University in agriculture and home economics to the residents of his county through personal visits, bulletins, and practical demonstrations. Furthermore it was his duty to render educational service not only in relation to agricultural production, but also in relation to economic problems including marketing, distribution, and utilization of farm products. (113 O. L. 82-83).

The initial legislation contained a clause which required the county commissioners to appropriate annually $1,000 if they wish to obtain the services of an agricultural agent. This amount was to be matched by the state. Under the present system the commissioners are empowered to levy a tax and to appropriate from the premium thereof or from the general fund to be paid to the state treasury to the credit of the agricultural extension fund an amount not to exceed $3,000 for each agent. Amounts in excess must have the unanimous consent of the commissioners. (113 O. L. 82-83).

All records are located in agricultural extension agent's office.

Experiments

689. EXPERIMENT FARMS

1936. 8 file boxes.

Reports to county agent of the results of experiments on various experiment farms in the county showing the value gained by certain agricultural methods. Chronologically arranged by dates of reports. No index. Handwritten on printed forms. 6 x 24 x 30.

690. SOIL CONSERVATION

1936—. 3 file boxes.

Record of farms of Washington County, where soil conservation is in progress, showing rotation of crops, tree planting to enrich and conserve soil. Alphabetically arranged by names of farm owners. No index. Handwritten. 12 x 14 x 30.

691. FEDERAL REPORTS

Approximately 1923—. 3 file boxes.

Copies of reports to Federal Bureau of agriculture showing results of valuable experiments to aid farmers and securing better crop production. Chronologically arranged by dates of reports. No index. Printed. 12 x 14 x 30.

Crop Curtailment and Loans

692. SEED LOANS

1931—. 1 file box.

Record of applications and grants of loans to farmers of the county to purchase seeds or crop planting. Alphabetically arranged by names of farmers obtaining loan. No index. Handwritten on printed forms. 12 x 14 x 30.

693. WHEAT

1933-1936. 1 file box. Discontinued.

Record of wheat curtailment in county showing acreage reduction of wheat for which each grower is to receive federal compensation according to the number of acres less the amount previously planted. Alphabetically arranged by names of farmers. No index. Handwritten on printed forms. 12 x 14 x 30.

694. CORN-HOG CONTRACTS

1933-1935. 2 file boxes. Discontinued.

Applications of farmers for federal grants in Washington County and statements of reduction in the usual production of corn and hogs. Alphabetically arranged by names of farmers. No index. Handwritten on printed forms. 12 x 14 x 24.

695. CORN-HOG PAYMENTS

1934-1935. 1 file box. Discontinued.

Record of payments made to hog and corn producers, for curtailment of production showing name of farmer, address, amount of curtailment and total amount of payments. Alphabetically arranged by names of producers. No index. Handwritten on printed forms. 6 x 7 x 24.

Reports

696. HOME ECONOMICS

1923—. 2 file boxes.

Reports on child feedings, maternity clinics, canning, and baking by members of the home economics clubs connected with the county extension department. Alphabetically arranged by names of members. No index. Handwritten. 12 x 14 x 24.

697. FRUIT

No date. 1 file box.

Growers' report of Washington County and other counties on fruit production, also soil testing reports in various orchard lands. Alphabetically arranged by names of growers. No index. Handwritten. 12 x 14 x 30.

698. 4-H CLUB

1923—. 2 file boxes.

Record of the 4-H club showing present enrollment, grades and accomplishment of each club; also individual progress record for each member. Chronologically arranged by years. No index. Handwritten. 12 x 14 x 28.

699. MONTHLY AND ANNUAL REPORTS

1935—. 2 file boxes.

Copies of miscellaneous reports of county agent to state department of agriculture showing business transactions and visitors to county agent. Chronologically arranged by dates of reports. No index. Handwritten on printed forms. 12 x 14 x 24.

700. REPORTS

No date. 2 filing cabinets.

Monthly reports of county extension agent to Ohio State University extension service on county farming activities, such as crop production and soil conservation, which are connected with the extension office. Chronologically arranged by dates of reports. No index. Handwritten. 84 x 72 x 24.

701. RECREATION ACTIVITIES
1923—. 1 file box.
Record of recreation activities of 4-H clubs including initiation reports, games, essays, and camping activities of various county club groups and club meetings throughout the year. Alphabetically arranged by names of clubs. No index. Handwritten. 12 x 14 x 30.

Miscellaneous

702. AGRICULTURE
1926—. 1 file box.
Miscellaneous correspondence between counties regarding developments and experiments in agriculture that are of mutual interest. Alphabetically arranged by names of counties. No index. Handwritten. 12 x 14 x 24.

703. LETTERS
1934—. 2 file boxes. Prior records destroyed.
Business letters and soil testing reports of Washington County as compiled by county extension agents through contact with farmers of the county. Alphabetically arranged by names of farmers. No index. Handwritten. 12 x 14 x 27.

704. COUNTY AGENT'S OLD RECORDS
1923-1934. 1 file box.
Record of material furnished; also monthly and yearly statistics of county agents expenditures for development of agriculture. Alphabetically arranged by names of agents. No index. Handwritten. 12 x 14 x 30.

The county dog warden, appointed by the Washington County commissioners in 1927, has as its duty the enforcement of the provisions of the General Code relating to licensing dogs, the impounding and destroying of unlicensed dogs, and paying of compensation for damages to livestock inflicted by dogs. This officer, like other county officials, is required to give bond conditioned for the faithful performance of the duties of his office. This bond, in the sum of not less than $500 nor more than $2,000 is filed with the county auditor. His compensation and tenure, like that of his deputies, is determined by the county commissioners. (108 O. L. pt. i, 535; 112 O. L. 348).

The warden is required to make a record of all dogs owned, kept, or harbored in his county; to patrol the county; and to seize and impound dogs more than three months of age found not wearing a valid registration tag. The last provision does not apply, however, to dogs kept in a regularly licensed kennel. Moreover, he is required to present to the commissioners weekly written reports of all dogs seized, impounded, redeemed, and destroyed, and to report all claims for damages to livestock inflicted by dogs.

In the performance of their legal duties, the dog warden and his deputies have the same police power as are conferred by statute upon sheriffs and police. They may summon the assistance of bystanders in performing their duties, and serve writs and other legal processes at any court in the county with reference to enforcing the provisions of the laws relating to dogs. (G. C. sec. 5652-7).

705. RECORD

1927—. 2 file drawers (labeled Dog Warden).

Record of all claims for damages to livestock inflicted by dogs showing name and address of claimant, number and kind, grade and quality, value, and nature of injury to animals, amount claimed for such injury less deduction for carcasses or pelts sold or used, net damages claim, and warden's estimate of net amount of injury. Chronologically arranged by dates of claims. No index. Handwritten on printed forms. 23 x 14 x 5.5. Commissioners' office, filing cabinet, south wall.

706. REPORTS

1927—. 3 file boxes (labeled Dog Warden).

Record copies of reports of county dog warden to the board of county commissioners of all dogs seized, impounded, redeemed or destroyed, showing name of owner, or harborer, if known, sex, breed, color, address where dog is kept or harbored, date seized or impounded, date disposed of, whether sold, redeemed, or destroyed, amount of fees and cost collected, and date paid into county treasury. Chronologically arranged by dates of reports. No index. Handwritten on printed forms. 23 x 14 x 5.5. Commissioners' office, south wall.

For commissioners' copies, see entry 11.

SELECTED BIBLIOGRAPHY FOR COUNTY HISTORY AND OFFICE ESSAYS

Documentary Sources

Acts of the General Assembly, 1803-1938 (117 volumes, published annually under state authority).

Baldwin, William Edward, ed., *Throckmorton's Ohio Code* (certified edn., Cleveland, 1936).

Carter, Clarence Edwin, ed., and comp., *The Territorial Papers of the United States* (4 volumes, Washington, 1934, in progress). Volumes II and III of this monumental work treat of the Northwest Territory.

Chase, Salmon P., comp., *Statutes of Ohio and the Northwest Territory, 1788-1883* (3 volumes Cincinnati, 1833-1835).

Commissioners' Journal [Washington County], 1797—. 20 volumes. This journal, as well as other records listed under the various offices included in the inventory, constitutes the most important source material on the history of Washington County.

Ford, Worthington Chauncey, and others, eds., *Journals of the Continental Congress* (34 volumes, Washington, 1904-1937).

Hammond, Charles, and others, eds., *Reports of Cases Argued and Determined in the Supreme Court of Ohio in Bank* . . . (20 volumes, Cincinnati, 1824-1852).

Hulbert, Archer Butler, ed., *The Records of the Original Proceedings of the Ohio Company* (Marietta Historical *Collections,* 3 volumes, Marietta, 1917). The author's induction constitutes the best history of the Ohio Company.

McCook, G. W. and others, eds., *Reports of Cases Argued and Determined in the Supreme Court of Ohio* . . . (132 volumes, Cincinnati 1852—).

Pease, Theodore Calvin, comp., *Laws of the Northwest Territory, 1788-1800* (*Illinois State Bar Association Law Service,* no. I, Springfield, 1925).

Report of the Joint Legislative Committee on Economy and Taxation of the Eighty-Sixth General Assembly (Columbus, 1926). In chapter xiii the Committee condemns the organization of county government in Ohio.

Shepherd, Vinton R., ed., *The Ohio NISI PRIUS REPORTS* (32 volumes. n. s., Columbus and Cincinnati, 1894-1934). Cases decided by common pleas, probate, and municipal courts of the state of Ohio.

United States Statutes at Large, 1776-1936 (49 volumes, United States Government Printing Office).

Journals, Diaries, Memoirs, and Travel Accounts

Brunet, Jacob, *Burnet's Notes on the Northwest Territory* (Cincinnati, 1847). An interesting contribution by a Cincinnati pioneer.

Celoron's Journal, Rev. A. A. Lambing, ed., *Ohio Archaeological and Historical Quarterly,* XXIX (1920), 335-396.

Harris, Thaddeus Mason, *The Journal of a Tour into the Territory Northwest of the Allegheny Mountains; made in the year, 1803 . . .* (Boston, 1805).

Melish, John, *Travels in the United States of America, in the years1806 and 1807, and 1809, 1810, and 1811 . . .* (2 volumes, Philadelphia, 1812). Volume II contains excellent materials treating of Marietta and vicinity.

Memoirs of Rufus Putnam and Certain Official Papers and Correspondence, Rowena Buell, comp., (Boston, 1903). This volume was published by the Colonial Dames of America in the state of Ohio.

Michaux, F. A., *Travels to the West of the Allegheny Mountains, in the states of Ohio, Kentucky, and Tennessee, and back to Charleston, . . .* (B. Lambert, tr., London, 1805). Contains valuable contemporary observations made by a Frenchman who was a member of the society of natural history at Paris.

Sargent, Winthrop, *Journal of the Winthrop Sargent, Secretary of the Territory Northwest of the Ohio River.* October 1, 1793-December 31, 1795 (n. p., n. d.). Typewritten copies of the text of the journal in the possession of William Butler Duncan, of New York City.

Biography

Cone, Mary, *Life of Rufus Putnam with Extracts From His Journal and an Account of the First Settlement in Ohio* (Cleveland, 1886). A good brief biography.

Cutler, Julia Perkins, *Life and Times of Ephraim Cutler* (Cincinnati, 1890). This biography, written by Cutler's daughter, is a bit laudatory.

Cutler, William Parker and Julia Perkins, *Life Journals and Correspondence of Reverend Manasseh Cutler, LL. D.* (2 volumes, Cincinnati, 1888). This biography reveals Cutler's part in the formation and history of Ohio Company.

Smith, William Henry, *The St. Clair Papers: The Life and Public Services of Arthur St. Clair* (2 volumes Cincinnati, 1882). Although inaccurate in detail, this is the best work on St. Clair.

Secondary Sources

Ambler, Charles Henry, *A History of Transportation in the Ohio Valley* (Glendale, California, 1932). An excellent study written by a careful student.

Adams, George Burton, *Constitutional History of England* (New York, 1921). A standard work.

Andrews, Israel Ward *Washington County, and the Early Settlement of Ohio* (Cincinnati, 1877). A centennial address delivered before a group of citizens of Washington County, Marietta, Ohio, on July 4, 1876.

Beach, Arthur G., *A Pioneer College: The Story of Marietta* (n. p. 1935).

Bond, Beverly W. Jr., *The Civilization of the Old Northwest: A Study of Political, Social, and Economic Development, 1788-1812* (New York, 1934). An excellent study in which the author develops the thesis that the Northwest was a laboratory in which the American colonial system was developed.

Bownocher, J. A., *The Occurrence and Exploitation of Petroleum and Natural Gas in Ohio* (Geographical Survey in Ohio, Bull. i, 4th ser., 1903).

Chaddock, Robert E., *Ohio Before 1850: A Study of the Early Influence of Pennsylvania and Southern Populations in Ohio* (Columbia University, *Studies,* XXXI, no. 2, New York, 1908).

Cross, Arthur Lyon, *History of England and Greater Britain* (New York, 1925). A standard textbook, but two sharp in outline.

Dickinson, C. E., *A History of Belpre, Washington County, Ohio* (Parkersburg, 1920).

Downes, Randolph Chandler, *Frontier Ohio, 1788-1803 (Ohio Historical Collections,* no. 3, Columbus, 1935). One of the most satisfactory treatments of the Ohio frontier-well documented.

Dyer, Albion Morris, *First Ownership of Ohio Lands* (Boston, 1911).

Heiges, R. E., *The Office of Sheriff in the Rural Counties of Ohio* (Findlay, Ohio, 1933) This volume has the usual limitations of a doctoral dissertation.

Hildreth, S. P., *Memoirs of the Early Pioneers Settlers of Ohio* (Cincinnati, 1854). Contains much viable information.

__________, *Pioneer History: being an account of the first examination of the Ohio Valley, and the early settlements of the Northwest Territory* (Cincinnati, 1848). Although an old work, this volume is interesting and informative.

Hinsdale, Burke Aaron, *The Old Northwest* (New York, 1888). An old work of great value.

Hockett, Homer C. *Western Influence on Political Parties to 1825: An Essay in Historical Interpretation* (Ohio State University Bulletin XXII, no. 3, Columbus, 1917). An excellent study.

Johnson, Allen, and Malone, Dumas, eds., *Dictionary of American Biography* (2) volumes, New York, 1922-1928). A monumental work.

Kennedy, Aileen Elizabeth, *The Ohio Poor Law and Its Administration* (Sophonisba P. Breckinridge, ed., *Social Service Monographs*, no. 22, University of Chicago Press, Chicago, 1934). A biting criticism of the administration of poor relief in Ohio prior to 1932.

Karraker, Cyrus Harreld, *The Seventeenth-Century Sheriff: A Comparative Study of the Sheriff in England and the Chesapeake Colonies, 1607-1689* (Chapel Hill, 1930). Although interesting, this volume does not supersede the earlier studies made of that office.

Lewis, Thomas William, *History of Southeastern Ohio and the Muskingum Valley* (3 volumes, Chicago, 1928).

McLaughlin, Andrew Cunningham, *The Confederation and the Constitution* (Albert Bushnell Hart, ed., *The American Nation: A History,* New York, 1904-1918, X). This is a standard work.

Mills, William C., *Archaeological Atlas of Ohio* (Columbus 1914).

Paxson, Frederic L., *History of the American Frontier 1763-1893* (Boston, 1924). A careful analysis of the western movement.

Peters, W. E., *Ohio Lands and their Subdivisions* (Athens, 1918).

Pollock, Sir Frederick, and Maitland, Frederic, *The history of English Law Before the Time of Edward I* (2 volumes, Cambridge, 1895). A standard work.

Pratt, Julius W., *Expansionist of 1812* (New York, 1925). An interpretation of western influences making for war.

Robinson, Louis N., *Penology in the United States* (Philadelphia, 1922). Although an old work, this volume contains many significant conclusions.

Roseboom, Eugene Holloway, and Weisenberger, Francis Phelps, *A History of Ohio* (New York, 1934). The most satisfactory history of Ohio– scholarly and impartial.

Schapiro, J. Salwyn, *Modern and Contemporary European History 1815-1925* (New York, 1923). A standard textbook. Especially good on the intellectual and social history of the period.

Sherman, C. E., *Original Ohio Land Subdivisions, Final Report, Ohio Cooperative Topographic Survey* (Mansfield, 1903).

Summers, Thomas J., *History of Marietta* (Marietta, 1903).

Trent, P. J., "Origin of the National Land System under the Confederation," (American Historical Association Annual *Reports,* 1905, I).

Williams, H. Z., and Bros., publication, *History of Washington County, Ohio . . .* 1788-1881 (Cleveland, 1881). This volume has the usual merits and defects of county histories.

Wrong, George M., *The Conquest of New France* (Allen Johnson, ed., *The Chronicles of American Series*, New Haven, 1918-1921, X). One of the best accounts of the struggle between France and England for supremacy in North America.

Magazine Articles

Anmann, H. R., "Development of the Judicial System of Ohio," *Ohio Archaeological and Historical Quarterly,* XLI (1932), 195-236.

Cutler, W. P., "Private Contract Provision in the Ordinance of 1787," *Magazine of American History,* XXII (1889), 483-486.

Dawes, E. C., "The Beginning of the Ohio Company and the Scioto Purchase," *Ohio Archaeological and Historical Quarterly,* IV (1895-1896), 1-29.

Dickinson, Reverend C. E., "The First Church Organization in the Oldest Settlement in the Northwest Territory," *Ohio Archaeological and Historical Quarterly,* II (1888-1889), 289-298.

Downes, Randolph Chandler, "Evolution of the Ohio County Boundaries," *Ohio Archaeological and Historical Quarterly,* XXXVI (1927), 340-477.

__________, "The Statehood Contest in Ohio," *Mississippi Valley Historical Review,* XVIII (1931-1932), 155-171.

__________, "Thomas Jefferson and the Removal of Governor St. Clair in 1802," *Ohio Archaeological and Historical Quarterly,* XXXVI (1927), 62-77. Reveals the antagonism between the Federalists and Republican parties in the Northwest.

Dunn, W. Ross, "Education in Territorial Ohio," *Ohio Archaeological and Historical Quarterly,* XXV (1926), 322-379.

Galbreath, C. B., "The Ordinance of 1787, its Origin and Authorship," *Ohio Archaeological and Historical Quarterly,* XXXIII (1924), 111-175.

Graham, A. A., "The Military Post, Forts and Battlefields Within the State of Ohio," *Ohio Archaeological and Historical Quarterly,* III (1890-1891), 300-311.

Hart, Albert Bushnell, "The Westernization of New England," *Ohio Archaeological and Historical Quarterly,* XVII (1908), 259-274.

Hulbert, Archer Butler, "The Methods and Operations of the Scioto Group of Speculators," *Mississippi Valley Historical Review,* I (1914-1915), 502-515.

Martzolff, C. F., "Early Religious Movements in the Muskingum Valley," *Ohio Archaeological and Historical Quarterly,* XXV (1916), 183-190.

Moats, Francis I., "The Rise of Methodism in the Middle West," *Mississippi Valley Historical Review,* XV (1928-1929), 69-88.

Morris, William A., "The Office of Sheriff in the Anglo-Saxon Period," *English Historical Review,* XV (1916), 20-46.

Pershing, B. H., "Winthrop Sargent," *Ohio Archaeological and Historical Quarterly,* XXXV (1926), 583-602.

Peters, Bernard, "The German Pioneers," *Ohio Archaeological and Historical Quarterly,* II (1888-1889), 55-59.

Shetrone, H. C., "The Indian in Ohio," *Ohio Archaeological and Historical Quarterly,* XXVII (1919), 274-510.

Stone, Frederick D., "The Ordinance of 1787," *Pennsylvania Magazine of History and Biography*, XIII (1889), 309-400.

Commissioners

*Appointed under territorial government***

William R. Putnam
Paul Fearing
Oliver Rice
Gilbert Devol
Jonathan Haskell
Simeon Deming
Isaac Pierce

*Elected under state government****

Nathaniel Hamilton, 1804
John Sharp, 1805
Paul Fearing, 1806
Nathaniel Hamilton, 1807
Joseph Barker, 1808
Paul Fearing (resigned), 1809
John Sharp (2 years), 1809
Nathaniel Hamilton, 1810
Daniel Goodno, 1811
Henry Jolly, 1812
Nathaniel Hamilton, 1813
Daniel Goodno, 1814
William Skinner, 1815
Ttitan Kemble, 1816
John B. Regnier, 1817
Daniel Goodno, 1818
Titan Kimble (resigned), 1819
John B. Regnier (died), 1820
Samuel Beach (2 years), 1821
Amzi Stanley (1 year), 1821
Daniel Goodno, 1821
Joseph Barker, 1822
William R. Putnam, 1823
Daniel H. Buell (resigned), 1824
Joseph Barker, 1825
Thomas White (1 year), 1825
William Pitt Putnam, 1826
Silas Cook (1 year), 1826
Anselm T. Nye, 1827
Seth Baker (1 year), 1828
Joel Tuttle, 1829
Jabesh F. Palmer (2 years), 1829
Ebenezer Battelle, 1832
William Pitt Putnam, 1833

*This list was compiled from the following sources: H. Z. Williams and Bro., pub., *History of Washington County, Ohio* (Cleveland, 1882); Thomas J. Summers, *History of Marietta* (Marietta, 1903); Carrington T. Marshall, ed., *A History of the Courts and Lawyers of Ohio* (*American Historical Society*., pub., New York, 1924); Martin R. Andrews, *History of Marietta and Washington County, Ohio* (Chicago, 1902); *Reports of Secretary of State*, 1880-1938.

**Of these Isaac Pierce served until 1804, William Putnam until 1805, and Simeon Deming until 1806.

***Until 1897 the year of election or taking office only is given. If the full term of three years was not served that fact is indicated wherever data was available.

Commissioners, continued

John D. Chamberlain, 1834
Robert K. Ewart, 1835
Daniel H. Buell, 1836
John D. Chamberlain, 1837
William Dana, 1838
Daniel H. Buell, 1839
John D. Chamberlain, 1840
James Dutton, 1841
Douglas Putnam, 1842
Hiram Gard, 1843
William West, 1844
Doutlas Putnam, 1845
Boyleston Shaw, 1846
Lewis H. Greene, 1847
Douglas Putnam, 1848
John Breckenridge, 1849
George Stanley, 1850
Douglas Putnam, 1851
Walter Curtis, 1852
Benjamin Rightmire, 1853
William Mason, 1854
Walter Curtis, 1855
Charles Dana, 1856
William R. Putnam, 1857
Joseph Penrose, 1858
Zachariah Cochrane, 1859
James McWilliams, 1860
J. J. Hollister, 1861
William Thomas, 1862
Anthony Sheets (resigned), 1863
J. J. Hollister, 1864
George Benedict, 1865
James Little (1 year), 1865-1866
Seymour Clough, 1867
George Benedict, 1868
Thomas Caywood, 1869
Mark Green (resigned), 1870
Joseph Penrose, 1871
Cyrenius Buchanan (2 years), 1871
John Hall, 1872
Pemberton Palmer, 1873
John Pool, 1874
John Potter, 1875
Moses A. Malster, 1876
John Hoppel, 1877
Philip Mattern, 1878
Robert Mullenix, 1879
William Thompson, 1880
Philip Mattern, 1881
William Thompson, 1882
B. J. Williamson, 1883
J. M. Fearson, 1883
J. M. Murdock, 1884
J. M. Farron, 1885
Mason Gorby, 1886
J. Warren Thorniley, 1887
Thomas Fleming, 1888
J. Warren Thorniley, 1889
John A. Gage, 1890
Mason Gorby, 1891
Samuel S. McGee, 1892
C. M. Grubb, 1893
John Randolph, 1894
Samuel S. McGee, 1895
C. M. Grubb, 1896
John Randolph, Sep 1897-Sep 1900
William L. Hadley, Sep 1898-Sep 1901
Henry Strecker, Sep 1899-Sep 1902
Daniel R. Shaw, Sep 1900-Sep 1903
William L. Hadley, Sep 1901-Sep 1904
Lewis J. Cutler, 1902-Sep 1908
Daniel R. Shaw, 1903-Sep 1906
James D. Ballentine, 1904-Sep 1907
Lindley S. Bingham, 1905-1908
S. M. Campbell, 1908-1911
J. W. Pryor, 1908-1911

Commissioners, continued

Alva M. Malster, 1908-1911
S. M. Campbell, 1910-Sep 1913
Alva M. Malster, 1910-Sep 1913
J.W. Pryor, 1910-Sep 1913
T. E. Dye, 1912-1915
George B. Henry, 1912-1915
Charles Schimmel, 1912-1915
T. E. Dye, 1914-Sep 1917
G. B. Henry, 1914-Sep 1917
Charles Schimmel, 1914-Sep 1917
C. H. Bingham, 1917-Sep 1919; 1919–
L. L. Dutton, 1917-1925
Harvey Thomas, 1917-Sep 1919
J. Wiley west, 1919-1925
H. C. McNeal, 1920
J. H. Fleming, 1926-Jan 1931
Martin McBride, 1924-Jan 1931
B. F. Oliver, 1924-Jan 1929
Kenneth Kearns, 1928-1933
T. W. Porter, 1928-1933
John Zimmer, 1930-Jan 1935
Roy R. Engle, 1932-1937
Thomas W. Porter, 1932-Jan 1937
J. F. McIntire, 1932-Jan 1937
C. Truman Wells, Nov 6 1934-1939
Roy R. Engle, Nov 3, 1936—
J. Clark Middleswart, 1936—
C. Truman Wells, Jan 1939—

Recorders*

Enoch Parsons, 1788-Apr 1790
Dudley Woodbridge, Apr 1790-Jun 1807
Giles Hempstead, Jun 1807-Jun 1814
George Dunlevy, Jun 1814-Jun 1817
Daniel H. Buell, Jun 1817-Oct 1834
James M. Booth, Oct 1834-Nov 1837
Daniel P. Bosworth, Nov 1837-Oct 1843
Stephen Newton, Oct 1843-Nov 1855
William B. Mason, Nov 1855-Jan 1862
Manly Warren, Jan 1862-May 1864
William Warren (appointed),
May 1864-Jan 1865
George J. Bartmess, Jan 1865-Aug 1866
A. T. Ward (appointed),
Aug 1866-Jan 1867
James Nixon, Jan 1867-Jan 1882
Joseph P. Ward, Jan 1882-Jan 1888
John W. Steele, Jan 1888-Jan 1894
John W. Athey, Jan 1894-Jan 1900
George W. Bonnell, Sep 1900-Sep 1906
John W. Lansley, 1906-Sep 1908
William T. Watkins, 1908-Sep 1913
Frank J. McCauley, 1913-Sep 1917
William M. Sprague, 1917-Sep 1921
Frank g. Simmons, 1921-Sep 1923
Ruth L. Sprague, 1923-Sep 1927
May Bell, 1927-1931
Katherine Rothley, 1931-Jan 1933
May Bell, 1933-Jan 1937
Julia A. Miller, 1937—

*Under the Territory the recorder, styled register until 1795, was appointed by the governor. Under the law of 1803 the associate judges appointed the recorder for seven years. The office became elective for a term of three years in 1829, two years in 1905, and four years in 1937.

Clerks of the Court of Common Pleas*

Return Jonathan Meigs, Sep 9, 1788-Jun 9, 1795
Benjamin Ives Gilman, Jun 9, 1795-Jul 1803
Edward W. Tupper, Jul 1803-Oct 31, 1808
Giles Hempstead, Oct 31, 1808-Jan 1, 1809
Levi Barber, Jan 1, 1809-Mar 1, 1817
George Dunlevy, Mar 1, 1817-Oct 31, 1836
Thomas W. Ewart, Oct 31, 1836-Oct 21, 1851
William C. Taylor, Oct 21, 1851-Feb 1852
George S. Gilliand, Feb 1852-Jul 1852
William C. Taylor, Jul 1852-Feb 1854
O. Lewis Clarke, Feb 1854-Feb 1857
Jasper S. Sprague, Feb 1857-Feb 1863
Willis H. Johnson, Feb 1863-Feb 1866
Jewett Palmer, Feb 1866-Feb 1872
Daniel B. Torpy, Feb 1872-Feb 1878
Christian H. Etz, Feb 1878-Feb 1884
J. M. Mitchell, Feb 1884-Feb 1887
Wesley G. Barthalow, Feb 1887-Feb 1893
L. E. McVay, Feb 1893-Feb 1899
Orlando Trotter, Feb 1899-Sep 1900
Elmer E. Trotter (appointed to fill unexpired term), Sep 1900-Feb 1902; and 1903-Aug 1905
A. A. Crawford, 1905-Aug 1908
Walter J. Dutton, 1908-Aug 1913
George P. Deshler, 1913-Aug 1917
A. L. Savage, 1917-Aug 1919
C. R. Williamson, 1919-1923
Katherine D. Thomas, 1923-1927
A.L. Savage, 1927-1929
Roy Morris, 1929-1935
Harry C. Barnes, 1935—

*Under the Territory the title for the clerk of the court of common pleas was prothonotary. This official was appointed by the governor. Under the state constitution of 1802 the court appointed its own clerk for a seven-year term; under that of 1851 the office became elective for a three-year term. The term was changed to two years in 1905 and to four in 1935.

Judges of the Court of General Quarter Sessions of the Peace

Joseph Gilman
Isaac Pierce
Robert Oliver
Dudley Woodbridge
Josiah Munroe
John G. Petit
Griffin Greene
William R. Utnam
Samuel Williamson
Joseph Barker
Ephraim Cutler
Henry Smith
Phillip Witten
Alvin Bingham
Thomas Stanley
Seth Cathcart
Robert Safford
William Harper
William Burnham
Joseph Buell

Judges of the Court of Common Pleas

*Judges under the territorial government***

Rufus Putnam
Benjamin Tupper
Archibald Crary
Joseph Gilman
Dudley Woodbridge
Robert Oliver
Daniel Loring
John G. Petit
Isaac Pierce
Griffin Greene
Ephraim Cutler
Peregrine Foster

President judges under the constitution of 1802 in District III which included Washington County

Calvin Pease, 1803-1808
William Wilson, 1808-1819
Ezra Osborne, 1819-1826
Thomas Irwin, 1826-1840
John E. Hanna, 1840-1847
Arius Nye, 1847-1850
A. G. Brown, 1850-1852

Associate judges under the constitution of 1802 in District III

Griffin Greene, 1803-1808
Joseph Buell, 1803-1810
Joseph Wood, 1803-1808
Esekiel Deming, 1808-1824
William Hempstead, 1808-1810
Paul Fearing, 1810-1817
Thomas Lord, 1810-1817
Henry Jolly, 1817-1824
John Sharp, 1817-1823
J. M. Chamberlain, 1823-1824
Walter Curtis, 1824-1837
Henry P. Wilcox, 1824-1825
Alexander Warner, 1824-1830
John Cotton, 1825-1847
Joseph Barker, 1830-1843
Oliver Loring, 1837-1847
Isaac Humphreys, 1843
Ebenezer Gates, 1843-1844
Joseph Barker, Jr., 1844-1852
Bial Stedman, 1847-1852
William R. Putnam, Jr., 1847-1852

Judges under the constitution of 1851 in District VIII which included Washington County

Simeon Nash, Gallipolis, Feb 1852-Feb 1862
William V. Peck, Portsmouth, Feb 1852-Feb 1859
Henry C. Whitman, Lancaster, Feb 1852-resigned Mar 1862
William W. Johnson, Ironton, Feb 1859-Mar 1872

Philadelphus Van Trump, Lancaster, Feb 1862-Aug 1866
John Welch, Athens, Feb 1862-Feb 1865
Philemon B. Ewing, Lancaster, Mar 1862-Nov 1862
Erastus A. Guthrie, Athens, Feb 1865-Oct 1875
James R. Groghan, Sep 1866-Nov 1866
Silas H. Wright, Logan, Oct 1866-died 1887
Martin Crain, Oct 1867-Feb 1872
William B. Loomis, Marietta, Jul 1868-Jul 1873
Henry A. Towne, Portsmouth, 1869
John J. Harper, Portsmouth, Feb 1872-Feb 1874
W. K. Hasting, Jackson, Mar 1872-Feb 1874
Tobias A. Plants, Pomeroy, Jul 1873-resigned 1875
Porter Du Hadway, Jackson, Feb 1874
David P. Hebard, Jan 1875-Oct 1875
John Cartright, Feb 1875-Oct 1884
Samuel S.Knowles, Marietta, Oct 1875-Jul 1883
Joseph P. Bradbury, Pomeroy, Oct 1875-Jan 1885
James M. Tripp, Feb 1879-Feb 1894
James S. Friesner, Logan, 1879
Albert C. Thompson, Portsmouth, Feb 1882-Oct 1884
Hiram L. Sibley, Marietta, Jul 1883-Jan 1897
E. V. Dean, Ironton, Sep 1884-Oct 1884
James W. Bannon, Portsmouth, Oct 1884-Feb 1887
F. C. Russell, Pomeroy, Jan 1885-Oct 1885
Rudolph DeSteiguer, Athens, Feb 1885-Feb 1897
Noah J. Dever, Portsmouth, Feb 1887-Feb 1897
Samuel Bright, Logan, Nov 1887-Nov 1888
Tall Slough, Lancaster, Nov 1888-died 1900
Joseph G. Huffman, New Lexington, Dec 1889-died 1896
William D. James, Waverly, Feb 1894-Feb 1899
Henry W. Coultrap, McArthur, Jan 1895
James E. Johnston, Feb 1896-Nov 1896
Joseph M. Wood, Athens, Feb 1897-Feb 1902
John C. Milner, Portsmouth, Feb 1897-Feb 1902
Davis W. Jones, Gallipolis, Jul 1898-Jul 1903
W. H. Middleton, Waverly, Feb 1899-1914
O. W. H. Wright, Logan, Dec 1899-Feb 1909
Charles W. McCleary, Lancaster, Aug 1900-Nov 1900
John G. Reeves, Lancaster, Nov 1900-Feb 1914
Henry Collins, Manchester, Feb 1902-Feb 1907
Albion J. Blair, Portsmouth, Nov 1904-1914
George E. Martin, Lancaster, Feb 1905-Feb 1911
Joseph P. Bradbury, Pomeroy, Feb 1905-Feb 1910
Edward E. Corn, Ironton, Feb 1906-1914
Charles E. Peoples, Feb 1911-1913
Virgil C. Lowery, Feb 1911-1913
James S. Thomas, Feb 1913-1914
Edward B. Follett, Jan 1, 1911-Dec 31, 1916

Resident judge under the constitutional amendment of 1912

David H. Thomas, Jan 1, 1917—

Judges of Probate Court*

Rufus Putnam, Oct 1788-resigned Dec 1789
Joseph Gilman, Dec 1789-resigned Dec 1796
Paul Fearing, Mar 1797-Mar 1803
Thomas W. Ewart, Feb 1852-Oct 1852*
Davis Green, Oct 1852-Feb 1855
William Devol, Oct 1855-Feb 1858
C. R. Rhodes, Oct 1858-Feb 1861
C. F. Buell, Oct 1861-Feb 1864
L. W. Chamberlain, Oct 1864-Feb 1870
A. W. McCormick, Oct 1870-Feb 1876
C. T. Frayzer, Oct 1876-Feb 1882
F. J. Cutter, Oct 1882-Feb 1888
William H. Leeper, Oct 1888-Feb 1894
David R. Rood, Oct 1894-Feb 1900
Charles H. Nixon, Oct 9, 1900-1906
Archa M. Farlow, 1906-1909
Albert L. Smith, 1909-1917
A. A. Schramm, 1917-1925
Frank F. Fleming, 1925—

*For the probate judges from March 1803 to February 1852, see the clerks of the common pleas court, as the probate court was merged into it during this period (Summers, *op. cit.,* 163).

Prosecuting Attorneys

Paul Fearing, Sep 9, 1788-Sep 9, 1794
Return Jonathan Meigs, Jr., Sep 9, 1794-Sep 9, 1798
Matthew Backus, Sep 9, 1798-Sep 9, 1808
William Woodbridge, Sep 9, 1808-Feb 5, 1815
Caleb Emerson, Feb 6, 1815-Apr 10, 1821
John P. Mayberry, Apr 10, 1821-Oct 30, 1829
Arius Nye, Oct 30, 1829-Aug 17, 1840
David Barber, Oct 26, 1840-Apr 3, 1845
Arius Nye, Apr 3, 1845-Mar 8, 1847
William D. Emerson, Mar 8, 1847-Mar 13, 1848
William S. Nye, Mar 18, 1848-Mar 8, 1850
Davis Green, Mar 18, 1850-Apr 5, 1852
Rufus E. Harte, Apr 5, 1852-Oct 4,1852
Samuel B. Robinson, Oct 4, 1852-Jan 1855
Charles R. Rhodes, Jan 1855-Jan 1857
Samuel B. Robinson, Jan 1857-Jan 1859
Charles R. Barclay, Jan 1859-Jan 1861
Frank Buell, Jan 1861-Apr 1861
Melvin Clarke, Apr 1861-Oct 11, 1861
William S. Nye, Oct 11 1861-Jan 1862
David Alban, Jan 1862-Jan 1868
Walter Brabham, Jan 1868-Jan 1870
Reuben L. Nye, Jan 1870-Jan 1872
Walter Brabham, Jan 1872-Jan 1874
Samuel B. Robinson, Jan 1874-Jan 1876
Frank F. Oldham, Jan 1874-Jan 1876
David Alban, Jan 1880-Feb 15, 1882
L.W. Ellenwood, Jan 1883-Jan 1886

Prosecuting Attorneys, continued

John W. McCormick, Jan 1886-Jan 1892
John C. Preston, Jan 1892-Jan 1898
Joseph C. Brenan, Jan 1898-Jan 1904
Wm. E. Sheldon, 1904-Jan 1906
Edward B. Follett, 1906-1910
Allen Thurman Williamson, 1910-1917
Robert M. Noll, 1917-1921
N. C. Kidd, 1921-1923
Everett E. Folger, 1923-1925
Verner E. Metcalf, 1925-1929
Frederick C. Myers, 1929-1931
Everett E. Folger, 1931-Jan 1933
Frederick C. Myers, 1933-1937
William M. Summers, 1937—

Coroners*

Charles Greene (Territory) 1788-1803
Joel Bowen, 1803-1806
Joseph Holden, 1806-1812
Alexander Hill, 1812-1814
Silas Cook, 1814-1816
Samson Cole, 1816-1818
Silas Cook, 1818-1820
John Merrill, 1820-1824
Griffin Greene, 1824-1834
Francis Devol, 1834-1836
Warden Willis, 1836-1838
Lawrence Chamberlain, 1838-1844
John T. Clogston, 1844-1846
Lewis Chamberlain, 1846-185
Finley Wilson, 1852-1853
James H. Jones, 1853-1855
Chauncey T. Judd, 1855-1857
Benjamin F. Stone, 1857-1859
Louis Soyez, 1859-1860
Allen M. Creghbaum, 1860-1864
Lemuel Grimes, 1864-1866
Simeon D. Hart, 1866-1868
Herman Michealis, 1868-1870
Philip Emrich, 1870-1872
Marcellus J. Morse, 1872-1874
T. C. Kiger, 1874-1876
Conrad Krigbaum, 1876-1880
J. F. Ullman, 1880-1882
John Bohl, Jr., 1882
B. C. Gale, 1883
J. B. Mellor, 1884
J. J. Neuer, 1886-1890
Frank E. McKim, 1890-
Osmer M. Willis, Kam 1896–Jan 1900
John B. McClure, Jan 1900-Jan 1904
R.W. Athey, 1904-1908
Clarence R. Sloan, 1908-1910
J. D. Parr, 1910-1912
F. J. Mitchell, 1912-Jan 1914
J. D. Parr, 1914-1916
Obed D. Green, 1916-Jan 1920
B. E. Guyton, 1920-1924
N. O. Whiting, 1924-Dec 1928
Mac. R. Sprague, 1928-1930
Fred E. Jackson, 1930-Dec 1934
Harry E. Dickson, Nov 6, 1934–1936
R. W. Riggs, Nov 6, 1936—

* "The list is believed to be correct from 1812 to the present time; there is some uncertainty as to the previous periods" (Andrews, *op. cit.* 431-435).

Sheriffs

Ebenezer Sproat, Sep 2, 1788-1802
William Skinner, 1802-1803
John Clark, 1803-1810
Timothy Buell, 1812-1814
Alexander Hill, 1814-1816
Timothy Buell, 1816-Oct 1820
Alexander Hill, 1814-1816
Timothy Buell, 1816-Oct 1820
Silas Cook, Oct 1820-Oct 1824
Jesse Loring, Oct 1824-Oct 1828
Robert R. Green, Oct 1828-Oct 1832
Jesse Loring, Oct 1832-Oct 1834
Benjamin M. Brown, Oct 1834-Oct 1838
John Test, Oct 1838-Oct 1842
George W. Barer, Oct 1842-Oct 1846
Junia Jennings, Oct 1846-Oct 1850
Jesse Hildebrand, Oct 1850-Jan 1853
Marcellus J. Morse, Jan 1853-Jan 1857
Mark Green, Jan 1857-Jan 1861
Augustus Winsor, Jan 1861-Jan 1865
Jackson A. Hicks, Jan 1865-Jan 1869
Samuel L. Grosvenor, Jan 1869-Jan 1873
George Davenport, Jan 1873-Jan 1877
William T. Steadman, Jan 1877-Jan 1881
Daniel B. Torpy, 1881-1885
I.R. Rose, 1885-1889
Arthur B. Little, 1889-1893
William B Dye, 1893-1897
J. S. McAllister, Jan 1897-Jan 1901
Jesse C. Morrow, Jan 1901-Jan 1905
Charles A. Owen, Jan 1905-Jan 1907
E. Clark, Jr., 1908-Jan 1913
Henry C. Posey, 1913-1917
Clyde A. Posey, 1917-Jan 1919
A. E. Roberts, 1919-1924
E. L. Yarnell, 1924-Jan 1927
Perley J. Way, 1927-1931
C. G. Thorn, 1931-Jan 1935
Arthur D. Mackey, 1935—

Treasurers

Jonathan Stone, 1792-1801
Jabez True, 1801-1817
Joseph Holden, 1817-1828
Weston Thomas, 1828-1830
Royal Prentiss, 1830-1832
Michael Deterly, 1832-1836
Ebenezer Gates, 1836-1838
Robert Crawford, 1838-1850
Abner L. Guitteau, 1850-1856
Stephen Newton, 1856-1858
Ebenezer B. Leget, 1858-1860
William B. Thomas, 1860-1862
Rufus E. Harte, 1862-1866
William B. Mason, 1866-1868
Lewis Anderson, 1868-1870
Ernest Lindner, 1870-1874
William S. Waugh, 1874-1878
William R. Goddard, 1878-1880
John Holst, 1880-1884
Walter Thomas, 1884-1886
Thomas J. Connor, 1886-1890
George W. Stanley, 1890-1894
G. J. Lund, 1894-1898
Henry P. Bode, 1898-Sep 1902
Frederick A. Dana, 1902-Sep 1906
S. Austin Coffman, 1906-1908
Herman H. Miller, 1908-Sep 1913
Adam C. Beach, 1913-Sep 1917
Casper Hopp, 1917-1919
Thomas W. Porter, 1919-1921

Treasurers, continued

W. C. Robinson, 1921-1925
H. H. Myers, 1925-Sep 1929
E. L. Yarnall, 1929-1931
Arza L. Savage, 1931-Sep 1935
Hammond Burton, 1935—

Auditors

Royal Prentiss, 1820-1825
William A. Whittlesey, 1825-1838
James M. Booth, 1838-1840
Joseph P. Wightman, 1840-1842
James M. Booth, 1842-1846
Sala Bosworth, 1846-1854
Horatio Booth, 1854-1856
Frederick A. Wheeler, 1856-1864
Zadok G. Bundy, 1864-1868
John V. Ramsey, 1868-1870
John T. Mathews, 1870-1876
Benjamin J. McKinney, 1876-1882
David H. Merrill, 1888-1894
W. A. Patterson, 1894-1900
C. C. Chamberlain, Oct 1900-Oct 1906
J. Marion Williams, Oct 1906-Oct 1908
Hammond Burton, Oct 1908-Oct 1913
W. B. Alexander, 1913-1915
J. Henry Best, 1915-1919
John F. Scott, 1919-Mar 1927
Frank J. McCauley, Mar 1927-Mar 1935
Arza R. Pryor, Nov 6, 1934
(unexpired term)
Fulton H. Quigley, 1935—

Infirmary Directors

Samson Cole, 1836-1842
Eben Gates, 1836-1842
Wyllys Hall, 1838-1842
James Dunn, 1842-1849
Thomas F. Stanley, 1842-1844
William R. Putnam, Jr., 1842-1845
Samuel Shipman, 1844-1847
Brooks Blizzard, 1845-1851
John Collins, 1847-1859
James M. Booth, 1849-1850
James Dunn, 1850–1861
James Dutton, 1850-1853
James S. Cady, 1853-1856
Robert B. Cheatham, 1860-1863
Junia Jennings, 1861-1870
John Dowling, 1862-1865
William West, 1863-1866
James Dunn, 1865-1868
F. A. Wheeler, 1866-1875
Samuel E. Fay, 1868-1871
H. W. Corner, 1870-1873
Charles Athey, 1871-1874
George W. Richards, 1873-1876
William Caywood (3d), 1874-1880
John Dowling, 1875-1878
Charles A. Cook, 1876-1879
John Dowling, 18781881
John Strecker, 1879-1882
Charles W. Athey, 1880-1886
John D. Templeton, 1881-1884
Henry Van Bergen, 1882-1885
William T. Harness, 1883-1886
Thomas D. Hoff,1884-1886
Robert G. Miller, Jr., 1885-1887

Infirmary Directors, continued

William G. Harness, 1886-1888
James F. Briggs, 1887-1890
Robert G. Miller, Jr., 1888-1891
William G. Harness, 1889-1892
James F. Briggs, 1890-1892
Russell O'Neall, 1891-1893
George Richards, 1892-1894
Russell O'Neall, 1893-1895
William Schnauffer, 1894-1896
George Richards, 1895-1897
Russell O'Neall, 1896-1898
William Cranston, 1897-1899
George W. Smith, 1899-1903
William Schnauffer, Jan 1897-Jan 1900
William Cranston, Jan 1899-Jan 1902
George W. Richards, 1898-1901 Deceased, Wm. Schnauffer appointed.
George W. Smith, Jan 1900-Jan 1903
J. K. Gregory, Jan 1901-Jan 1904
Reuben E. Hull, 1902-Jan 1905
George W. Smith, 1903-Jan 1906
J. K. Gregory, 1904-Jan 1907
S. S. Stowe, 1904-Jan 1908
Minor M. Dye, 1905-1908
John B. Smith, 1906–
Tom McDermott, 1908–
J. O. Dutton, 1908–
Alex Clark, 1908–
Jasper O. Dutton, 1910-Jan 1913
G. B. Henry, 1910-Jan 1913
Tom McDermott, 1910-Jan 1913

Surveyors*

Levi Barber, Nov 1805-Jul 1816
William R. Putnam, Jul 1816-Oct 1826
William R. Browning, Feb 1827-May 1832
Levi Bartlett, Nov 1841-Oct 1851
L. W. Chamberlain, Oct 1851-Dec 1861
R. W. St. John, Dec 1861-Dec 1864
Samuel N. Hobson, elected Oct 1864, resigned
Daniel F. Dufer, Jan 1881-1884
A. A. Hollister, 1884-1887
William Eldridge, 1887-1893
Daniel F. Dufer, 1893-1896
Charles E. Gard, (appointed) Jan 1865-Dec 1865
John A. Plumer, Feb 1866-Jan 1875
J. P. Hulbert, Jan 1875-1881

*From 1803 to 1831 the surveyor was appointed by the court of common pleas and commissioned by the governor. From 1831 to 1908 he has been elected for a three-year term and since 1906 for a two-year term.

Surveyors, continued

Daniel F. Dufer, Jan 1881-1884
A. A. Hollister, 1884-1887
William Eldridge, 1887-1893
Daniel F. Dufer, 1893-1896
Levi Bartlett, 1896-1902
Arthur F. Cole, 1902-1908
A. A. Hollister, 1909-1913
W. P. Mason, 1913-1915
Charles M. Weeks, Sep 1915-Sep 1917
W. P. Mason, 1917-Sep 1919
E. Frank Gates, Sep 1919-1923
George E. Carr, elected 1923, failed to qualify
Charles M. Weeks, 1925-Jan 1929
Guy W. Elis, Jan 1929-Jan 1937

Engineer*

Cecil W. Stacy, 1936—

*An act in 1935 changed the title from surveyor to engineer.

Governmental

All addresses refer to Marietta, Ohio, unless otherwise noted

Auditor
205 Putnam Street
https://auditorwashingtoncountyohio.gov/

Board of Elections
204 Davis Avenue
Suite B
https://www.boe.ohio.gov/washington

Clerk of Courts
205 Putnam Street
https://washingtongov.org/250/Clerk-of-Courts

Commissioners
223 Putnam Street
https://washingtongov.org/238/Board-of-County-Commissioner

County Home
845 County House Lane
https://washingtongov.org/114/County-Home

Court of Common Pleas
205 Putnam Street
https://washingtongov.org/269/Common-Pleas-Court---General-Division

Common Pleas Court, Juvenile Division
Courthouse Annex
205 Putnam Street
https://washingtongov.org/306/Common-Pleas-Court---Juvenile-Division

Common Pleas Court, Probate Division
Courthouse Annex
205 Putnam Street
https://washingtongov.org/317/Common-Pleas-Court---Probate-Division
Dog Warden
309 Fourth Street
https://washingtongov.org/120/Dog-Warden

Engineer
103 Westview Avenue
https://washingtongov.org/286/Engineer

Health Department
340 Muskingum Drive, Suite B
https://washingtongov.org/137/Health-Department

Municipal Court
259 Butler Street
https://www.mariettacourt.com/

Prosecutor
205 Putnam Street
https://washingtongov.org/319/Prosecutor

Recorder
205 Putnam Street
https://washingtongov.org/324/Recorder

Sheriff
309 Fourth Street
https://www.washingtoncountysheriff.org/

Soil and Water Conservation
21330 State Route 676, Suite E
https://washingtoncountyswcd.com/

Treasurer
205 Putnam Street
https://washingtongov.org/328/Treasurer

Veterans Service
706 Pike Street Suite 1
https://www.wcvsc.com/

FamilySearch
https://www.familysearch.org/search/catalog

FamilySearch is a free website with digitized records. Digitized court records for Washington County include: Auditor, Board of Elections, Chancery Court, Children's Home Trustees, Circuit Court, Common Pleas, County Commissioners, District Court, Justice of the Peace, Probate Court, Recorder, School Board (Fourth District), Supreme Court, and Treasurer. Some of these records may be listed under a different division, Many early deeds pertain to the earliest settlers of the Ohio Company Purchase, Northwest Territory. It should be noted that many other sections are listed which may include books abstracted by individuals or organizations.

Campus Martius Museum
601 Second Street
Marietta
https://mariettamuseums.org/

Marietta has the distinction of being the first permanent organized settlement in the Old Northwest Territory. The museum has the list of French law suits on file at the museum with a date range is 1793-1802; Northwest Territory...court records, 1789-1808. Also located at the museum are marriage records and certificates dating from 1789-1804 and 1825 to 1841. (To learn more about the settlement of the area, see *The Pioneers* by David McCullough.)

Washington County Chapter, Ohio Genealogical Society
P. O. 2174
Marietta
https://www.washogs.org/

The website lists maps, city directory fo 1871-1872, cemeteries, children's home, epidemics, high school graduates 1853-1904, and Ohio Company Purchasers. Listings on the site link to many other locations helpful in researching Washington County.

Heritage Books by Jana Sloan Broglin:

Additions and Corrections to the W.P.A. Inventory of Adams County, Ohio: West Union

Additions and Corrections to the W.P.A. Inventory of Allen County, Ohio: Lima

Additions and Corrections to the W.P.A. Inventory of Ashland County, Ohio: Ashland

Additions and Corrections to the W.P.A. Inventory of Athens County, Ohio: Athens

Additions and Corrections to the W.P.A. Inventory of Belmont County, Ohio: St. Clairsville

Additions and Corrections to the W.P.A. Inventory of Cuyahoga County, Ohio: Cleveland

Additions and Corrections to the W.P.A. Inventory of Fulton County, Ohio: Wauseon

Additions and Corrections to the W.P.A. Inventory of Geauga County, Ohio: Chardon

Additions and Corrections to the W.P.A. Inventory of Hamilton County, Ohio: Cincinnati

Additions and Corrections to the W.P.A. Inventory of Hancock County, Ohio: Findlay

Additions and Corrections to the W.P.A. Inventory of Lake County, Ohio: Painesville

Additions and Corrections to the W.P.A. Inventory of Lorain County, Ohio: Elyria

Additions and Corrections to the W.P.A. Inventory of Lucas County, Ohio: Toledo

Additions and Corrections to the W.P.A. Inventory of Medina County, Ohio: Medina

Additions and Corrections to the W.P.A. Inventory of Montgomery County, Ohio: Dayton

Additions and Corrections to the W.P.A. Inventory of Muskingum County, Ohio: Zanesville

Additions and Corrections to the W.P.A. Inventory of Seneca County, Ohio: Tiffin

Additions and Corrections to the W.P.A. Inventory of Trumbull County, Ohio: Warren

Additions and Corrections to the W.P.A. Inventory of Washington County, Ohio: Marietta

Additions and Corrections to the W.P.A. Inventory of Wayne County, Ohio: Wooster

Hookers, Crooks and Kooks, Part I: Hookers

Hookers, Crooks and Kooks, Part II: Crooks and Kooks

Lucas County, Ohio, Index to Deaths, 1867–1908

Mason County, Kentucky Wills and Estates, 1791–1832, Second Edition

www.ingramcontent.com/pod-product-compliance
Lightning Source LLC
Chambersburg PA
CBHW071352290326
41932CB00045B/1520

9780788449536